D1156992

The Republican Party

A HISTORY

The Republican Party

A HISTORY

William Starr Myers, Ph.D.
PROFESSOR OF POLITICS, PRINCETON UNIVERSITY

ILLUSTRATED

The Century Co.
NEW YORK LONDON

First printing March, 1928

PRINTED IN U. S. A.

TO THE MEMORY OF

MY MOTHER

LAURA VIRGINIA STARR MYERS

1850–1894

PREFACE

Students of politics throughout the world who are impressed by the practical as well as the theoretical aspects of political science are well aware of the necessary part that political parties play in actual government. There are those whose viewpoint is that of Washington's Farewell Address and other like opinions of a century and more ago, who would do away with all parties and party organizations, with nothing to substitute in their place. But it is with the conviction that parties are the natural and necessary organs of government and administration that I have undertaken to tell the plain story of the Republican party, one of the two great political organizations that between them have ordered the affairs of the United States for many years. Though their failures have been great, yet also their successes have been remarkable. This is especially true when one remembers the general indifference of the average American citizen toward political affairs, except from the standpoint of personal prejudice or selfish advantage. Few Americans have gotten beyond the emotional stage of political interest and have come to that of intelligent participation. Since ignorance of the most elementary facts of our political history also accompanies this popular indifference, some knowledge of the unique history of one of the great present-day parties may help to a better appreciation of the problems of government. As has been well said by one of our recent political leaders, "Things do not happen. They are brought about."

I desire to give much more than the usual trite and routine expression of thanks and appreciation to those who have undergone the labor and weary grind of reading and criticizing my manuscript. Among them must be mentioned my friend and neighbor, Dr. Herbert Adams Gibbons, at whose suggestion this book was written; also my colleagues in the department of politics of Princeton University, Professor Edward Samuel Corwin and Professor Walter Lincoln Whittlesey; and especially and above all, my wife. Mr. Malcolm Oakman Young, reference librarian of the university library, has been most helpful, as always.

WILLIAM STARR MYERS.

Princeton, New Jersey,
October 27, 1927.

Contents

Illustrations

The Republican Party

A History

Chapter I

INTRODUCTION

DURING the month of February, 1926, an active local Republican party organization in New York city held a largely attended meeting. The subject for discussion was the "World Court" and the expediency of the recent action of the United States Senate in ratifying, at the demand of President Coolidge, the protocol that established the international tribunal. This action leading to the ultimate membership of the country was rightfully appreciated as a step toward greater American participation in world affairs. The speaker for the occasion had just concluded an historical and legal discussion in which mere partizan politics was kept rigidly in the background, when a woman in the back of the room rose to her feet and in a voice tense with lacrymose emotion announced that she was a "Jefferson Democrat from the state of Virginia, and also a devoted follower of that other great Democrat and martyred hero, Woodrow Wilson, who gave up his life for the cause of peace, and should have adequate recognition and glory for doing so." Of course, this "stump speech," possibly premeditated to disturb a meeting of members of an opposing party, aroused immediately a partizan reply, the former speaker stressing his side of the unending discussion of the Wilson policies following the armistice of 1918. But the important point of the incident lies in the fact that not only was the "woman in question" guilty of bad manners, but also entirely inconsistent in the statement of her political belief. In the first place, those who protest their Jeffersonian Democracy may be entirely correct from the standpoint of the political philosophy and doctrines of one of the founders of American politics, but when the word "Democracy" is meant to imply a strict following of the present party of that name and at the same time is used in connection with the above-named philosophy of Jefferson, there is an inconsistency that is of decided importance.

"The logical foundation of the Republican party was laid by Thomas Jefferson just seventy years before its actual appearance," says Professor Arthur N. Holcombe of Harvard University.[1] "The resolution, which he introduced into the Congress of the United States in 1784 [under the Articles of Confederation] for the organization of territorial governments in the great empty regions of the West which the larger states had recently ceded to the Union, was designed to prevent the extension of slavery into any of those regions." He adds, further, that "it is not without significance that the popular conventions, which actually founded the present Republican party, were held in the states of the old Northwest, several of them on the anniversary of the adoption of the Northwest Ordinance, and chose for the name of their new party that which Jefferson had preferred for the party which he himself had founded. The Republican tradition was born one hundred and forty years ago, though the political organization to which it is now attached did not come into existence until a full half of this long period had passed."

We also have other and weighty testimony showing the same tendency of thought in no less a person than Abraham Lincoln himself, the patron saint of present-day Republican politics, in a letter he wrote to a Boston committee in the year 1859, in reply to an invitation to attend a "festival" in Boston on Jefferson's birthday. He pronounced himself a thor-

[1] "Political Parties of To-day," 156.

ough disciple of Jefferson and found in the principles of Jefferson "the definitions and axioms of free society." [2]

In contrast to this, and of equal importance from the standpoint of the consistency of present-day followers of Woodrow Wilson who at the same time style themselves "Jefferson Democrats," we have a statement from Wilson himself, who said at the time he was President of Princeton University, and presumably was stating his real convictions without thought of political necessities, "I am not a Jeffersonian Democrat, because no one knows what kind of a Democrat Jefferson really was." [3] This is in sharp contrast to the very definite ideas of Lincoln on the subject, and those who knew President Wilson well and followed closely his course while the head of the nation will realize that he spoke the truth, and this fact possibly will explain the reason for many of his later acts which were not thoroughly understood at the time, or since.

But the inconsistent statement of the woman quoted above should not be stressed too much, for she merely was an illustration of the lack of knowledge of certain of the events in American history which is only too common among the rank and file of our citizens, men and women, and also of the fact that the majority of them, whether of the Republican or the Democratic party, vote not from conviction but from inherited prejudices, force of habit, or direct personal as contrasted to public or national benefit.

On Tuesday, November 3, 1925, the Republican voters of Essex county, New Jersey, reëlected to the state legislature Hunter Lindsay by a majority of about 9000 over his nearest Democratic opponent, a total of 68,382 votes being cast for him. Mr. Lindsay had died about three weeks before this

[2] The letter is in "Works of Abraham Lincoln" (Nicolay and Hay), V, 124–7.

[3] Statement made in the course of an informal discussion of politics with several members of the Princeton faculty on May 8, 1908, which was heard by the present writer and written down at the time. "Ever since I have had independent judgments of my own I have been a Federalist." Letter of Wilson to Professor A. B. Hart, under date of June 8, 1889, quoted by Ray Stannard Baker in "The Life and Letters of Woodrow Wilson," "New York Herald Tribune," October 17, 1927.

election took place. Essex county contains among its people, in Newark and various suburban cities and towns, as intelligent citizens as may be found in any like area in the country, and yet this election of a dead man to office actually took place. It is true that many of the Republican voters frankly stated their belief that "a dead Republican was better than a live Democrat," while others consciously took this means of preventing the return of a Democratic member of the legislature; yet there is no question that a large number of citizens voted for Mr. Lindsay in blissful ignorance of his death. The Democrats of New York city exhibited a somewhat similar performance in the fall of 1915, and like cases of such voting have occurred in other sections of the United States. The citizens merely voted the party label.

A leading business man in one of our largest cities recently told the writer that he would always vote for a Republican, "because the worst Republican always was better than the best Democrat," and at the same election a Democratic business man remarked that "he would vote for a yellow dog if it was on the Democratic ticket, because it was bound to be better than any Republican." These were intelligent, well-informed, educated men, who meant what they said, and were willing to support their statements by well thought out arguments. In both cases the underlying reason was loyalty to party, and the belief that in that party alone was to be found good administration and national safety.

The superficial onlooker, or the theoretical student, most naturally will sneer at such exhibitions of hidebound political action, especially that class of persons who, as Walter Hines Page deliciously remarked, are accustomed to "mistake self-indulgence and criticism for the intellectual life." They rightly will point out the oft-repeated evasions, inconsistencies, and lack of principle on the part of politicians, the vague platitudes and pious piffle of party platforms, and the absolute turn-about for seeming party expediency on the part of more or less cowardly office-holders. Also the statement repeatedly has been made, at various times in the political history of the country, that there is no difference between the parties. There is a large amount of truth in this saying, and yet we find the same continuing loyalty to party, the same self-denying contributions of time, money, and personal services—and not always for actual personal benefit, but even in many cases from a sense of real patriotism and public spirit. This is what holds together the rank and file of regular party voters, who may be counted literally by the millions, and who "stand hitched" for year after year, no matter what may be the success or failure of the party ticket at the polls.

The answer to this problem of practical politics will lie in part in the hands of the psychologist. But there also are certain practical reasons for such loyalty, as worked out in the experience of several generations of American citizens and which, as will be shown later on, have a real basis in the history of the United States, even running back to the British politics of their ancestors. Among such reasons lies the fact of the necessity of community action on the part of our people if they would successfully conduct the affairs of government. They must work together whether they will or no, and it has been found in all self-governing countries that political party offers the best means, and in most cases the only means, of accomplishing this. At any one time a party is composed of those who will work together in a practical manner, and for practical purposes, in order to supply the community feeling or spirit of coöperation necessary to conduct the common affairs of the country, whether these latter be local, state or national, according to the orthodox division of interests as worked out in American history.

The political leaders at any given time must offer inducements in the form of candidates, promises, issues, or whatever may be necessary in order to induce the voters to stand together and secure the administration of the government according to their desires, or what they may imagine to be such. The problem is one of coördination rather than alienation. Again to quote Professor Holcombe, "the so-called principles of a political party are merely the justification which is offered for the responses of their members to the problems which changing circumstances present for solution." [4]

It is hardly an exaggeration to say that in the formation and continuity of political party existence this coöperation or group loyalty comes first, the worth and ability of candidates second, and principles last. This is the best explanation of the plain facts of the oft-repeated instances of dishonesty, graft, self-seeking, and incompetence in office that repeatedly have marred the history of American politics, are an outstanding evil to-day, and will continue to be such until our people become aware of the causes of evil that degrade our public life and demand otherwise. When right and just principles of coöperation are open to our practical political leaders as a basis of support, they will willingly, in most cases, drop the questionable and selfish or dishonest policies and cheerfully accept that which is clean, upright, and efficient, for one absolute and unswerving basis of action is always accepted by them without question, and that is that they must "give the people what they want." When our people are sufficiently convinced that they "want" honest and efficient government they will get it, and not before.

It is the purpose of the following pages to narrate the story of the origin, development, and continued existence of the Republican party of to-day, one of the two great political organizations that have shared between them the direction of the government of the United States for nigh on to seventy-five years. The oft-repeated problem of the coördination of interests, the more or less persistent tendencies in political thought, and the personalities that took the lead in molding or directing these great influences upon human welfare all go to make a story of success and failure, of lofty ideal or materialistic purpose, that must be known if the American people are to accomplish all that was expected of them by those who founded our nation, or gave their best of life or fortune in order that it might continue to live.

[4] A brilliant discussion of this whole problem is contained in Professor Holcombe's "Political Parties of To-day," especially pages 348 *et seq.*

Chapter II

THE HISTORICAL BACKGROUND

EVEN the most casual observer of world affairs will be struck by the fundamental difference between parties and elections in Great Britain and the United States, and those in the countries of Continental Europe and in practically all other self-governing democracies. British and American politics is based upon the two-party system, and this system extends generally throughout the British self-governing dominions as Canada, Australia, and South Africa. While for a time there may be more than two major parties, as during the years 1912 to 1914 in the United States, and during the past ten years in Britain or Canada, yet in the long run the swing is always back to the system of a party in power and a party in opposition. Much of the difficulty which has come upon France since the World War, and nearly led that country to financial destruction in 1926, has been due in direct cause to the multiple party system, and the lack of national unity and coördination in parliamentary affairs. The same may be seen in Belgium and Holland, in Italy before Mussolini's great work for political unification, in Germany and the Succession States of eastern Europe. So universal is the multiple party system, or lack of any system, leading to *blocs,* factional and local politics, that it would seem near the truth to say that this is the normal tendency in countries of popular government. In sharp contrast, we have the experience in successful government of Great Britain, and in the United States and other countries of British origin, with their peculiar devotion to two major parties, and two alone, and the inevitable rule that third parties either must take the place of one of the preexisting rivals, or else dwindle and disappear after taking part in a few electoral campaigns.

It should not be forgotten that the United States is primarily British in law and political institutions. There is no more essentially British document than the Constitution of the United States and our two-party system is part of our British heritage. This same system is the direct result of British history and goes back to the closing years of the reign of King Charles II, when there was sharp controversy as to the succession to the throne after that shrewd and conscienceless king should have ended his selfish and disgraceful existence.

One party, soon to be known as the "Tories," believed in the divine right of kings, and that the crown should go to Charles's Catholic brother, who later succeeded to the throne as James II. The other party, or "Whigs," desired the substitution of some other member of the royal line, in order to secure a Protestant succession, and also to restrain the aggressive use of executive authority so dear to the heart of the Stuarts. This struggle came to a sharp crisis at the time of the "Glorious Revolution" of 1688, the flight of James II, and the succession of William and Mary. It was more than half a century before the struggle between these two rival forces was changed to other objectives, and the opposition to the Hanover line finally disappeared in the general acceptance of George II and George III as the "rightful" kings, and the recalcitrant Jacobites and other legitimists transferred their convictions of "divine right" to the then occupants of the throne. But this struggle turned political life in England, and later in Scotland and the other parts of the British kingdom, into the two-party groove. During all this time politics was essentially based upon ideals and convictions that struck to the very fundamentals of human life and thought, and which held together, in more or less closely joined union, the mass of people who had sufficient civil rights to make them articulate, and this in spite of the almost total lack of party organization and machinery considered so essential to political existence at the present day.

While it is dangerous to dogmatize, yet it is hardly an exaggeration to say that the Tories stood for authority in church and state, believed in the divine right of kings, and were in many cases still loyal to the exiled Stuart kings. They were in large part made up of "high church" Episcopalians and Presbyterians, Roman Catholics, and conformists in the broadest sense. On the other hand, the Whigs believed in the divine right of the people as represented in Parliament, a more popular government of state and church, and contained the large body of "low church" and nonconformist population that foreshadowed the political and religious tendencies of British peoples for the years to come. A person did not lightly change his politics in those days, for it would mean a change in the most fundamental religious and political beliefs, and the average Britisher accepted the division between Whigs and Tories as natural and inevitable, and the two-party system was the practical outcome.

We inherited this along with the other British institutions and prepossessions, and the American Revolution was, in a sense, a British civil war, in which the party of the people, or Whigs, fought at first for popular rights and then for independence, while the party of the king, or Tories, fought for the upholding of British authority and the maintenance of royal prerogative. The war resulted in a Whig triumph, and the Tories were annihilated. But the essentially British party names were acclimated to American politics, and soon had lost their foreign connotation.

The events of the "critical period" that led up to the formation and adoption of the national Constitution caused a temporary alignment into Federalists and anti-Federalists, two factions of the Whigs who believed in or opposed a strong National Government in contrast to a continuation of the semi-sovereign position of the thirteen separate states leagued together at this time under the Articles of Confederation. Added to these groups were also those who had divided during the war into what has been known as the "military party" and the "party of Congress," or those who were interested in business and commercial pursuits on the one hand, as against the agricultural and frontier elements on the other.

When the Constitution was adopted and Washington began his administration as the first President, he attempted a nonpartizan conduct of the affairs of the nation, including in his cabinet men of varying views of national policy. But the inevitable happened, and by the end of his first administration there was a clear-cut line of division of the former Whigs into two groups soon to be known as the Federalist party, led by Washington and Hamilton, and the Republican-Democratic party, led by Jefferson and Madison.

We have here the first political alignment which was destined to have such enduring effect upon all our subsequent history, the present Republican and Democratic parties being descended, in inherent tendencies at least, from their Federalist and Republican-Democratic predecessors.

The Federalists, in general, stood for a strong National Government, a loose construction of the Constitution, the protection of property, and the advancement of commercial and industrial interests. These principles were inherited by the Republican party of to-day at the time of its founding and first successes in the years 1854 to 1860. Jefferson's Republican-Democratic party, on the other hand, believed government to be a necessary evil and the less of it the better, stood for individual liberty even to the endangering of law and order, strong local or state governments as the best guarantee of all this, and a strict construction of the Constitution. Much of these tendencies, at least, has come down to the present day in the Democratic party, which had its real origin in the leadership of Andrew Jackson and his shrewd and able colleagues, who knew how to use the arts of a demagogue to attract the attention and then loyalty of the plain people, without incurring actual demagoguery itself. But the principle of individual liberty was snatched away from the Democratic party by the Republicans of seventy years ago, when they took their stand firmly upon the exclusion of slavery from the new lands of the West and its gradual and inevitable abolition from all the states of the Union.

Jefferson's election in 1800 put the strict-construction, states' rights party in power. But its leader, by the purchase of Louisiana in 1803, not to mention the Non-Intercourse and Embargo acts that followed within the next five years, extended the bounds of loose constitutional construction much farther than ever had been dared by Hamilton or any of the high-arch Federalists. The Jefferson party was becoming used to the assertion of strong national authority, and this attracted many Federalists into the fold. Added to this was the death of Hamilton, which removed the ablest leader from the Federalist party, and the downright treason of many of its New England members during the war of 1812 and the events that culminated in the Hartford convention, all of which resulted in the virtual suicide of the party as a national organization and its disappearance except as a local faction in several states of the Union. The "Era of Good Feeling" followed, Monroe won his second election almost by default in 1820, and the American people, busily occupied in the economic development of the country, seemed to forget politics for a while, only to be aroused again by the personal squabble for office on the part of a number of the ablest national leaders in the campaign of 1824, and the election of John Quincy Adams by the House of Representatives, due to the lack of a majority for any candidate in the Electoral College.

Now emerges one of the greatest political leaders, as distinguished from statesmen, that the country has ever seen, in the person of Andrew Jackson. This is not to say that he was no statesman whatever, but certainly he would rank in that capacity below a dozen or more men in nineteenth-century American history, while he was the embodiment of the natural-born leader with an unerring instinct for the popular desires and the superficial means of satisfying them—at least so far as appearances went. "He was very ignorant. . . . While he had keen intuitions, he never thoroughly understood the merits of any question of politics or economics. But his was in the highest degree the instinct of a superior will, the genius of command. If he had been on board a vessel in extreme danger, he would have thundered out his orders without knowing anything of seamanship, and been indignantly surprised if captain and crew had not obeyed him. . . . His friends would sometimes exercise much influence upon him in starting his mind in a certain direction; but when once started, that mind was beyond their control. His personal integrity was above the reach of corruption. He always meant to do right; indeed, he was always convinced of being right." [1] In fact, it is hardly an exaggeration to say that Jackson believed, as have many other public men before and since his time, that there were just two sides to any and every question, a right and a wrong side. Of course, he held the right side; and those who opposed him and favored the wrong did so for either one of two reasons—they were fools and did not know the difference between right and wrong, or else they were knaves; they had intelligence enough to know he was right, and yet opposed him for reasons that could not be otherwise than dishonest or corrupt.

Jackson's policies of executive aggression, war on the United States Bank, strong nationalism and strict constitutional construction at the same time, naturally alienated large and diverse sections of the people. Although he drew his strength from the agricultural and frontier elements of the population who had been so true to Jefferson in the past, yet at the same time he appealed to the rising industrial elements who were growing in power and numbers due to the departure of the country from the early agricultural simplicity of life which had been so desired and advocated by their early political leader. Henry Clay and John Quincy Adams led that wing of the old Jefferson party that had advanced to the advocacy of policies of strong nationalism as embodied in the "American system" of protective tariffs and internal improvements at the hands of the Federal Government, and had been loosely known as "National Republicans"—the second "Republican" party

[1] Carl Schurz, "Henry Clay," I, 321, 323.

in American history. They promptly accepted Jackson's challenge on the bank and other economic questions, and among other allies were aided by Calhoun and his strict-construction, states' rights followers, who were aroused to a pitch of ecstatic rage over Jackson's prompt and patriotic action in squelching nullification and all treasonable attempts to make a breach in the national Union.

This collection of "political odds and ends," as the late Henry Jones Ford well called it, primarily anti-Jackson in composition, adopted the name of "Whig" party in 1834; while Jackson's followers sloughed off the "Republican" part of their Jeffersonian name and called themselves "Democrats," a name more or less consistently carried by their political descendants up till the present time. The discarded "Republican" half of the name was appropriated some twenty years later by the new and vigorous party which during succeeding years was to banish to retirement for two thirds of the time the party now seemingly triumphant and invincible under the picturesque and brilliant leadership of Andrew Jackson.

During the period now under discussion the development of American political institutions was in large part dependent upon the advancing frontier. This was involved in such questions as internal improvements, increasing looseness of constitutional construction, and the disposition of the public lands. But this ordinary course of two-party politics, based more or less on divergent theories of constitutional and economic questions, was rudely disturbed as though by the hand of Fate when there loomed on the political horizon the portentous and sinister issue of slavery, destined permanently to wreck the Whig party and to cause a new and more coördinate party to rise in its place, and also to split up the "Jackson Democrats" or bring them to political banishment for years at a time.

It is a well-known fact that the founders of our National Government were anything but favorable to slavery, but were restrained in their hostility to the institution by the need to conciliate the southern slave states, especially the Carolinas and

Georgia, in order that they might ratify the Constitution and enter the new and more perfect Union. Furthermore, they anticipated the gradual decay of the institution and its abolition within the near future. This reasonable anticipation was shattered by two events—the invention of the cotton gin by Eli Whitney in 1793 and the steady westward extension of settlement into the Mississippi Valley and the Southwest. Whitney's invention vastly increased the production of cotton and the monetary profits therefrom. "Tidewater South Carolina and Georgia produced practically all of the cotton crop in 1791. . . . By 1834 the Southwest had distanced the older section. What had occurred was a repeated western movement; the cotton-plant first spread from the seacoast to the uplands, and then . . . advanced to the Gulf plains, until that region achieved supremacy in its production."[2]

As a forecast of what was to come some years later, slavery appeared as an issue in 1790, during the second session of the First Congress. A discussion was precipitated by a petition from the Quakers protesting against the continuation of the slave trade. The House of Representatives finally resolved that the slave trade could not be abolished until 1808, and that Congress had no authority to interfere with slavery within the states. By act of March 2, 1807, the foreign slave trade was abolished after January 1, 1808, while in 1820 the slave trade was made piracy, with the nominal penalty of death. "It was the Mississippi Valley as an area for expansion which gave the slavery issue its significance in American history. But for this field of expansion, slavery might have fulfilled the expectation of the fathers and gradually died away."[3] The first crisis as the result of this expansion came in the struggle over Missouri during the years 1818 to 1820. The "Tallmadge Amendment" passed the House of Representatives, placing a gradual emancipation restriction upon the new state, but this was thrown out by the Senate. Finally, the Missouri Compromise became law on March 3, 1820, which admitted Missouri as a

[2] F. J. Turner, "Rise of the New West," 46, 47.
[3] F. J. Turner, "The Frontier in American History," 201.

slave state, but prohibited any other extension of slavery beyond the line of 36° 30′. This postponed the slavery struggle for twenty years.

Southern pro-slavery opinion, whetted to aggressiveness by the growing world demand for cotton, the increasing value of slaves, and the desire to extend the area of agricultural interests supported by slave labor, was roused to greater efforts by the instinct of self-preservation due to unadmitted conviction that in reality slavery was out of date and outgrown everywhere by the ordinary progress of civilization. An oarsman in a rapidly flowing river must row steadily against the adverse current in order merely to stand still, and must expend much greater effort if he would advance against the stream. So the Southern owners of slaves must be especially aggressive if they would prevent the gradual extinction of their "peculiar institution," and were convinced of the necessity of further extension of slave territory if they would make safe the political future. Added to this was the wrath and sense of injustice aroused in the South by the activities of the militant Abolitionists, who attracted exaggerated attention by their radicalism, their intensity of devotion, and their fanatical activities. Of them, Theodore Roosevelt well said, "the cause of the Abolitionists has had such a halo shed around it by the after-course of events, which they themselves in reality did very little to shape, that it has been usual to speak of them with absurdly exaggerated praise. Their courage, and for the most part their sincerity, cannot be too highly spoken of, but their share in abolishing slavery was far less than has commonly been represented; any single non-abolitionist politician, like Lincoln or Seward, did more than all the professional Abolitionists combined really to bring about its destruction. The abolition societies were only in a very restricted degree the causes of the growing feeling in the North against slavery; they are rather to be regarded as themselves manifestations or accompaniments of that feeling. The anti-slavery outburst in the Northern states over the admission of Missouri took place a dozen years before there was an abolition society in existence. [Mr. Roosevelt evidently means, of the radical Garrisonian school] . . . They belonged to that class of men that is always engaged in some agitation or other; only it happened that in this particular agitation they were right." [4]

The pro-slavery forces of the South, blocked from their field of territorial expansion within the then bounds of the Union by the Missouri Compromise, turned their attention at first to the Southwest. In that section a number of southerners had emigrated with their slaves into Mexico, settled what later became known as Texas, and revolted and proclaimed their independence on March 2, 1836. The issue of the annexation of Texas, ardently supported by the Southern slaveholders in general, became a critical problem of American politics. More and more the North and West became convinced of the evil of human bondage and its logical contradiction of the fundamental ideals for which the country had stood, in theory at least, since the adoption of the Declaration of Independence. They realized that the annexation of new slave territory, with the inevitable organization and admission of new slave states, would buttress the peculiar institution that was supposed gradually to be dying out. But the popular and essentially American doctrine of continental expansion was too strong for them when hitched up to the willing yoke of the pro-slavery forces, and Congress finally, by joint resolution, declared Texas annexed as a state of the Union. This resolution was signed by President Tyler and became law on March 1, 1845. Texas formally accepted this act and became a state of the Union within the same year.

But with Texas the United States had annexed a war. Polk, a man of moderate abilities in statesmanship, was keen enough to appreciate the possibilities of the office of President. He dominated and led the Democratic party during the four years of his administration in a way that was a decided reminiscence of Andrew Jackson and an anticipation of Woodrow Wilson. Himself a pro-slavery man and an expansionist, this combination of qualities could only result in a policy that

[4] "Life of Thomas H. Benton," 158–160.

led straight to a war of aggression. The invasion and conquest of Mexico was the result, followed by new and enormous additions of territory in 1848. Slavery had been abolished in Mexico by decree of President Guerrero on September 15, 1829; the annexation of this territory to the United States did not change its status from freedom to slavery; so the whole question of the extension of slavery, as settled in the American territory of that time by the Missouri Compromise, was reopened again by the problem of what to do with the new accessions. It stood to reason that the North and West would not lightly see the pro-slavery forces acquire this new source of strength without vigorous attempts to prevent it, while the pro-slavery leaders of the South never would lose, if they could help it, this wonderful opportunity for great and almost unlimited increase of strength.

Soon after the Mexican War began, Polk on August 8, 1846, sent a message to Congress asking for an appropriation of two million dollars to "settle the boundary question with Mexico." This was enough to show, beyond question of doubt, what had been in his mind during all of his manipulation of the diplomatic relations with Mexico. The same day a bill was introduced into the House of Representatives to make the appropriation, when David Wilmot, a Pennsylvania Democrat, at once introduced his celebrated "Proviso," which crystallized the whole issue of freedom and slavery within the United States and led directly to the rise of the "Free Soil" movement and the founding of the present Republican party.

The text of this celebrated measure was as follows:

"Provided, That, as an express and fundamental condition to the acquisition of any territory from the Republic of Mexico by the United States, by virtue of any treaty which may be negotiated between them, and to the use by the Executive of the moneys herein appropriated, neither slavery nor involuntary servitude shall ever exist in any part of said territory, except for crime, whereof the party shall first be duly convicted."

It appears that the Wilmot Proviso in reality originated with Jacob Brinkerhoff, who was a Democratic member of Congress from Ohio. He had opposed the annexation of Texas and had tried so to amend the resolution of annexation as to exclude slavery, at least from the western and northwestern parts of the territory annexed. He now seems to have wished to put Polk's administration in a difficult situation, so the Proviso was the means he used for this purpose. Since he had lost his influence with the Democratic party, he wished the measure to be introduced by some other member of the party. Wilmot was a good man for this service, since he stood well with the South, due to his support of the annexation of Texas, and his vote for the Walker Tariff. Therefore, Brinkerhoff wrote the Proviso and arranged for Wilmot to introduce it. [5] The Proviso was adopted by the House, with little or no excitement, by the vote of 87 to 64. The bill was taken up by the Senate on August 10. A motion was made to strike out the Proviso, but it is probable that the measure would have passed, nevertheless, had not Senator John Davis of Massachusetts, well-meaning but garrulous, talked it to death. Congress adjourned before final action was taken. Had Senator Davis not been prone to the evil which to-day is so great a source of temptation to the "Pat" Harrisons, Caraways, La Follettes and other self-appointed spokesmen of the "pee-pul," the Proviso would have been passed and the whole history of the country changed. This is just another illustration of the fact that most evils of the present day are old ones, and the waste of the people's time and patience is certainly not the least of them.

Strange to relate, the Southern political leaders do not seem to have been awake to what was going on, or to what so greatly threatened to take away from them what they were convinced they had newly won, and wreck their hitherto successful plans for slavery extension. On the other hand, the politicians throughout the country, timid as always, had no desire to arouse

[5] Garrison, "Westward Extension," 255–260.

a new controversy over slavery, for they were face to face with the preparations for the national campaign of 1848, and they did desire to evade every issue that might make more difficult their task of uniting the interests necessary for success in the Presidential election. But facing them was the fact that there had just been an enormous annexation of territory, including California, New Mexico, and what has later been incorporated into several of the states of largest area in the Union. The Southerners began to realize what was meant by the movement behind the Proviso, and political trouble at once began. The Democratic leaders, in order to stave off any party controversy over the issue, took up the doctrine which they designated "squatter sovereignty": to make no determination at present about slavery or freedom in the new territory, but wait until the land became settled and was ready for statehood, then let the inhabitants make their own decision—one of those instances of beautiful theory, so characteristic of the self-styled *intelligentsia,* where fact and practical experience are overlooked as minor matters of rude and impolite significance, while the results always come later with the inexorable quality of cause and effect. Although raised to the point of political ecstasy by Douglas a few years later and always with disastrous consequence, "squatter sovereignty" was too vague to be practical, except for purposes of deferring an issue to a future time—which, it was devoutly hoped, might never arrive.

It should be noted in passing that during the few years preceding the period now under discussion the Abolitionists, forsaking the usual political and moral agencies for anti-slavery agitation, formed the Liberty party in 1840. Following a convention held at Warsaw, Genesee county, New York, in December, 1839, a second convention met at Albany, New York, and founded the Liberty party. The meeting was made up of abolitionists from the eastern part of the country, there being not one delegate from the Northwest, where, as will be seen, the main strength of the Republican party of some fifteen years later was to lie. The new party nominated James G. Birney of New York for President and Thomas Earle of

Pennsylvania for Vice-President. But 7069 votes were cast for this party in the election of 1840, the anti-slavery men in general, who from now on must be distinguished from the more radical Abolitionists, preferring to support Harrison and Van Buren, the respective Whig and Democratic nominees. Not discouraged by this small showing, the Liberty party leaders kept hard at work agitating and organizing, and held their first real national convention at New York city on May 12, 1841. Delegates were present from most of the northern and western states, the party was formally organized, and even then it made nominations for the campaign of 1844 in the persons of Birney and Thomas Morris of Ohio. Adjournment was made for two years, subject to the call of the Central Committee. Pursuant to this action a second nominating convention met at Buffalo, New York, in the latter part of August, 1843, many northwesterners being present; Birney and Morris were unanimously renominated, and in the election of the next year the party vote increased to 62,300. Most important of all, the Liberty party vote in New York, most of which came from the Whig party, according to contemporary belief, was enough to throw the state to Polk and cause the defeat of Henry Clay, the idol of the Whigs. They never forgave the Liberty party, and its already great unpopularity was largely increased. The party seems to have reached its maximum strength, especially in the Northwest, about the year 1846, but it soon became evident that the voters of the nation who were anti-slavery in sympathy would not leave their parties for a third party movement, and slavery itself must become a vital and all-absorbing subject of popular interest before the old parties would make it an issue, or a widespread movement for a new party develop after the wreck of one of the two great organizations. This was accomplished as the final result of the struggle over the Mexican annexations, the beginnings of which already have been discussed in connection with the Wilmot Proviso. The next step came soon after, in the split in the Democratic party during the campaign of 1848.

For some years there had been a division in the Democracy

of New York state, which became so bitter during Polk's administration that two definite factions were formed, ready to fight to the death for state and national party supremacy. These were known as the Hunkers and Barnburners, or might be designated as Regulars and Radicals. The Hunkers were the organization "stand-patters," who were said by their opponents to have little principle but merely to "hunker" after office. They supported Polk and his administration, especially in the matters of the Mexican War and the tenderness, if not outright sympathy, toward slavery. Among them were many state leaders soon to be known, with other prominent Democrats in the North and West, as "Northern men with Southern principles," a description soon reduced to the nickname of "Doughfaces." The Barnburners were in large part the more liberal or radical in thought, but were still loyal to Martin Van Buren and the extreme tenets of Jacksonian Democracy, and had never forgiven Van Buren's defeat for the nomination in 1844. They were rather unfriendly to slavery, and in many cases had opposed the annexation of Texas and the Mexican War. They now were moving toward a more decided hostility to the slave interests, and especially opposed the extension of slavery into new or hitherto free territory. The Wilmot Proviso came as a convenient expression of their hitherto inchoate policy, and they cheerfully accepted their new name of Barnburners, bestowed upon them by their factional opponents. This name arose from the political campaign story of the Dutchman who burned down his barn in order to get rid of the rats which infested it—the application being apparent that these reform elements were perfectly willing to destroy the great national Democratic party in order to effect the "minor" objective of the restriction of slavery.

The first important national convention in the Presidential campaign of 1848 was that of the Democrats, who met at Baltimore on May 22. The candidates nominated were Lewis Cass of Michigan and William O. Butler of Kentucky. The platform was a rehearsing of old principles and evasion of slavery. Dissatisfied with their treatment, the New York

Barnburners withdrew and began to look around for political allies who might assist them in making their more liberal principles effective.

The Whigs met at Philadelphia on June 7. General Zachary Taylor of Louisiana, a southern slaveholder of little political interest, was nominated, with Millard Fillmore, of New York, for the second place on the ticket. No platform was adopted and the slave issue was entirely ignored. Evidently the Whigs were persuaded that their "best bet" was a repetition of the "old hero" type of emotional campaign, so successful at the hands of the Jackson Democrats on several occasions, and in their own experience with William Henry Harrison. But there was a small group of anti-slavery men, several of them from Ohio, who were dissatisfied and ready for some positive action.

The Barnburners took the first step toward the formation of an anti-slavery party, and held a convention a few days later at Utica, New York, where delegates from several other states, northeast and northwest, joined them in the nomination of Martin Van Buren for President. This led to a later and more extended movement that culminated in a convention at Buffalo on August 9. There were representatives from seventeen states, totaling about 300 delegates. The name of "Free Democracy" was adopted as the formal name of the new party, but it has been generally known in history as "Free Soil," due to the outstanding characteristic of its platform. The nominees were Martin Van Buren for President and Charles Francis Adams of Massachusetts for Vice-President.

The above-named platform is the important fact with regard to this party, since it laid the foundation for the issues so soon to be adopted by the new Republican party of six years later. The outstanding features of this platform are contained in the following summary:

That slavery in the several states of this Union which recognize its existence depends upon state laws alone, which cannot be repealed or modified by the Federal Government, and for which laws that Government was not responsible. We therefore propose no interference by Congress with slavery within the limits of any state.

It was the settled policy of the nation not to extend, nationalize, or encourage, but to limit, localize, and discourage slavery; and to this policy, which should never have been departed from, the Government ought to return.

In the judgment of this convention, Congress has no more power to make a slave than to make a king; no more power to institute or establish slavery than to institute or establish a monarchy. No such power can be found among those specifically conferred by the Constitution, or derived by any just implication from them.

It is the duty of the Federal Government to relieve itself from all responsibility for the existence or continuance of slavery wherever the Government possesses constitutional authority to legislate on that subject, and is thus responsible for its existence.

The true and in the judgment of this convention the only safe means of preventing the extension of slavery into territory now free is to prohibit its existence in all such territory by an act of Congress.

We accept the issue which the slave power has forced upon us; and to their demand for more slave states and more slave territory our calm but final answer is, no more slave states and no more slave territory. Let the soil of our extensive domains be ever kept free for the hardy pioneers of our own land, and the oppressed and banished of other lands seeking homes of comfort and fields of enterprise in the New World.

There must be no more compromises with slavery; if made, they must be repealed.[6]

This was rather a strong defiance of the aggressive and powerful slave interests, hitherto so strong in the Democratic party, and whose hold on political leadership in that organization was to last for more than a decade. While decidedly anti-slavery, it was by no means Abolition, at least in the sense

[6] The full text of the platform may be found in E. Stanwood, "History of the Presidency," 239–241.

of the term as used by Garrison, Gerrit Smith, or radicals of that stamp, but it did offer a constructive and sound program upon which could unite all those people who, while opposed to the institution of slavery, yet saw the difficulties and dangers in immediate emancipation, both in the field of politics, and economics or social welfare. It was the enunciation of a sound process of reform by evolutionary rather than revolutionary methods, and it was just this feature that soon was to appeal so strongly to the statesmanship of a man like Abraham Lincoln. Van Buren, a man of great ability but adept in political manipulation and proper evasion of unpleasant and critical issues, must have squirmed with inward trepidation when he accepted the platform, but he did so, saying that the exclusion of slavery from free soil was an object "sacred in the sight of heaven, the accomplishment of which is due to the memories of the great and just men long since, we trust, made perfect in its courts."

The Liberty or Abolition party, which had nominated John P. Hale for President at a convention held in New York city in November, 1847, withdrew its candidates and indorsed Van Buren, Anti-slavery Whigs, in New York and many other northern districts, generally supported Taylor, while those of the same political stripe in Ohio and other western sections supported the Free Soil party. Nevertheless, Van Buren actually received more votes than Cass in the three states of New York, Massachusetts, and Vermont, and ran strongly in Wisconsin. The splitting of the vote in the three states first mentioned was sufficient to defeat Cass and elect Taylor, since the latter carried several southern states and was a candidate upon whom the various forces of men strongly devoted to the Union could unite their efforts. The election was a foreshadowing, although faint as yet, of the political strength ere long destined to swing into the Republican party, which was led to final victory by Lincoln in the election of 1860 and upon a distinctly Free Soil platform.

But Taylor's success did not settle the question of the disposition of California and other territory recently annexed from Mexico. An united effort was made by the leaders of both national parties to make a final settlement of the slave issue by means of a compromise which should end the struggle for all time. But while this often may be accomplished in matters of purely political expediency, yet there can be no compromise on moral questions, and slavery inevitably partook of that character. This became more and more recognized as time went on, not only by the anti-slavery elements in the North and West, but also by the pro-slavery elements in the South, who advanced from a position of moral defense of slavery as an institution, to that of its advocacy as a decidedly moral and social good. When absolutely honest and sincere people are convinced of the moral and religious justification of their respective views, and are willing to support them to the end, armed conflict is inevitable. But few were the people who at this time had the prophetic insight to see it.

The Compromise of 1850 was an attempt to place slavery beyond the pale of practical political issue. Taylor, who developed into a President of strength and ability, and even of statesmanlike qualities, has never received adequate recognition for the stand he took for the Union, and the policy of settling matters a step at a time, but settling them, rather than that of attempting to settle everything at once—and really settling nothing. His untimely death gave the compromisers their chance, with the assistance of the gentlemanly and pliant Millard Fillmore. Although this resulted in the people actively entering upon a process of self-deception, which caused the disappearance of the Free Soil party, and the eclipse of the political power of the Abolitionists, the resultant political calm was but temporary, and the storm that broke ended only in the horrors of the Civil War.

Chapter III

THE KANSAS-NEBRASKA BILL AND INEVITABLE CONFLICT

THE Compromise of 1850 was typical of Henry Clay, and was a fitting and concluding masterpiece of the political life of that gay eupeptic son of Kentucky. Clay was born to poverty and the hard discipline of want. To that fact probably is due his first great success, but it came too early, and he soon learned the art of following the line of least resistance to such an extent of adeptness that it often resulted in real mental laziness. Naturally bright and able, he could see to the heart of any problem, but never *went* to it. Therefore, his solution usually was superficial and of temporary effect.

The aforenamed Compromise well illustrates these weaknesses. It settled definitely the admission of California as a free state, and also the boundary of Texas. So far, this was "all to the good," but the organization of Utah and New Mexico as Territories, without mention of slavery, and the abolition of the slave trade in the District of Columbia were but half measures that merely deferred to the near future an inevitable contest. The Fugitive Slave Law was but a pyrrhic gain for the South, and that at the expense of exasperation and dismay at the North, when its people had the most disagreeable, not to mention atrocious, features of slavery brought to their very doors at the hands of slave-catchers and national enforcement officers.

And yet Clay plumed himself on his third great success in the line of "great pacificator," and went to his grave in the happy thought that he had again "saved the Union," forgetting that it never is possible to compromise a moral issue. The majority of the people in the United States soon were to come to the conviction that slavery violated the fundamental instincts of morality and the laws of God, or else were as firmly convinced that it was a great moral good, of Divine origin, and fraught with the imperative duty of a superior to a subordinate race. The train was well laid for a fine explosion, and one Stephen A. Douglas soon was to apply the match—to his own astonishment and political undoing.

Clay's influence and the sincere and honest attempts of his colleagues in this legislative activity had such a good pedagogical effect on public opinion that not only were they able to act upon their own sincere convictions that the "Compromise was a finality," but also to fool the major part of the American people into agreeing with them. And this delusion lasted for over three years. It was defended by Lewis Cass and Douglas among northern Democrats, and by Rufus Choate and Daniel Webster among the Whigs, while Clay, Crittenden, Alexander Stephens, Cobb, and Foote strongly supported it in the South. Under this quieting influence occurred the congressional elections of 1850. The Whigs lost ground, the Barnburners returned to their old party, and the Free Soil party crumbled away, just as did its later model the Progressive party in 1914. The old party names still had an attenuated hold upon the American mind, but this was to last only a short time longer, when the greater crisis was to cause a new political alignment. All opposition was not stilled, and the old-line partizans of both parties saw the ominous success of fusion efforts in Ohio, where Benjamin R. Wade, an anti-slavery Whig, was elected to the United States Senate, Charles Sumner, a Free Soil Democrat, was chosen to the same body from the state of Massachusetts, while George S. Boutwell also was elected Democratic Governor of the latter commonwealth by the same political tactics.

The political leaders were not forgetful of the approaching presidential campaign of the year 1852, so on January 22, 1851, was issued a pronouncement signed by forty-four members of Congress, composed by Stephens and bearing at its head the name of Henry Clay. It opposed the renewal at any time of the sectional quarrel and declared against the support of any candidates for President, Vice-President, Congress or a state legislature of whom it was not a well-known fact that they condemned all disturbance of the Compromise and any further agitation of the slave question in any form. President Fillmore, the gentlemanly occupant of the White House in succession to the virile Taylor, also had intimated in his recent annual message to Congress that he would use his veto to protect the precious legislation of which such exaggerated hopes were entertained.

There now was the practical problem before the leaders of preserving the old party lines, interesting the people in other matters of legislation than slavery, and preventing the formation of any sectional political organizations. Moral issues such as temperance reform and the management of penal and correctional institutions were good outlets for reforming enthusiasm, while the remarkable economic expansion of the country seemed destined completely to occupy the energies of a vigorous and confident people.

It was under such conditions that the campaign of 1852 was fought and won by the Democrats. They called together their convention at Baltimore on June 1 and nominated Franklin Pierce of New Hampshire for President, who was mainly known for his handsome presence and his innocuous character. William R. King of Alabama was designated for the office of Vice-President, and the platform was a safe statement of belief in the Compromise as a "finality." The Whig convention met at the same city on the fifteenth of June and nominated General Winfield Scott for President and William A. Graham of North Carolina for Vice-President, the embattled hosts being unable to escape from their obsession that only with the aid of a military hero would they be able to march to certain victory. Their platform—for they really had one this time—stood by the Compromise, but without the word "finality," and added the cautious statement that this devotion should last until further legislation might be rendered necessary by time and experience.

The Free Soil Democrats, in spite of their reverses two years before, did not give up, but met at Pittsburgh on August 11 and nominated John P. Hale of New Hampshire and George W. Julian of Indiana for President and Vice-President, placing them on a platform that strongly opposed slavery and the Compromise of 1850 as well. There was a stagnation in their appeal to popular interest, and their vote fell off nearly fifty per cent. at the polls in November when compared with that of Van Buren at the preceding presidential election, showing that a new crisis was needed to shake the people out of their complacency and seeming indifference.

Pierce was overwhelmingly elected, his good looks and convivial habits being appropriate to the era of good political feeling that was being foisted upon an obedient electorate, and the Whig party was fairly crushed. Probably the fact that the slave interests had gotten the advantage in the Compromise deal resulted in the alienation or in the lack of interest among the anti-slavery people and caused many of them to remain away from the polls. Since there were more of this kind of people in the Whig than in the Democratic party, it was the former that suffered the most from indifference, with the oft-repeated result, so common at the present day, that the "stay-at-home" vote settled the election.

Suddenly an entirely new party, based on issues of a decidedly new character, appeared and seemed for a time destined to offer to the dissatisfied members of the old parties a haven of refuge, with a brand-new set of principles well calculated to appeal to the emotions of all sorts of people. This was the American, or "Know-Nothing," party, which began to affect elections in an astonishing way, individuals often being elected to office who had not been publicly known as candidates. Or the tickets of the two old parties were "split" and only those candidates succeeded who were known to hold the views of the new party. A secret organization, known as the "Order of the Star-Spangled Banner," had been worked out on a plan formulated in the state of New York about the year

1849. It was put into practical effect in the year 1852 as one of a number of societies opposed to the influence of foreigners and of Roman Catholics in elections. It rapidly extended its influence, but did not have any marked effect until the year 1854. It became especially strong in the states of Massachusetts, New York, Pennsylvania, and Maryland, and in the spring of 1855 it carried the states of New Hampshire, Rhode Island, and Connecticut.

As the Irish Catholics and Germans, against whom it mainly was directed, were in large part Democrats, the new party offered special attractions to disgruntled Whigs, and they went into it literally by the thousands. But just at the time of its seeming great success it ran squarely against the slave issue, revived in an especially aggravated form by the Kansas-Nebraska Bill, as soon will be narrated. Added to this was the fact that although it called itself the "American Party," and professed what at a later date was called "one hundred per cent. Americanism," yet it had in it the seeds of inevitable decay, for it was based, in spite of its professions, upon two essentially un-American issues—racial and religious prejudice. It did not operate as a final alternative to the slave issue, but merely served to pry loose many congenital Whigs from their early political foundations, and thus prepared them for their entry into the new Republican party soon to be formed.

The state of forced political calm described above which followed the passage of the Compromise of 1850 was rudely broken up by the action of Stephen Arnold Douglas, the Democratic senator from Illinois, who had gradually won his way to a position of outstanding leadership and influence in his party and the nation. Douglas, in early life, was not unlike Clay. Born to poverty, in the state of Vermont, in the year 1813, he had attended the district schools, was apprenticed to a cabinetmaker, and at the age of seventeen removed to Ontario county, New York, attending Canandaigua Academy. He studied law, drifted West in 1833, and in the following year was admitted to the bar at Jacksonville, Illinois. The next year he became a district state's attorney, then followed service in the state legislature, an interval as commissioner of the land office at Springfield, and at the age of twenty-seven he became secretary of state of Illinois in 1840. Meanwhile he had helped organize the Democratic party in the state and soon became one of its leading lights. Almost immediately this infant prodigy of an office-holder became a judge of the state supreme court and in 1845 was elected to the House of Representatives at Washington, being advanced two years later to the Senate, where he held a position of leadership and great influence for the rest of his life, until his comparatively early death in the year 1861.

He was like Clay in that his early success had the same bad effects of superficiality and mental laziness, and there was added a streak of the demagogue. This vitiated much of his work as a statesman until the last two years of his life, when suddenly he seemed to realize a sense of responsibility and became a changed man, rising to such heights of statesmanship and patriotism that his death was little short of a national calamity. These events will be discussed in turn, for the story of American politics of necessity must have much to say of Douglas, and unwittingly he became a moving cause in the formation of the Republican party.

The immediate congressional events leading up to the introduction of the Kansas-Nebraska Bill had their inception on December 5, 1853, when Senator A. C. Dodge of Iowa gave notice to the Senate of his intention to introduce a bill for the organization of a government for a new Territory of Nebraska. He did this on December 14, and the measure was referred to the Committee on Territories, of which Douglas was chairman. A duplicate of the Dodge bill was introduced in the House of Representatives on December 22 by J. G. Miller of Missouri and referred to the House Committee on Territories, of which W. A. Richardson of Illinois was chairman. On January 4, 1854, Douglas formally introduced a bill from his committee to organize the Territory of Nebraska and permit it to enter the Union "with or without slavery." The same day Senator Archibald Dixon of Kentucky, a Whig, offered an amendment providing for "squatter sovereignty," or the determination of the slave or free character of the new territory at the time it applied for statehood and according to the desire of the then inhabitants thereof. On January 23 Douglas reported a second bill, dividing the territory into two parts, naming the northern and southern parts Nebraska and Kansas respectively, and definitely incorporating the doctrine of "squatter sovereignty." It also stated that the slavery restriction of the Missouri Compromise was superseded by the principles of the Compromise of 1850, and "is hereby declared inoperative." It is thought Douglas was forced into this action by the Dixon measure, and it is known he had conferred with both President Pierce and Jefferson Davis, the secretary of war. Evidently he did not appreciate the moral background of the slavery controversy and was acting on the grounds of political expediency.

There are many theories with regard to what these grounds may have been, influence being traced to Missouri politics and the rivalry between the two senators, Atchison and Benton. Also, there is no question that Douglas already had his eye on the Presidency, and might hope to curry favor with the strong and dominant Democratic leaders of the South. But did he realize the alienation of Northern sentiment that was bound to follow? Says Professor Allen Johnson:[1] "When, . . . under the pressure of conditions for which he was not responsible, he yielded to the demand for the repeal of the Missouri Compromise, he failed to see that revulsion of moral sentiment that swept over the North. It was perfectly clear to his mind, that historically the prohibition of slavery by Federal law had had far less effect than the North believed. He was convinced that nearly all, if not all, of the great West was dedicated to freedom by a law which transcended any human enactment. Why, then, hold to a mere form, when the substance could be otherwise secured? Why should Northerner affront Southerner by imperious demands, when the same end might

[1] "Life of Douglas," 271.

be attained by a compromise which would not cost either dear? Possibly he was not unwilling to let New Mexico become slave territory if the great Northwest should become free by the operation of the same principle. Besides, there was the very tangible advantage of holding his party together by a sensible agreement, for the sake of which each faction yielded something."

On the other hand, recent researches would tend to give a more logical and specific reason for Douglas's action, and this lay in the location of a proposed transcontinental railroad. It was realized by thoughtful people of the time that speedier communications between the widely separated sections of the vast continental republic were an absolute necessity if the nation were to endure united and without future territorial and national division. Seventy years before this time George Washington, with rare insight and statesmanship, had been foremost in stressing the imperative necessity of this policy. Of course, the first question now was the route the great continental railroad should follow, for the determination of this question meant the economic prosperity and even rapid settlement of the central and western country for years to come. Jefferson Davis was now at the head of the War Department, and surveys for the railroad were largely the future work of the army engineers. Undoubtedly Davis would prefer that the railroad have its eastern terminus in some Southern city, as New Orleans, thus adding enormously to the wealth and the growth of the southern sections of the country. On the other hand, the location of the transcontinental railroad somewhat along the lines of the present Southern Pacific system would be a direct blow at the future prosperity of the new and rising cities of St. Louis and Chicago, and the latter was within the state of Illinois and therefore under the especial care of Douglas himself. What better bargain could be made than to give the South the direct benefit of the opening to slavery of the land hitherto held to freedom by the Missouri Compromise, and provide the slave interests with the political and economic advantages of great development, gaining in return the transcontinental railroad which might give at once to Chicago and St. Louis the vast trade of the Mississippi Valley and the developing West, and thus guarantee their future greatness and prosperity? This was an opportunity too good to be lost, and Douglas was not the person to let it pass by, especially when he was more or less blind to the storm of opposition he was about to raise, and which ultimately changed the whole course of history. There is good reason to believe that this bargain was probably the underlying cause of all the political and legislative maneuvering mentioned above, and at least it offers an explanation more convincing than all the surmises and speculations that have occupied the attention of historians for the past seventy or more years.[2]

Whatever the underlying motives may have been, the Kansas-Nebraska Bill was the cause of an explosion that veritably blew to pieces the political and moral unity of the country, and aroused such feelings of hatred and vindictiveness that the effects are finally vanishing only after nearly three quarters of a century of hostility and sectionalism. The debate in both houses of Congress was bitter and long drawn out. The bill passed the Senate on March 3 by the vote of 37 to 14, made up of 28 Democrats and 9 Southern Whigs for the measure, while those opposed were 2 Free Soilers, 6 Northern Whigs, one Southern Whig (John Bell of Tennessee), 4 Northern Democrats and one Southern Democrat (Houston of Texas).

The bill passed the House of Representatives on May 22 by the vote of 113 to 100. This vote may be analyzed as follows: yeas, 101 Democrats and 12 Southern Whigs; nays, 42 Northern Democrats, 2 Southern Democrats, 45 Northern Whigs, 7 Southern Whigs, 4 Free Soilers. The disintegration of the two old parties may well be seen, and is ample evidence of the readiness even on the part of office-holders to break

[2] Correspondence between Jefferson Davis and George B. McClellan, then an officer in the engineers of the United States army, tends to substantiate this theory.

away from old alignments and unite along new lines of cleavage.

The effects of the Kansas-Nebraska Bill are well summed up by Professor T. C. Smith, who says:[3] "No act more fateful in character ever passed the Congress of the United States, for it set in motion the train of political changes which led straight to the Civil War. It was the direct cause of a radical alteration of northern political feeling, of the total failure of the compromising or Union party of 1850, and of the destruction of both the national parties. The suddenness of its introduction, the recklessness of its disturbance of the territorial situation, were such as to make an instant powerful impression, and the members of Congress who passed it realized, when the session finally ended in August, that they had begun a political revolution whose end no man could foresee."

The outcry over the country was instantaneous. The North felt that in the repeal of the Missouri Compromise the South had violated its solemn faith, and was no more to be trusted in any way. The pro-slavery leaders saw their advantage and were not slow to profit by it, meanwhile standing firm on the position that simple justice was being done, that the territories were the property of the entire people, and that any citizen of the United States had the right to go into the common national domain and take his movable property of any kind—slaves, horses, furniture, cattle, or anything else—with him. Of course, the obvious answer was that the common domain was the property of the people of the United States only in their corporate capacity and thus subject to the determination of the will of the corporate body; but people in a state of emotional excitement and engaged in acrimonious argument seldom stop to think clearly or logically, and the American people of seventy-five years ago were no exception to this rule.

The various churches and their ministers were especially active in the controversy, deeming it to be of direct effects in its moral and religious implications. This was especially

[3] "Parties and Slavery," 107–8.

true of New England, and the sermons preached throughout the land often formed the sentiments and laid the foundations for the convictions that were soon to be expressed in the new party about to be organized. Everybody "went to church" in those days. A petition signed by 3050 clergymen of various denominations in New England sent a typical protest to Congress. It condemned the Kansas-Nebraska Bill as "a great moral wrong, a breach of faith eminently unjust to the moral principles of the community, and subversive of all confidence in national engagements; a measure full of danger to the peace and even the existence of our beloved Union, and exposing us to the righteous judgment of the Almighty." [4]

A rather humorous twist is given to the reception of this petition by Congress due to the fact that William M. Tweed, of later malodorous Tammany memory, was at that time a Democratic member of the House of Representatives, and delivered himself with characteristic hypocrisy as follows: "Alas, alas, such a profanation of the American pulpit was never before known. The head of the devout follower droops!" He does not state whither the devout head "droops," but we may suppose it was to undisturbed contemplation of future and characteristic graft and peculation.[5]

By using strong party pressure on the Democratic majority in both houses of Congress the Kansas-Nebraska Bill had been forced through, but the results were party disintegration and more or less of chaos. Any crystallization of sentiment into new party organization was delayed by the activity and seeming success of the American or Know-Nothing party as narrated above. Added to this was the fact that for the present no great Northern leaders emerged, so the anti-slavery feeling developed slowly along political lines and more or less at random. For some time opponents of the legislation, who deserted the old parties on that account, were content to be known merely as "anti-Nebraska" men, and even were so designated in official rolls of state legislatures or other bodies.

[4] Nicolay and Hay, "Lincoln," I, 361.
[5] L. W. Spring, "Kansas," 13.

The first and most outstanding instance of this party demoralization was the long struggle over the organization of the new or Thirty-fourth Congress, which was elected in the fall of 1854, the same year that saw the Kansas-Nebraska legislation. In the new House of Representatives, "as nearly as any classification could be made," there were "108 anti-Nebraska members, nearly 40 Know-Nothings, and about 75 Democrats. The remaining members were undecided. The proud Democratic majority of the Pierce election was annihilated." [6] Beginning on December 3, 1855, the House struggled for two months to elect a speaker, and only succeeded on February 2, 1856, in electing Nathaniel Prentiss Banks, who represented Massachusetts in Congress from 1853 to 1857, and was at first a "coalition Democrat," then a "Know-Nothing," then a "Republican." This was accomplished on the one hundred and thirty-third vote, or more or less formal ballot, and only after the adoption of a special "rule" permitting a plurality election.

It is of special interest to note that friends and foes of Banks repeatedly designated his supporters as "Republicans," thus referring to a movement, or series of movements, that had begun throughout the country, and mainly in the Northwest, for the organization of a new party to meet the changed political conditions. Many of the present members of Congress had taken part in these efforts, and the election of Banks was in a sense the *début,* on a national stage, of the new organization that soon was to sweep the country and hold in its hands the destinies of the nation for the larger number of years since that time. From Speaker Banks to President Coolidge is the span of the past life of the Republican party as we know it to-day, and the basis for all present and future forecasts as to the immediate development of many important political institutions of the United States. It is now necessary to trace the local beginnings of this party, soon to become of such national importance.

[6] Nicolay and Hay, "Lincoln," I, 363.

Chapter IV

THE FOUNDING OF THE REPUBLICAN PARTY

THE Kansas-Nebraska Bill brought about the disruption of the Whig party and the final separation of the Northern from the Southern members of that organization. Furthermore, Democrats of Free Soil tendency throughout the North, whether or not they had ever coöperated with the party of that name, were now permanently alienated in large numbers from Southern pro-slavery domination. If these elements could be amalgamated with the more conservative wing of the Abolitionists, and with all others who were of a more or less liberal or progressive tendency, it would be possible to form a party that would be strong enough to afford some opposition to the aggressive policy of the Jackson-Democratic party, now hopelessly in bondage to reactionary influence in all that affected social or moral issues.

This amalgamation now was successfully accomplished, but not all at once, or in any one place. Rather was there a synchronous rising at many places and in many widely separated parts of the nation. It is a matter of great interest that the lead was taken in the old Northwest and soon seconded elsewhere, but mainly in New England. Frederick Jackson Turner points out the underlying reasons for this.[1] "Slavery was a sectional trait that would not down, but in the West it could not remain sectional. It was the greatest of frontiersmen who declared: 'I believe this government cannot permanently endure half slave and half free. It will become all one thing or all the other.' " Both Lincoln and Jefferson Davis were from Kentucky and thus typical products of the new

[1] "The Frontier in American History," 29–30, 138, 198, 217.

West. "The Mississippi Valley had rejuvenated slavery, had given it an aggressive tone characteristic of frontier life," and "a map showing the location of the men of New England ancestry in the Northwest would represent also the counties in which the Free Soil party cast its heaviest votes." Of course, this unity of feeling and inherited characteristic which so underlay and modified the thought and belief of the great western section of our country offered fertile ground for a unified political movement, and the wide-reaching and spontaneous uprising was the result. As Professor T. C. Smith well has pointed out, "it is a mistake to disregard local political history in the United States; for, as a matter of fact, half the political battles of the period before the Civil War were fought out in state legislatures and state elections, and Congress did little more than ratify the results." [2]

Many men in many places have laid claim to suggesting the name "Republican" for the new party about to be formed, and several with more or less of valid right. As a matter of fact, the name was a logical one, from theoretical, sentimental, and historical reasons. "Jefferson had originated the policy of slavery restriction in his draft of the ordinance of 1784," hence the name by which his followers later became known "became singularly appropriate, and wherever the Free Soilers succeeded in forming a coalition in 1854 it was adopted without question." [3] Also, there was the necessity of attracting to the new party many thousands of former Democrats if the new organization was to have any prospect of carrying elections or controlling the country, and therefore the use of the old Jefferson political name, discarded when Jackson re-formed the earlier party into the "Democratic" party of some twenty years before, was of telling effect, for now a claim could be made that there was a revival of real Jeffersonian principles. That this plea was effective soon was shown, with the result that the old-line Democrats attempted to throw contempt upon the young party by calling it the *black* Republican, or "nigger-

[2] "The Liberty and Free Soil Parties," 298.
[3] Nicolay and Hay, "Lincoln," I, 359.

loving," party. When individuals cease argument and begin "calling names," it is a rather good sign of consciousness of waging a losing fight, and this was amply demonstrated within four or five years.

Says Holcombe:[4] "The original spirit of the Anti-slavery Republicans was the spirit of the Declaration of Independence, of the Land Ordinance of 1785, and of the Northwest Ordinance of 1787. Of the first of these great documents Thomas Jefferson was the author; he had a leading part in the preparation of the second; his ideals were embodied in the third. In these three documents the fighting principles of the Anti-slavery Republicans were first set forth. The interests to which the Anti-slavery Republicans were most strongly devoted were those which had most loyally supported the Jefferson policies. Thus the spirit as well as the name of the original Jeffersonian party was revived by the party of Lincoln, of Seward, and of Chase."

Finally, Thomas Jefferson was greater as a social reformer and politician than he was as a statesman. His political philosophy was often vague, contradictory, and inconsistent. Therefore, his teachings were especially useful to those who would weld a more or less incoherent mass into a united whole, which could coöperate upon a basis sufficiently broad to include all sorts and kinds of political elements. "Republicans" of 1854 could all point to Jefferson as the apostle of social freedom, and no matter what their political views might be, there was little difficulty in finding in the writings and sayings of the sage of Monticello something that might justify their own peculiar or otherwise contradictory political beliefs.

During the winter and spring of the year 1854, while Congress was struggling over the Kansas-Nebraska legislation, and before the leaders of the old party organizations were quite ready to join any movement for a new organization, people began to discuss the matter at a lively rate and local bodies began to fuse together. There were fortunately many individuals with a moral and political conscience and a lively

[4] "Political Parties of To-day," 249–50.

interest in politics who were not bound down by the lure of office or the fear of losing political prizes already won. In many places regular committees of the old Whig, Democratic, and Free Soil parties united to call "Anti-Nebraska Conventions." [5] The newspapers, especially in the Northwest, joined in the movement. Probably the meeting which especially deserves the credit for leading the way in the organization of a new party was that held at Ripon, Fond du Lac county, Wisconsin; and Mr. Alvan E. Bovay, a prominent member of the Whig party who lived in that town, was the prime mover in calling the convention, and also in the use of the name Republican for the new party.[6]

Ripon was, and still is, a small town southeast of the center of the state of Wisconsin, even having a total population of less than 4000 in the census of 1920. Mr. Bovay, who later held the rank of major in the Nineteenth Wisconsin Infantry in the Civil War, was born in the state of New York in 1818 and lived for a while in New York city. He later became a lawyer and settled in Ripon in 1850. In 1852 Mr. Bovay, while on a visit to New York city, said to Horace Greeley, with whom he long had been acquainted, that inevitably there must be a new party formed on the basis of the exclusion of slavery from the territories. Greeley asked him what he would name the new party, and Bovay replied, "Republican." While the Kansas-Nebraska Bill was before Congress, he wrote Greeley on February 26, 1854, saying: "Your paper is now a power in the land. Advocate calling together in every church and schoolhouse in the free states all the opponents of the Kansas-Nebraska Bill, no matter what their party affiliations. Urge them to forget previous political names and organizations, and to band together under the name I suggested to you at Lovejoy's Hotel in 1852. I mean the name

[5] See T. C. Smith, "The Liberty and Free Soil Parties," 288, 296.

[6] The following account of the Ripon and Jackson meetings has been drawn in large part from Henry Wilson, "The Rise and Fall of the Slave Power," II, 408–13; Francis Curtis, "The Republican Party," I, 173–192. Also see an article by Charles M. Harvey in the magazine "The Chautauquan," September, 1897 (Vol. XXV, No. 6), 643–648.

'Republican.' It is the only one that will serve all purposes, present and future—the only one that will live and last." Greeley approached such a decision only by slow stages, but on June 24, after the Kansas-Nebraska Bill had been enacted, he suggested the name "Republican" in an editorial article in the "Tribune."

Meanwhile Bovay had been at work in a practical manner. Along with two other men of Ripon, a Mr. Bowen and a Mr. Baker, who were respectively a Democrat and a Free Soiler, he issued a call for a public meeting to consider the situation caused by the legislation then pending in Congress. This meeting took place in the Congregational church in Ripon on February 28, 1854, and a resolution was passed to the effect that if this legislation should pass, old party organizations must be disregarded and a new party, to be called the Republican, should be formed, based solely on the issue of opposition to the extension of slavery.

It will be remembered that the Kansas-Nebraska Bill passed the United States Senate on March 3. The Ripon leaders decided not to wait longer but called a second meeting for March 20, in which men of all parties were to participate. Mr. Bovay wrote, many years later, that he "went from house to house and from shop to shop and halted men on the street to get their names for the meeting of March 20, 1854. At that time there were not more than a hundred voters in Ripon, and by a vast deal of earnest talking I obtained fifty-three of them. . . . We went into the little meeting held in a schoolhouse Whigs, Free Soilers, and Democrats. We came out of it Republicans, and we were the first Republicans in the Union."

By the vote of this meeting the local committees of the Whig and Free Soil parties were dissolved "and a committee of five—three Whigs, one Democrat, and one Free Soiler—was chosen to begin the task of forming a new party." Mr. Charles M. Harvey rightly says that "at these two meetings was started the earliest systematic work begun anywhere in the country to bring about the coalition of the enemies of slavery extension, who were eventually fused into a homogeneous and aggressive party, adopting the name Republican."

There were a number of other local movements of more or less importance, which will be mentioned presently, but the next great step in the final organization of a new party, and the step usually accepted by historical judgment as being the actual beginning of the Republican organization, was taken when a state convention was held, a little over three months after the Ripon meeting, at Jackson, Michigan, on July 6, 1854. The events leading up to this meeting were as follows:

The anti-slavery elements in the Democratic party in Michigan held a convention at Jackson on February 22, 1854, at which resolutions of a strong character were passed, declaring that slavery was sectional and freedom national, and denouncing the current attempts in Congress to repeal the Missouri Compromise to be an "infamous outrage on justice, humanity, and good faith." These were words well calculated to rouse the emotional resentment of the free-soil element in both old parties, and upon this platform also was nominated a state ticket headed by Kinsley S. Bingham for governor, and containing two former Whigs. This was a direct bid for fusion of anti-slavery elements, and results of a striking character were not long in coming. "The Detroit Tribune," under the editorial leadership of Joseph Warren, who appropriately bore a name of outstanding significance in the struggle for American freedom, began a definite campaign in the columns of his paper to bring about a fusion of all elements in the state, no matter what previously had been the party membership, in a movement to carry the next election in the cause of liberty. Of course, one of the most important problems was to induce the Democrats to withdraw their ticket, since the Whigs had made no nominations whatever, and thus both old parties would be put upon the same footing and the general movement for a state-wide organization might begin anew. It is fortunate for the success of the movement that there existed a person with such clear insight into practical politics and such common sense as Mr. Warren, for only on this basis was there any chance for gaining results rather than a mere temporary coalition. The state of Michigan then was peopled by inhabitants of old American stock, far above the average in education and intelligence, and we can see this section of the American people at its best.

The leaders of the "Free" Democratic party saw the logic and sense of the efforts of Mr. Warren, and the ticket nominated at Jackson on February 22 was withdrawn at a convention held at Kalamazoo. This being accomplished, a call which had appeared in "The Detroit Tribune" and later in the "Free Democrat" was signed by more than ten thousand names. It was addressed "to the people of Michigan," and stated that "a great wrong has been perpetrated. The slave power of this country has triumphed. Liberty is trampled under foot. The Missouri Compromise, a solemn compact entered into by our fathers, has been violated, and a vast territory dedicated to freedom has been opened to slavery. This act, so unjust to the North, has been perpetrated under circumstances which deepen its perfidy. . . . Such an outrage upon liberty, such a violation of plighted faith, cannot be submitted to. This great wrong must be righted, or there is no longer a North in the councils of the nation. The extension of slavery, under the folds of the American flag, is a stigma upon liberty. . . . The safety of the Union—the rights of the North—the interests of free labor—the destiny of a vast territory and its untold millions for all coming time—and finally, the high aspirations of humanity for universal freedom, all are involved in the issue forced upon the country by the slave power and its plastic Northern tools."

In the light of these facts, skilfully stated in order to arouse both moral and sectional fears, an invitation was given to "all our fellow citizens, without reference to former political associations, who think that the time has come for a *Union* at the North to protect liberty from being overthrown and downtrodden, to assemble in mass convention on Thursday, the 6th of July next, . . . at Jackson, there to take such measures as shall be thought best to concentrate the popular sentiment of this state against the aggression of the slave power." [7]

The convention was attended literally by hundreds of leading and influential citizens from all parts of the state, men who represented all varieties of anti-slavery and progressive opinion. The crowd was so great that it overflowed the largest hall in the town. It was a beautiful summer day, so the convention was adjourned to meet in an oak grove "situated between the village and the county race course, on a tract of land then known as 'Morgan's Forty.' The growth of Jackson has since covered this historic ground with buildings, and the spacious grove has dwindled [1880] to a few scattered oaks shading the city's busy streets. A rude platform erected for speakers was appropriated by the officers of the convention, and about it thronged a mass of earnest men."

The shrewd and effective leadership which had carried the movement thus far was not wanting in this mass meeting "under the oaks," for such controversies and differences of opinion and conviction as might exist among such a heterogeneous crowd of men were smoothed out in private conference and secret committee deliberations. There was promptness, unity of feeling, great earnestness, and enthusiasm. Levi Baxter, a Free Soiler, was temporary chairman of the convention and David S. Walbridge, a Whig, was chosen permanent president. The crowd was then divided up into sections representing the four congressional districts in the state, and these sections chose their respective representatives on a committee on resolutions. Jacob M. Howard of Detroit, a leading Whig, who later was to loom large in national affairs as Republican senator from Michigan, was chosen chairman of this joint committee. He already had prepared the draft of a platform and in advance of the time for the meeting of this convention. This platform was considered by the committee sitting under a clump of trees on the outskirts of the "oak

[7] For the text of this call, also for a full account of the Jackson convention, see "The Life of Zachariah Chandler," published by "The Detroit Post and Tribune" (1880), 104–116.

grove," at what later became the intersection of Franklin and Second Streets in the city of Jackson. There were "no material modifications" made in the platform, but it was adopted substantially as prepared by Mr. Howard. Two resolutions, dealing exclusively with state affairs, were added on the motion of Austin Blair.

Joseph Warren later stated that in a correspondence with Horace Greeley the latter had suggested the name "Republican" in a letter received by Warren a day or two before the Jackson convention. Howard had contended that the name "Democrat-Republican" was appropriate for the new party they intended to form, but Warren handed him Greeley's letter on the day of the convention and after Howard had been chosen chairman of the committee. Warren urged the adoption of the name, which was done, and it was included, as will be seen, in the platform. There seems to have been little or no discussion over this plank. Thus the train of events would seem to be fairly complete, leading from Alvan E. Bovay through Horace Greeley to Joseph Warren and Jacob M. Howard, and thence to the committee on resolutions and the convention itself, with the formal adoption of the name "Republican," which the party since has borne for nearly three quarters of a century.

The platform itself was long, and followed numerous addresses from men of different political antecedents, which roused the meeting to a pitch of excited determination. It was issued in the name of "the freemen of Michigan, assembled in convention in pursuance of a spontaneous call, emanating from various parts of the state, to consider upon the measures which duty demands of us, as citizens of a free state, to take in reference to the late acts of Congress on the subject of slavery and its anticipated further extension." It then resolved that "the institution of slavery except in punishment of crime is a great moral, social and political evil"; that it is "a violation of the rights of man as man and . . . like imprisonment for debt, but a relic of barbarism as well as an element of weakness in the midst of the state."

After this strong pronouncement of faith, the constructive measures and statement of policy followed, being drawn up by Howard with shrewdness and a keen sense of political effect. These were stated in part in the following words:

"We . . . publicly proclaim our determination to oppose by all the powerful and honorable means in our power, now and henceforth, all attempts, direct or indirect, to extend slavery in this country, or to permit it to extend into any region or locality in which it does not now exist by positive law, or to admit new slave states into the Union.

"The Constitution of the United States gives to Congress full and complete power for the municipal government of the territories thereof, a power which from its nature cannot be either alienated or abdicated without yielding up to the territory an absolute political independence, which involves an absurdity. . . . The exercise of this power necessarily looks to the formation of states to be admitted into the Union; and on the question whether they shall be admitted as *free* or *slave* states Congress has a right to adopt such prudential and preventive measures as the principles of liberty and the interests of the whole country require. . . . This question is one of the gravest importance to the free states, . . . is one which we hold it to be our right to *discuss;* which we hold it the duty of Congress in every instance to determine in unequivocal language, and in a manner to *prevent* the spread of slavery and the increase of . . . unequal representation. In short, we claim that the North *is a party to the new bargain, and is entitled to have a voice and influence in settling its terms.*

"The repeal of the Missouri Compromise . . . is an act unprecedented in the history of the country, and one which must engage the earnest and serious attention of every Northern man. As Northern freemen, independent of all former parties, we hold this measure up to the public execration, for the following reasons: It is a plain departure from the policy of the fathers of the republic in regard to slavery. . . . It actually admits *and was intended to admit* slavery into said Territories [Kansas and Nebraska]. . . . It was sprung upon the country stealthily and by surprise. . . . On the part of the South it is an open and undisguised breach of faith. . . . It is also an undisguised and unmanly contempt of the pledge given to the country by the present dominant party at their national convention in 1852, not to *'agitate the subject of slavery in or out of Congress.'* . . . It is greatly injurious to the free states, and to the Territories themselves, tending to retard the settlement and to prevent the improvement of the country by means of free labor, and to discourage foreign immigrants resorting thither for their homes. . . . One of its principal aims is to give the slave states such a decided and practical preponderance in all the measures of government as shall reduce the North, with all her industry, wealth and enterprise, to be the mere province of a few slave-holding oligarchs of the South—a condition too shameful to be contemplated. . . . As openly avowed by its Southern friends, it is intended as an entering wedge to the still further augmentation of the slave power by the acquisition of the other Territories."

The following program of action was laid out in resolutions, that—

"The obnoxious measure to which we have alluded ought to be *repealed,* and a provision substituted for it, prohibiting slavery in said Territories, and each of them.

"After this gross breach of faith and wanton affront to us as Northern men, we hold ourselves absolved from all *'compromises.'* . . . We now demand measures of protection and immunity for ourselves; and among these we demand the *repeal of the fugitive slave law,* and an act to abolish slavery in the District of Columbia.

"We notice without dismay certain popular indications by slaveholders on the frontier of said Territories of a purpose on their part to prevent by violence the settlement of the country by non-slaveholding men. To the latter we say: Be of good cheer, persevere in the right, remember the Republican motto, *'The North will Defend You.'*

"Postponing and suspending all differences with regard to political economy or administrative policy, in view of the imminent danger that Kansas and Nebraska will be grasped by slavery, and a thousand miles of slave soil be thus interposed between the free states of the Atlantic and those of the Pacific, we will act cordially and faithfully in unison to avert and repeal this gigantic wrong and shame.

"In view of the necessity of battling for the first principles of republican government, and against the schemes of an aristocracy, the most revolting and oppressive with which the earth was ever cursed, or man debased, we will co-operate and be known as *Republicans* until the contest be terminated.

"We earnestly recommend the calling of a general convention of the free states, and such of the slaveholding states, or portions thereof, as may desire to be there represented, with a view to the adoption of other more extended and effectual measures in resistance to the encroachments of slavery; and that a committee of five persons be appointed to correspond and co-operate with our friends in other states on the subject."

It will be seen at once that these resolutions offered a clean-cut and cleverly formulated program well calculated to appeal not only to the anti-slavery sentiment of the people of Michigan, but also throughout the North, and thus offered a real beginning of party organization with a practical objective that easily might be made effective in Congress. It was first of all designed to be preventive of the extension of slavery, thus affording the opportunity for that institution to die a natural death, as being against the progress of civilized society. On the other hand, it was not aggressively abolition in the radical and political sense of the term, but would appeal to the cautious as well as the soundly progressive elements of the population of the country. But it necessarily must be sectional, and on this rock it split the country and its success led directly to secession and civil war.

These resolutions were adopted "almost unanimously." Then Isaac P. Christiancy, who was the chairman of a committee of sixteen appointed by the recent convention at Kalamazoo, announced the withdrawal of the "Free" Democratic state ticket recently nominated and the abandonment of the organization of that party. The convention at once appointed a committee of ninety, made up of three representatives from each of the senatorial districts of the state, in order to nominate a state ticket for the coming election, and the convention adjourned until the evening.

This later session on the same day was held in a village hall and both a state central committee was chosen and the state ticket, nominated by the committee mentioned above, was unanimously indorsed. At its head was placed Kinsley S. Bingham for governor, who recently had withdrawn from the "Free" Democratic nomination, and the entire ticket was made up of three Free Soilers, five Whigs, and two anti-Nebraska Democrats.

When the news of what had been done at Jackson spread throughout the state, there was great popular indorsement. A number of old-line Whigs, unreconciled to the disbanding of their cherished party organization, called a convention which met at Marshall on October 4, but the representation and leadership of this meeting already were committed to the new Republican movement, and they skilfully used the convention for the purpose of indorsing the actions and nominations of the Jackson convention. This made the contest a straight-out fight between the new Republican party and the old-line Democrats, who had nominated John S. Barry to head their ticket. Zachariah Chandler, later the radical leader and Republican senator at Washington, did yeoman service in organizing the new party throughout Michigan, and was dubbed by the Democratic papers the "traveling agent of the new Abolition party." But the Democrats were playing from the very first a losing game, and the Republicans carried the state by a vote of 43,652 for Mr. Bingham, to 38,675 for Mr. Barry, electing also the entire state ticket, three of the four Congressmen and a legislature which contained an overwhelming anti-Nebraska majority in both branches. This hold was gradually strengthened, the members of the Jackson convention dominating for years the political fortunes of the state.

The various movements elsewhere looking toward the formation of a new party are of importance, for they gradually coalesced with the Michigan organization, although no one of them dominated the rest, and a national party was the result. One of the first of these was in Washington, D. C., where about thirty members of the House of Representatives were called together by Israel Washburne, Jr., of Maine, for consultation concerning the crisis now upon the country. They met on May 9, 1854, in the rooms of Thomas D. Eliot and Edward Dickinson of Massachusetts. There was unanimity in the judgment of the hopelessness of checking the slave power by means of present political organizations, although several were loath to leave the Whig party, still hoping against hope that the organization of the latter might be used for future political purposes. While this was sound strategy in general, in the recognition of the use for forces of unity and coöperation of historic names and existing organizations, yet the disintegration of the Whig party had gone too far, and its death and disappearance as a national force were inevitable. The majority of those present expressed themselves as convinced that a new party was inevitable, showing their appreciation of actual facts, and the name "Republican" was agreed upon, after discussion, as being most appropriate for the purpose.[8] It was shortly after this that Mr. Washburne addressed a meeting at Bangor, Maine, in which he stated that "every true Republican must take the place, if not the name, of that wise conservative party, whose aim and purpose were the welfare of the whole Union and the stainless honor of the American name."

If we except this last-named meeting, the first real movement in New England looking toward the formation of a new party was made in Vermont, where the Whigs met in a state

[8] Curtis, "The Republican Party," I, 178–9; Wilson, "Rise and Fall of the Slave Power," II, 410–11. Dr. Bailey, editor of the "National Era," was a moving spirit in the call of the Washington meeting.

convention on June 8, 1854, and passed resolutions urging those people in Vermont and "all the other states" who were opposed to the extension of slavery to coöperate and, in case there be a national convention for this purpose, to send delegates to it. On June 16 there was issued a call for a state convention of "all persons who are in favor of resisting by all constitutional means the usurpations of the propagandists of slavery." This second convention met on July 13, chosen because it was the anniversary of the enactment of the Ordinance of 1787, at which anti-slavery resolutions were passed, with the added sentiment that "we propose, and respectfully recommend to the friends of freedom in other states, to coöperate and be known as Republicans." A fusion delegation of three men was chosen to represent the state at any national convention and a state ticket was nominated. A little later a fusion ticket to take its place was made up by the state committees of the parties and elected at the polls, at which election a legislature was chosen which sent to the United States Senate Jacob Collamer and Lawrence L. Brainard, who were respectively an anti-slavery Whig and a Free Soiler.[9]

Massachusetts was the next New England state to follow suit, although the movement to form the Republican party was confused and its efforts delayed by the rise and success of the Know-Nothings. Soon after the passage of the Kansas-Nebraska Bill, Samuel Hoar started a movement in Concord looking toward more effective opposition to the slave power. A meeting was held in this famous old town which was attended by leading citizens, including Charles Francis Adams, Henry Wilson, G. F. Hoar, and R. W. Emerson. It decided, however, that in view of the fact that a call already was in circulation, signed by large numbers of citizens, and calling for a popular convention of the people of the state to meet at Worcester, they should take no further action but merely coöperate with this wider movement. It is said that this call

[9] Wilson, "Rise and Fall of the Slave Power," II, 411–12; Curtis, "The Republican Party," I, 192–3; J. B. McMaster, "History of the People of the United States," VIII, 209–10.

for a convention was signed by people of all parties and especially by business men.

The Worcester convention met on July 20, 1854, at the city hall, and grew to such size that after an estimated number of 1500 people were present, it adjourned to the common. Judge Oliver B. Morris of Springfield was chosen president, and a platform was adopted including the usual anti-slavery resolutions, and also stating that "in co-operation with the friends of freedom in other states, we hereby form ourselves into the *Republican Party* of Massachusetts." Still another convention was held at Worcester on September 7, at which Charles Sumner was a dominating influence, and which nominated Henry Wilson for Governor. Henry Wilson himself says[10] that "in these conventions no prominent Whigs or Democrats took part, and few members of those parties were present. Being composed mainly of Free-Soilers, the Whig and Democratic presses naturally united in pronouncing 'fusion' a failure." Says James Ford Rhodes,[11] "The people of Massachusetts were all, with the exception of a few Democrats, so strongly opposed to the repeal of the Missouri Compromise that the question could not be made a political issue. The contest was virtually between the Whigs and Know-Nothings, and the Whig discomfiture was complete." The Know-Nothings swept the state and controlled the legislature, which sent Henry Wilson, the Republican nominee for governor, to the United States Senate. His hatred for foreigners and Catholics was a convenient addition to his anti-slavery sentiments in his ambition for political success.

It rouses a sense of humor to learn that in the September convention of the Republicans (or Free Soil Democrats, or whatever they were) at Worcester, Amasa Walker had made an earnest speech, received with "great applause," in which he stated that the contest pending in the country was one "between Slavery, Romanism and Rum, on the one side, and Freedom, Protestantism and Temperance, on the other." This

[10] "Rise and Fall," II, 414.
[11] "History of the United States," II, 65.

omelet of present-day issues or prejudices would hardly be to the taste of the contemporary "Democratic party of Thomas Jefferson and Woodrow Wilson," giving it full credit for its hybrid intellectual ancestry, in the year of grace 1928! Of course, the organization of the Republican party was merely delayed in Massachusetts by Whig stubbornness and Know-Nothing success, for it swept the state in the Presidential election of 1856 by a vote of nearly two to one over all opponents combined.

Both the states of Maine and New York have made claims, accepted by many people, to be the scene of the founding of the Republican party, but it seems a settled fact that Wisconsin and Michigan should be given the credit. Thus the claim is made that on August 7, 1854, there assembled at Strong, a little village in Franklin county, Maine, the first regularly organized convention of delegates that assumed the title of Republican in a formal manner. It was made up of Free Soilers, Whigs, and "Morrill Democrats," and nominated a candidate for senator, but was unsuccessful in the fall election.

The New York situation, as might be expected, was more complicated. A Mr. A. N. Cole of Allegany county many years later claimed to have been the "Father of the Republican Party" not only in this state but also in the nation. It appears that he was the moving spirit in a caucus of anti-slavery men who met at Friendship on May 16, 1854, and called a nominating convention that met in Angelica on October 15, following. Both towns are in Allegany county. At this convention there were nominations for county officers, who were later elected at the polls, using the name Republican at the instance, it is said, of Horace Greeley.[12] However that may be, there were numerous local anti-slavery movements under various names in New York, and Henry Wilson is correct in saying that the lead was taken in opposition to the Kansas-Nebraska issue by the Whigs, who held a convention early in the summer.[13] This

[12] Curtis gives a full and exhaustive account of these New York state movements, with the rival claims, in I, 202–6, 208–10.

[13] "Rise and Fall," II, 413–14.

met under the lead of William H. Seward and Thurlow Weed, adopted resolutions, and nominated an anti-Nebraska ticket. On August 17 an anti-Nebraska convention met at Saratoga. Horace Greeley was present and introduced resolutions which indorsed the movements in various states that already had taken steps looking toward the formation of a new party. This convention took no action, however, but adjourned to meet at Auburn on September 26. A resolution to organize a new party was introduced at the adjourned convention but was not adopted. "The Whigs having by their platform and ticket put themselves in substantial accord with the sentiments of the convention, it was deemed expedient to retain the Whig organization and to contest the election under its auspices. The ticket was successful, and Myron H. Clark and Henry J. Raymond were elected governor and lieutenant-governor" at the fall election.

Probably the best explanation of this Whig success is given by James Ford Rhodes,[14] who says that owing to timidity both Seward and Weed, the one the leading anti-slavery man in the state or perhaps in the Union, and the other his more than astute political manager, successfully opposed all attempts to disband the organization of the Whig party and create a new political party in its place. Seward was exceedingly anxious to secure his own reëlection to the United States Senate, which he accomplished during the coming winter, but events soon after out-distanced him, and he was forced to take a stand in favor of the new party, which he loyally supported from that time. But his delay in coming to the front cost him the position of dominating leadership which he easily could have assumed and held, probably might have led to his own nomination for President and election, if not in 1856, almost certainly in 1860. His hesitation gave the opening later filled so fully by his greater rival, Abraham Lincoln.

Before ending this long-drawn-out but necessary narration of the various movements to form the new party, mention must be made of both Ohio and Wisconsin. In the former state

[14] II, 67–70.

a convention was held at Columbus on July 13, which did not adopt the name Republican but nominated anti-Nebraska candidates for Congress, all of whom were later elected at the polls. Also, at Madison, Wisconsin, a state convention met the same day and resolved that "we accept the issue forced upon us by the slave power, and in defense of freedom will co-operate and be known as Republicans." It should be pointed out that the thirteenth of July was the anniversary of the enactment of the Ordinance of 1787. On this date met in 1854 the state conventions of Indiana, Ohio, Vermont, and Wisconsin. This was a shrewd move to impress upon the popular mind throughout the United States the fact that the new organization was founded upon an historic and traditional American doctrine, that of prohibition of the further extension of slavery into new territories and states.

In conclusion, it may be said that, like Topsy, the Republican party was not "founded" in the common acceptance of the term but just "grew." It was the expression of a widespread sentiment, soon to harden into a public opinion that was all-powerful, and destined to change the future of the United States and even of the whole world.

Chapter V

THE CAMPAIGN OF 1856

THE movement to form the Republican party was widespread but not uniform throughout the North and West, due to the slow crystallization of public opinion. As already stated, this latter was caused by the hesitation of Seward, Weed, and many others of the more prominent leaders to give this movement that strength and direction which were so necessary for a complete organization on a nation-wide basis, and also to the rise of the Know-Nothing or American party. Nevertheless, within the space of about twelve months following the passage of the Kansas-Nebraska Act, eleven Republican senators were sent to Washington and anti-Nebraska majorities were secured in fifteen states. Also there were one hundred and twenty members of the House of Representatives from the North who were opposed to such legislation. They were strong enough, after the long and desperate fight already described,[1] to force the election of N. P. Banks as speaker, and to pass, by a majority of fifteen, a resolution that "in the opinion of this House, the repeal of the Missouri Compromise of 1820, prohibiting slavery north of 36° 30′ was an example of useless and factious agitation of the slavery question, unwise and unjust to the American people."

Douglas had been hissed off the platform in Chicago when he attempted to make a plea in justification of his activity in support of the Kansas-Nebraska Bill, and new leaders were coming to the front in Illinois—especially Lincoln, who was just beginning to grow to the stature of political manhood. Naturally all this political activity reacted with renewed force

[1] *Ante*, page 39.

upon the South, and the Whig party in that section rapidly disintegrated. It was impossible for its leaders to justify the anti-slavery activity of the northern wing of the organization, and the southern Democracy received great accessions of strength, becoming more than ever the citadel of the pro-slavery interests. While sectionalism thus became rampant, it is not to be considered an accepted fact that sectionalism and disunion were synonymous terms. No matter how strong the sympathy with slavery and with sectionalism might be, there were literally hundreds of thousands of people in the South who still believed it possible to hold such views and yet maintain the Union unimpaired. It was only such "fire-eaters" as Barnwell Rhett, Yancey, Quitman, and the like who saw keenly into the future and prepared more or less consciously for inevitable conflict.

The year 1855 found the Republican party organized definitely in several more states in the North and West of that day, and the foundations laid for a concerted movement in the Presidential campaign of 1856. Ohio saw the nomination of Salmon P. Chase for governor on the Republican ticket, and his election by nearly 15,000 majority over the Democrats, although the latter had the more or less open support of many Whigs and Know-Nothings. Pennsylvania, then a rock-ribbed support of Democracy and all that pertained to it, fell into line when a Republican convention was held at Pittsburgh on September 5, and a ticket was put into the field for the state election. Although an organization, ready for future emergencies, was thus put upon its feet, the state held true to its old political beliefs and the Democrats carried the election as usual.

The results in Massachusetts and New York were much the same. After preliminary meetings at Boston on August 16 and 30, a state convention was called by anti-slavery leaders and met at Worcester on September 20. At first the Know-Nothings had given signs of coöperation, but bolted. The Republicans, who definitely took this name in a series of resolutions, nominated a candidate for governor. He was defeated and the Know-Nothing governor, Henry J. Gardner, was reëlected at the polls. A like attempt to form a fusion of Republicans and Whigs in New York failed for the same reason —that, like the Know-Nothings in Massachusetts, the Whigs still refused to desert or disband their old party organization.

Connecticut was even more confused, with elections during most of the decade from 1850 until 1860 carried by one or another of the various factions that struggled for the mastery. Various mass conventions which supported the Republican movement were held from time to time, and the state was carried by Frémont in 1856 on a plurality vote, but the first regular Republican convention, called by the means of a state committee, was held in 1858. Conditions in Illinois, which brought Lincoln to the front, will be considered in the following chapter.

But the time now was coming for a general union of all these more or less local movements into a national organization; and, as might be expected, the dazzling and exciting prospect of a Presidential election was the common impulse that set the minds of the people, and their more or less halting leaders, toward the discovery of some broad basis of coöperation. There was an issue upon which men of more or less degrees of radicalism or liberalism might safely unite with those of a more conservative temper. That was the old Free Soil platform or principle of 1848, that slavery should not be extended to any new territory. But the accompanying statement that the institution should not be interfered with wherever established by state law met the scruples of those who would stand by a "Jeffersonian" or strict construction of the Constitution. The next task was to find a "good candidate," and upon these foundations of principle and personality build up a national party as the expression of a desire for national coöperation. Of course, organization would go along with this, but it could only become complete when elections were carried. Then, as now, nothing succeeded like success, and also there would be spoils for the taking.

A book of more or less journalistic character, consisting of articles written by John Tweedy of Danbury, Connecticut, and originally published several decades ago in "The Hartford Courant," states [2] that on June 19, 1855, there was organized in Washington, D. C., a small club that adopted a platform in which the statement was made that "we do associate ourselves together under the name and title of The Republican Association of Washington, D. C." On January 17, 1856, an appeal was published, largely under the influence of this club, which urged the formation of like clubs throughout the nation. This appeal, in the form of a circular, was signed by Daniel R. Goodloe, H. S. Brown, and Lewis Clephane, committee. On the same day (January 17), as is well known, there also was issued a call for a national convention to meet at Pittsburgh, Pennsylvania, on February 22 following. This was dated Washington, D. C., and signed by A. P. Stone of Ohio, J. Z. Goodrich of Massachusetts, David Wilmot of Pennsylvania, Lawrence Brainard of Vermont, and William A. White of Wisconsin. Other signatures subsequently were added, and this call stated that the undersigned were "chairmen of the State Republican Committees of Maine, Vermont, Massachusetts, New York, Pennsylvania, Ohio, Michigan, Indiana and Wisconsin." [3]

Representatives from twenty-three states were present at Pittsburgh on the day named, and they came from all the free states and Maryland, Virginia, South Carolina, Kentucky, and Missouri as well. As will be seen, these latter were merely local enthusiasts and represented no real anti-slavery movement of a political character whatever.

The convention overflowed with enthusiasm and listened to many speeches from the anti-slavery leaders present, stirring up a remarkable feeling of unity and coöperation. John A. King, son of Rufus King, and later governor of New York, was the temporary chairman, and the venerable Francis P. Blair of Missouri was elected permanent president. A National Executive Committee was chosen by name, with the power to add to its number one member from each state not repre-

[2] "A History of the Republican National Conventions," 3.
[3] Curtis, I, 250. Stanwood, 269.

sented and to fill vacancies; also, the recommendation was made that in each state a complete organization of state and county committees be formed; and finally a national nominating convention was called for the seventeenth of June, 1856, the anniversary of the battle of Bunker Hill. It will be noted that the early Republican leaders had a keen eye for history, and their good judgment was vindicated repeatedly. The national convention, it was decided, should consist of delegates from each state equal in number to double the number of its representation in both houses of Congress.

Politicians in those days were never sparing in words, as has been seen ere this, and the Pittsburgh convention ran true to form. It issued an address of length, closing with three resolutions. These declared against the extension of slavery to new territory, pledged aid to Kansas in its fight against the usurped authority of lawless invaders, and condemned the national administration of Franklin Pierce as "identified with the progress of the Slave Power to national supremacy" which the Republican party had a "leading purpose" to "oppose and overthrow."

About a month later, on March 27 to be exact, the Executive Committee appointed by the Pittsburgh convention met at Washington, D. C., and issued a formal call for the Philadelphia convention, to consist of three delegates from every congressional district and six delegates-at-large from each state. This was an addition of fifty per cent. to the number usually considered ample for the proper representation of states in the national conventions of the various parties, but it had the decided advantage of allowing wide and varied representation, and also a number sufficient to guarantee plenty of that essential commodity for electoral success—enthusiasm.

Of course, the one great problem before all others, if the young party was to have any prospect of success, was the choice of candidates. The hesitation of Seward during the preceding year, when he delayed the decision to join the new organization, was sufficient to prevent his success as a leader at this late moment. Chase of Ohio was too strong a Democrat to suit Whig and Know-Nothing converts, and both these men had been anti-slavery to such a degree that they might alienate more hesitant elements in the border states, at least. James Ford Rhodes says [4] there was a canvass by means of views in the press, private correspondence, public addresses, and open discussion, and that the choice of Frémont was practically decided upon before the convention met. He was lighted upon some time during the course of the winter of 1855-56, and at the proper time he issued a letter plainly stating his views upon the issues involved in the national crisis. It also gave formal notice that he was a candidate for the nomination. He had been a Democrat, but not to such a prominent extent as to arouse enmity from former members of other parties. The German elements throughout the country, now looming large on account of recent immigration, were strongly in his favor. But he was not obnoxious to the Know-Nothings, it being said that he "had no political antecedents." In other words, the one question of availability overshadowed all others, as so often in the political history of our country, especially during this period, and before the office of President began that process of development into national party leadership so characteristic of the twentieth century and at the hands of such men as Theodore Roosevelt and Woodrow Wilson.

But not all Republicans were satisfied with the prospect of the dashing and effervescent Frémont. The erratic and unbalanced character of his later actions, not to mention his actual incompetency during the Civil War, all of which cost Lincoln much worry and the country most dear, are ample proof of the present sound judgment of the Republicans of more conservative and statesmanlike tendency, who began to rally around the candidacy of Justice John McLean, a member of the Supreme Court of the United States; and this candidacy of McLean was probably responsible for the Dred Scott decision. It shows how one extreme leads to another, for if Frémont was dashing, certainly McLean was not—and if for no other reason, most certainly on account of his seventy-one

[4] II, 174–82.

Photograph from Brown Brothers

JOHN CHARLES FRÉMONT

years, for he was born in Morris county, New Jersey, in the year 1785. Age and judicial experience were certain antidotes to too great enthusiasm in a new and radical cause.

But the eminent justice had real claims to respect and even veneration. He had been a Representative in Congress from the state of Ohio, postmaster-general in the cabinets of James Monroe and John Quincy Adams, and an appointee to the Supreme Court at the hands of Andrew Jackson, thus holding the latter office for nearly twenty-seven years. And he soon gave signs of being "willing," for he began to write letters to define his position on the leading issues of the day, which of course aroused the familiar and somewhat justifiable cry of "politics" in a judicial position, not to mention judicial impropriety. There was no question that McLean was far more capable for the Presidency than Frémont, but availability won the day, and the latter was nominated.

All historians are united in the opinion that the first great Republican national convention, which met at Music Fund Hall in Philadelphia on June 17, 1856, was composed of men who were of singular patriotism, unselfish idealism, and unusual integrity. It should be noted that the early Republicans went into their party with the spirit of real crusaders; and not merely enthusiasts at that, but also men of common sense who knew what they wanted, why they wanted it, and for reasons they were not afraid openly to express. Spoils and personal profit were conspicuous by their absence from any influence, for success was too remote in prospect to attract the mere place-hunter or potential grafter. This high moral enthusiasm, fanned to a white heat by later warfare on the actual battlefield, lasted for years and did untold good in its accomplishment for our country, although at times it was used by designing demagogues or callous criminals for their own benefit. All this was inevitable, but it should not cause later generations of Americans to forget the high moral character and purpose of these early Republicans.

The convention was more of a mass meeting than a regular convocation of delegates chosen by technically legal party machinery. They came together to organize victory, and had common sense enough to conduct their business without overlooking what was practical, as well as what was honest and ideal. Robert Emmet, Irish born and a former Democrat of New York, was the temporary chairman, proposed by Edwin D. Morgan of New York, chairman of the National Committee, and Henry S. Lane of Indiana, a former Whig, was chosen permanent president. There was little scrutiny of credentials, but it was found that there was a total of 565 delegates present, representing every free state, also Delaware, Maryland, Virginia, and Kentucky. There were also representatives from the territories of Kansas, Minnesota, Nebraska, and from the District of Columbia. Among the delegates were such men as James G. Blaine, Charles Francis Adams, E. R. Hoar, David Wilmot, Thaddeus Stevens, Alphonso Taft, Joshua R. Giddings, Zachariah Chandler, Owen Lovejoy, John M. Palmer, and Samuel C. Pomeroy. They were all roused to a high pitch of enthusiasm by various "spellbinders," among whom Senator Henry Wilson of Massachusetts and Owen Lovejoy of Illinois were most successful. A National Committee was chosen and the convention then proceeded to the most important business before it, the adoption of a platform and the nomination of candidates.

David Wilmot, of "Wilmot Proviso" fame, was chairman of the Committee on Platform, and he reported that document. The most important passages are given in order that the principles upon which the Republican party entered upon its first national campaign may be clearly understood. These were as follows:

"This convention of delegates, assembled in pursuance of a call addressed to the people of the United States, without regard to past political differences or divisions, who are opposed to the repeal of the Missouri Compromise, to the policy of the present administration, to the extension of slavery into free territory; in favor of admitting Kansas as a free state, of restoring the action of the federal government to the principles of Washington and Jefferson; and who propose to unite in presenting candidates for the offices of President and Vice-President, do resolve as follows:

"That the maintenance of the principles promulgated in the Declaration of Independence and embodied in the Federal Constitution is essential to the preservation of our Republican institutions, and that the Federal Constitution, the rights of the States, and the union of the States, shall be preserved.

"That with our republican fathers we hold it to be a self-evident truth, that all men are endowed with the unalienable rights to life, liberty, and the pursuit of happiness, and that the primary object and ulterior designs of our federal government were to secure these rights to all persons within its exclusive jurisdiction; that, as our republican fathers, when they had abolished slavery in all our national territory, ordained that no person should be deprived of life, liberty or property without due process of law, it becomes our duty to maintain this provision of the Constitution against all attempts to violate it for the purpose of establishing slavery in any Territory of the United States, by positive legislation prohibiting its existence or extension therein; that we deny the authority of Congress, of a territorial legislature, of any individual or association of individuals, to give legal existence to slavery in any Territory of the United States, while the present Constitution shall be maintained.

"That the Constitution confers upon Congress sovereign power over the Territories of the United States, for their government, and that in the exercise of this power it is both the right and duty of Congress to prohibit in the Territories those twin relics of barbarism, polygamy and slavery.

"The dearest constitutional rights of the people of Kansas have been fraudulently and violently taken from them; . . . all these things have been done with the knowledge, sanction, and procurement of the present administration; and that for this high crime against the Constitution, the Union, and humanity, we arraign the administration, the President, his advisers, agents, supporters, apologists, and accessories, either before or after the fact, before the country and before the world, and that it is our fixed purpose to bring the actual perpetrators of these atrocious outrages, and their accomplices, to a sure and condign punishment hereafter.

"Kansas should be immediately admitted as a State of the Union, with her present free constitution.

"The highwayman's plea, that 'might makes right,' embodied in the Ostend circular, was in every respect unworthy of American diplomacy, and would bring shame and dishonor upon any government or people that gave it their sanction.

"A railroad to the Pacific Ocean, by the most central and practicable route, is imperatively demanded by the interests of the whole country, and the Federal government ought to render immediate and efficient aid in its construction; and, as an auxiliary thereto, the immediate construction of an emigrant route on the line of the railroad.

"Appropriations by Congress for the improvement of rivers and harbors, of a national character, required for the accommodation and security of our existing commerce, are authorized by the Constitution, and justified by the obligation of government to protect the lives and property of its citizens."

This was a clear-cut statement of the Free Soil doctrines as enunciated by the followers of Van Buren in 1848, and there was judicious addition of "old-line Whig" doctrine of internal improvements, with additional and direct reference to such present controversies as the immediate admission of Kansas and the condemnation of the Ostend Manifesto, which has not ceased to cause patriotic Americans even of the present day to blush with shame at the unprincipled and disgraceful pronouncement of the intention, in the year 1854, to seize the island of Cuba without shadow of right or justification. An especial fillip was given to this platform declaration by the Republicans due to the fact that the authors of the manifesto issued at Ostend were John Y. Mason, Pierre Soulé, and—James Buchanan! This last-named gentleman had, only two weeks before, been nominated by the Democratic national convention at Cincinnati for President of the United States. It may not be always tactful, but it is certainly delightful, to be able to call your political opponent a "highwayman"—and with at least a shadow of truth!

As has already been stated, the nomination of Frémont was a prearranged affair, and probably would have been made by acclamation had not Thaddeus Stevens of Pennsylvania begged for delay, declaring that Justice McLean was the only man who could carry the state of Pennsylvania. This caused the name of McLean to be placed before the convention, both his name and those of the other candidates, with the exception of Frémont, previously having been withdrawn. An informal ballot was taken, with the result that Frémont received 359 votes, McLean 196, Charles Sumner 2, Nathaniel P. Banks 1, and William H. Seward 1. A formal ballot at once followed, in which Frémont received 520 votes, McLean 37, and Seward 1. This nomination of Frémont at once was made unanimous.

McLean's strength came mainly from Maine, New Hampshire, New Jersey, Pennsylvania, Delaware, Ohio, Indiana, and Illinois. A scene of wild enthusiasm followed the declaration of Frémont's nomination. A large white banner was raised on the platform bearing the legend: "John C. Frémont for President of the United States." Also, in front of the platform was raised a United States flag bearing the same inscription; that was before the days when the "principles of proper respect for the flag" had been codified by conscientious patriotic organizations. Banners were displayed from the windows to notify of the nomination those outside, and there were the usual "cheers from the streets."

The convention adjourned until the next day, when the name of William L. Dayton of New Jersey was placed before the convention for the Vice-Presidential nomination. This was followed by that of Abraham Lincoln of Illinois. John Tweedy gives interesting details of this latter proposal.[5] He states that Hon. John Allison of Pennsylvania said he had been "requested to nominate as a candidate for the Vice-Presidency, Abraham Lincoln of Illinois. He knew him to be the prince of good fellows, and an old-line Whig." Colonel William B. Archer,

[5] "History of the Republican National Conventions," 25–6.

also of Illinois, said he had been acquainted with Lincoln for thirty years and knew him well. He was born in "gallant Kentucky," was now in the prime of life, about forty-seven years of age, and enjoying remarkably good health, and he knew him to be as pure a patriot as ever lived. Judge Spaulding of Ohio then asked, "Can he fight?" Archer replied with great emphasis, "Yes! Have I not told you he was born in Kentucky? He's strong mentally; he's strong physically; he's strong every way." Judge John M. Palmer of Illinois, himself the "Gold" Democratic candidate for President in 1896, seconded the nomination of Lincoln. He said that he had been an old-line Democrat and was very sorry for his last vote. He had known Lincoln long and knew he was a good man and a hard worker in the field, although he had never heard him speak, "for when he was on the stump I always dodged. He is my first choice and I am going to name my first boy after him. We can lick Buchanan anyway, but I think we can do it a little easier if we have Lincoln on the ticket with John C. Frémont."

An informal ballot was taken, with the result that Dayton received 253 votes, Lincoln 110, N. P. Banks 46, David Wilmot 43, Charles Sumner 35, Jacob Collamer (of Vermont) 15, and nine other men votes in lesser number. A formal vote then was taken, during the course of which Judge Palmer, in behalf of the Illinois delegation, withdrew the name of Lincoln. He said that Illinois "knew that in Abraham Lincoln we had a soldier tried and true. We offered him to the Republican party of the United States for the position that we have indicated, but we are content to prefer harmony and union to the success even of our cherished favorite." This formal vote showed Dayton to be the unanimous choice of the convention.[6]

In nominating John Charles Frémont for the Presidency the Republican party, as already stated, had decided, after careful thought, that availability was the prime necessity, for a new party could not do otherwise than center all its energies

[6] This account of the convention of 1856 is drawn mainly from Rhodes, I, 174–186; Stanwood, 269–273; Curtis, I, 255–262; Wilson, II, 511–514; Tweedy, 9–29.

in getting out as large a vote as possible, and success along this line was the basis upon which any hope for future extension and continued existence must depend. William L. Dayton, the running-mate of Frémont, was a native of New Jersey and in the forty-ninth year of his age. He graduated from Princeton, studied law, and was admitted to the bar. He occupied various state offices, finally serving continuously in the United States Senate after the year 1842. He was a "free-soil Whig," and had thus been a colleague of Frémont when the latter was Democratic senator from California.

We learn from contemporary campaign literature that Frémont was the son of a "French gentleman, who visited this country from political causes," and his wife Anne Beverley Whiting of Gloucester county, Virginia, and was born in Savannah, Georgia, in 1813, thus being forty-three years of age when he received the nomination. He entered a law office in Charleston at an early age, and through the aid of a friend was placed in a private school in the same city. At the age of fifteen he entered the junior class of Charleston College, "and might have made a brilliant career there, had it not been for the fascinations of a fair West-Indian girl, whose beauty ran counter to the academic regulations. . . . He was expelled by the Faculty; and this serious rebuke awoke him to a sense of the responsibilities which he owed to his widowed mother." [7]

After this auspicious beginning of romantic life, he became teacher of mathematics on board the sloop of war *Natchez,* and after his return from a three years' cruise "he received the honorary degree of Master of Arts from the college which had been reluctantly compelled to treat his youthful irregularities with rigor." He now surveyed the railroad line between Charleston and Augusta and assisted in exploring mountain passes between South Carolina and Tennessee. Next he assisted in surveying the sources of the Mississippi and Missouri rivers, and in 1838 was appointed from civil life to a commission as second lieutenant in the topographical engineers of the United States army. "In 1841, having been for some

[7] See the "Criterion" (New York, 1856), 7–9.

years on terms of intimacy with the family of the Hon. Thomas H. Benton, of Missouri, he married Jessie, the second daughter of that respected senator. The match was not approved by the young lady's father, and consequently had to be performed clandestinely by a Roman Catholic priest, in the absence of any other clergyman bold enough to officiate." Exploring expeditions followed, of remarkable boldness and success, throughout the Rocky Mountain region, gaining for Frémont the popular name of "The Pathfinder." "In his third expedition he first visited Mariposa, first hoisted the American flag in California, and, in company with Commodore Stockton, made the conquest of that modern Eldorado. For this he was afterwards courtmartialed and dismissed from the service—a sentence which the President revoked, at the same time restoring his rank and ordering him to rejoin his regiment. But Frémont did not wish to expose himself a second time to the jealousy of the West Point officers: he resigned and organized a fourth expedition out of his own funds. After this he settled on his Mariposa purchase, and was the first United States senator elected by California." This was his sole political experience, but his romantic life, with instances both of physical bravery and enthusiastic daring worthy the most approved modern standards of "movie" production, were great assets in his appeal to a young, vigorous, and high-spirited political party. The *naïve* biographical account quoted above concludes by narrating Frémont's trip abroad and honors received there, and his return to America and residence in New York city since the year 1855. It also adds this quaint and delicious sentence: "Col. Frémont is of a spare figure, but remarkably compact and symmetrical; his eyes are very piercing, his head well formed and finely balanced, and his whole appearance is a justification of the obstinate attachment which his wife exhibited to his fortunes."

At this later day we well can see that he would have been impossible as a President of the United States. But his popular appeal was great, especially in contrast to the Democratic candidate, James Buchanan of Pennsylvania, of retiring and evasive cordiality, who was one of the most consummate adepts, in American political history, in the art of following the line of least resistance and "side-stepping" unpleasant issues. The remains of the old-line Whigs and the Know-Nothings nominated that very respectable gentleman, ex-President Millard Fillmore, but it soon became apparent that the real contest lay between Frémont and Buchanan.

The Republicans took their platform, and perhaps one third of their membership, from the old Jefferson-Jackson Democratic party, and placed especial emphasis upon the Declaration of Independence, the Northwest ordinance and other typically Jeffersonian measures. They added a strong declaration for internal improvements, with an undercurrent of loose construction of the Constitution, which was especially well calculated to appeal to old-line Whigs of the Clay or Webster stripe. The Democrats repeated past platform promises, with indorsement of the old Virginia-Kentucky resolutions, "squatter sovereignty," and the Monroe Doctrine. The Whigs, with consciousness of aristocratic conservatism in the face of political *parvenus* or southern reactionaries, stated their faith in the Constitution of the United States and the "absolute necessity for avoiding geographical parties."

The followers of Frémont and Dayton went into the campaign with a vim and enthusiasm seldom equaled in American political history. The whole movement was placed upon a basis of moral enthusiasm that at times savored of spiritual exaltation. Especially active were ministers of practically all the Protestant churches, who preached sermons of such soul-reaching power that their followers were fired to ever-renewed zeal and even a species of spiritual consecration. The faculties of the colleges and universities of that day, literary men of the most intellectual school, charitable and philanthropic leaders, added their support in no uncertain terms. This moral exaltation is almost unique in American politics, and for once there was a party of principle, from which the professional office-seeker and the spoilsman were conspicuous by their absence.

The people of the South, sincerely convinced that their cause was just—that slavery was a righteous institution and their own interests in direct danger of unfair, not to mention unconstitutional, interference or even destruction—were deeply wounded in spirit. The office-holders of a Democratic persuasion found this feeling a fine motive to work upon. The demagogue was in his element, and the timid and confused were relieved in mind when they could find such vociferous, if not unselfish, leadership.

Two things were of the greatest help to Buchanan. The more aggressive of the leaders of the South began to make the statement, based upon determined purpose, that they would cause their states to secede from the Union if Frémont were elected. Many people both at that time, and since, have maintained that this was mere political "bluff," but there was perhaps more than an element of truth in the threat. At least, it was sufficient to stir the timid and hesitant to the depths of their being, and they went in droves into the camp of the Democrats. But there was another and more potent influence. The level-headed, thoughtful men of common sense, who are always the ones to look beneath the surface and study political and other problems from their very foundations, well could sense the extreme danger in the crisis. And, at the same time, they more and more doubted the ability of Frémont to cope with it if he were elected and this crisis came to a head. Added to this were charges, not entirely disproved to the satisfaction of this conservative element, of speculations and business indiscretions in California. These seem to have been believed in that state, which in the subsequent election went to Buchanan by an overwhelming vote nearly equal to the votes for Fillmore and Frémont combined—Frémont running a bad third in the contest. In fact, there is little doubt that Frémont appealed to the emotional and unthinking, to that element always existing in every time and among every people who run after the bizarre, the spectacular, the new. Had they lived to-day they would have said they were "intrigued" by him, and felt an "urge" to vote for him—and then written articles in this strain and for their own reading in so-called "journals of opinion." But the sober, common sense of the American people seldom runs that way, and Rhodes is right when he says that the Republican cause was much stronger than its candidate. "Bleeding Kansas" was much more potent than "Free speech, free soil, and Frémont."

This cause, and its essential soundness, was the reason for the remarkable record that the new national party made at the November election. Thirty-one states took part in it. Buchanan carried nineteen, including Pennsylvania, New Jersey, Indiana, Illinois, California, all the slave states but Maryland, and received 174 electoral votes. Frémont carried eleven states—Connecticut, Iowa, Maine, Massachusetts, Michigan, New Hampshire, New York, Ohio, Rhode Island, Vermont, and Wisconsin, with 114 electoral votes. Fillmore carried Maryland, and received only the eight electoral votes of that state. The popular vote was: Buchanan, 1,838,169; Frémont, 1,341,264; Fillmore, 874,534. Buchanan received 1,226,290 in the free states, 611,879 in the slave states. Fillmore totals in the free and slave states were 394,642 and 479,892 respectively. Rhodes points out that the only votes Frémont received in the slave states were: Delaware, 308; Maryland, 281; Virginia, 291 (and this contained what later became West Virginia during the Civil War); Kentucky, 314. Not a vote was cast for him in Alabama, Arkansas, Florida, Georgia, Louisiana, Mississippi, Missouri, North Carolina, Tennessee, and Texas. The electoral votes of South Carolina were still cast according to the will of the legislature.

The Republican party was entirely sectional, and in this fact lay its greatest handicap. It now can be seen, after the lapse of these many years, that the defeat of 1856 was in reality a good thing for the new party. It came as an overwhelming blow, at first to dampen the enthusiasm of those who suffered merely from emotionalism. But the steady building up, the slow process of bringing the conservative but progressive people around to its support—above all, the emergence of Abraham Lincoln from obscurity and his readiness to assume prominence—were all worth waiting for. And with every passing year the North and West were becoming stronger, both politically and economically, and bound more and more closely together by the lengthening bands of railroads, which in the main ran significantly from East to West and *not* from North to South. The South, as in all communities based upon slave labor, was steadily weakening, in spite of its surface appearance of strength and prosperity. Everything was carrying it toward inevitable tragedy, and defeat, from which a greater country and a greater Union were to grow.

Chapter VI

ABRAHAM LINCOLN

THE political situation in the state of Illinois has purposely been overlooked in this narrative, for it came to its greatest importance after the campaign of 1856, when Abraham Lincoln rose to national prominence. This state gave Buchanan a plurality of 9159, the total votes being: Buchanan, 105,348; Frémont, 96,189; Fillmore, 37, 444. Douglas, the great Democratic leader in the North and West, still had enormous influence, and his prestige was a great asset to his party. It was remarkable that the Republicans had done so well, and they hoped for accessions from the disintegrating Whig party that might put them within striking distance of future political control of the state. What was needed above all else was a leader who might challenge the supremacy of Douglas. They found this leader in Abraham Lincoln.

Of recent years we have had a succession of biographies of this most elusive and stupendously great man; elusive because wonderful in his depths of character, great on account of the simplicity of his treatment of seemingly insoluble problems. One of the most brilliant of the stories of the life of this man is the biography by Professor Nathaniel Wright Stephenson, which gives a remarkable analysis of the mental and spiritual growth of Lincoln from boyhood until the full flower of his undoubted genius. As pointed out by that writer, Lincoln was a typical child of the dwellers in the forest, or in the silence of the frontier. He inherited and enjoyed in the fullest measure the three forest luxuries of dreaming, companionship, and humor, and these exerted a dominant influence upon his entire career.

Abraham Lincoln was born near Hodgenville, Kentucky, on February 12, 1809, and lived in that state about eight years. Although hard times were not unknown, yet he lived what might be called a fairly comfortable peasant life both here and for the ten following years in Indiana. By the age of eighteen or nineteen he had grown to the height of six feet and four inches, and was known for his unusual muscular strength. In the spring of 1830 the family moved to Illinois and the next year Lincoln started out for himself, having meanwhile made two trips down the Mississippi River as a boatman to New Orleans. He became both clerk in a store and then an unsuccessful candidate for the state legislature at the age of twenty-three.

There followed an independent attempt to set himself up in business, which ended in financial failure and a load of debt. However, he came across a complete edition of Blackstone's "Commentaries" by accident, became absorbed in their reading, and this old legal classic had a large share in giving to America one of its very greatest statesmen, for it determined him to become a lawyer.

It was just about this time, as pointed out by Professor Stephenson,[1] that Lincoln suddenly seemed to "find himself" both spiritually and mentally. "In him had come to a head the deepest things in the forest life: the darkly feminine things, its silence, its mysticism, its secretiveness, its tragic patience." He also had "that instinct to endure, to wait, to abide the issue of circumstance, which in the days of his power made him to the politicians as unintelligible as once he had been to the forest huntsmen. . . . In the grown man appeared a quietude, a sort of tranced calm, that was appalling." All these, of course, at first were latent. A sweet, auburn-haired village maiden, the best that New Salem had to give, revealed Lincoln to himself. Ann Rutledge, the daughter of a tavern-keeper, was his first love. She was nineteen years old when she first met Lincoln. Three years later they became engaged, and this

[1] "Abraham Lincoln," 26–27, 39, 47. See also W. E. Barton's great "Life of Abraham Lincoln," I, 211–222.

relation was terminated in a few months by her sudden death of malarial fever in August, 1835.

A period of violent grief and depression followed. Lincoln, naturally morbid and introspective, was inconsolable, and only gradually recovered his normal poise and self-control. But the scar was deep and took long to remove. He was no longer the same man. "His friends had no suspicion that in his real self, beneath the thick disguise of his external sunniness, he was forever brooding, questioning, analyzing, searching after the hearts of things both within and without." But all the time Lincoln was growing in mind and spirit, a living example of the rule, as old as the human race itself, that there is no growth without pain, whether in the physical, mental, or spiritual sphere. And Lincoln's true greatness consisted in the fact that his growth never really stopped. As will shortly be seen, this growth continued until the day of his death, and was the dominating force in his life and his public services.

Professor Stephenson makes an observation that should never be forgotten. "The mighty energy that was in Lincoln, a tireless inexhaustible energy, was inward, of the spirit; it did not always ramify into the sensibilities and inform his outer life." When once this great brooding spirit was possessed by the force of some problem, it worked over it in silence and, undisturbed by clamor or selfish outside influence, it worked its way through to a solution. And this is what happened when Lincoln turned his attention seriously to a study of the problem of slavery.

Early in the year 1837, while a member of the Illinois legislature, he brought in a resolution that never was passed. It stated the significant belief that "the institution of slavery is founded on both injustice and bad policy; but that the promulgation of abolition doctrines tends rather to promote than to abate its evils." This of course led directly to a later acceptance, as a practical policy, of the Free Soil doctrine soon to be imbedded in the Republican platform—that slavery should not be interfered with in the states where already it was established, but also that its further extension should be absolutely prohibited. Left thus to itself, it gradually would die out, as against the progress of civilization and humanity. It was its inevitable disappearance that impressed Lincoln, but it required the aggressiveness of the slave leaders in the Kansas-Nebraska and other policies to arouse him and bring him to the front as a leader in the Illinois branch of the Republican party. The extension of his influence to national scope was only a matter of time.

But Lincoln's comparative failure when a member of Congress during the years 1847-49 caused him to feel that his public career was ended. He turned his attention to his practice of law, where he was gaining an ever-extending influence. When Douglas returned to the state of Illinois, following his furtherance of the Kansas-Nebraska legislation, in the autumn of 1854, he made a bold attempt to justify his course, as well as to resume his position of dominant leadership in the Democratic party and the public opinion of the state. Lincoln was put forth to answer him and succeeded so well that he became a potential candidate for the United States Senate. This again aroused his interest in politics; and although he finally withdrew for strategical reasons and gave his influence in the Illinois legislature toward the election of Lyman Trumbull, yet he now definitely was committed to the Republican cause, his former conservative Whig traditions and membership making easy the transference of his allegiance to this new form of opposition to Douglas and also to pro-slavery Democracy. He did not formally ally himself with the new party until some time during the early part of the year 1856, but his name, as we have seen, was proposed for the nomination for Vice-President on the ticket with Frémont. There is also the report that he made a powerful speech at the state Republican convention at Springfield a short time after, and during the same year.

Douglas broke with the Buchanan administration when it was proposed to admit Kansas with the pro-slavery Lecompton constitution, which had been foisted upon the voters of that territory by a shrewd species of "heads I win, tails you lose" sort of strategy. This policy was a denial of the doctrine of

Photograph from Brown Brothers

REPUBLICANS IN NOMINATING CONVENTION IN THEIR WIGWAM AT CHICAGO, MAY, 1860

"squatter sovereignty" for which Douglas so strongly had stood, and which he had diligently used to excuse himself from the charge of total giving over of self to the interest of the pro-slavery forces. The great and supreme need, if Douglas was to hold his position of leadership in the Democratic party and survive the vendetta of the southern supporters of Buchanan, was to secure a reëlection to his seat in the United States Senate. This seat would become vacant following the elections of 1858.

The Republicans were going through a period of doubt and depression. The defeat of Frémont had discouraged the more effervescent, emotional spirits; and also, prospective office-holders began to doubt the chances for political pie at the hands of the new party. But the rift in the Democratic ranks aroused their drooping spirits, and they saw in the Douglas bolt the chance to compass the defeat of the Buchanan forces at the polls. It is true that Horace Greeley, usually right in theory and wrong in practical politics, favored the withdrawal of all opposition to Douglas by the Republicans of Illinois and the reëlection of Douglas as a means of embarrassing the Democratic party, but fortunately wiser counsels prevailed, and Lincoln was formally chosen to contest the seat.

When Lincoln formally accepted this nomination at the hands of the Republican organization, and it was decided that the election of members of the legislature should be on the ground of their support of Lincoln or Douglas, he made one of the greatest speeches of his life, and one that did much to clarify the whole national situation. It became almost a new platform for the Republican party, and began the train of events that led to party triumph and the election of Lincoln to the Presidency. This was summed up in one great paragraph: "A house divided against itself cannot stand. I believe this Government cannot endure permanently half slave and half free. I do not expect the Union to be dissolved. I do not expect the house to fall, but I do expect it will cease to be divided. It will become all one thing or the other. Either the opponents of slavery will arrest the further spread of it and place it where the public mind shall rest in the belief that it is in the course of ultimate extinction; or its advocates will push it forward till it shall become alike lawful in all the states, old as well as new, North as well as South."

The challenge was at once taken up by Douglas, who knew that his political life depended upon his success in this campaign. The two candidates began a campaign that took rank as one of the most important events in American history. Following a custom of the time, Lincoln challenged Douglas to joint debate. The number of meetings was to be seven, the opening speaker to have an hour and a half, followed by two hours for his opponent. The first speaker then was to have thirty minutes for a rebuttal, giving a total of two hours to each side.

People took their politics seriously in those days, especially the speaking part of it. Lacking the radio, moving pictures, automobiles, and other amusements of a later day, and even being much more circumscribed in their life by bad roads, no telephones, rural mail, or other conveniences and means of enlightenment, they were much more isolated, and looked upon a great debate as a social function, as well as a means of keeping abreast of the times. Newspapers were more rare and much more expensive to-day, so it was often the custom for entire families to travel miles, and make an all-day picnic of the affair, giving recreation to the children and relief to the women of the household from the grueling, grinding cares of their drab and uninteresting life.

Douglas accepted Lincoln's challenge, stating that he would make the opening speech at the first encounter. This would permit him to open and close four out of the seven debates. Lincoln pointed out this fact, so typical of Douglas, but made no objection. It was a brave challenge on his part, for he was pitting himself against one of the shrewdest, ablest, and most popular men of his time. Furthermore, Douglas was an accomplished orator, especially along the lines of the flamboyant speech more popular some years ago than during this more prosaic day of tabloids and motion-pictures. "Slick," that most expressive and well-understood bit of present-day American slang, would be a most fitting description of the man, and his long career of intellectual demagoguery had made him adept in appealing to the crowd and playing upon mob psychology. In character and method he was merely a more crude Henry Clay. Self-made, risen from poverty, early success also had spoiled him, and he too seldom went to the heart of a problem, although he knew as well as Clay where it could be found. In addition, he had the habit of confusing subject and extraneous matter, speaking about rather than on a subject, and his seeming bluntness of moral perception could not fail to appeal to the sympathies of the unthinking—but only of the unthinking, as he was to find out to his cost. He was a little man, his legs too short for his body, but his activity, energy, and driving force had earned for him the name of the "Little Giant."

Contrasted with Douglas was Abraham Lincoln—tall, awkward, "gawky," ungainly, more slow of speech, and with a high-pitched voice, that was not always pleasant. He had a wonderful power of clear expression, his use of the English language was masterly, and his speeches had a literary flavor that might not appeal to the crowd but made wonderful reading afterward. He was profound in thought, but also shrewd enough to lead his opponent into many a trap, and make his political life anything but a bed of roses. It was the old case of an altogether successful politician of great experience meeting a man he considered a newcomer in the field.

This debate was the sensation of the hour in Illinois, and had a resounding repercussion all over the country. Lincoln, at least, was advertising the Republican party as well as himself, and doing it at the expense of Douglas. He met the seemingly overwhelming blow of the Dred Scott decision, which came from the Supreme Court the year before and was virtual denial of the constitutionality of the Republican platform, but turned its effect adroitly upon Douglas. As Woodrow Wilson well has said,[2] the opinion of the court in this case "sustained the whole southern claim. Not even the exercise of squatter

[2] "Division and Reunion," 198–9.

sovereignty could have the countenance of law; Congress must protect every citizen of the country in carrying with him into the Territories property of whatever kind, until such time as the Territory in which he settled should become a State, and pass beyond the direct jurisdiction of the federal government. Those who were seeking to prevent the extension of slavery into the Territories were thus stigmatized as seeking an illegal object, and acting in despite of the Constitution." Douglas of course took advantage of this, and seemingly had the Republican party helpless in the face of the decision. But Lincoln did not overlook the fact that if the Free Soil principle of no further extension of slavery were unconstitutional, so also was that of squatter sovereignty, of which Douglas was the strongest exponent. So he directly asked Douglas in the course of the debates how he would answer this point.

Douglas could not evade, nor did he try to. He answered with his usual cleverness in the debate at Freeport, and hence his position is known as the "Freeport doctrine." Douglas said that the decision stood, and that neither Congress nor a territory could expressly prohibit slavery in a territory, but that *practically* slavery could not exist unless supported by *local police* regulations. Therefore, he concluded that a territory might effectually exclude slavery, and in spite of the Dred Scott decision, by failing to pass or enforce these necessary police laws, or by "unfriendly legislation."

Of course this took with the crowd, who were convinced that Douglas had Lincoln "in a hole." But his opponent knew well what he was doing, and by this simple means really destroyed any chances that Douglas might have for becoming President, as the latter hoped from the future result of the contest of 1860. In standing by the Dred Scott decision, which was the sum of iniquity to the anti-slavery elements in the Northern wing of the Democratic party, he broke down that citadel of his strength. But by showing also how the decision could be evaded or gotten around, he increased the opposition to him in the South, already aroused by his fight against the Lecompton constitution, and thus, so to speak, fell between two stools.

sides—of the essential wrong of slavery on the Northern side, and of the serious danger to their "peculiar institution" on that of the South. John Brown's insane Harper's Ferry raid in October, 1859, did nothing but add fuel to the flames, and make less and less possible the settlement by peaceful means. And of course, as might be expected, it was just the pacifist and other unbalanced elements of radicals and mid-nineteenth century *intelligentsia* who went into ecstasies of delight, and utterly failed to see or appreciate their own silly inconsistency. The world changes but little as time goes on—or at least such self-styled "liberals" remain much the same as a disintegrating and unbalanced force. They forget that true liberalism is constructive and always has been throughout the world's history. John Brown was a consecrated fool, without even the prospect of a "holy grail" to permit him to masquerade as an American Parsifal. And as always, the sincere fool without common sense was the most dangerous influence imaginable. He made war inevitable, and immediate, and removed whatever faint shadow of peaceful solution might remain. Lincoln in his wisdom saw this, and rightly condemned Brown in no uncertain terms.

But the problem still remained, for Lincoln's friends, of bringing him more to the attention of the East. This was accomplished, in a measure, by his Cooper Union speech. An interesting story is connected with this, which was told the writer by one of the principal actors, the late Judge Charles C. Nott, who was himself appointed to a Federal judgeship by Lincoln, and who lived many years, becoming a resident of Princeton, New Jersey.[3]

During the winter of 1859-60 Judge Nott was chairman of the Republican City Committee in New York, and this set of men, mainly young and enthusiastic in a new cause, followed the policy of inviting the leading Republicans over the country to come to the city and address them. This was a sensible means of advertising Republican doctrines as well as the men

[3] This was told in a conversation on February 22, 1912, and written down, in part, at the time.

who advocated them. Nott had heard of Lincoln, and became attracted by his reputation, so he suggested that the secretary of the committee write and invite Lincoln to come East and make one of these addresses. Lincoln replied that he would be glad to come, but would require $300 as a fee. When the committee met and this letter was read to them, they were practically unanimous in their opinion that this fee was too high, and that they could not afford it, as their funds were very limited. Judge Nott, practically alone, insisted that they must have Lincoln come on, and finally, on account of this insistence and their regard for their young leader, the members of the committee told him to go ahead and engage Lincoln, although it practically exhausted their treasury. Years later Judge Nott humorously remarked, and with some show of reason, that he had made Lincoln President by giving him his chance to advertise himself to the East.

Lincoln then accepted the invitation, and the date was set for February 27, 1860, at Cooper Union, although the church of the Rev. Henry Ward Beecher in the neighboring city of Brooklyn was first suggested. It was decided to make the event as important as possible, and in order to give it "tone" William Cullen Bryant, then one of the leading intellectuals in New York, was invited to preside over the meeting, and accepted. As the time drew near for the address, Judge Nott became more and more apprehensive that it might be a failure. He knew that Lincoln had been invited and the heavy drain made upon the committee's treasury largely out of personal regard for him, and this feeling of personal responsibility increased when the designated evening arrived. Cooper Union was filled, and with the most cultured and intelligent people that the city could offer. When Nott saw Lincoln, his apprehension increased, for the Westerner was of anything but prepossessing appearance. Nott described him as the "worst-dressed man he ever had seen," lanky, tall, and awkward, who looked as though his clothes had been thrown at him, and there had stuck. Both sleeves and trousers were too short for him, the latter of the length commonly sneered at as "high waters," and when Lincoln raised his arms, his red woolen underwear showed forth at the wrists.

Bryant made a graceful introduction, and Lincoln rose to speak. At once a chill seemed to come over the temper of the audience and the thermometer dropped to "freezing." But almost the first words of the speaker aroused attention. He spoke in his usual high-pitched voice and made few gestures, mainly emphasizing his words by nodding his head as he leaned over the reading desk. His transparent honesty, sincerity, and clarity of thought now gripped the audience, and he held these people in the hollow of his hand until the end, thrilling them with his statement, since become almost a classic, that, "wrong as we think slavery is, we can yet afford to let it alone where it is, because that much is due to the necessity arising from its actual presence in the nation; but can we, while our votes will prevent it, allow it to spread into the national territories, and to overrun us here in these free states? . . . Let us not be slandered from our duty by false accusations against us, nor frightened from it by menaces of destruction to the Government. . . . Let us have faith that right makes might; and in that faith let us, to the end, dare to do our duty as we understand it."

The speech was a great success and made a profound impression. Judge Nott was exceedingly relieved, but humorously added that so little did he realize the future greatness of Lincoln that he merely escorted him carrying his own little traveling bag to a street car or bus, and gave him directions how to reach his hotel, leaving him entirely to his own devices. The next morning the newspapers were outspoken in their praise, and Lincoln was a marked man in New York city from that time. Lyman Abbott heard the speech, and telling of his feelings, as he remembered them fifty years after, said that he was carried away with enthusiasm, and "I then became a Lincoln man and have remained one ever since."

We now know why Lincoln insisted upon the $300. This was due to the fact that his eldest son, Robert Todd Lincoln, was a student at Phillips Academy at Exeter, New Hampshire, and Lincoln could not afford to send him the money for him to return home for the Christmas vacation. Therefore, when the invitation came to make the address in New York, he placed the fee at a sum sufficient to pay for the trip East to see his son, and the day following his Cooper Union address he went to New England, making a number of speeches on his way, including Providence, Rhode Island; Concord, Manchester, and Dover, New Hampshire; and Hartford, Meriden, and New Haven, Connecticut. In all, he gave eleven addresses, and thus became known to some of the Eastern leaders. This was to stand him in good stead when the national convention met at Chicago a few months later.

It should be remembered that Lincoln was an active aspirant for the Presidential nomination. He was early known as the "Rail Splitter," due to the fact that when the Illinois state convention met at Decatur on May 10, 1859, he entered the hall as a spectator, and at that moment Governor Richard J. Oglesby announced that he had a contribution offered to the convention by an old Democrat from Macon county. Then old John Hanks brought in two rails which he and Lincoln had split together in 1830, and bearing the inscription: "Abraham Lincoln. The Rail Candidate for President in 1860." The delegates went wild. Lincoln addressed them and told of his experiences as a laborer thirty years before. The convention went on record for Lincoln, and thus his candidacy was officially launched. Governor Oglesby himself was the author of this theatrical byplay,[4] and had himself hunted up Hanks and then driven with him ten miles out into the country west of Decatur to the site of Lincoln's first Illinois farm. Here Hanks found and identified the rails, and two of them were brought back with them and hidden until the day of the convention.

Lincoln also made speeches through various parts of the West, and wrote many letters to personal and political friends. These latter went hard to work, knowing that although Seward was the outstanding candidate, yet his earlier prominence in national politics had won him many enemies. Democrats would

[4] See Barton, I, 413–15.

not want to vote for him, nor would old-line Whigs be apt to follow whole-heartedly such an old Democratic "war horse" as Salmon P. Chase, who was the other candidate of outstanding prominence.

It is now known that Lincoln, knowing the potential power of the German and other recent immigrant vote, made every attempt to secure its influence, even buying a German-language newspaper, the "Illinois Staats-Anzeiger," at that time recently established and edited by Dr. Theodore Canisius of Springfield. According to an agreement drawn up in Lincoln's handwriting and signed on May 30, 1859, the ownership was vested in Lincoln, and Canisius was to edit the paper, which was to support strongly the Republican party. On December 6, 1860, this ownership was conveyed to Canisius, Lincoln having been elected President a month before.[5]

Altogether it may be judged that Lincoln was a "dark-horse" candidate for the Presidency, disguised under the name of a "favorite son" of Illinois. The plan of his shrewd friends was to secure for him the place of second choice with as many delegates as possible, calculating that Seward, Chase, and the other leading aspirants would "kill each other off"—a form of political strategy not unknown on many later occasions, and used with triumphant effect.

The Republican national convention of 1860 met in Chicago on Wednesday, May 16, in a building erected especially to house it. This was the celebrated "Wigwam," built at a cost of $7000 by the Republicans of Chicago. It was a small edition of the New York Crystal Palace, built of boards, and held ten thousand people comfortably. It stood on the corner of Lake and Market Streets and was admirable for its acoustic excellence, so that a voice could be heard with ease throughout the entire building. It can be seen how the party had grown since the days of the Philadelphia convention of four years before; and the crowds in attendance were enormous for that day.

[5] Barton, I, 421–4. See also letter of the late Albert J. Beveridge, quoted in "New York Herald Tribune," May 2, 1927.

While the Democratic party was split in two and almost demoralized as it entered the Presidential campaign, the Republicans were filled with enthusiasm and had every prospect of success. The elections of the preceding autumn of 1859 had been largely in their favor. They had carried every Northern state in which an election had been held, with the exception of four—California, New York, Oregon, and Rhode Island—and these latter were lost only by small margins or by the means of fusion movements in opposition. Therefore the professional office-holders and others of spoils tendency were more ready to jump on the Republican bandwagon than had been the case in 1856. The Presidential nomination would be well worth the having, and popular interest and anticipation were intense.

Murat Halstead, who attended all four of the national conventions of the year as the correspondent of "The Cincinnati Commercial," wrote at the time his observations and experiences, which were published in the form of a pamphlet entitled "Caucuses of 1860," and the following account of the Chicago convention is mainly drawn from his brilliant and authentic narrative.

With great frankness Halstead tells of the large amount of whisky, champagne, and other convivial liquors imbibed on the trains to Chicago, as well as throughout the time of the meetings and the caucuses in between. "A portion of the Republicans are distressed by what they see and hear of the disposition to use ardent spirits which appears in members of their supposed to be painfully virtuous party. And our Western Reserve was thrown into prayers and perspiration last night by some New Yorkers, who were singing songs not found in hymn-books." Horace Greeley attended as a delegate from Oregon, his personal and vindictive enmity to Seward and Thurlow Weed, the latter's manager, preventing his securing the position of delegate from New York. He favored the nomination of Edward Bates of Missouri, but finding that to be impossible, swung over to Lincoln on the ground of anything to beat Seward. He was considered one of the lions of the convention, and Halstead noted that "the way Greeley is stared at as he shuffles about, looking as innocent as ever, is itself a sight. Whenever he appears there is a crowd gaping at him. . . . The Seward men have badges of silk with his [Seward's] likeness and name, and some wag pinned one of them to Horace Greeley's back . . . and he created even an unusual sensation as he hitched about with the Seward mark upon him."

The scenes when the doors of the Wigwam were opened to the general public were exciting, to say the least. Three doors about twenty feet wide were simultaneously thrown open. Three torrents of men roared in, and rushed headlong for front positions. The standing room, which held 4500 persons, was packed in five minutes. The galleries were open only to "gentlemen accompanied by ladies," and held nearly 3000 people. There was much hilarity, also many curious performances in the efforts to gain admission to this part of the building. Ladies to accompany gentlemen were decidedly in demand; schoolgirls were found on the street and given a quarter each to see a "gentleman" safely in. Says Halstead: "Other girls, those of undoubted character (no doubt on the subject whatever), were much sought after as escorts. One of them being asked to take a gentleman to the gallery, and offered half a dollar for so doing, excused herself by saying she had already taken two men in at each of the three doors, and was afraid of arrest if she carried the enterprise any further. An Irish woman, passing with a bundle of clothes under her arm, was levied upon by an 'irrepressible' [intoxicated], and seeing him safely into the seats reserved for ladies and accompanying gentlemen, retired with her fee and bundle. Another 'irrepressible' sought out an Indian woman who was selling moccasins, and attempted to escort her in. This was a little too severe, however. He was informed that she was no lady—and the point was argued with considerable vehemence. It was finally determined that a squaw was not a lady. The young Republican protested indignantly against the policeman's decision, claiming equal rights for all womankind."

The convention was called to order by Edwin D. Morgan

of New York, chairman of the National Republican Committee, and he nominated David Wilmot for temporary president. Upon taking the chair, Wilmot made a strong anti-slavery speech. He was rather a poor presiding officer, and there was general relief when George Ashmun of Massachusetts was chosen permanent president and took the chair. His rulings were clear and prompt, and he held the convention remarkably well in hand, in spite of its irascibility and emotional vagaries. Norman B. Judd of Illinois, Lincoln's friend, presented to the convention on behalf of the mechanics of Chicago a gavel made of the oak of the flagship of Commodore Perry, the *Lawrence*. It was received with "terrific cheering." The routine business of organization being effected, the convention adjourned—while the real business of the committee room and caucus got under way and lasted throughout the night.

The next morning, Thursday, May 17, the Seward men made a great demonstration in the form of a procession. They formed in front of their headquarters, the Richmond House, and wearing badges marched four abreast, being led by a band in splendid uniform and playing a current musical success—"Oh, Isn't He a Darling?" Heedless of the clouds of dust from the Chicago streets, they marched along with great enthusiasm. The crowds were greater than ever, both in and outside the Wigwam.

The morning session was taken up with reports of the committees, especially on credentials and rules, which were not adopted without some sparring, with "keen sharpshooting" and "bitter and incisive sarcasm." Then came the platform report, and it was received with great enthusiasm. Each section of it was greeted with tumultuous applause, especially the ones dealing with the homestead laws and the tariff, the latter causing the Pennsylvania delegation to go into "spasms of joy," the whole delegation rising and swinging hats and canes.

Here occurred an incident that might have resulted most seriously for the Republicans in the approaching campaign. Joshua R. Giddings of Ohio, the old anti-slavery veteran of many a political fight, arose amid much confusion and moved the inclusion of the clause from the Declaration of Independence contained in the 1856 platform, that declared that all men were endowed by their Creator with unalienable rights such as life, liberty, and the pursuit of happiness. This had been omitted by the Platform Committee in an effort to tone down the radical character of the party declarations, in order to attract more conservative people from both the old parties. Giddings made an emotional speech in favor of his amendment and aroused great enthusiasm, at least among the spectators, but the convention voted it down, holding it unnecessary. One delegate said he believed in the Ten Commandments, but did not think it necessary to include them in the platform.

Giddings quickly arose and started for the door. He considered everything lost, even honor, for the Declaration of Independence had been voted down. A dozen delegates begged him not to go, but he proceeded as far as the New York delegation, where he was given assurances that the amendment would be tried again, and he took a seat in the rear of the room. A little while later, George William Curtis of New York obtained the floor and in a clever and tactful speech renewed Giddings's motion in a slightly different form. He closed by saying, "I rise simply to ask gentlemen to think well before, upon the free prairies of the West, in the summer of 1860, they dare to wince and quail before the men who in Philadelphia, in 1776—in Philadelphia, in the Arch-Keystone state, so amply, so nobly represented upon this platform to-day—before they dare to shrink from repeating the words that these great men enunciated." This was received with "terrific" applause, and the amendment was at once approved, followed by the adoption of the entire platform. It was a great personal triumph for Curtis.

This platform, upon which Lincoln successfully won his victory, was a clever piece of political construction. It is important to note its main provisions. The opening section stated that "the history of the nation, during the last four years, has fully established the propriety and necessity of the organization and perpetuation of the Republican party, and that the causes which called it into existence are permanent in their nature, and now, more than ever before, demand its peaceful and constitutional triumph." Then followed the plank reaffirming the principles of the Declaration of Independence and the Constitution of the United States, thus placing the party firmly upon the principle of Jeffersonian Republicanism —a shrewd move to catch Democratic votes. Next came a condemnation of all threats of disunion, followed by a declaration that "the maintenance inviolate of the rights of the states, and especially the right of each state to order and control its own domestic institutions according to its own judgment exclusively, is essential to that balance of power on which the perfection and endurance of our political fabric depends." This should have been sufficient to disprove any charges of abolitionism, or an intent to interfere with slavery in the Southern states, and only the blind emotionalism of the Southern "fire-eaters" could overlook such denial of any attempts at hostile aggression.

The same subject was amplified by several succeeding sections, which may be summed up as follows: "The present Democratic administration has far exceeded our worst apprehensions, in its measureless subserviency to the exactions of a sectional interest. . . . The new dogma that the Constitution, of its own force, carries slavery into any or all of the Territories of the United States, is a dangerous political heresy, at variance with the explicit provisions of that instrument itself. . . . The normal condition of the territory of the United States is that of freedom; . . . as our republican fathers, when they had abolished slavery in all our national territory, ordained that no person should be deprived of life, liberty, or property without due process of law, it becomes our duty, by legislation, whenever such legislation is necessary, to maintain this provision of the Constitution against all attempts to violate it; and we deny the authority of Congress, of a territorial legislature, or of any individual, to give legal existence to slavery in any territory of the United States.

. . . Kansas should of right be immediately admitted as a state under the Constitution recently formed and adopted by her people."

After this statement of orthodox Republican or Free Soil principles followed several planks shrewdly intended to catch various elements of the Northern and Western population, and insure their allegiance to the party irrespective of their feelings about slavery. These latter principles are a forecast of much of the Republican policy during succeeding years, and even to the present day, furnishing a sort of unity of policy during the whole period of Republican domination of the National Government.

Of course the most important of these dealt with the tariff, and was the means by which Pennsylvania was changed from a bourbon Democratic to a Republican alignment. It is significant that the delegation from this state received the plank with such an outburst of approval. It read, "while providing revenue for the support of the General Government by duties upon imports, sound policy requires such an adjustment of these imposts as to encourage the development of the industrial interests of the whole country; and we commend that policy of national exchanges which secures to the workingmen liberal wages, to agriculture remunerating prices, to mechanics and manufacturers an adequate reward for their skill, labor, and enterprise, and to the nation commercial prosperity and independence." By this means the Republican party began that process of uniting in its ranks the business and industrial interests without which, as not only American history but that of other self-governing countries shows, it is impossible to continue political domination. With it, a political party is intrenched, and in a perfectly legitimate way, provided one believes in nation-wide material prosperity as a requisite for a happy and contented people.

The homestead plank, mentioned above, protested against "any sale or alienation to others of the public lands held by actual settlers, and against any view of the free-homestead policy which regards the settlers as paupers or suppliants for public bounty," and demanded "the passage by Congress of the complete and satisfactory homestead measure which has already passed the House." This was an appeal to the farmers of the Northwest, as also was the section on immigration, which stated the opposition of the party to "any change in our naturalization laws, or any state legislation by which the rights of citizenship hitherto accorded to immigrants from foreign lands shall be abridged or impaired; and in favor of giving a full and efficient protection to the rights of all classes of citizens, whether native or naturalized, both at home and abroad." Last and not least of these provisions was a declaration that "a railroad to the Pacific Ocean is imperatively demanded by the interests of the whole country; and that the federal government ought to render immediate and efficient aid in its construction; and that, as preliminary thereto, a daily overland mail should be promptly established."

The whole platform was a clever and able statement of special Republican views with regard to the slave issue, and also the preparation of an economic basis of doctrine upon which could be brought about the coöperation of the agrarian, industrial, and commercial interests of the country. It built not alone for the present campaign but also looked to the future of a well-established and permanent national political party.

The adoption of this platform was so immediate and so hearty, that the convention really outran its program. Seward had the prestige of leading candidate, and at that time the advocates of such other men as Bates, Lincoln, Chase, and Cameron were practically in despair. The Seward leaders sensed victory, and demanded that the convention begin balloting at once. Had this taken place, it is probable that Seward would have received the nomination; but just then it was announced that the secretaries of the convention were not yet provided by the printers with the necessary tally-sheets. This fact possibly changed American history in a most profound way. In spite of the protests of the New York delegation, the convention adjourned soon after six o'clock until the next day.

Halstead has interesting comment upon this New York delegation. He states that they are of a "class unknown to Western Republican politicians. They can drink as much whiskey, swear as loud and long, sing as bad songs, and 'get up and howl' as ferociously as any crowd of Democrats you ever heard, or heard of. They are opposed, as they say, 'to being too damned virtuous.' They hoot at the idea that Seward could not sweep all the Northern states, and swear that he would have a party in every slave state, in less than a year, that would clean out the disunionists from shore to shore. They slap each other on the back with the emphasis of delight when they meet, and rip out 'How *are* you?' with a 'How are you hoss?' style, that would do honor to Old Kaintuck on a bust. At night those of them who are not engaged at caucusing, are doing that which ill-tutored youths call 'raising hell generally.' Wherever you find them, the New York politicians, of whatever party, are a peculiar people." One can only wonder how congenial George William Curtis found himself with his brother-delegates.

The real work of the convention with regard to the nomination for President was done during the night of Thursday and before the reassembling on Friday morning. The delegates from Pennsylvania, New Jersey, Indiana, and Illinois made strenuous efforts to swing votes away from Seward, for they insisted that the New York candidate could not carry their states in the fall. They said they considered "success rather than Seward," and made their first breach in his ranks among the delegates from Vermont and Virginia. It was argued that Vermont would cast its electoral votes for any candidate that might be nominated, while Virginia just as surely would cast its votes against him. The Chicago papers of Friday morning contained a last appeal to the convention not to nominate Seward. The Cameron men, finding that their man had absolutely no hope, but that either Seward or Lincoln would be nominated, decided to throw their vote to Lincoln at such a time as to have credit for his nomination if it were made. Also, Lincoln's friends, in specific violation of his instructions to them, promised a cabinet place for Cameron if Lincoln were President.

After the preliminary exercises, the names of candidates for the nomination were presented without the laudatory addresses so characteristic of later days. They were presented for the most part by the chairmen of the different delegations. William H. Seward was nominated by William M. Evarts of New York. Abraham Lincoln was nominated by his friend Norman B. Judd of Illinois; William L. Dayton was nominated by Thomas H. Dudley of New Jersey; Simon Cameron by Andrew H. Reeder of Pennsylvania; Salmon P. Chase by D. K. Carter of Ohio; Edward Bates by Francis P. Blair, Jr., of Missouri; and Justice John McLean by Thomas Corwin of Ohio. Lincoln's nomination was seconded by Caleb B. Smith of Indiana (later secretary of the interior in Lincoln's cabinet), by Columbus Delano of Ohio, and William M. Stone of Iowa. His strength thus lay mainly in the Northwest. The nomination of Seward was seconded by Austin Blair of Michigan and Carl Schurz of Wisconsin. The only names that caused great applause were those of Lincoln and Seward, ovations worthy of modern days being accorded their names.

The convention then began to ballot. The names of the New England states were called first, and it at once became evident that the strength of Seward in that section was not so great as had been claimed. The New York delegates looked at each other in a significant way when the vote of Virginia went eight for Seward and fourteen for Lincoln. Here was seen the result of the work during the previous night, for this state had been considered solid for Seward. The secretary of the convention announced the result of the first ballot to be: Seward, 173½; Lincoln, 102; Bates, 48; Cameron, 50½; McLean, 12; Chase, 49; Wade, 3; Dayton, 14; Reed (of Pennsylvania), 1; Collamer, 10; Sumner, 1; Frémont, 1. Whole number of votes cast, 465; necessary to a choice, 233.

On the second ballot, the votes of Vermont and Pennsylvania were thrown to Lincoln, as well as scattering votes from

© *Brown Brothers*

ABRAHAM LINCOLN

Last portrait. Made one week before he was assassinated

elsewhere, so the result was: Seward, 184½; Lincoln, 181; Chase, 42½; Bates, 35; Dayton, 10; McLean, 8; Cameron, 2; Clay (Cassius M.), 2. There was great confusion while this ballot was being counted. It was known that while Seward and Lincoln were about even, yet Lincoln was the second choice of most of the delegates who were voting for the minor candidates.

The convention at once proceeded to the third ballot, and many people kept tally so that they knew the result before the secretary gave formal announcement that the vote was: Seward, 180; Lincoln, 231½; Chase, 24½; Bates, 22; Dayton, 1; McLean, 5; Clay, 1.

Lincoln thus needed just one and a half votes to nominate him, and, says Halstead, "in about ten ticks of a watch, Carter of Ohio was up. . . . Every eye was on Carter, and everbody who understood the matter at all knew what he was about to do. He is a large man with rather striking features, a shock of bristling black hair, large and shining eyes, and is terribly marked with the small-pox. He has also an impediment in his speech which amounts to a stutter. . . . He had been quite noisy during the sessions of the Convention but had never commanded, when mounting his chair, such attention as now. He said, 'I rise (eh), Mr. Chairman (eh), to announce the change of four votes of Ohio from Mr. Chase to Mr. Lincoln.' The deed was done. There was a moment's silence. The nerves of the thousands, which through the hours of suspense had been subjected to terrible tension, relaxed, and as deep breaths of relief were taken there was a noise in the Wigwam like the rush of a great wind, in the van of a storm—and in another breath the storm was there. There were thousands cheering with the energy of insanity."

With a partial restoring of order, many men struggled to get the floor, and a number of states changed their votes to Lincoln. When the votes finally were announced, Lincoln had 364 votes out of a total of 466, with 234 necessary for a choice, and was declared nominated. Meanwhile the New York delegation, disappointed and quiet, had sat in their seats.

There were cries of "New York! New York!" but they continued to sit silent. The state was prepared to move that the nomination be made unanimous, but not out of order. When the vote was regularly declared, Evarts arose and, standing on the secretary's table, "handsomely and impressively expressed his grief at the failure of the convention to nominate Seward, and in melancholy tones moved that Lincoln's nomination be made unanimous." John A. Andrew of Massachusetts, later the "war governor" of that state, followed Evarts. He was a short man, inclined to be portly, and was asked to mount a table, which he did. He, too, seconded the nomination of Lincoln, followed by Carl Schurz to the same effect. After several other speeches of a like character, the vote was taken and the convention adjourned for dinner.

Nicolay and Hay give the following as their summary of the reasons for the nomination of Lincoln: "The credit of the nomination is claimed by many men, and by several delegations, but every such claim is wholly fictitious. Lincoln was chosen not by personal intrigue, but through political necessity. The Republican party was a purely defensive organization; the South had created the crisis which the new party was compelled to overcome. The ascendancy of the free states, not the personal fortunes of Seward, hung in the balance. Political victory at the ballot-box or a transformation of the institutions of government was the immediate alternative before the free states.

"Victory could be secured only by the help of the electoral votes of New Jersey, Pennsylvania, Indiana, and Illinois. It was therefore a simple problem: what candidate could carry these states? None could answer this question as well as their own delegates and these, when interrogated, still further reduced the problem by the reply that Seward certainly could not. These four states lay on the border land next to the South and to slavery. Institutions inevitably mould public sentiment, and a certain tenderness towards the 'property' of neighbors and friends infested their people. They shrunk from the reproach of being 'abolitionists.' They would vote for a conservative

Republican; but Seward and radicalism and 'higher law' would bring them inevitable defeat." [6]

During this dinner recess was held a caucus of the chairmen of the delegations, at which New York was requested to name a candidate for Vice-President, but declined. When the convention resumed its sittings it nominated Hannibal Hamlin of Maine on the second ballot. Cassius M. Clay was the only competitor of Hamlin who made any impression, and the outside influence was for him. At one time there were loud calls of "Clay!" from the spectators. But Hamlin was nominated on the grounds of political availability, as usual with the candidates for the Vice-Presidency. He was geographically far removed from Lincoln, and was a former Democrat. He had been governor of his state, and at this time was United States senator. Halstead caustically remarks: "It was deemed judicious to pretend to patronize the Democratic element, and thus consolidate those who were calling the convention an 'old Whig concern.' They need not have been afraid, however, of having it called an old Whig affair, for it was not 'eminently respectable' nor distinguished for its 'dignity and decorum.' On the other hand, the satanic element was very strongly developed."

The delegates were worn out with excitement and liquor and soon departed for their homes. Halstead well points out that the outstanding fact of this convention was the defeat of Seward rather than the nomination of Lincoln, and as such it was looked upon by the eastern Whig elements, especially the more conservative people, such as four years before had wavered, and then refused to support Frémont. Meanwhile, Lincoln had remained quietly at home in Springfield, Illinois, where he received the news of his success. He went first of all to inform his wife. The next day the committee appointed by the convention to notify him arrived in Springfield, and Mr. Ashmun made a short notification address. Lincoln replied, with exquisite taste, as follows: "I accept the nomination tendered me by the convention over which you presided, of

[6] "Lincoln," II, 263–4.

which I am formally apprised in a letter of yourself and others acting as a committee of the convention for that purpose. The declaration of principles and sentiments which accompanies your letter meets my approval, and it shall be my care not to violate it, or disregard it in any part. Imploring the assistance of Divine Providence, and with due regard to the views and feelings of all who were represented in the convention, to the rights of all the states and the territories and people of the nation, to the inviolability of the Constitution, and the perpetual union, harmony, and prosperity of all, I am most happy to coöperate for the practical success of the principles declared by the convention." The committee then passed into Lincoln's library, where they were introduced to Mrs. Lincoln and were given light refreshments, but no wine or strong drink of any kind.

The Republicans entered the campaign with great confidence. This was due to the split in the Democratic party and the nomination of two candidates by the respective wings. The causes of this were deep, and represented the essential differences between the Northern and Southern wings and their attitudes toward slavery, especially as shown at the time of the Free Soil campaign in 1848. The immediate occasion was a series of events which had begun with the introduction in the United States Senate by Jefferson Davis of a set of resolutions on February 2, 1860, which demanded that Congress should guarantee slave property in the territories. These were an ultimatum from the South, and on this basis the Democrats of the North must unite. Of course it was impossible for them to do this, and when the Democratic national convention met on April 23 at Charleston there was a secession of the delegates from eight of the states of the far South. They had demanded an inclusion of a plank somewhat to this effect, and the Douglas men refused. After several days of useless attempts to unite the convention upon a candidate under the Democratic "two thirds rule," an adjournment was taken to Baltimore on June 18 following. When the convention again met, it nominated Douglas for President, and later the National Committee nominated Herschel V. Johnson of Georgia for Vice-President. The Cincinnati platform of 1856, upon which Buchanan had been elected, was reaffirmed, which meant that the party pledged itself to stand by the Dred Scott decision, or any future decision of the Supreme Court which dealt with the rights of property in the various states and territories.

The seceding Democrats met at Baltimore on June 28 and nominated John C. Breckinridge of Kentucky for President (at that time the Vice-President in the Buchanan administration) and Joseph Lane of Oregon for Vice-President. Its platform was of course a reaffirmation of the extreme southern position with regard to slavery. To add to the political complications, the various remnants of the old-line Whigs and Know-Nothings already had met in a convention at Baltimore on May 9 under the name of the Constitutional Union party. They nominated John Bell of Tennessee for President and Edward Everett of Massachusetts for Vice-President, upon the platform of "the Constitution of the country, the Union of the states, and the enforcement of the laws." The members of the convention were of a more conservative type, and their more advanced age was evident. It is interesting to note that their platform in fact became the bedrock of Lincoln's plan of action after the South had attempted secession and the Civil War had begun. This party died immediately following the election, but many of its members in the border states went into the Republican party by way of this ephemeral organization, and when they finally were faced with the actual attempt by the South to disrupt the Union.

The news of Lincoln's nomination was not received with very great enthusiasm by the more intelligent and conservative members of the Republican party. He appealed to the common people, and also to the more or less radical elements which it included. The more educated realized that Lincoln was almost an unknown quantity, had had very little experience in governmental affairs, and would have to face the most critical situation in the history of the country since the

Constitution was adopted. Charles Francis Adams of Massachusetts made a speech in the House of Representatives at Washington on May 31, just about two weeks after the Chicago convention adjourned, which discussed the subject "The Republican Party a Necessity." It was a strong argument in favor of the party but did not once mention the name of Lincoln, its candidate. Edward Bates of Missouri at first hesitated to take part in the campaign, and was only persuaded to do so after some pressure from party leaders. Seward was bitterly disappointed by his failure to receive the nomination; his friends had planned and arranged for a great celebration at his home in Auburn, New York, when the expected news of his success should come from Chicago. But he threw himself into the campaign and loyally supported Lincoln and Hamlin, as did Chase and Cameron. James Ford Rhodes considers Seward's work in this campaign as perhaps the most brilliant of his career.

The campaign gradually grew in enthusiasm. The almost certain prospect that the Democratic split would give the Republicans the victory carried them to renewed courage. Experienced office-holders and trained professional politicians scented the prospective spoils, jumped on the bandwagon in droves and gave their aid, of the most practical kind. The marching organization known as the "Wide-Awakes," with oilcloth capes and torchlights, marched in long processions, overflowing with enthusiasm and singing their campaign song of "Old Abe Lincoln came out of the wilderness, Down in Illinois." While the other parties took up this custom, yet the Republicans used it with the greatest enthusiasm and success. The Whig elements remembered their success in 1840 in the "hard cider" campaign for Harrison and Tyler—"Tippecanoe and Tyler too." While the cider was not featured, there was plenty of "licker" in these pre-prohibition days of 1860, and it was used judiciously for purposes of excitement and popular enthusiasm. It should be remembered that in those days much was done by enthusiasm which now is accomplished by party organization.

In contrast to these elements of the usual "practical" kind

of politics, there was the fact that such intellectual and religious leaders as Henry Ward Beecher, Oliver Wendell Holmes, John Greenleaf Whittier, William Cullen Bryant, George William Curtis, and James Russell Lowell were active in their support of Lincoln. It was the last named who put his finger on the point of main strength of the Republican cause when he wrote, "It is in a moral aversion to slavery as a great wrong." The German and other foreign elements in our citizenship, hostile to slave labor as always, rallied in thousands around the Lincoln banner. Lincoln himself remained in Springfield after his nomination, except for one journey to Chicago and one to visit his stepmother. He made no speeches, nor did he make or allow to be made any formal declarations except the party platform.[7]

Stanwood says that in the South there was a grim determination to win a victory if in any way possible, but not to submit to defeat. It soon was realized everywhere but among the few enthusiasts of their followers that neither Douglas, Bell, nor Breckinridge could carry the country, and that the best that might be hoped by their partizans was that through a division of the electoral vote no one would get the required majority and the election be thrown into the House of Representatives. As in 1856, there were threats that the election of the Republican candidates would mean secession and the breakup of the Union. The Lincoln men laughed at this and refused to believe that their opponents in the South should be taken at all seriously. Douglas, after speaking in the South, openly stated his belief that the country was in more danger than at any other time in his experience of public life. Seward countered the threats by saying a few days before the election: "For ten, aye for twenty years these threats have been renewed, in the same language and in the same form, about the first day of November every four years when it happened to come before the day of the Presidential election. I do not doubt but that these southern statesmen and politicians think they are going to dissolve the Union, but I think they are going to

[7] Barton, I, 445.

do no such thing." This shows that most of the people in the North and West refused to take seriously the threats of the South, and they were totally unprepared for what happened when Lincoln was elected and the lower South seceded. Douglas went South to urge the people to submit if Lincoln should be elected, and stated openly at Norfolk, Virginia, when questioned, that there would be no justification for the South to withdraw from the Union in case of Republican success. He repeated this view at other places and in more emphatic form, stating that he would do all in his power to aid the United States Government in maintaining the supremacy of the laws against all resistance to them, "come from what quarter it might." He added that he hoped the President of the United States, whoever he might be, would copy Andrew Jackson and his attitude toward the nullifiers of 1832. Douglas thus was showing a new character—he rapidly was leaving the pose of a demagogue, so often seen in the past years of his public life, and was showing in its place the attributes of a courageous and patriotic statesman. His untimely death within the year following was a grievous loss to his old opponent, Lincoln, and to the cause to which the latter then was dedicating his life.

Meanwhile there had been a strong and earnest attempt to make a fusion of all anti-Republican elements on a ticket; or with the implied or express agreement that whichever ticket should receive a plurality should receive the electoral votes necessary to a majority and thus cause an election. Both Breckinridge and Bell expressed their willingness to retire in favor of some Union candidate acceptable to all, but Douglas refused, saying it was impracticable. Fusion was accomplished in certain close states. Even had this been the case everywhere, it is probable that only the votes of Oregon and California would have been lost to Lincoln.

The early elections, which took place in the states of Indiana, Maine, Ohio, and Oregon, forecast Republican success. The party elected governors in Indiana and Pennsylvania, and these had been considered doubtful states during the negotiations of the delegates to the Chicago convention. When the

Photograph by Brown Brothers

ABRAHAM LINCOLN AND HIS CABINET

votes were counted on the night of November 6 it was soon found that Lincoln had received 180 electoral votes and was elected. Breckinridge received 72, Bell 39, and Douglas but 12. The popular vote was far otherwise. Thirty-three states participated in the election. Lincoln carried every Northern state but New Jersey, where there had been fusion, but even in that state he received three out of the seven electoral votes, since that number of the fusion candidates for elector had been "scratched" by the voters. Bell carried the three border states of Kentucky, Tennessee, and Virginia—the last by only 358 plurality. On the other hand, he nearly carried Georgia, Louisiana, Maryland, and North Carolina, which states he lost by small margins to Breckinridge; and Missouri, which he lost to Douglas by less than five hundred votes. The popular vote totaled 1,857,610 for Lincoln; 1,291,574 for Douglas; 850,082 for Breckinridge; 646,124 for Bell. The combined opponents received a majority of 930,170 over Lincoln, who thus was a minority President for his first administration.[8] In each house of the newly elected Congress the Republicans would be in a minority against a combination of their opponents—eight in the Senate and twenty-one in the House of Representatives. By the withdrawal from Congress of the senators and representatives from the seceding states, this condition was changed and there was a Republican control of both houses during the last five or six weeks of the Buchanan administration. It is especially interesting to note that during this time laws were passed to organize the territories of Colorado, Dakota, and Nevada, without any provision to prohibit slavery in them. The showed that in spite of the platform and principles of the Republican party, there need be no fear on the part of the

[8] Horace Greeley, "American Conflict," I, 328, gives an analysis of the vote as follows, after making an apportionment of the fusion votes: Free states—Lincoln, 1,831,180; Douglas, 1,128,049; Breckinridge, 279,211; Bell, 130,151. Slave states—Lincoln 26,430; Douglas, 163,525; Breckinridge, 570,871; Bell, 515,973. Lincoln's majority over Douglas was 566,036. Breckinridge lacked 135,057 of a majority in the slave states, which thus did not vote outright for secession. See article by W. E. Dodd, "The Fight for the Northwest," "American Historical Review," July 1911 (Vol. XVI, 774–88).

South of aggressive action against that section when that party should come into control with the inauguration of Lincoln. But the party meanwhile could do nothing to stem the tide of secession, due to the supineness and even cowardice of the Buchanan administration, and the fact that it was in large part an executive duty, and not that of the legislature, to meet such a crisis. Things continued to go from bad to worse until Lincoln was inaugurated, and even then for some five or six weeks longer, until he could "learn the ropes" and gain real control of the Government.

Chapter VII

SAVING THE UNION

LINCOLN followed exactly the same policy during the time between his election on November 6, 1860, and his inauguration on March 4, 1861, that he had chosen during the period of the campaign which saw his triumph at the polls. For the most of the time he remained quietly at home in Springfield, "thinking his way through," as was shown to be his custom when great problems confronted him. And also, he evidently was not at first impressed with the danger of secession. When South Carolina made good her threats on December 20 and announced her "dissolution of the Union" with the "other states united with her under the compact entitled the Constitution of the United States of America," he refused to take the matter too seriously and still hoped that better counsels would prevail. But events went from bad to worse as other Southern states joined the movement, and he then adopted the policy of attempting to allay excitement and thus gain time for study and experience to show him the way out. He generally was not of a disposition to hunt trouble, but would wait until the necessary moment before acting; but when that came, he could be inexorable in carrying out his purposes. The following pages will furnish ample evidence of this trait.

Seward now came to the front and desired to bring about some form of unity between the Union and the South, as we may begin to call these two opposing sections. As Professor Stephenson well says,[1] if the Union were to be preserved, the Republicans must pledge themselves to some new form of compromise, dealing with the South as a unit, or what might

[1] "Lincoln," 111–15.

be called an *imperium in imperio*. There must be some kind of pledge of non-interference with the South, not merely as regards slavery, but also Southern life, institutions, and traditions generally. There must also be opportunity for Southern expansion, even if it meant further annexations of lands to the south of us. Seward sent his friend and manager, the astute and able Thurlow Weed, to Springfield to discuss the matter with Lincoln. He carried Seward's proposal that the plan known as the Crittenden Compromise be made the basis of dealings with the Southern leaders. This plan, proposed by Senator John J. Crittenden of Kentucky in a last frantic attempt to prevent further secession and thus to save the Union, would have revived the old Missouri Compromise line of 36° 30′ and extended it to the Pacific, guaranteeing it by an amendment to the Constitution. Added to this was to be a repeated guarantee of non-interference with slavery where it already existed and a favorable attitude toward the enforcement of the fugitive slave laws. Lincoln long ago had come to the point of a conviction that if slavery were held within definite boundaries it would inevitably become extinct, as against the progress of civilization. He therefore would not enter into any policy for further expansion, and declined any additional compromise other than non-interference with the South in its intrastate concerns. He prepared a memorandum for the consideration of the Republican members of the Senate in which he proposed that the Fugitive Slave Law should be enforced by an act of Congress "with efficient provisions," that opposing legislation such as the "personal liberty laws" in certain states of the North ought to be repealed, and that "The Federal Union must be preserved." [2] This was not satisfactory to the Southern leaders, and five more states had joined South Carolina in secession by February 4, 1861. These were Georgia, Alabama, Mississippi, Louisiana, and Florida, and on that same day a convention of representatives from these six states met at Montgomery, Alabama, and adopted a provisional constitution for "The Confederate States of America,"

[2] Frederic Bancroft, "Life of Seward," II, 10 (note).

on February 8, and the next day elected Jefferson Davis of Mississippi president, and Alexander H. Stephens of Georgia vice-president. Texas ratified this action on February 23, and thus the lower South had formed a new and revolutionary government of seven states. A permanent constitution for the Confederacy was adopted March 11, 1861, and went into force in 1862.

A century before this time abolition of slavery was very popular in the South, with the exception of South Carolina and Georgia, and this movement had grown under the influence of such men as Washington and Jefferson. The change in Southern opinion and feelings became more pronounced after 1833. This was due to attempted negro insurrection in the South, but especially to the rabid and revolutionary excesses of the Abolitionists. Writing in the year 1870, Thomas Jefferson Randolph of Virginia admirably summed up this change by saying: "After the adjournment of the [Virginia] legislature in 1833 the question was discussed before the people fairly and squarely, as one of the abolition of slavery. I was reëlected on that ground in my county. The feeling extended rapidly from that time in Virginia, Kentucky and Missouri until Northern abolitionism reared its head. Southern abolition was reform and appeal to the master; Northern abolition was revolution and an appeal to the slave. One was peaceful and the other mutually destructive of both races by a servile insurrection. The Southern people feared to trust to the intervention of persons themselves exempt by position from the imagined dangers of the transition." This is one of the best statements of the underlying causes of hostility between the two sections that ever was written.[3]

Another excellent statement of the views of many conservative Northerners is that of General McClellan:[4] "I was thoroughly opposed to slavery, regarding it as a great evil, especially to the whites of the South, but in my opinion no

[3] Quoted in B. B. Munford, "Virginia's Attitude Toward Slavery and Secession," 51.

[4] "Own Story," 33.

sweeping measure of emancipation should be carried out, unless accompanied by arrangements providing for the new relations between employers and employed, carefully guarding the rights and interests of both. . . . No real statesman could ever contemplate so sweeping and serious a measure as sudden and general emancipation without looking to the future and providing for its consequences; four and a half millions of uneducated slaves should not suddenly be manumitted without due precautions taken both to protect them and to guard against them." It is probable that these words also contain the views of Lincoln at this time, but he was great enough statesman soon to see that conditions had so changed as the result of actual warfare that immediate emancipation was a necessity.

The South felt that it was faced with the accession to power of a sectional party, matching its own sectionalism, and one with which at that time the Abolitionists were in alliance, although we shall see that these extremists, disruptive as usual, soon gave Lincoln more than his share of trouble ere the war had proceeded but a few months. In addition, the new party had definitely adopted the policy of a protective tariff, and this had been anathema to the South since the days of Calhoun and Nullification. It should not be forgotten that the Civil War was caused by the mutual rivalry and incompatibility of two sections based on different and mutually hostile economic and social systems. The immediate cause was sectionalism, kept alive and irritated by slavery until it resulted in attempted secession. The people of both sides were, in the major part, of the same American birth and ancestry, trained to separate lines of thought and life, but both alike sincere, patriotic, and honest. They fought for what they thought and believed to be right. In fact, there was nothing else for them to do, and such divergent tendencies will always rise at different times in the history of humanity, showing how silly and ignorant is the cry of the "pacifist" that all wars must cease and that war must be "outlawed." This never will come until after the passage of many generations from the earth, when all people are not only civilized but have the same kind of civilization.

This consummation can be only a gradual growth. No sane person wants or desires war, but there are worse things than war, such as dishonest and dishonorable peace. No matter how we may differ with regard to the relative merits of the Union and the Confederate causes, and the present writer sympathizes with the cause of the so-called North, yet there is no doubt that to-day we may say that both sides in this terrible and tragic contest were right. They fought and suffered for their country.

During the winter of 1860-61 Lincoln was besieged and his life made miserable by hordes of office-seekers and spoilsmen. Many men whose conversion to the Republican party had been very recent were hungry for the spoils of office, and he was fairly persecuted from now on until the day of his untimely death, five years later. He well knew the value and need of party solidarity, and how much this solidarity depended upon selfish satisfaction and the enjoyment of loaves and fishes, so he played the game of patronage honestly, but of necessity with partizanship. He was a practical politician.

If spoils and favors offered the necessary basis for that kind of coöperation, such as we have seen unfortunately is needed in some measure for the organization and existence of all political parties, he also must find some other basis that would appeal to the people at large. He at first tried to stave off hostilities, but when war came, he gradually moved to the conviction that the one underlying basis for the very being of the Republican party must be the preservation of the Union. On this golden mean he could unite extreme radicals such as the Abolitionists, and also conservatives from both the old Whig and Democratic parties. He met with furious opposition from both sides, and throughout the first of his administrations he had to strive for this bond of unity, only succeeding in the fall of 1864. In accomplishing this he not only was a great politician but also had developed into a great statesman. He had the insight to perceive that the future of the democratic type of government depended in large part upon the success of this great experiment in the United States. Republics were hardly respectable as yet, and the failure of America would set back the advance of democracy for many generations. Therefore, as Lincoln told Horace Greeley some time later, he did not so much care whether he preserved the Union with slavery or without slavery, or half slave and half free, but he was determined to preserve the Union. If he succeeded in that, democracy was safe for the time at least, and slavery was irrevocably doomed.

Lincoln's first practical political task, of course, was now that of forming his cabinet. John G. Nicolay and John Hay, who were his private secretaries during his Presidency, were in a position to know much of the "inside workings" of this period, and their account of his solution of this problem is most authentic.[5] Lincoln began to plan the cabinet while sitting in the telegraph office in Springfield as he received the returns of the election on the evening of November 6, 1860, and the final choices were substantially as he then planned them. Said Lincoln: "When I finally bade my friends good night and left that room, I had substantially completed the framework of my cabinet as it now exists." It was characteristic of the man that he put aside all matters of rivalry, jealousy, or personal profit, and chose several of his strongest opponents in the Chicago convention. His main idea was to include the leading men of the different elements that went to make up the more or less chaotic Republican party, to make a united force behind his administration, and carry through the great and critical tasks he now knew were before him. There were seven cabinet portfolios at that time, and he chose four former Democrats and three former Whigs, saying that he himself would make up the balance.

Early in December he offered the post of secretary of state to his brilliant and somewhat conceited rival, William H. Seward. The latter accepted the offer toward the end of the month. He next offered the attorney-generalship to Edward Bates of Missouri, whom he had known for eight years, and this offer was accepted. The announcement of these two appointments did much to inspire confidence in the prospective

[5] "Lincoln," III, 345-74.

administration, for both men were leaders who held the confidence of large sections of the people. A third place also was promptly determined, that of secretary of the interior, which went to Caleb B. Smith of Indiana. He was a man of moderate but sound ability, and possibly the least well known of the entire cabinet. His appointment was on account of geography and expediency, but also was upon sound grounds of common sense. These three men were of Whig antecedents, and their choice by Lincoln was therefore more easy. When he turned to former Democratic elements, the trouble increased. For secretary of the treasury he chose Salmon P. Chase of Ohio, an able, brilliant man, vain and ambitious, at times jealous and suspicious, but of "spotless integrity" of character. Pennsylvania's representatives were especially desirous that this office should go to one of her citizens, on account of the influence its occupant of necessity would have upon the fiscal policies of the administration, with especial regard to tariff problems—for protection was the prime requisite for the further expansion of her industries. Simon Cameron was therefore put forward as a rival claimant, and Lincoln, after some hesitation, made Cameron a tentative offer of the Treasury, followed by a more definite offer of the War portfolio. There was the promise made by Lincoln's friends at the Chicago convention, and he was not the kind to fail in his part of a bargain. But now came bitter and persistent attacks upon Cameron from the ranks of Pennsylvania politicians themselves, and Lincoln was perforce compelled to withdraw his offer. Cameron was the center of charges reflecting gravely upon his character, but there has never been any proof that they were more than political innuendo. He now has the general reputation of having been personally honest, but allied with political friends who were rightly subject to suspicion—as only too often has happened in the political history of the United States, both before and since that time.

The matter was in a state of suspense, much to the embarrassment of Cameron and his friends, until Lincoln went to Washington the latter part of February. Here he was thrown into a perfect maelstrom of political intrigue, but managed to keep his head clear and finally to make his own decisions. "Willard's," then the principal hotel, was never in its history more busy nor more brilliant. Here Mr. Lincoln and his suite had spacious and accessible rooms, and here, during the six or eight working days which intervened between his arrival and the inauguration, was the great political exchange where politicians, editors, committeemen, delegations, congressmen, governors, and senators congregated, and besieged the doors of the coming power from morning till midnight.[6]

Lincoln early had in mind the appointment of Gideon Welles of Connecticut to the post of secretary of the navy, and this soon was settled. The next question was the recognition of the border states, for he was very anxious to give to his administration as much of a national character as possible. Lincoln had caused his friends to approach John A. Gilmer of North Carolina, but was met with a rebuff. This was repeated when other more weak or tentative "soundings" were made among the leading Union men from that section of the country. For this reason, although Bates came from the slave state of Missouri, Lincoln decided to give another cabinet seat to a border state, and at once there was great rivalry between the friends of two Maryland men—Montgomery Blair of Democratic and Henry Winter Davis of Whig antecedents. The latter was one of the most brilliant and able men that the state of Maryland ever produced, but Lincoln finally decided upon Blair, and the position of postmaster-general was offered and accepted.

Lincoln now went ahead, and the offers and acceptances of Chase and Cameron to the offices of the Treasury and War departments were made definite, and all seemed settled, when suddenly Seward shocked Lincoln by sending him, on March 2, a letter in which he withdrew his acceptance of the position of secretary of state. Lincoln held the matter over until after the inauguration, and then a personal conference straightened things out and Seward renewed his acceptance. It is probable

[6] Nicolay and Hay, III, 367.

that the pulling and hauling of the partizans of the different candidates, especially the friends of Chase and Cameron, had caused whisperings to go around which were detrimental to the reputations of those who already were on the cabinet slate. Seward must have heard these and, being rather vain and feeling a sense of humiliation at the advancement of another to the office of President which he felt of right should have come to him, he decided to remain out of the administration. Lincoln was especially skilful in reconciling diverse interests, and prejudices and used his influence upon Seward.

The Senate met in special session on March 5 and the names of the proposed cabinet were presented and at once confirmed. The appointees almost immediately took the oath of office, and the first cabinet meeting was held on the evening of March 6. But it now is necessary to narrate the events leading up to Lincoln's inauguration, and the beginning of his great administration as President, which was to lay firmly the foundations upon which were built up the later successes of the Republican party.

Lincoln left Springfield on Monday morning February 11, 1861. It was a dark and rainy day, and gloom seemed to be the keynote of the whole party that accompanied him. In a voice filled with emotion, Lincoln delivered this beautiful little parting address from the rear platform of the train: "My friends: No one, not in my situation, can appreciate my feeling of sadness at this parting. To this place, and the kindness of these people, I owe everything. Here I have lived a quarter of a century, and have passed from a young to an old man. Here my children have been born, and one is buried. I now leave, not knowing when or whether ever I may return, with a task before me greater than that which rested upon Washington. Without the assistance of that Divine Being who ever attended him, I cannot succeed. With that assistance, I cannot fail. Trusting in Him, who can go with me, and remain with you, and be everywhere for good, let us confidently hope that all will yet be well. To His care commending you as I hope in your prayers you will commend me, I bid you an affectionate farewell."

Of course, Lincoln and his family were accompanied by a number of political and official friends. The trip filled up nearly two weeks, the journey leading him by way of Indianapolis, Cincinnati, Columbus, Pittsburgh, Cleveland, Buffalo, Albany, New York city, Trenton, Philadelphia to Harrisburg. Here he was alarmed by reports that there was a plot to assassinate him as he passed through Baltimore. The entire party returned to Philadelphia and from there he went alone to Washington by night, accompanied only by Allan Pinkerton and his friend Ward H. Lamon. They reached Washington at six o'clock on the morning of Saturday, February 23, and went to the Willard Hotel. Lincoln was joined there that evening by the remaining members of his family. There was much ridicule of this hasty entry, as might be expected, but such cheap political capital is beside the point, and one thing is certain—Lincoln was no coward. He took the advice of his advisers, and any person the least familiar with the history of that troubled period knows that excitement and enmity were aroused to such a pitch that there was a decided possibility that some unbalanced fanatic might be insane enough to vent his personal spite upon the leader who embodied the character of the hated Republican party—so far as one element of the population was concerned.

The inauguration passed off without untoward incident. There had been great apprehension that some violence might be attempted, and the city was heavily guarded by regular army troops, under the command of the aged general-in-chief, Winfield Scott, a Virginian who remained thoroughly loyal to the Union, although his own state attempted secession. He stationed soldiers along the whole line of march, and bayonets could be seen on the housetops along Pennsylvania Avenue.

On the trip to Washington, Lincoln's genius seemed to be in eclipse. His speeches were banal and empty. At first almost flippant, he completely lost a wonderful opportunity to rally the people around him, and a deepening sense of solemnity as he neared the national capital did not arouse any more enthusiasm or trust on the part of the people. On the other hand,

Douglas touched the right spot when he said that Lincoln was typically "a man of the atmosphere that surrounds him. He has not yet gotten out of Springfield. . . . He does not see that the shadow he casts is any bigger now than it was last year. It will not take him long to find it out when he has got in the White House." [7] And this was absolutely true.

Lincoln began to recover himself with his inaugural address. Standing on the rude platform at the east front of the unfinished capitol, he read this to a crowd somewhat less than usual but eager to hear what he might have to say on the burning subject of the hour. It was carefully drawn up to meet the specific occasion. He first made the categorical statement that there was no reasonable excuse for the apprehension on the part of the Southern states that their property and their peace would be endangered by the accession of a Republican administration to power. He quoted from one of his own speeches in which he had said, "I have no purpose, directly or indirectly, to interfere with the institution of slavery in the states where it exists. I believe I have no lawful right to do so, and I have no inclination to do so." He also quoted from the Chicago platform the statement that it was essential to maintain inviolate the rights of the states to order and control their own institutions, and denouncing lawless invasion by armed force, no matter under what pretext. He then went on to argue against the legality and the expediency of attempted secession, but followed with a clear and explicit statement that "to the best of my ability I shall take care, as the Constitution enjoins upon me, that the laws of the Union be faithfully executed in all the states." He went on further: "I trust this will not be regarded as a menace, but only as the declared purpose of the Union that it *will* constitutionally defend and maintain itself. In doing this there need be no bloodshed or violence, and there shall be none unless it be forced upon the national authority. The power confided to me will be used to hold, occupy and possess the property and places belonging to the Government and to collect the duties and imposts; but beyond what

[7] Allen Johnson, "Life of Douglas," 461.

may be necessary for these objects, there will be no invasion, no using of force against or among the people anywhere." He closed with the fine passage, said to be the joint work of Lincoln and Seward:[8] "In *your* hands, my dissatisfied fellow-countrymen, and not in *mine,* is the momentous issue of civil war. The government will not assail *you.* You can have no conflict without being yourselves the aggressors. You have no oath registered in heaven to destroy the government, while *I* shall have the most solemn one to 'preserve, protect, and defend it.' I am loath to close. We are not enemies but friends. We must not be enemies. Though passion may have strained it must not break our bonds of affection. The mystic chords of memory, stretching from every battlefield and patriot grave to every living heart and hearthstone all over this broad land, will yet swell the chorus of the Union, when again touched, as surely they will be, by the better angels of our nature."

This address was received with varying feelings in the North and West, while the people of the South paid but little attention to it. Hostility was too great, and the temper of the people had been worked up to a high pitch of excitement. When it is remembered that the Southern states had in reality voted for the Union by over one hundred thousand, for this is the plain indication of Breckinridge's minority of over 135,000 in the November election, the unanimity of opinion now shown in the Confederacy may seem cause for wonder, but the explanation is remarkable leadership. The strong aggressive men who had made the move to carry the South out of the Union were the natural product of an aristocratic economic society which was well calculated to train leaders, no matter what it did for the remainder of the population, as Hinton R. Helper well had pointed out in his book on the "Impending Crisis."

McClellan says that in the early part of 1861 it became almost impossible for any Northern man to travel in the Southwest without being subjected to gross insults or to personal maltreatment. J. B. Jones, who occupied the position of clerk

[8] Stephenson, 137. The entire message may be found in J. D. Richardson, "Messages and Papers of the Presidents," VI, 5–12.

in the War Department of the Confederacy, typically relieved himself of his overcharged emotions by writing as follows in his diary: "The wrath of the Southern chivalry will some day burst forth on the ensanguined plain, and then let the presumptuous foemen of the North beware of the fiery ordeal they have invoked. The men I see daily keeping time to the music of revolution are fighting men, men who will conquer or die, and who prefer death to subjugation. But the Yankee has no such motive to fight for, no thought of serious wounds and death. He can go back to his own country; our men have no other country to go to. . . . Full many ensanguined plains will greet the horrific vision before this time next year; and many a venal wretch coming to possess our land, will occupy till the day of final doom a tract of six feet by two in some desolate and unfrequented swamp. The toad will croak his requiem, and the viper will coil beneath the thistle growing over his head." [9]

On the other hand, the few Unionists in that section did not mince words in reply. "Parson" Brownlow wrote the following likewise typical letter:

"KNOXVILLE, April 22, 1861

"General GIDEON J. PILLOW:

"I have just received your message through Mr. Sale requesting me to serve as chaplain to your brigade in the Southern army: and in the spirit of kindness in which this request is made, but in all candor, I return for an answer, that when I shall have made up my mind to go to Hell I will cut my throat and go *direct* and not travel round by way of the Southern Confederacy. I am

"Very respectfully, etc.,

"W. G. BROWNLOW"

We in this more fortunate and happy day of complete reconciliation hardly can imagine that such feelings existed in this land of ours, but the above well illustrates what Lincoln had to deal with, and the reasons why at first he must go slowly,

[9] "Rebel War Clerk's Diary," I, 42, 77–8.

for his whole idea was to force the South to be the aggressor. At first he was almost too deferential to the members of his cabinet, seeming almost overawed by their greater experience and wide political influence. They had been old party leaders for the most part, but now were to turn their attention to consolidating the Government, and that necessarily meant also the Republican party, which was charged with its administration. It is doubtful whether any other man than Lincoln could have worked with such a cabinet of strong individualists, and force them to coöperate, and the fact that he did this, and succeeded, is ample proof of his political genius.

Seward was the most difficult at first, and seemed filled with the conceit that he was to be the moving power in the administration. He advised Lincoln in all sorts of matters, whether in his own executive Department of State or not, and it took several kindly but firm rebuffs on the part of the ever-patient but decided Lincoln to put him in his place. When finally "put" there, he accepted the leadership of his more able chief and loyally stood by him until the day of the accomplishment of Booth's foul work. But now he even undertook to give assurances to Southern leaders as to the policy of the administration, and without Lincoln's consent or even knowledge. The repudiation by the President, and the following of his own policy, caused charges of double-dealing by the South, for which Lincoln was in no way to blame.

Of course, the first great problem was the determination of policy with regard to Fort Sumter, still held by a few United States troops, although situated in Charleston Harbor. The Confederate Congress early had taken over jurisdiction of the matter of Fort Sumter by a resolution passed on February 12, and then General Beauregard was appointed to command the Southern forces in South Carolina. He took command on March 6, by authority of the departments of War of both the Confederacy and the state of South Carolina. Major Robert Anderson, who commanded the small Federal forces at Charleston, withdrew all his men from Fort Moultrie to Fort Sumter, and there was besieged by the Southern troops. His provisions soon began to run short, and the specific problem was now put squarely before Lincoln whether or not he should reinforce the fort. An investigation of the feasibility of reinforcement was made by Lincoln's order, and by March 29 all the cabinet except Seward and Smith were for carrying it through. Lincoln decided to reinforce, and ordered an expedition to sail for that purpose "as early as April 6th next."

The very day of April 6 James E. Harvey, who had been appointed by Lincoln and was about to go as Minister to Portugal, treacherously telegraphed to Judge A. G. Magrath, one of the South Carolina leaders, the information that Lincoln intended to provision Sumter. Harvey was a newspaper correspondent in Washington, who served eight years at Lisbon as the representative of the country he so foully betrayed. He was a native of South Carolina, hence probably felt some sympathy with the people of that wayward state. He evidently was at this time totally forgetful of the fact that the people of South Carolina always have stressed honor and sincerity as the prime requisites for a gentleman. Under instructions from the Confederate Government at Montgomery, Beauregard demanded surrender of the fort on April 11. Major Anderson promised that he would surrender if not reinforced by April 15. A relieving force of United States vessels arrived off Charleston Harbor on the night of April 12-13. Fire was opened upon the fort at 4:30 A.M. on April 12. Although no one was killed, the defenses were rendered untenable and Anderson surrendered on the evening of the thirteenth. He evacuated the fort on Sunday, April 14, with drums beating and flags flying and was carried north by the relieving squadron.

The die now was cast. The United States flag had been fired on and the South had definitely become the aggressor. The question above all others was, What will Lincoln do? He did not hesitate. Had he done so for a moment, much less made a public speech on the canting theme of "too proud to fight," we should be two countries to-day. The American people have good reason to be thankful that in 1861, at least, they had a President who did not need to be shoved into war in order to preserve the national honor and defend the country. Although Lincoln was the head of a nation torn in two, he also was without promise of definite support in a war policy by the people of his own section of the country. It is the present writer's own deliberate opinion that had Lincoln had in the North and West alone one half of the support that Woodrow Wilson had throughout the entire nation in 1917, the Civil War would have ended in two years at most. Lincoln had to *form* public opinion, not be swept along by it.

The news from Fort Sumter reached Washington on Sunday morning, April 14. Lincoln called together his cabinet, now become a unit, and after reading to them a proclamation, he issued it on the fifteenth, calling into the service of the United States 75,000 militia to suppress combinations against the laws of the nation and to cause such laws to be enforced. Three weeks later he called for an additional 42,000 and ordered increased enlistment in the regular army and the navy. There was great popular response to this appeal and by July 1 there were more than 300,000 men in the field. But four of the slave states, which believed in the right of secession but had opposed its exercise, seceded when the call for troops was issued, on the ground that they were opposed to the coercion of the South. These states were Arkansas, Virginia, North Carolina, and Tennessee. The last named took action on June 24, and thus completed the bounds of the eleven states of the Southern Confederacy. Had Lincoln permitted the Union to be broken up without any opposition, it is probable that for a time at least the dividing line between the two countries would have been the southern boundaries of North Carolina, Tennessee, and Arkansas.

There were strong secession movements in the three remaining border states of Maryland, Kentucky, and Missouri, but these were finally saved to the Union by local military and political forces, directly aided by the strong arm of the National Government. Since slavery was established in all of them, Lincoln went slowly with regard to that institution, and only gradually came to an anti-slavery policy that possibly might alienate these states. It is a matter of special significance that Douglas came out in support of Lincoln and the coercion of the South in no uncertain terms, even "stumping" the North and West and rallying the "War Democrats" around the National Union. While engaged in this most important and patriotic work he was taken ill and died on June 3. His wholehearted support of Lincoln had been invaluable, and his death was a grievous loss to his country. But his work remained, and it is estimated that a million northern Democrats were heartened and inspired to sacrifice all political prejudice and partizanship in order to fight for and sustain their country.[10] As Senator O. H. Browning of Illinois (who succeeded Douglas at Washington) later told Lincoln, the Republican party could not put down the rebellion—no party could do it; it required a union of all loyal men in the free states to give success, and without that union there would be disastrous failure. To this Lincoln fully assented,[11] but he had great difficulty in holding together his own party with its diverse elements, and also in retaining the steady support of a majority of the Democrats. He finally came to the one basis of coöperation possible, that of preservation of the Union, which led him into direct complications with the extreme pro- and anti-slavery elements that existed in varying degrees in both the North and West.

From the military standpoint two facts are of supreme importance—the blockade of the ports of the South by the Federal navy and the search of the North for generals. On April 19 Lincoln issued a proclamation declaring the Southern ports blockaded. This was a virtual recognition of the belligerency of the Confederacy, for a nation can only close and not blockade its own ports. But if closed, there then would be legal difficulty in seizing a ship that had left or was bound to a closed port after it had passed the three-mile limit. On the

[10] See Allen Johnson, "Douglas," 475–89, for an account of these brilliant closing days in the life of Douglas.

[11] Barton, II, 154.

other hand, a blockade runner can be apprehended after leaving home waters whenever and wherever there is sufficient proof that the vessel is bound to or proceeding from a port that is effectively blockaded—that is to say, where the blockade is maintained by a force sufficient really to prevent access to the port of the enemy. Thus for reasons of efficiency Lincoln wisely took the risk of any international complications and *blockaded* the Confederacy. He was eminently justified by the outcome. For four long years day in and day out the navy watched the Southern ports, on the stormy Atlantic coast as well as at the Gulf ports, both in summer and in winter weather, and gradually starved out and broke the back of the Confederate states. Our people to-day are only beginning to realize that it was the navy, as much as the army, that won the Civil War.

When hostilities began, the major portion of the officers of outstanding ability in the regular army resigned their commissions and entered the Confederate forces. The South was fortunate in getting her great commanders almost at once, for both Lee and Stonewall Jackson, as well as Joseph E. Johnston, Longstreet, J. E. B. Stuart, N. B. Forrest, and others were well placed in power by the beginning of 1862 at latest. On the other hand, public opinion in the North, excited by a too-careless estimate of Southern strength, forced a Union advance in July, 1861, that terminated in the rout at Bull Run and also practically ended the military prominence of Irvin McDowell, the commander. Lincoln then called McClellan from western Virginia, made him commander-in-chief, and he organized and trained the superb Army of the Potomac. There was no question of the ability of McClellan, and also of his deliberation, while certain traits of character made him difficult to coöperate with. He was one of the best educated, most refined of gentlemen, of finest moral fiber and religious sincerity, but at first neither Lincoln nor he understood each other. Added to the trouble was the fact that McClellan being a Democrat, there was a certain element of cheap Republican politicians who made it their business to prevent a mutual

Photograph by Brown Brothers

LINCOLN'S FIRST INAUGURATION

understanding. Lincoln finally sized up McClellan, understanding him rather completely by the fall of 1862. McClellan looked upon Lincoln as socially crude and "impossible"; it was a matter of real moment to him that even after the President had been in the White House for eight months he had not as yet learned the use of a handkerchief—and seldom or never carried one! McClellan had a contempt for his superior that never wore off, and not until about the year 1865 or 1866 did he really begin to understand what a stupendously great man Lincoln was.

When McClellan was foiled in his Peninsular campaign against Richmond he was virtually superseded by John Pope. The sharp defeat of Pope at second Bull Run caused McClellan's hasty recall over the protests of Lincoln's cabinet. McClellan succeeded in driving Lee back at Antietam on September 17, 1862, but was so slow in his succeeding operations that Lincoln relieved him and put Burnside in his place. The latter made the bloody sacrifice at Fredericksburg on December 13 and was succeeded by Joseph Hooker. Then came Chancellorsville, followed by Lee's invasion of Pennsylvania in June of 1863. Just before the opening of a new and great battle Hooker was deposed and Meade put in his place—and Meade "held strong" and won the battle of Gettysburg. This was the turning point of the war. By that time Grant had loomed up in the West, with such aides as Sherman, Sheridan, and Thomas to assist him. Also, Lincoln, as we shall see, was meanwhile working hard to get sufficient power in his own hands to be able to support through thick and thin a man he might place in supreme control. He only succeeded during the spring of 1864, and in March of that year he gave the power to Grant, who carried through the war to a successful conclusion. But the pulling and hauling of demagogues, contractors, and selfish politicians of both parties, playing upon the susceptibilities of headstrong though honest and patriotic officials of the Government, wrecked many a military plan and caused countless suffering, defeat, and loss of life. The political behind the military strategy of the Civil War never yet has been sufficiently studied, but when fully known it will add a sorry chapter to American history, but also add anew to the glory of Abraham Lincoln, who withstood it all and triumphed. The South had much of the same experience, which shows that democratic government is no bar to personal and political selfishness.

One of the greatest sources of evil was the so-called "Committee on the Conduct of the War," instituted in December, 1861, as a joint committee of Congress, its members totally without military experience and under the chairmanship of Senator Benjamin F. Wade of Ohio, who was headstrong, honest, and politically unscrupulous, but ably seconded by his fellow-member Senator Zachariah Chandler of Michigan. Says Stephenson:[12] "Though armed with no weapon but publicity, its close connection with Congressional intrigue, its hostility to the President, the dramatic effect of any revelations it chose to make or any changes it chose to bring, clothed it indirectly with immense power. . . . Its mode of procedure was in constant interrogation of generals, in frequent advice to the President, and on occasion in threatening to rouse Congress against him. . . . Whoever disagreed with them was instantly an object of distrust; any plan that contradicted their views was at once an evidence of treason." Their first victim was General Charles P. Stone, who had been charged with responsibility for the defeat at Ball's Bluff during the previous October. Their treatment of Stone is an outstanding disgrace in American history. He was thrown into prison without trial, after being "investigated" by this ruthless band of political fanatics, and finally released upon parole and the charges dropped.

Their power was vastly increased by a cabinet change. During January, 1862, Cameron fell into disrepute. There were scandals in the War Department, but it never has been determined how responsible he was for them. His enemies were active, and Lincoln to placate them kicked Cameron up-stairs by appointing him Minister to Russia. Chandler and Wade now urged the appointment of one of the strongest, ablest, and

[12] "Lincoln," 205.

most enigmatic figures in American history. To keep the peace, Lincoln appointed him to the War portfolio, and the committee now had a representative in the President's cabinet. This man was Edwin M. Stanton of Ohio. He instituted close relations between his department and the committee, and was hardly above using his position in Lincoln's confidence to instruct and inform the Committee on the Conduct of the War whenever he felt sure, in his own judgment, that the committee and the interests of the country at large would be the beneficiaries by such instruction.

The writer of this narrative has tried for many years to form a fair and just estimate of Stanton, and must acknowledge his complete failure. There is no doubt of Stanton's ability, driving force, and patriotism. He was in a position where the grafters he balked and the treason he uncovered would cause his name to be covered with vilifications in reprisal. On the other hand, the probable double-dealing in his treatment of McClellan, who had urged his appointment, and later of Andrew Johnson, while still a member of the unfortunate President's cabinet, are a dark stain upon his reputation. Stanton may have been either a much maligned patriot, or a masterful and accomplished liar and hypocrite, with a probability of the latter.

There is no doubt that Lincoln put Stanton in his cabinet for purposes of political strategy, and kept him there not only on that account but because of his outstanding executive ability. Masterful in his handling of men, the great President was able to add one more to his collection of strong cabinet individualities, and later acquired an influence over him that amounted not only to respect but even to affection. Lincoln was able to outmaneuver the Committee on the Conduct of the War and other enemies both inside and outside Congress, especially during the period when Grant was in supreme control; but they gradually formed an opposition that took the bit in their teeth and bolted when the war closed, Lincoln was removed by the assassin's bullet, and Johnson's honest but utterly tactless personality was unable effectively to oppose them. The tragedy of Southern reconstruction was the result, and the Republican party is unjustly suffering from their sins of omission and commission to-day. But that is a later part of the story, and the story of their opposition to Lincoln in his handling of the slavery question must now be narrated.

As soon as war measures were actively undertaken, the treatment of slaves in the region of military operations became a pressing problem. Should the Union forces treat them as free, or return them to their owners who now were in active rebellion against the Government? Could this same Government consistently retain them and use them for its own purposes? General Benjamin F. Butler, that able, strange, and sinister figure in American politics for the next two decades or more, characteristically and cleverly cut the gordian knot on May 27, 1861, by declaring them "contraband of war" and thus subject to confiscation. Congress met on July 4 in special session at the call of Lincoln, and on August 6 passed a Confiscation Act. This provided that any slave who worked on Confederate fortifications should be confiscated by the United States Government.

And now loomed up our old friend John C. Frémont as a major-general in the Union army and placed in command of the military district of the West, comprising the states of Illinois, Kentucky, Missouri, and Kansas, with headquarters at St. Louis. On August 30 he issued a proclamation declaring martial law throughout the state of Missouri, and emancipating the slaves of such persons as were in armed rebellion against the laws of the United States. This headlong and rash policy caused great embarrassment to Lincoln. It attempted to force his hand and cause him to outrun the sentiment of the North and West, especially that of the border states in addition, and thus might result in a split in the support that Lincoln was endeavoring to work up behind his administration. Lincoln promptly disavowed the act of Frémont, and this proper action caused an estrangement between the early standard-bearer of the Republican party and its present political leader. Frémont actively identified himself a short time later with the radical opponents of Lincoln, but probably for political reasons was continued in his position as a general officer, much to the embarrassment and misfortune of the Union arms. He proved himself, as might have been expected, very incompetent, and must have caused many a sincere and patriotic Republican to thank Heaven for the defeat in 1856. It well can be imagined what kind of a President Frémont would have made, even in times of peace, much less during a great national crisis. Fortunately, his political effectiveness was soon dissipated and he sank into deserved oblivion.

Lincoln never was an Abolitionist, in the radical sense, and now moved toward a conservative and common-sense method of gradual emancipation by means of compensation. On March 6, 1862, he sent a message to Congress in which he recommended a policy of compensated emancipation in the "slave states." This, of course, referred to the border states, although it did not rule out any other part of the South that might be willing to coöperate. On April 10 he had an interview with the delegations from the border states in which he urged them to adopt this policy, but they gave him little encouragement. A second interview four months later was no more successful, the border states practically declining to entertain his proposals. Meanwhile, about the middle of April, Congress passed an act abolishing slavery in the District of Columbia, which also provided for the compensation of loyal owners at a rate not to exceed $300 per slave, and that any of these emancipated negroes who might desire to go, should be colonized in Hayti or Liberia at a cost not to exceed $100 for each person. It should be remembered that Lincoln steadily and consistently advocated the colonization of the negroes in some definite place, either in America or even across the Atlantic. He foresaw the great and seemingly insoluble problem of the two races, which since has arisen and plagued both, and tried to avert its portentous consequences. During May, 1862, General David Hunter, a more or less incompetent general of the Frémont type, who commanded the military district including Georgia, Florida, and South Carolina, issued a proclamation declaring the slaves in this district free. Lincoln likewise disavowed this, and of course the opposition of the radical abolitionists to the administration increased in proportion. However, he approved on June 19, 1862, the act of Congress which prohibited slavery in all territories of the United States, present and future, and thus the Republican party completed the pledges of its platform in 1856 and 1860. The Republican leaders of that day never have received proper recognition for their sincerity and consistency. A second Confiscation Act, passed and signed during July, 1862, provided for the emancipation of all slaves of rebels and abettors of treason.

But Lincoln now had come to the point of taking one of the greatest and most important steps of his career. He had arrived at a belief in the necessity for military emancipation and the arming of the blacks. Also, the question of the effects abroad were not overlooked.

The Government and certain aristocratic elements in Great Britain were decidedly hostile to the cause of the Union, and sympathized openly with that of the South, especially following the *Trent* affair, while the great middle classes, not then so vocal and influential in British politics as they became after the Reform Bill of 1867, were in large part deeply sympathetic with the cause of the North. They recognized the Republican party as occupying close analogy to the position of the Liberal and Tory Democratic elements in their own politics, and especially were aware of the fact that their country always had stood against human slavery, which was not recognized in the English common law. Lincoln also knew that for years, especially since the abolition of slavery in the British West Indies by act of Parliament of 1833, British people had been pointing the finger of scorn and sarcasm at the United States, which professed the great principles of the Declaration of Independence and yet stultified itself by keeping millions of human beings in bondage. If the Civil War could now be turned from one merely to save the Union into a contest upon which depended the abolition of slavery, Southern sympathizers in Great Britain and many parts of Europe would be absolutely silenced.

And this is exactly what Lincoln accomplished by his Emancipation Proclamation. The hopes of the Confederate Government, that it might secure formal recognition and aid from abroad, went glimmering, and a turn for the worse came in the fortunes of the South which finally went to the lengths of destruction.

Lincoln called together his cabinet on July 22, 1862, and read to them a proposed proclamation of emancipation. He intended to free all slaves in the states then in rebellion, using his war powers as President for the purposes of confiscation of this form of Southern property. Seward wisely suggested that the issue of the proclamation be postponed until some military victory made it appear with increased strength and significance, rather than during the then time of defeat and despondency; otherwise it might seem like the last despairing "shriek" of a defeated and retreating power. Lincoln at once saw the shrewdness and sense of this proposal and laid the draft aside.

McClellan met and stopped the invading Lee at Antietam on September 17, and on the twenty-second of the same month Lincoln issued the Proclamation, to take effect on the following January 1, 1863, provided in the meantime the rebellious states did not lay down their arms and submit to the authority of the National Government. Of course, this did not apply to the border slave states, or those portions of the South such as eastern Tennessee and western Virginia that still adhered to the cause of the Union. Lincoln could not permanently fix the status of the slaves. That was only accomplished by the Thirteenth Amendment to the national Constitution, which finally passed Congress by the necessary vote on February 1, 1865, and was declared ratified by the states by a proclamation of the secretary of state dated the eighteenth of the following December. Of course the final question of the abolition of slavery in the South depended entirely upon the success or failure of the North in defeating the rebellion, and in bringing back the Confederate states under the authority of the national laws and government.

Lincoln thought that this new policy would cement the

various factions of the Republican party, and offer a new basis for coöperation. To his sorrow the immediate results were exactly the opposite. The conservative elements were shocked by this use of extreme war powers, while even the radicals were disgruntled, extending of course to what Professor Stephenson well designates as the "Jacobins," or Vindictives, of the Committee on the Conduct of the War and their more or less active friends throughout the country. These latter, if autocratic power were necessary to win the war, wished it to be placed in the hands of Congress. Lincoln wisely judged that these powers should be in the hands of the executive. The same rivalry between the executive and legislative powers or parts of government that arises repeatedly in the history of all democratic governments thus came to a critical issue, as it did following the World War, and even has existed in lesser importance but equal strength between the United States Senate and President Coolidge in this present day. The people then, as now, usually sided with the executive in the long run; and thus only in some vital and more or less theatrical contest can Congress overthrow the executive. Public opinion is more easily centered on one outstanding person than on many individuals, and also the people feel they can see who is really responsible when the President acts, rather than look to over 500 congressmen, by no means united among themselves.

The pro-slavery elements in the North raised a bitter protest against the Emancipation Proclamation. The Democratic party at once seized upon this discontent and began to charge that no longer was the war being waged to save the Union, but that white men were asked to sacrifice their lives to give not only freedom but also social equality to the black man. That cry of "nigger domination" which for nearly sixty-five years has been used by demagogic Democrats to scare timid souls into voting their ticket now was "worked overtime," and the hiss of the so-called "Copperheads," who soon were more or less actively engaged in definite plans to overthrow the Federal Government, joined in the chorus. Other high-handed or even arbitrary acts, which Lincoln thought necessary in order to save the Union cause from impending defeat, also aroused great popular opposition. His suspension of the writ of *habeas corpus,* interference with the jurisdiction of the courts, and use of the military at the polls in the border states, since generally justified by the best historical judgment, at that time only added to the fears of the conservatives and gave opportunity to his enemies, of both patriotic and treasonable stripe.

But Lincoln was looking to the future. Great statesman that he was, he also knew whereon he was building anew the foundations of an old but reënforced Union. He had implicit faith that the people would decide rightly if only given time, and while he might appear to lose in immediate popularity and strength, yet he was willing to take the risk, in the hope that the rank and file of our population, which he was in the habit of fondly calling the "plain people," would soon understand his objects, and indorse and support his policy. In fact, several years before, in his first joint debate with Douglas, at Ottawa, Illinois, on August 21, 1858, he had enunciated a principle which now had become the fundamental basis of his policy. Said he: "Public sentiment is everything. With public sentiment, nothing can fail; without it, nothing can succeed. Consequently, he who molds public sentiment goes deeper than he who enacts statutes or pronounces decisions. He makes statutes and decisions possible or impossible to be executed."

The fall elections of 1862, which immediately followed the Emancipation Proclamation, were a decided setback for Lincoln and his administration. New York, New Jersey, Pennsylvania, Ohio, Indiana, and Illinois did not support him, while the New England states, the border states, with Minnesota, Iowa, Kansas, California, and Oregon went Republican or sent sufficient supporters of the administration to Congress to prevent the opposition from having control of it. The Democrats increased their strength in the House of Representatives from forty-four in the Thirty-seventh to seventy-five in the Thirty-eighth Congress, in whose hands would lie the determination of the future conduct of the war. New York elected Horatio

Seymour, Democrat, by a majority of nearly 10,000, while the Democratic majorities were 4000 in Pennsylvania (in spite of the high protective tariff of the war finance), 7000 in Ohio, and 17,000 in Lincoln's own state of Illinois. Some of the Republicans were very hostile to him, and he had always to meet, even in his own nominal supporters, the opposition of the "Jacobins." Things looked very ominous for 1864, and the Republican party seemed to face early and complete defeat. The state of Nevada was admitted to the Union in 1864, and this gave two more Republican senators, as well as one representative. This perennial "rotten borough" constituency, still a grotesque travesty upon real representative government, was created largely on account of the critical exigencies of Civil War politics.

Chase soon came into prominence through his handling of the Treasury Department and the national finances in time of war. When the special session of Congress began on July 4, at the call of Lincoln, the national debt of the country stood at about $76,000,000. While this was considered large for the times, it was a mere drop in the bucket compared to increases in the next few years. The policy generally followed by the administration was to stimulate the industrial resources of the country as much as possible, and then tax them for the support of the war. For this reason high protective tariff duties were laid, much to the gratification of Pennsylvania and other industrial districts, and heavy direct and indirect taxes were imposed in addition. "In levying these taxes the motto seemed that of 'Donnybrook fair'—'when you see a head, hit it!' " It is interesting to know that in August, 1861, Congress also levied a direct tax of $20,000,000 on real estate, apportioned among the states according to population. Chase received great praise for his handling of the finances, and especially for his part in the passage of the National Banking Act of February 25, 1863, by means of which banks were chartered by the Federal Government and a market was provided for the national bonds. This was secured by the provision of the act which required that each bank must deposit with United States officials an amount of these bonds equal to one third of its paid-in capital. He also began the sale of bonds to the public in popular denominations through the banking house of Jay Cooke & Company of Philadelphia and Washington.[13]

Chase has been much criticized for giving his consent, although only after long hesitation, to the issue of legal-tender notes of the United States known as "greenbacks"—so called because the backs were printed in green ink. Not having the coin to pay for supplies that were needed, these notes were issued and given the quality of legal tender in payment of all debts, except for the payment of import duties. They of course steadily deteriorated as their amount was increased by three issues, until the total amount authorized was above $400,000,000. Gold rose until it reached 250 on June 30, 1864, and even went to 285 on the succeeding July 11, when the Confederates under General Jubal A. Early were threatening the capture of Washington. Throughout part of this time a paper dollar was worth about forty cents in gold. Fractional specie currency disappeared from circulation, and small notes of from five to fifty cents, known in popular parlance as "shinplasters," were issued. Even postage stamps, with all their gummed-up inconvenience, and many private tokens were used. When the war closed, about $400,000,000 in greenbacks faced the Government for redemption. They lasted for several decades as a menace to sound finance and government solvency, and played a great part in politics as a forerunner of Bryanism and other heresies which the Democratic party later tried to swallow—and digest. Their issue vastly increased the cost of the war through inflation, and Chase must share a certain part of the blame due to his giving his consent—although the emergency was great and business was in a precarious condition.

People of the present time, awed by the stupendous fame of Lincoln, make the common mistake of assuming that he was popular and highly regarded throughout his Presidency. Nothing could be further from the truth. The measures discussed above, with his strong handling of the affairs of the

[13] See E. P. Oberholzer, "Jay Cooke, Financier of the Civil War."

National Government, caused bitter opposition, so that as the time drew near for the election of 1864 it appeared to be doubtful that he could be chosen for a second term. His growth during the years since his inauguration in March, 1861, was almost miraculous, and with it came a deepening of spirit, until he emerged a profoundly religious man, although reserved and even peculiar in his mode of expressing these religious convictions. So deep was his insight, so profound his judgment, that often his purposes escaped the comprehension of the average person, much as he delighted to appeal to the "common people," and the popular hesitancy that inevitably followed easily could be swayed into momentary distrust. But always the thoughtful elements in our population were more and more impressed by the soundness of his statesmanship, until a "ground swell" arose that finally swept him back into power, and even into final popularity. After his tragic death an appreciation of his greatness burst upon the senses of the American people and then of the world, like a vivid light, and that without organized propaganda or the emotional exaggeration that is so characteristic of present-day fashions in hero worship. The real statesman always can afford to wait the judgment of history. Lincoln's great repute is ample proof of this fact.

Lincoln made no secret of his personal belief that it would be best for the country if his administration were continued in office. He made the remark that it was not good policy to "swap horses while crossing a stream," and this homely phrase attracted the attention of the people. The radicals, restless and unbalanced, thought that they might forestall his nomination by holding an early convention and putting some one else in the field. A number of calls were issued for a convention to meet at Cleveland, Ohio, on May 31, 1864, one especially being addressed "To the Radical Men of the Nation."

The Cleveland convention was neither large nor were men of great prominence in attendance. General John Cochrane of New York presided, and a platform was adopted which professed the usual constitutional principles but significantly added that "the question of the reconstruction of the rebellious states belongs to the people, through their representatives in Congress, and not to the executive." Also, "the confiscation of the lands of the rebels, and their distribution among the soldiers and actual settlers, is a measure of justice." Of course there was, as might be expected, that age-worn and threadbare issue of all disappointed and disgruntled politicians of only one term for the President, as well as the direct election of the President and Vice-President by the people, forgetting that practically this is accomplished by the usage of moral compulsion of presidential electors to vote for the party nominee.

John C. Frémont was nominated for President and General Cochrane for Vice-President. In his letter of acceptance Frémont, with bad taste and characteristic foolishness, bitterly attacked Lincoln as showing "incapacity and selfishness," "disregard of constitutional rights," "violation of personal liberty and liberty of the press," "feebleness and want of principle," and charged that if "he had proved faithful to the principles he was elected to defend, no schism would have been created"! [14]

The real significance of this convention and events soon to transpire cannot be understood without its relation to what has become known in history as the "Wade-Davis Manifesto." This will be more fully explained following an account of the nominating convention which met in Front Street Theater, Baltimore, on June 7 and 8, 1864, and put Lincoln in the field for a second term. The call for this convention was addressed to those "who desire the unconditional maintenance of the Union, the supremacy of the Constitution, and the complete suppression of the existing rebellion, with the cause thereof, by vigorous war, and all apt and efficient means." It was issued on February 22, 1864, in the name of "the executive committee created by the National Convention held at Chicago on the 16th day of May, 1860," and carefully avoided the use of the name "Republican."

The "Union National Convention," as it named itself, was called to order by Senator Edwin D. Morgan of New York,

[14] Henry Wilson, III, 546–9.

the chairman of the Republican National Committee. Dr. Robert J. Breckinridge of Kentucky, a near relative of former Vice-President John C. Breckinridge, now actively engaged in the cause of the Confederacy, was chosen temporary chairman, and he made a strong plea for the Union and for the nomination of Lincoln. As illustrating the feeling of the times, he said that "no government has ever been built upon imperishable foundations which foundations were not laid upon the blood of traitors, the only imperishable cement of free institutions." This ranks well with the silly mouthings of Thomas Jefferson, half a century or more before, about the necessity that the "tree of liberty" be watered with the blood of tyrants every twenty years—only it was more agreeable in providing for the killing off of enemies rather than possible friends.

There was a squabble in the convention about the admission of delegates from Southern states and territories, but these were finally admitted and given the right to vote. A permanent organization was effected by the election of former Governor William Dennison of Ohio as president. He urged the prosecution of the war for the Union to a successful conclusion, no matter what the cost, and in fact this was the keynote of the entire convention proceedings. It was a "Union" convention in fact as well as in name.

The platform, reported by Henry J. Raymond of New York, was adopted unanimously. In no uncertain terms it pledged the convention "as Union men . . . to do everything in our power to aid the government in quelling by force of arms the rebellion now raging against its authority, and in bringing to the punishment due to their crimes the rebels and traitors arrayed against it." Also, it approved the determination of the Government "not to compromise with the rebels, or to offer them any terms of peace except such as may be based upon an unconditional surrender of their hostility and a return to their just allegiance," and called upon the Government "to maintain this position and to prosecute the war with the utmost possible vigor to the complete suppression of the rebellion."

The opposition to slavery was likewise uncompromising. It was condemned as "the strength of this rebellion, and as it must be, always and everywhere hostile to the principles of republican government. Justice and the national safety demand its utter and complete extirpation from the soil of the republic." While the proclamations and war measures against this institution were indorsed, an amendment to the Constitution was favored to "prohibit the existence of slavery within the limits or the jurisdiction of the United States." Of course, this made slavery the real issue of the campaign, in addition to that of the preservation of the Union, and marks the consummation of the change in the Republican party from its anti-slavery character in 1860 to that of abolition in 1864. In times of crisis matters move with incredible swiftness, and never is the outcome what might have been anticipated.

Next in importance to the above, or possibly of even greater importance as we view these events in the light of over sixty years of time, was the unqualified indorsement of Abraham Lincoln and his administration. This was worded so clearly that no one could mistake the meaning, which is especially important in the light of the opposition, both secret and open, that soon was to crystallize in the North to oust Lincoln and even to compel his withdrawal from the contest for the Presidency. It stated that the convention approved "the practical wisdom, the unselfish patriotism, and the unswerving fidelity with which Abraham Lincoln had discharged, under circumstances of unparalleled difficulty, the great duties and responsibilities of the presidential office." The convention also approved "the measures and acts which he has adopted to defend the nation against its open and secret foes," and "approved especially, the proclamation of emancipation and the employment as Union soldiers of men heretofore held in slavery."

This was a statement of "unconditional Union" principles without fear or favor, and shows sound courage and strong leadership on the part of the administration forces. The planks in favor of foreign immigration, "a speedy construction of the railroad to the Pacific coast," and of gratitude to the soldiers in the army and navy, were more or less perfunctory, and of course should be taken on the ground of political expediency. There was, however, a dash of vigor in the strong reiteration of the Monroe Doctrine, when it is remembered that at this very time France under its charlatan emperor, Napoleon III, was busily engaged in violating this American policy by its machinations in Mexico. Truly, courage and sound patriotism were not wanting in these Republican leaders of 1864.

When it came to nominations, on June 8, Lincoln received the votes of every delegate except those from Missouri, who had been instructed to vote for General Grant. The vote then was made unanimous. In its Vice-Presidential nomination the convention cast aside Vice-President Hamlin on grounds of expediency, and chose in his stead Andrew Johnson of Tennessee, an old-school Democrat, who had been conspicuous for his loyalty to the Union in spite of the rebellion of his own state. Little did they know what tragedy was to center upon this choice, for the career of Johnson is a tragedy, as also is that of Lincoln, although in a different sense. And on this choice depends the greatest handicap of the Republican party up to the present day, in the menace of the "solid South," which always arises to defeat its purposes, and which has been of such unfortunate effect on the South itself, in handing it over to leadership based upon the issues of the past instead of those of the twentieth century.

Lincoln accepted the nomination in modest terms, as might have been expected, telling of his gratitude that he had been thought "not unworthy," and in his formal letter of acceptance stated that he "heartily approved" of the platform. Characteristically, Andrew Johnson was more lengthy as well as more vociferous, saying that treason was "worthy of the punishment of death." He accepted the platform as in accord with his "public acts and opinions heretofore made known" and called upon his Democratic friends to "justly vindicate their devotion to true democratic policy and measures of expediency."

The Democratic party held its convention on August 29

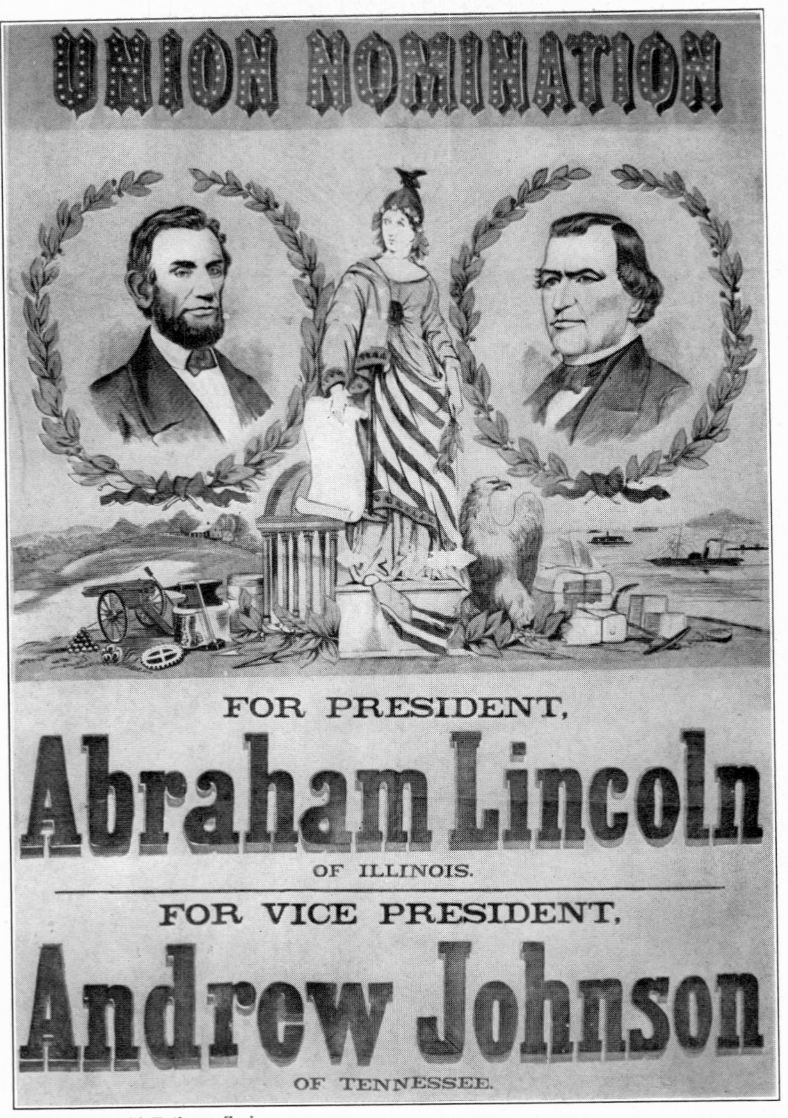

Courtesy Herald-Tribune-Zerbe

A RARE OLD POSTER USED DURING THE CAMPAIGN FOR THE ELECTION OF LINCOLN AND JOHNSON, 1864, RECENTLY DISCOVERED IN FLUSHING, N. Y.

at Chicago. Former Governor William Bigler of Pennsylvania was its temporary chairman, and Governor Horatio Seymour of New York its permanent presiding officer. Its platform declared the war a "failure," for the immediate cessation of hostilities, and to restore the Union by peaceable means. This miserable compromise with disloyalty gave a stigma to the Democratic party which, largely due to the efforts of such men as Grover Cleveland, Alton B. Parker, and Woodrow Wilson, it has only outgrown within recent years. Had only Douglas been alive, he possibly might have saved the party from itself and provided for a real two-party system, of undoubted loyalty to the Union, during the years of sorrow and dismay that were immediately to follow the Civil War.

The Chicago convention nominated General George B. McClellan for President and George H. Pendleton of Ohio for Vice-President. Of course, this put McClellan in a difficult situation. Had he only had the sound judgment to decline the nomination, he probably might have been elected President at some later day, possibly in 1872 or 1876, if not 1884, for he was a very young man at this time. He could not look his old soldiers in the face and tell them that their fighting had resulted in failure, especially under his own leadership. But now he was prevailed upon by political pressure to accept the nomination, which he did while at the same time repudiating the platform. There is no doubt that McClellan was thoroughly loyal to the cause of the Union. His honesty, sincerity, and patriotism are unquestioned. But he conscientiously felt that it was his duty to try and save the country from Lincoln and the Republican party, which were bent on destroying the Constitution of the United States and wrecking the nation! In other words, he was totally without guile as a politician, and fell into the hands of designing politicians who used him as a convenient weapon in the attempt to beat Lincoln at all costs.

And at first it seemed as though they were to succeed. In the long-drawn-out and agonizing struggle of Grant against Lee in the Wilderness of Virginia, with its terrible bloodshed and seeming uselessness, there came a great feeling of gloom and despair over the North and West. Peace at any price became the watchword with people otherwise sound and patriotic in their feelings. It appeared as though success to the arms of the Union soldiers was farther off than ever, showing how hard it often is accurately to gage contemporary events, for the Confederacy even then was undermined with weakness and went down in a complete crash eight or ten months later. The results of the blockade were having their inevitable effect, although not yet understood or appreciated by the public. Added to this was the political conspiracy mainly engineered by the "Jacobins," or Vindictives, and other radicals of a more or less emotional nature who joined them.

The whole controversy between Lincoln and the radicals turned upon the rivalry between Congress and the President, and this centered in their respective theories with regard to the attitude to be taken by the United States Government toward the Confederate states. The crisis was precipitated by the virtual conquest of Louisiana, Arkansas, and Tennessee. Lincoln always held, and, as the present writer considers, correctly, that the Southern states were never out of the Union. That what had taken place was the destruction of legal government in each state, and the substitution of revolutionary government therefor. Also, that a state could not legally secede from the Union, any more than a county could secede from a state, for a state was *legally* or *constitutionally* only an administrative district of the United States, endowed for some purposes with sovereign *powers,* but *not sovereignty.* Therefore, the process of dealing with the Confederate states was primarily one of *restoration,* at the hands of the executive, and not *reconstruction,* which would require the action of the legislative department. The Vindictives or radicals at once challenged this. When Lincoln attempted to *restore* Louisiana and Arkansas, not content with their undoubted right to debar senators and representatives from those states if they thought expedient, they passed, on July 2, 1864, under the leadership of Henry Winter Davis of Maryland and Senator Benjamin F. Wade of Ohio, a bill providing for Congressional reconstruction of the Southern states. As Congress was about to adjourn, Lincoln killed this bill by a "pocket veto."

Lincoln showed characteristic courage and statesmanship by this action, just at the time of his campaign for reëlection, and in further support of his position he issued a proclamation in which he calmly stated that he would not bind himself to any one form of procedure, but would be willing to give his support if any state should present itself for restoration to the Union under the Wade-Davis plan. Meanwhile, Horace Greeley, busy and more or less politically futile as often happened, urged a wild-goose attempt to bring about peace by negotiation at a meeting with Confederate commissioners at Niagara Falls. Lincoln wisely did not oppose him, but sent Greeley as a delegate. The whole thing ended in a fiasco, and Greeley then tried to shift the blame to Lincoln. In the state of popular discouragement this was serious for Lincoln, and now the radicals, led by Wade and Davis, issued their celebrated "Manifesto," which appeared in "The New York Tribune," Greeley's own paper, on August 5, 1864. It was a public appeal to "check the encroachment of the Executive on the authority of Congress, and to require it to confine itself to its proper sphere." It also charged Lincoln with the design to "hold the electoral votes of the rebel states at the dictation of his personal ambition." This Wade-Davis Manifesto was the direct beginning of the struggle over reconstruction which later was to be waged between Andrew Johnson, who tried his best, in an awkward, tactless, and incompetent manner, to carry through Lincoln's policy, and Congress under the undisputed leadership of these same radicals, Thaddeus Stevens being substituted for Henry Winter Davis, who died in December, 1865. Had Lincoln lived, undoubtedly he could have checked and defeated his rabid opponents, and one of the darkest tragedies in American history would have been obviated. He was the one and only man who could have carried the people with him, especially after the triumph of the overthrow of the Southern Confederacy. As it was, he now remained silent and gave no reply to the Manifesto, which soon happily recoiled upon the heads of its backers, due to the victories of the Union forces in the field. Meanwhile, the Vindictives showed their enmity by passing a resolution that the electoral votes of any states restored under Lincoln's plan should not be counted. They followed this with the celebrated "Twenty-second Joint Rule," according to which the consent of each house of Congress was made necessary to count the electoral vote of a state if it were disputed. This gave a strategic power over elections to the radicals for some years to come, but was dropped in 1876 at the time of the Hayes-Tilden contest, when the House of Representatives was controlled by the Democrats.

Definite attempts now were made to induce Lincoln to withdraw from the race, and he was told by his advisers that most certainly he would be defeated. To add to his difficulties, Chase, who long had been sympathetic with the radicals and thought himself far above Lincoln in character and ability, after many threats finally resigned. For some time the cabinet had been divided into two cliques or sections, headed for the most part by Seward and Chase. Lincoln actually often met his cabinet in two sections or dealt with them individually, because he could not get them to coöperate sufficiently to carry on the business of the administration. Only a man of his broad-minded tolerance and self-effacing statesmanship could have carried through the work of his administration with such divided support; but Lincoln had an eye to practical politics, and by his tactful though dominant personality he gave the necessary unity that otherwise would have been lacking. Meanwhile, he had held secure the support of the personal followings of these members, or else had rendered them impotent. He now shrewdly appointed Senator William P. Fessenden of Maine to succeed Chase in the Treasury Department. Fessenden was sympathetic with the radicals, although not entirely allied with them. He was a man of honesty and ability, whom the radicals could not consistently refuse to confirm on account of "senatorial courtesy," and yet who had sense enough to support Lincoln loyally in his administration and cabinet activities.

On August 23, 1864, and against the advice of many of his

political managers, Lincoln put the draft into renewed effect, in order to fill up the frightful losses in Grant's armies. That same day he held a cabinet meeting and asked his ministers to put their initials upon a folded paper which he handed them. He did not tell them what it contained, but as later disclosed it was a memorandum stating the probability that he would not be reëlected, but made plain his determination to coöperate with the President-elect between the election and inauguration, in order to save the Union, as it would not be possible to do so afterward. Lincoln was nothing if not self-sacrificing and courageous, and it was just this characteristic, when understood, that appealed to the people and caused them suddenly to turn to him and strongly to support him during the last few months of his life.

On September 2 came the news that Sherman had captured Atlanta. The war could no longer be called a failure, and one of those strange and sudden changes in popular psychology, so elusive and yet so powerful in their influence upon public opinion, came with astounding swiftness. A quick turn in the political tide toward Lincoln was the inevitable result. "Every shell from Sheridan's guns knocks a plank from the Chicago platform. Go to the gallant Farragut, who, lashed to the mast amid a storm of leaden hail, went on to victory, and ask him if the war is a failure; go to Sherman, who steadily advanced the old flag until he planted it on the principal stronghold in Georgia, and ask him if the war is a failure; go to Grant, who is cutting every artery of the Rebellion, and ask if the war is a failure; go to the gallant Sheridan, whose gleaming bayonets sent the Rebel hordes like a whirlwind up the Valley, and ask him if the war is a failure. Go ask your 'deluded brother' Early, whose army was driven in squads to the mountains, if the war is a failure. . . . The great battle of the Republic is to be fought at the ballot-box. It is for us to say whether the war is to go on, or whether we shall bring back that gallant army with their cheeks mantled with the blush of shame. Let us send to the army a victory that it can carry to the enemy on the point of the bayonet." Thus said the future Senator from

Michigan, Julius C. Burrows, in a campaign speech.[15] Radical newspapers began advocating Lincoln's reëlection, and radical orators, Wade included, went upon the stump for the same purpose. Lincoln now threw a sop to them by requesting the resignation of their pet aversion from his cabinet, Montgomery Blair, the postmaster-general. Blair acquiesced with fine spirit, for he understood exactly the peculiar circumstances, and he nobly and magnanimously went upon the stump and advocated Lincoln's reëlection. It is this kind of patriotism and self-sacrifice that makes politics something more than a mere scramble for office and personal advancement. Whether connected with this event or not, the fact remains that the day before Blair's resignation Frémont and Cochrane withdrew. The radical fiasco was now complete, and the Vindictives were routed for the time being. But not forever, as Andrew Johnson was to find out to his cost a few months later.

The campaign from now on was conducted with unity and effect on the part of the Republicans and Union men generally. It was characterized by "solemnity" rather than idle clamor, and the people of the North and West, those "plain people" whom Lincoln so often praised as being his great reliance, did not fail him at this time. The voting took place on November 8, and Lincoln carried every state that took part in the election but New Jersey, Delaware, and Kentucky. He received 212 electoral votes (one of the Nevada electors died before the election) and McClellan received 21. The Northern states had practically all taken measures to permit the soldiers to cast their ballots in the field. The total vote was: Lincoln, 2,213,665 at home and 116,887 in the field, a total of 2,330,552; McClellan, 1,802,237 at home, 33,748 in the field, a total of 1,835,985. This gave Lincoln a majority of 494,567.

An analysis of these election returns will show that a possible change of 60,000 votes in certain doubtful or strategic states would have meant the defeat of Lincoln and the election of McClellan. If the years 1860 to 1864 inclusive were taken,

[15] Quoted in W. D. Orcutt, "Burrows of Michigan and the Republican Party," I, 119.

the number of foreigners naturalized to vote during that period would reach an astounding total. These new citizens were permitted, in spite of the fact that many of them, by means of fraud and falsification of records, had not been here the statutory time for length of residence, to vote upon the destiny of the United States. It is doubtful if at any time in modern history a people ever were so careless about the existence of their country, at the same time that they were pouring out blood and treasure like water in the sincere attempt to "preserve" that same country. It is one of the anomalies of American history.[16] But, nevertheless, the vindication of Lincoln was looked upon as complete, and succeeding events soon were to show that the Union was saved. And for the first time in his life Lincoln really was "popular." Nothing succeeds like success, and in addition the people now began to understand him, which meant that the politicians of a professional variety began to understand him too.

[16] See W. S. Myers, "American Democracy Today," 17–18, for numbers of naturalizations in leading cities in 1864.

Chapter VIII

ANDREW JOHNSON—AND TRAGEDY

As pointed out by Stanwood,[1] the election of 1864 was the first time in our history that any states had deliberately declined to choose electors for the choice of a President. In some of the eleven Confederate states Union governments had been set up under the patronage of Lincoln, who was committed to their legality. The consent to the erection of the state of West Virginia by one of these governments, that of Virginia, was given as required by the provisions of the Constitution of the United States. But Congress refused for the time to accept the legality of this act, and did not admit senators or representatives from the new state. On the other hand, elections were held in Louisiana and Tennessee, where Lincoln's plan of restoration had been put into effect. In January, 1865, a joint resolution was passed by both houses declaring that no valid election had been held in the eleven rebellious states, which were mentioned by name, and that "no electoral votes shall be received or counted from said states." Lincoln was opposed to such action, which virtually declared against the legality of the governments in Louisiana and Tennessee which he recognized, although Congress refused to do so. Of course the "Twenty-second Joint Rule" took care of this, and Lincoln dropped the matter. When the same question arose a few months later concerning the other nine states of the South he was dead, and Johnson inherited the struggle.

As already mentioned, Lincoln now entered upon the only period of his life in which he really enjoyed popular approval. He now was enabled to make necessary changes in the membership of his cabinet, placing William Dennison of

[1] 308–12.

Ohio in the vacancy as postmaster-general to succeed Montgomery Blair. Attorney-General Bates resigned the last of November, 1864, and James Speed of Kentucky was appointed in his place. Lincoln showed his great magnanimity, and also made a great stroke of state in cementing his party, when he appointed during December his critic and jealous rival, ex-Secretary Chase, to succeed as Chief Justice of the supreme court Roger B. Taney, who had died two months before. Seward, Stanton, and Welles still remained. Lincoln faced his second administration with his cabinet complete and functioning, with a wonderful series of victories won under Grant, Sherman, Sheridan, and Thomas to forecast the speedy collapse of the Confederacy, and undoubted popular support of a striking and effective character. His inaugural address was one of the greatest speeches of his life, and deservedly ranks among the great state papers of history.

It was a short *résumé* of the contrasting conditions between March, 1861, and March, 1865. Written in a spirit of conciliation and forgiveness, it made no uncertain statement of the intention to carry through the war to a final and successful conclusion, no matter what the cost, and closed with the really sublime paragraph: "With malice towards none, with charity for all, with firmness in the right as God gives us to see the right, let us finish the work we are in, to bind up the nation's wounds, to care for him who shall have borne the battle, and for his widow and his orphans, to do all which may achieve and cherish a just and a lasting peace among themselves and with all nations."

Poor Andrew Johnson began his national service under the worst possible conditions. It was widely believed that the Vice-President was intoxicated when he was inaugurated. He later stated he had been ill, and merely was given a drink of liquor for medicinal purposes. However that may be, Johnson's inaugural address was incoherent, and Lincoln and the audience were both surprised and deeply pained. Lincoln never said a word to Johnson, or openly expressed any anger whatever.

The war soon was over. Richmond fell on April 3, 1865, and Lee surrendered on April 9 at Appomattox village. The terms were most generous as given by Grant with the approval of Lincoln. The President was in Virginia near the scene of these closing events and returned to Washington on April 9. April 14 was the regular cabinet meeting, and General Grant was in the city and invited to be present. A policy of reconstruction was discussed, and Lincoln made it plain that he wanted no proscriptions. "I hope there will be no persecution, no bloody work after the war is over. No one need expect me to take any part in hanging or killing these men, even the worst of them. . . . We must extinguish our resentments if we expect harmony and union. There is too much of a desire on the part of some of our very good friends to be masters, to interfere with and dictate to those states, to treat the people not as fellow-citizens; there is too little respect for their rights. I do not sympathize with these feelings." Most significantly he also had remarked: "I think it providential that this great rebellion is crushed just as Congress has adjourned and there are none of the disturbing elements of that body to hinder and embarrass us. If we are wise and discreet we shall reanimate the states and get their governments in successful operation, with order prevailing and the Union reëstablished before Congress comes together in December."

Lincoln was shot that night in Ford's Theater by the fanatic John Wilkes Booth, and died early the next morning. Andrew Johnson at once quietly took the oath of office as President, and immediately undertook to carry out the above policy of Lincoln, and almost to the letter. In this he was opposed and bitterly defeated by the Vindictives, soon come to complete power. Some one has defined statesmanship as the right art of changing things from what they are toward what they ought to be. Lincoln thus showed the greatest statesmanship, and has ranked as one of the greatest men of all countries and all times. Unfortunately, Andrew Johnson was not a statesman, and in addition he lacked the tact, political ability, and judgment to conduct safely the administration and the country through the period of readjustment that necessarily must follow such a civil war.

Johnson was born in Raleigh, North Carolina, on December 29, 1808. He was the son of very poor parents and his father died when the child was only about four years old. At the age of ten he was apprenticed to a tailor, and virtually taught himself to read. He became a tailor, went to Greenville, Tennessee, and married a woman of some refinement who taught him to write; it was not until years later that he learned to write with ease. Nevertheless, he did not strike people as rough and ignorant when he became President. But he seemed to lack the faculty of inspiring proper respect. He had been a Democratic member of Congress from Tennessee during the years 1843-53; governor of Tennessee 1853-57; United States senator 1857-62; and had refused to give up his seat when Tennessee seceded. Lincoln appointed him military governor of Tennessee and he held this office until 1864, in which year he was elected to the Vice-Presidency. He was a man of ability, courage, good judgment of *measures* but not of men, and always had the unfortunate faculty of tactlessly doing the *wrong* thing at exactly the right time! His Democratic antecedents caused him strongly to be suspected by the partizan Republicans, and especially by the Vindictives when he attempted to carry out Lincoln's plans with regard to reconstruction. On the other hand, the aristocratic and defeated ex-Confederate leaders looked down upon him as "poor white trash," not forgetting their own unfriendly relations with him before the war. Had he been an able and shrewd political leader, he might easily have rallied a strong Lincoln Republican party behind him and retained with it the support of the "war Democrats." As it was, he was soon almost without any backing, and suffered bitter political defeat and near disgrace in consequence.[2]

[2] J. T. Trowbridge thus describes Johnson at the White House, when receiving ex-Confederates asking pardon: "I should scarcely have recognized the President from any of his published pictures. He appeared to me a man rather below the medium height, sufficiently stout, with a massy, well-developed head, strong features, dark, iron-grey hair, a thick, dark

As might well have been expected, the news of Lincoln's assassination caused widespread panic at the North. Rewards were offered for the arrest of Jefferson Davis and other Confederate leaders, and the wildest stories were repeated, charging them with attempts to introduce yellow-fever germs from the tropics into the Northern cities, also reflecting upon the personal morals of Davis. Nothing seemed to be too ridiculous to be believed. Johnson at first seemed to lose his head, and was very vindictive, saying that "treason must be made odious." Booth's accomplices were executed in June after trial by a military commission, and Wirz, formerly the notorious and contemptible commander of the Confederate military prison at Andersonville, Georgia, was executed in November for cruelty and mismanagement. Aside from the unfortunate casting of Davis and other leaders into prison, these were practically all the political executions or punishments handed out at the conclusion of the great conflict—a record equaled by no other country or people on earth. This is a proud page in the annals of the Republican party.

And soon came a gradual relaxation of the animosity of the North, and also of Johnson. The President came especially under the influence of Lincoln's cabinet, and Seward in particular. Samuel Bowles says, under date of Fort Kearney, Nebraska, May 24, 1865:[3] "Among the present limited number of troops on the plain are two regiments of infantry, all from the rebel army. They have cheerfully re-inlisted into the federal

---

complexion, deep-sunk eyes, with a peculiarly wrinkled, care-worn look about them, and a weary expression generally. His voice was mild and subdued, and his manner kindly. He shook hands with none. To each applicant for pardon he put a question or two, sometimes only one, and dispatched him with a word of promise or advice." "The South," 79. Later, when in Greenville, Tennessee, Trowbridge adds: "Every man knows 'Andy Johnson.' He has a good reputation for honesty, but I was told he was 'hard on money matters.' A prominent citizen who knew him intimately said to me: 'Johnson is a man of much greater ability than he has ever had credit for. When he was a tailor, he did his work well—always a good honest job. He has many good traits, and a few bad ones. He is surly and vindictive and a man of strong prejudices, but thoroughly a patriot,'" 238.

[3] "Across the Continent," 11. See also Barton, "Life of Lincoln," II, 313–15.

service. . . . They are known in the army as 'white-washed rebs,' or as they call themselves, 'galvanized Yankees.'" By the end of the month of May all opposition to the Union armies on the part of the Confederates had ceased. As has well been said, the North, at least officially, believed that the old Union had been maintained. The South believed that they had been conquered by an alien power and a new Union created.

Johnson and the Republican administration now had before them a twofold problem. In the first place, the North and West must be brought back to normal conditions. The army and navy were to be reduced, contractors, provost marshals, etc., to be done away with, military encroachments upon the rights of the citizens removed, and civil powers everywhere restored. On the other hand, the South was completely prostrated in both an economic and political sense, and in the very depths of destitution. Its people must in many cases be actually clothed and fed, normal governments must be restored, and four millions of helpless and incapable blacks taken care of.

Trade and blockade restrictions were removed during the summer of 1865. Unfortunately, the administration made a grievous, and in the light of common sense an unpardonable mistake, in garrisoning many parts of the South with negro troops. This naturally caused enmity among the Southern whites and discontent among the ex-slaves. The latter did not as yet understand what freedom meant, but began flocking from the farms to the coast or to the cities. To meet this emergency the famous "Freedmen's Bureau" had been created as a war measure by act of Congress of March 3, 1865, to exist for one year after the conclusion of the war. General O. O. Howard was the appointed head, a man of the highest character and patriotism. The bureau was in general good in its higher, and indifferent or even sometimes venal and dishonest in its lower ranks of officials. It was violently opposed by the Southerners, who thought it intrusive and designed to stir up the negroes against them.

It will be remembered that Lincoln's plan had been that of reorganizing state governments in the South by means of

Union sympathizers, and that he thought it was an essentially executive problem to accomplish this. The wrath of the Vindictives had been stirred by this, and the Wade-Davis Manifesto was the direct result. Lincoln never gave up his contention, but merely bided his time in order to carry through his policy when opportunity offered. In 1864 constitutional conventions had been held and governments started in Tennessee, Louisiana, and Arkansas. But the Virginia government located at Alexandria, which pretended to act for the whole state, was a farce by Lincoln's own admission.

Johnson took up and attempted to carry out Lincoln's policy. On May 9, 1865, he formally recognized Francis H. Pierpont as governor of Virginia, and aided the governments of Tennessee, Arkansas, and Louisiana, already organized. But on May 20 he stopped the attempts of the ex-Confederates in other states to start their own governments. However, on May 29 he issued a proclamation to carry out the organization of the remaining seven states. This required an *unqualified* (instead of Lincoln's qualified) oath to support all laws and decrees touching slavery, and excepted from amnesty more classes of persons than those excepted by Lincoln. The same day the reorganization of North Carolina was begun by the appointment of W. W. Holden as provisional governor, and he, like the other governors, was directed to assemble a constitutional convention of delegates to organize a government. The radicals desired Johnson to include a requirement for negro suffrage, but Johnson wisely opposed this. The various constitutional conventions met during the summer and winter of 1865-66—Texas being the last, in April, 1866.

These conventions followed instructions from Washington with more or less fidelity. First of all, they annulled the ordinances of secession. South Carolina and Georgia *repealed,* thus maintaining a constitutional validity for their attempted secession; Florida annulled, and the others declared the ordinance "null and void." North Carolina added the phrase, "null and void from the beginning." In the second place, slavery was declared forever abolished. Finally, the Confederate state debts were repudiated, as was right and proper, since they had been incurred for revolutionary purposes; but South Carolina added to her foolish recalcitrancy by refusing to do even this. The above acts of this state and Georgia merely handicapped Johnson in his attempts to carry through a policy of wise restoration, and played into the hands of their enemies, who were only waiting the moment to attack. Following this, state legislatures were elected in the fall, and the National Government used strong influence to compel them to ratify the Thirteenth Amendment. All obeyed except Mississippi, another instance of political madness. Provisional governors now gradually gave way to regular civil governments, and war conditions likewise gradually ceased. Finally, on April 2, 1866, Johnson formally declared the war at an end in all the "seceded" states except Texas, and in this state and "everywhere in the United States" on August 20, 1866.

Johnson became more and more conservative in his policy, stopped confiscation altogether, and gave it as his opinion that property, except slaves, must be restored to the former owners when they were pardoned. The radicals, especially the Vindictives, thought there had been undue haste, and desired proscription of the Confederate leaders, extensive confiscation of plantations, enfranchisement of the negroes, and the postponement of political reorganization until the continued ascendancy of the Union party might be insured. This soon came to mean the Republican party.

There is no doubt of Johnson's desire to form an administration party in the country; he generally appointed to office in the South former Whigs and opponents of secession, and there was some chance of this. The Whigs still existed in the South as a more or less organized party, but were finally, as we shall see, forced into the Democratic party by negro suffrage.[4] Had Lincoln lived and carried through his policy of

[4] Sidney Andrews, "The South Since the War," 135–6, says (October, 1865): "I find that I, in common with many other persons of the North, was entirely wrong in supposing that the Whig and Democratic party, as distinct political organizations, died at least ten years ago. . . . Here in North Carolina I discover with proper amazement, that the old parties are

political "restoration" and amnesty, with negro suffrage extended only to the exceptional members of that race, this Whig nucleus could easily have been compacted into a strong southern Republican party, and the "solid South" never would have come into being. As will be shown, this political bloc is the unfortunate legacy of the Vindictives to the Republican party of to-day. Lincoln foresaw it, and would have prevented it.

In order properly to understand the great political struggle that now ensued, and upon the facts of which has depended so much of political party history, it is necessary to give in outline a summary of the three main theories of the status of the Southern states which soon developed and upon which various politicians acted.

First and most important of all was that of Abraham Lincoln.[5] He recognized the continued existence of the states in rebellion as states of, and in, the Union. He regarded the rebellion against the United States within these states as the act of a combination of disloyal persons, and not as the act of the states at all. In other words, it was the work of individuals as such, who had overthrown the loyal governments within these states, but the states themselves were not disloyal, because they could not be. They were, in fact, impersonal entities, incapable of committing treason or any other wrong. According to this view the process of reconstruction consisted merely in putting the loyal element in a state in control of the government. Lincoln's plan, it must be reiterated, was based upon the belief that the work of reconstruction was an executive problem.[6]

---

both alive, and neither of them a whit older or less pugilistic than it was twenty years ago. To be an 'old line Whig' is to be a perfect gentleman, while to be an 'old line Democrat' is to be a vulgar fellow outside the pale of good society; or, on the other hand, to be an 'old line Democrat' is to be a man of good sense and sound opinions, while to be an 'old line Whig' is to be a conceited fool and a bloated aristocrat."

[5] J. W. Burgess, "Reconstruction and the Constitution," 9.

[6] W. A. Dunning states Lincoln's theory of sovereignty as follows: "The nation is sovereign, the states are local organizations subordinate to the nation. The general government represents the nation, and is limited in no way by the local state governments, but only by the federal Constitution. Of this Constitution, however, the departments of the central govern-

Johnson had undertaken to act upon the above theory. He "proposed a rapid and forgiving reconstruction by the executive, . . . to pardon the rebel leaders, upon special personal application, as an act of high executive grace, and to amnesty everyone else in a body; and upon the basis of their re-established loyalty to use the old electorate of the South in reconstruction." [7] He at once was met by the two other diametrically opposite theories which, however, might be used interchangeably in order to defeat him.

The second theory was that especially championed by Thaddeus Stevens and the most extreme of the radicals or Vindictives. According to this theory,[8] "the territory once covered by the states which had seceded from the Union was nothing now but a conquered district, whose future condition depended upon the will of the conqueror. If states should ever be erected there again, it must be accomplished by virtue of that provision in the Constitution which declares that 'new states may be admitted by Congress into this Union.' This theory involved the admission that secession had been temporarily successful. This Mr. Stevens frankly acknowledged. He said: 'Unless the law of nations is a dead letter, the late war between the two acknowledged belligerents severed their original contracts, and broke all the ties that bound them together.'" Of course, the statement of principle and fact in this last sentence is tacitly accepted by those people of the South to-day who insist upon calling the Civil War a "war between the states"; and they thereby acknowledge the legality of all the policy of reconstruction as carried through by the radicals or Vindictives.

John W. Burgess states that it was Mr. Shellabarger of Ohio who, not satisfied by either of the above theories, did more than anybody else to state the third theory, upon which

---

ment are the final interpreters. The limitations of the Constitution therefore, are practically guarded only by the mutual responsibility of the departments in action, and their accountability to the people in the elections." "Essays on Civil War and Reconstruction," 14.

[7] Burgess, 32, 34–5.

[8] Burgess, 58.

the majority of the Republicans in Congress, both restrained radicals and moderate conservatives, finally based their policy. Says Mr. Burgess:[9] "Briefly stated, that theory was that while secession was a nullity legally from the beginning, and could not take the territory occupied by the states attempting it, or the people inhabiting that territory out of the Union, or from under the rightful jurisdiction of the United States government and Constitution for one instant, yet it worked the loss of the state status in the Union, and from a legal point of view left this territory and the inhabitants of it subject exclusively to the jurisdiction of the United States government, a status from which they could be relieved only by the erection of states anew upon such territory, an operation which could be effected, under the Constitution of the United States, only by the co-operation of Congress with the loyal inhabitants of such territory."

The present writer believes that the first theory outlined, as the one maintained by Lincoln, was the correct one, and that a large part of the so-called reconstruction legislation of the next few years was unconstitutional, unless upon the attenuated ground of providing "a republican form of government" for the former Confederate states, or as "necessary and proper" in order to terminate an insurrection already ended! On the other hand, while regretting the mistakes then made and acknowledging the disastrous results of radical policy not only upon the prostrate South but the whole country as well, it must be admitted that at that time, at least, the majority of the people supported Congress in greater or less degree, being disgusted and driven to it by the bungling and mistaken policies of Andrew Johnson.

It will be remembered that just before his death Lincoln rejoiced that the new, or Thirty-ninth, Congress, elected in the autumn of 1864, would not meet until December, 1865. Johnson made his first mistake in not calling a special session, and making a frank effort to coöperate with the more conservative elements in both houses who had been following the leader-

[9] "Reconstruction and the Constitution," 59–60.

ship of Lincoln. Johnson was not the elected President, and necessarily must be handicapped by this fact in the popular estimation, while his continuing to go ahead on the Lincoln plan merely added to the suspicion and enmity of the Vindictives, who had been biding their time.

On December 2, 1865, two days before the beginning of the regular session, a Republican Congressional caucus met. Thaddeus Stevens—foremost of Vindictives, strong, brave, unashamed, and politically ruthless—assumed leadership and his program was decided upon. This may be summed up in a few words. It was decided to claim that reconstruction was the business of Congress alone; that all things done toward restoration by both Lincoln and Johnson should be regarded as tentative and subject to the final decision of Congress; and that Congress should refuse representation to the ex-Confederate states until it had pronounced any reconstructed governments to be valid and satisfactory. In the meantime, the clerk of the House, contrary to the usual custom, was not even to call the names of the claimants to seats, and a joint committee of fifteen was to be appointed to consider the whole matter. All this was carried out to the letter when Congress met on December 4.

In explanation of this it should be remembered that the radicals were facing a real danger to Republican party supremacy in the future. D. M. Dewitt has well summed this up in his brilliant work on "The Impeachment and Trial of Andrew Johnson" [10] by observing that "the dominating motive of the opposition to the Lincoln-Johnson plan of reconstruction

[10] P. 23–4. Dewitt says further, in description of Stevens: "This man was probably the most remarkable of the time. In his seventy-fourth year, his once stalwart form was enfeebled not only by age but by disease. His cavaderous countenance was surmounted by a brown wig, and from under beetling brows flashed eyes whose fire the flight of years seemed to have made only the more intense. A cripple from birth, one of his legs terminating in a mere bunch of flesh, his deformity, it is likely, had embittered his spirit. . . . Though kindly to individuals with whom he came in personal association and by nature not a man of blood, he was the very soul of vindictiveness toward classes who embodied principles or customs he detested, and he would not hesitate to wade through seas of blood to redress the wrongs of the poor and downtrodden." 24–5.

was the conviction that its success would wreck the Republican party, restore the Democrats to power and bring back the days of Southern supremacy and Northern vassalage. As Thaddeus Stevens with his customary frankness said in his first speech at this session: 'With the basis unchanged, the eighty-three southern members, with the Democrats that will in the best times be elected from the North, will always give them a majority in Congress and in the electoral college. They will at the very first election take possession of the White House and the halls of Congress.' And the most exasperating feature of the whole perplexing situation was that this catastrophe (to the minds of the entire majority the most disastrous they could contemplate) was being brought about by an Executive of their party's own choice. The President with his cabinet appeared to be pressing on with headlong eagerness a restoration of the Union which could not but prove fatal to the ascendancy of the party which had borne the heat and burden of administration during the war, a result which the President, supported by his old-time party associates, seemed to regard with the utmost equanimity."

Nor was this at all discreditable to the radicals. The only difficulty was that when Stevens rightly foresaw the "solid South" in alliance with the northern Democrats, so characteristic of national politics since that day, he and his fellow-radicals took exactly the means to consolidate and bring about this alliance. Had they had real statesmanship, instead of a policy colored by partizanship of the most short-sighted nature, they would have seen that the Whig and other opposing elements to the Democracy in the South, especially when united with the numerous body of men who originally had not wanted secession but only had been coerced into "going with their states" by the radical Democrats, offered an opportunity to build up a strong and in some cases overwhelming Republican party. This would have enabled the party to become truly national, and reunited the country fifty years before the World War, instead of being merely in process of present accomplishment since that later crisis. But this is just the difference between the statesmanship of a Lincoln and the partizanship of such men as Stevens, Sumner, Stanton, Chandler, and others of their type.

Johnson also must bear his share of the blame. There is no question that he opened negotiations with various Democratic leaders in the hope of rallying members of that party behind the administration.[11] Also, the ex-Confederates failed badly in their statesmanship. Their sending Alexander H. Stevens of Georgia (recently Vice-President of the Confederacy), and other like leaders in the rebellion, to Washington to occupy seats in the Senate and House of Representatives may have been human, but it was unpardonable blindness to the real situation. Following this came "black codes" and other special laws for the control of the newly freed negroes. These were understandable, but showed no political judgment whatever. Of course, the suspicions of the radicals, already aroused by Johnson, were increased, and the South paid bitterly for its rashness. Sidney Andrews, the newspaper correspondent already quoted, says further in this connection:[12] "I everywhere encounter more or less of the feeling which a Cuthbert (Georgia) man expressed in this terse and forcible language: 'I hope every district in the state will elect a man for Congress who can't take that damned test oath. I want to see the Yankees try it on; if Georgia isn't a free sovereign state, I think, by God, it's time we knew it.' This practical reaffirmation of the dogma of state rights is something of every-day witness to any one travelling here. The people hold to it just as strongly today as they did five years ago; and the moral of this election (November 1865) is, that the supremacy of the state is above that of the nation. . . . The merchant of Columbus who said in the public parlor of the hotel one evening so loudly that half a dozen persons heard him, 'I'm in favor of having our men go to Congress and to take their seats anyway, whether the damned Yankees are willing or not,' only put in strong

[11] See W. S. Myers "Self-Reconstruction of Maryland," 28–30.
[12] "South Since the War," 330–33.

phrase an idea I have heard half a dozen times in more cautious language."

The Joint Committee on Reconstruction, decided upon in the caucus of December 2, was promptly authorized and appointed. Stevens was chairman of the House section, and Fessenden of Maine of the Senate section, as well as of the entire committee. Fessenden had returned to the Senate a short time before Lincoln's death, and had been succeeded by Hugh McCulloch as secretary of the treasury. As yet the purpose of Congress was not necessarily that of rejecting Johnson's plans entirely, but merely to assert the right of Congress to a voice in determining the matter.[13] The elements opposing the President, says Dunning, [14] were (1) the extreme lovers of the negro who, on abstract grounds of a belief in human equality and natural rights, demanded full civil and political privileges for the freedmen; (2) the radicals or partizan politicians, who wanted to humble the Democratic party by means of the negro vote; and (3) "the representatives of an exalted statesmanship, who saw in the existing situation an opportunity for decisively fixing in our system a broader and more national principle of civil rights and political privilege." This third group assumed a sort of leadership during the first part of this session of Congress, but lost it to the radicals later. Also, there were many Republicans who at first were willing to use their votes in Congress to support the administration. They still were under the spell of Lincoln's genius, and possibly a tactful and sympathetic attitude toward them on the part of Johnson might easily have consolidated them into an administration Republican party holding the control of a majority of Congress. Johnson, by his extreme and undignified behavior, soon alienated them and threw most of them into

[13] Dunning points out ("Essays," 58) that during the war the President acted upon the necessity of military command, and Congress upon the "necessary and proper" clause of the Constitution. While the two departments of government worked with some degree of unanimity during the war, they disagreed and opposed each other during reconstruction. Congress then got the upper hand.

[14] "Essays," 85–6.

the arms of the radicals. However, his first annual message (written by George Bancroft) was a dignified, able, and conservative document. It allayed opposition for a few weeks; but the final break came in February, 1866.

This was in large part precipitated by the senseless and reactionary legislation passed by the newly established state governments in the South, which so alarmed the radicals in Congress that they passed a bill extending the life of the Freedmen's Bureau. Johnson met this by vetoing the bill on February 19, 1866, on the grounds of its unconstitutionality. Even though he honestly might be of this opinion, yet he easily could have justified the bill as a war measure, for war conditions had not yet been officially ended by Johnson's proclamation of April 2. Following this, Johnson made an offensive and abusive personal attack upon the Congressional leaders in a stump speech at the White House on February 22. This is a typical sentence: "I look upon as being opposed to the fundamental principles of this government and as now laboring to destroy them: Thaddeus Stevens of Pennsylvania, Charles Sumner and Wendell Phillips of Massachusetts. [A voice, "Forney."] I do not waste my fire on dead ducks." Both Johnson's followers and those who desired to be were filled with disgust and dismay. Justifiable contempt is the last thing under which a public man may prosper. His enemies took advantage of this situation and on March 2 the gauntlet was thrown down to Johnson by a concurrent resolution passed by Congress to the effect that no senator or representative should be admitted to Congress from a rebellious state until Congress had declared that state entitled to representation. Open warfare now was on, and the result must be political and personal, not to mention economic tragedy—at least as far as the South was concerned. The blame for this must be apportioned among Johnson, the radicals, and the South itself.

The radicals now attempted to secure for the negroes through the courts what had formerly been secured for them by means of military power, and passed the Civil Rights Bill, which declared them citizens of the United States. This bill was vetoed by Johnson and passed over his veto on April 6, 1866. The Joint Committee on Reconstruction now took charge of the whole matter of Southern reconstruction and on April 30 reported measures for reconstruction. This proposed a Fourteenth Amendment, which was substantially as passed on the following June 13. This amendment made "all persons born or naturalized in the United States, and subject to the jurisdiction thereof," citizens both of the United States and of the state in which they reside; it provided for a reduction of the Congressional representation of any state that should deny the franchise to any male citizens of voting age; excluded from Federal office the most prominent officials of the late Confederacy until Congress should pardon them; and invalidated all debts and obligations "incurred in aid of insurrection or rebellion against the United States." It was a fair attempt to secure the results of the war and prevent further rebellion. The plan also provided that the states ratifying the amendment should have representation in Congress, and in addition certain high ex-Confederate officials were declared ineligible for office. In July a bill finally was passed over Johnson's veto to continue the Freedmen's Bureau for two years. Just at this time Tennessee, having ratified the Fourteenth Amendment, was restored to its state status by the passage of a bill on July 24.

Both parties now turned to the Congressional campaign for the Fortieth Congress, which was to be elected at the polls in November. It is interesting to note that during that same month of July, 1866, there had been three changes in Johnson's cabinet, Dennison, Speed, and Harlan (appointed 1865) relinquishing the portfolios of postmaster-general, attorney-general, and the interior respectively, and being succeeded by Randall of Wisconsin, Stanbery of Ohio, and Browning of Illinois. All three were Republicans, so Johnson remained true to his adopted party.

The preparations for the fall elections began early. Johnson and his friends were actively engaged in the attempt to build up an administration Republican party, while the radicals strove to prevent this and gain complete control of the Republican organization. It is said that during the summer of 1866 Johnson removed 1283 postmasters from office, and the same process went on in the Treasury Department with its custom house and internal revenue officials.[15] On August 14 there met at Philadelphia a "National Union Convention," which had been called as the result of a movement begun by a political club in Washington, D. C., the previous March. It had among its delegates such Republicans as Montgomery Blair, Thurlow Weed, John A. Dix, Edgar Cowan, Henry J. Raymond, James R. Doolittle, and Randall and Browning of Johnson's cabinet. James G. Blaine sneeringly says [16] that among the "Copperheads" present were Clement L. Vallandigham, Fernando Wood, Edward J. Phelps, and among the Democrats were Samuel J. Tilden, John P. Stockton, Joel Parker, William Bigler, Asa Packer, James E. English, Robert C. Winthrop, and Reverdy Johnson. The members entered the hall arm in arm, led by General Couch of Massachusetts and J. L. Orr, an ex-Confederate from South Carolina, which led the radical newspapers to dub the convention "Noah's Ark." This convention declared for conciliation, restoration, and asserted the constitutional right of the Southern states to representation in Congress. Vallandigham withdrew on account of objections to his presence.

To offset this Johnson movement, the radicals had a "Loyal Unionists' Convention," which met at Philadelphia on September 3, and contained such prominent Republicans with different shades of view as Simon Cameron, Horace Greeley, James A. Garfield, Rutherford B. Hayes, Stanley Matthews, Zachariah Chandler, Carl Schurz, Lyman Trumbull, and John W. Forney; also such Southern representatives as H. C. Warmoth, Albion W. Tourgee, John Minor Botts, and William G. Brownlow. Extremely bitter attacks upon Johnson and his policies were made both in speeches and in a set of resolutions. It is probable that this gathering had great effect in rallying

[15] Dewitt, 108.
[16] "Twenty Years of Congress," II, 220 *et seq.*

the rank and file of Republican voters to the support of the radical plan of reconstruction.

The issue for the radicals is well stated by Blaine.[17] "The one objective point . . . was the adoption of the Fourteenth Amendment. It was evidently the unalterable determination of the Republicans to make that the leading feature of the campaign, to enforce it in every party convention, to urge it through the press, to present it on the stump, to proclaim it through every authorized exponent of public opinion. They were determined that the Democratic party of the North should not be allowed to ignore it or in any way evade it. It was to be the shibboleth of the Republican canvass, and the rank and file in every loyal state were engaged in its presentation and its exposition." Added to this objective was the defeat of Johnson's friends and the wresting of all party control from them. The New Orleans riot, on July 30, had the worst kind of political effect and aided the radicals greatly.

Johnson now undertook to bestir himself, and took advantage of the laying of the cornerstone of a monument to Stephen A. Douglas in Chicago on September 6 to make a series of political speeches by "swinging around the circle," as it was called. He left Washington August 28, taking Seward, Welles, Randall, Grant, and Farragut with him. This form of political campaigning by a President is now looked upon as a normal method of arousing and informing public opinion. But sixty years ago, before the emergence of the President as a great political leader (no matter who may hold the office), a political and constitutional phenomenon of the last twenty-five or thirty years, such procedure was looked upon askance, and also the feelings of the people were outraged by the lack of dignity and the cheap plane upon which Johnson placed his arguments. His whole purpose seemed intent on carrying over the country the unfortunate impressions aroused by his speech on the preceding February 22, and there was a resultant public disgust and contempt that proved disastrous to his cause. The

[17] "Twenty Years," II, 228.

radicals chuckled with glee as their enemy thus delivered himself into their hands.

When the election day came in November, Johnson was heavily defeated. Congress would be overwhelmingly against him, and made up of 143 Republicans, meaning radical supporters, and 43 Democrats. There was no doubt that the old party of Lincoln's opponents, the Vindictives, now were in power, and ruthlessly they went ahead, while the South at first, and then the country at large, suffered as a result. To add to the strength of their position, the South again played directly into their hands, and during the fall and winter of 1866-67 all the Southern states (except Tennessee, already "reconstructed") refused to ratify that radical "shibboleth," the Fourteenth Amendment. Had they pocketed their pride and done so, it would have been well for them—but this was almost too much to expect of human nature.

The radicals, encouraged by their overwhelming indorsement at the polls throughout the North and West, did not wait for the meeting of the new or Fortieth Congress, but went ahead in the short or "lame duck" session of the Thirty-ninth Congress yet remaining and passed, mainly over Johnson's consistent veto, the acts they considered necessary to put their policies into immediate effect. Lincoln was now merely a name to conjure with and to rally voters to the Grand Old Party—but his plans, according well with sound statesmanship, were entirely overlooked or probably forgotten. The radicals had received a new mandate from the people. They had found a new basis for popular coöperation founded upon feelings of revenge toward the South and personal hatred of Johnson. It was rather low in the moral scale, but relieved by protestations of help to the downtrodden freedmen—and effective.

On February 6, 1867, Stevens reported in the House of Representatives the Military Reconstruction Act, which passed by the most high-handed steam-roller method and became law over Johnson's veto on March 2. It declared the Lincoln-Johnson state governments in the South to be unconstitutional, and set them aside, assuming the power of Congress to do so, and divided up the South into five military districts. The states were to be restored to their normal position in the Union only after a reorganization on the basis of general negro enfranchisement and limited rebel enfranchisement. The act, in reality, provided no machinery for putting its provisions into effect. However, pursuant to an act passed by the Thirty-ninth Congress before its expiration on March 4, which called the Fortieth Congress into immediate session, the newly elected Congress met on the same day, and a Supplementary Reconstruction Act became law, also over Johnson's veto, on March 23. These two acts are possibly the most unjust and probably as unconstitutional as any legislation that was enacted by the national legislature. This second law provided that the five district commanders in the South were to register the voters, who were to be tested by an oath of loyalty; hold an election for delegates to a state convention; call a convention to reorganize or make a state constitution; call an election to ratify the constitution; and send the ratified constitution to Congress. As Zebulon B. Vance of North Carolina well said, if the Southern states could not constitutionally secede from the Union, certainly Congress could not constitutionally put them out.

Of immediate sinister purpose was another act passed on March 2 by the old Thirty-ninth Congress before its adjournment, known as the Tenure of Office Act. According to its provisions the President could not remove any executive official from office without the consent of the Senate, or else he would be guilty of a misdemeanor and be punished with fine or imprisonment. Furthermore, orders to the military forces could be issued only through the general in command of the army, and the President could not assign him to duty away from Washington or relieve him from duty except at the said general's own request, or with the previous approval of the Senate. All doubt concerning the constitutionality of this act has been recently removed by the decision of the United States Supreme Court in the case of Meyers *vs.* United States, December, 1926. At the time, it was severely criticized, but the Supreme Court, still under the shadow of its criticism at the period of the Dred Scott case of ten years before, and evidently cowed into extreme reticence by the high-handed and ruthless attitude of the Vindictives in Congress, was but a broken reed upon which any one might attempt to lean. It is said, and probably with truth, that Edwin M. Stanton was the instigator of this act, and this sinister conspirator now had developed as the secret enemy of Johnson in his own cabinet, and the direct representative of the Vindictives. The unconstitutionality of an attempt to take the control of the military forces of the country out of the hands of the President was of little influence to restrain the radicals when they placed this authority in the hands of such an undoubted friend as the secretary of war, and of a potential friend, because active political candidate for the Presidency, General U. S. Grant, the commander of the army. Meanwhile, Congress adjourned its special session on July 19, 1867, after passing still another supplementary act on reconstruction, increasing the power of the military, and drafted by the scheming and astute Stanton.

Of course, the leaders of Congress desired to take away from Johnson as much power as possible, in the hope that they thus could prevent his carrying out any of his policies during the time when Congress was not in session. Johnson, on the other hand, although he vetoed or protested against the radical program of legislation, was careful to carry it out after it became the law of the land, and in this way he prevented his enemies from taking any action to remove him from office as they had threatened. It is known that the Judiciary Committee of the House of Representatives were hunting for grounds of impeachment as early as January, 1867.

Johnson evidently felt that Congress now had gone too far, or the provocation became too great for his irascible nature longer to bear. On August 5 his first blow in retaliation fell upon Stanton, whom he naturally desired to get rid of, for in spite of that gentleman's plausible excuses, there were grounds for wide suspicion that he was closely in league with Johnson's opponents in the radical camp. Stanton's apologists explain that Stanton felt it his conscientious duty to remain in the cabinet and play this *rôle* of double-dealing, in order to save the country from destruction at the hands of Johnson, Seward, Welles, and the others of the old Lincoln Republicans who supported the President at this time. This excuse is hardly sufficient, and Stanton's checkered career offers too many points for criticism to convince the judicially minded that this case of double-dealing is justified, when that gentleman had probably been guilty of the same practice on many other occasions.[18] However that may be, on August 5, 1867, Johnson requested Stanton's resignation from the office of secretary of war. Stanton refused, and Johnson by order suspended him and appointed Grant secretary of war *ad interim.*

Congress met in November. George S. Boutwell of Massachusetts, now coming to the front as one of the radical leaders, moved the impeachment of the President. But he evidently was too hasty, or there still remained in a majority of the representatives a sense of decency and conservatism. The House defeated this motion on December 7 by a vote of 108 to 57. Among those who voted in the negative were N. P. Banks, John A. Bingham, James G. Blaine, James A. Garfield, Henry L. Dawes, and Elihu B. Washburne. On December 12 Johnson sent to the Senate a message giving his reasons for removing Stanton. With keen sarcasm and straight hitting he characterized the action of Stanton as follows: "Mr. Stanton holds the position unwillingly. He continues in office only under a sense of high public duty. He is ready to leave when it is safe to leave, and as the danger he apprehends from his removal then will not exist when Congress is here, he is constrained to remain during the interim. . . . He says, in effect, that while Congress is away he must remain, but that when Congress is here he can go. In other words, he has lost confidence in the President. He is unwilling to

[18] See Dewitt, *passim,* but especially 592–6.

leave the War Department in his [the President's] hands or in the hands of anyone the President may appoint or designate to perform its duties. If he resigns, the President may appoint a Secretary of War that Mr. Stanton does not approve: therefore he will not resign. But when Congress is in session the President cannot appoint a Secretary of War which the Senate does not approve, consequently when Congress meets Mr. Stanton is ready to resign." He added, when discussing the constitutionality of this act in the same message, these damning words with regard to Stanton, and showed his (Stanton's) duplicity beyond any contradiction, either at that time or since. It should be remembered that this was included in a formal message of the President to Congress. "It was a grave question of constitutional law, in which I would, of course, rely most upon the opinion of the Attorney General and Mr. Stanton, who had once been Attorney General [in Buchanan's cabinet]. Every member of my cabinet advised me that the proposed law was unconstitutional. All spoke without doubt or reservation, but Mr. Stanton's condemnation of the law was the most elaborate and emphatic. He referred to the constitutional provisions, the debates in Congress, especially to the speech of Mr. Buchanan when a Senator, to the decisions of the Supreme Court, and to the usage from the beginning of the government through every successive administration, all concurring to establish the right of removal as vested by the Constitution in the President. To all these he added the weight of his own deliberate judgment, and advised me that it was my duty to defend the power of the President from usurpation and to veto the law."[19]

Strange as it may be to relate, but a fact throwing a flood of light on the whole policy of the radicals, on January 13, 1868, the Senate refused to concur in the suspension of Stanton and, in spite of his sanctimonious expressions of patriotic duty during the absence of Congress only, that gentleman resumed his office as secretary of war. Grant gave

[19] Richardson, "Messages and Papers," VI, 585, 587.

up at once, in spite of the fact that Johnson claimed, and with the support of others in a position, to know that Grant had let Johnson understand that he would stand by him and refuse to relinquish his office as secretary of war even if Congress should decline to concur in the suspension of Stanton, so that a test case might be made of it. Johnson charged Grant with cowardice and desertion, and never forgave him. It is probable that Grant took refuge in a possible misunderstanding of words and was only too anxious to get out of the controversy. The Republican nomination for President was only a few months off and looked very tempting.

Johnson was nothing if not courageous, and on February 21 he ordered Stanton to leave office, and appointed General Lorenzo Thomas *ad interim*. Stanton refused to leave, and there were now two men claiming to be secretary of war. Whether this was good politics on the part of Johnson is doubtful. He had only a little more than a year to serve as President, and had he merely with dignity acquiesced in the action of Stanton and the radicals, it is possible a wave of sympathy might have swept over the people, who were mystified and wondering what this quarrel was all about. The radicals were quick to say it was a contest to preserve the Union from a more sinister and secretive method of destruction at the hands of Johnson and the ex-Confederates. Johnson's defiance of them played right into their hands, and also gave opportunity for the impeachment charges his enemies were seeking.

On February 24, 1868, the House of Representatives passed a resolution that the President be impeached of high crimes and misdemeanors in office. This may seem monstrous politics to-day, but in those times of excitement the move was supported by some of the very ablest and best men in public life, and any judgment can only be given in the light of this fact. The House selected seven managers to conduct the case for the prosecution—John A. Bingham, George S. Boutwell, Benjamin F. Butler, John A. Logan, Thaddeus Stevens, Thomas Williams, and James F. Wilson. The Senate

TICKET OF ADMISSION TO THE IMPEACHMENT TRIAL
OF PRESIDENT JOHNSON

organized as a trial court on March 5, with Chief Justice Chase presiding, and the trial began on March 13. Johnson had as defending counsel ex-Judge Benjamin R. Curtis, William M. Evarts, T. A. R. Nelson, and W. S. Groesbeck. It soon was found that even under the Tenure of Office Act there was a possibility that Johnson was legally justified in removing Stanton, for the act declared that every officer whose appointment required the consent of the Senate should be entitled to hold his office until his successor should be duly appointed; but there was a provision which limited the tenure of cabinet officials to "the term of the President by whom they may have been appointed and for one month thereafter." Stanton had been appointed by Lincoln in 1862.

It soon developed that the real attack on Johnson was based upon grounds of general political expediency. "Ben" Butler, with characteristic effrontery, told the Senate in his argument, "as a constitutional tribunal solely, you are bound by no law, either statute or common, which may limit your constitutional prerogative. . . . You are a law unto yourselves, bound only by the natural principles of equity and justice, and that *salus populi suprema lex*." This is ample illustration to what depths this low politician was willing to descend. The trial ended on May 26, the first test vote having come on May 16. Johnson was acquitted by the margin of a single vote, 35 voting guilty, 19 voting not guilty, thus lacking the two thirds majority. There were only twelve Democrats in the Senate, and it soon was known that they would support Johnson. Of course, he was doomed unless seven of the Republicans should refuse to follow the radicals and vote for acquittal. It is a cause for lasting satisfaction both to Americans in general and to the Republican party in particular, then worst led of any time in its long history, that these seven men were found. And it was understood that one or two others were willing, if necessary, to break from their party and vote for acquittal. The radical leaders early let it be known that any Republican doing this would absolutely end his political career, and it is a shame upon their memories that they "made good." These seven Republicans, who overlooked all questions of personal profit and remained true to their convictions no matter what the sacrifice, were Fessenden of Maine, Fowler of Tennessee, Grimes of Iowa, Henderson of Missouri, Ross of Kansas, Trumbull of Illinois, and Van Winkle of West Virginia. Although their political careers practically ended from this time, yet they deserve to be held in high honor by Republicans of this day, for they remained true to the traditions of their party as led by Abraham Lincoln, and showed themselves above fear and above reproach.

Dewitt makes this caustic and true comment upon the whole trial: "In truth the entire impeachment trial was, in effect, as much a convention of the Republican party to put Andrew Johnson out, as the assembly to meet in Chicago was a convention of the Republican party to put General Grant in. Indeed, but few of the majority of senators thought it obligatory to hold themselves aloof from discussing the merits of the case out of court."[20] It will be interesting to note how the rank and file of Republicans, at first carried away by the vociferous cries of the radicals that the beloved Union was in danger and disgusted by the rough and even coarse speeches and actions of Johnson, were strong in their support of these proceedings. But soon they began to doubt the wisdom and even the fairness. The unsavory news from the South also disquieted them. At last, by a gradual process of change, they more and more returned to the plans and counsels of the dead Lincoln, and the Republican party gradually sloughed off many of its old leaders and came to new life and promise under such men as Rutherford B. Hayes, James A. Garfield, and a newer generation that arose during the quarter century after the close of hostilities. The radicals, of course, would not give up without a struggle, and it required the experience of the graft and disgrace of the administration of the honest but dull Grant to awaken the people to the real condition of things, although this was delayed by the weak

[20] "Impeachment and Trial," 517.

and inept policy of the Democratic party, still bearing the stigma of disloyalty to the Union. Had Douglas lived, a man concerning whose loyalty to the Union there could have been no shadow of doubt, he might have reorganized the Democrats into a vital party of opposition. His death possibly is second in effect only to that of Lincoln, in causing the legal and political chaos into which the affairs of the country fell for the decade following the close of the Civil War.

Stanton immediately left office when the result of the impeachment proceedings became known, and Johnson appointed in his place General John M. Schofield of the regular army, a man of ability and the highest integrity. The Senate confirmed the nomination, and for the remainder of Johnson's administration there was a sort of armed neutrality between the White House and the halls of Congress. During all this period the President's cabinet, and the other Republican officials in charge of governmental affairs, were a very able set of men. The administration thus was conducted with great efficiency, in spite of the rather hectic aspect of national politics and the crisis in the relations between the executive and legislative departments. The army and navy were rapidly disbanded to a peace footing and the people of the North and West enjoyed a fair degree of prosperity.

Johnson returned to private life on the fourth of March, 1869, a defeated and disappointed man. He was honest but incompetent for the office under such trying circumstances. Of one thing we may be sure: he was, with the exception of Andrew Jackson, probably the best hater that ever lived in the White House. He emerged for a short time in the year 1875 as senator from Tennessee. He made a vitriolic attack upon the floor of Congress upon Grant, then President, and soon after went home to die—satisfied.[21]

[21] A good illustration of Johnson's utter lack of political ability is found in the fact that on January 17, 1867, he sent a telegram to Lewis E. Parsons, ex-provisional governor of Alabama, in which in guarded words he practically advised the state of Alabama against supporting the ratification of the Fourteenth Amendment. (See E. McPherson, "History of the Period of Reconstruction," 352, note.)

Chapter IX

THE ADMINISTRATION OF GRANT

THE Democratic party gained a number of victories in the northern states in the fall elections of 1867, so that the enormous Republican majorities of 1866 seemed threatened in the Presidential campaign of 1868. New York and Pennsylvania were carried by the Democrats, and Ohio was saved by the Republicans by only about 3000 majority. That state also defeated a negro-suffrage amendment by 50,000, and in addition a like enfranchising measure was defeated in Michigan, Minnesota, and Kansas. The Republican leaders felt that they needed a popular candidate who might sweep all before him; and, fortunately for them, they had such a man in General Grant, at this time probably the most popular man in the North and West.

Ulysses Simpson Grant had been a Democrat before the war and, as he himself says,[1] he voted for Buchanan in 1856; and only the lack of a legal residence in 1860 prevented his voting for Douglas. At first the radicals feared his party orthodoxy and leaned toward Chase for the nomination, but Grant's bitter quarrel with Johnson threw him into the radical camp and he came out a full-fledged Republican—and thereby made sure of the nomination. This is not to say that Grant was merely a time-server. He was absolutely honest and sincere, but a perfect child when it came to political finesse—as the country later learned to its cost. The radicals also had the added consolation of knowing that they had "reconstructed" seven states and "readmitted" them to the Union, with the

[1] "Personal Memoirs," I, 215-6.

expectation that their electoral votes would all go to the Republican candidate. This was especially guaranteed by extensive disfranchisement of the whites in Alabama, Arkansas, and Louisiana, and the enfranchised blacks were being trained in the proper way of voting the Republican ticket. It also was very natural that the freedmen should do this, for they rightly appreciated the fact that they owed the ballot alone to the work of the radical Republicans in Congress. Nebraska had been admitted to the Union in 1867 over the veto of Johnson, and its three votes were considered safe for the Republican ticket.

Various local state and district conventions early began to instruct or declare for Grant, so that the coming national convention would be merely a ratification of the popular choice for the nomination. This body met in Crosby's Opera House, Chicago, on Wednesday, May 20, and completed its work in two days. It was called to order by Marcus L. Ward of New Jersey, the chairman of the Republican National Committee. Bishop Matthew Simpson of the Methodist Episcopal Church offered prayer. Carl Schurz, now a resident of Missouri, was unanimously chosen temporary chairman and in his address urged that they "fearlessly acknowledge that the career of the Republican party will not be ended till the great trusts proclaimed in the Declaration of Independence, in the fullest meaning of the term, have become a living reality on every inch of American soil." The Committee on Permanent Organization had some controversy, General Daniel E. Sickles of New York, who lost a leg as well as a military reputation at Gettysburg, being the choice of many of its members. One of them urged that it "would arouse great enthusiasm in the convention when General Sickles, if chosen, came forward with only one leg and on crutches."[2] Finally, the choice fell upon General Joseph R. Hawley of Connecticut for permanent president, and he aroused great enthusiasm when, in his speech, he stated that "for every dollar of the national debt the blood of a soldier is pledged. Every bond, in letter and spirit, must be sacred as a soldier's grave." This was of course a challenge to the soft

[2] J. Tweedy, "Republican National Conventions," 88–9.

money, repudiation sentiment now becoming prominent in the counsels of the Democratic party.

On the morning of the second day the platform was reported and adopted with amendments. It was rather conservative and very sound in its economic principles. Fortunately, platforms were not at that time of the inordinate length and stuffy sameness of platitudes as those of the different parties to-day, and the provisions of 1868 can easily be summarized. Of course, the convention "congratulated the country on the assured success of the reconstruction policy of Congress" and sententiously stated that "the guarantee by Congress of equal suffrage to all loyal men at the South [meaning negroes] was demanded by every consideration of public safety, of gratitude, and of justice, and must be maintained; while the question of suffrage in all the loyal states properly belongs to the people of those states." There followed an admirable condemnation of "all forms of repudiation as a national crime" and declared for "the payment of the public indebtedness in the uttermost good faith to all creditors at home and abroad not only according to the letter, but in the spirit of the laws under which it was contracted." This was a decided and admirable stand for sound finance in the face of the "greenback" and "soft money" craze now affecting the Democratic party, and destined to do so for the next thirty or more years. Honor should be given the Republican leaders of that day, no matter what other mistakes they may have made in this time of stress and strain during the aftermath of a colossal civil war, for standing for honest business principles in national finance and governmental policy.

According to Stanwood,[3] the hot-heads among the radical members of the convention desired to express in the platform special condemnation of the seven Republican senators who had prevented the conviction of Johnson at the time of the impeachment. Most fortunately, saner counsels prevailed and the convention was content to state that those who voted for his conviction were in the right. They "took it out" on Johnson, however, in no uncertain terms, saying that "the corruptions

[3] "History of the Presidency," 318.

which have been so shamefully nursed and fostered by Andrew Johnson call loudly for radical reform." This was mere partizan hatred, and we now know that there was little or no cause for such charges, Johnson himself being thoroughly honest and sincere, although so often sadly mistaken. Not content with the above statement, the charge was amplified in a second and long plank, including among many things the assertions that Johnson had "acted treacherously to the people who elected him and the cause he was pledged to support," had "perverted the public patronage into an engine of wholesale corruption," and had been "justly impeached for high crimes and misdemeanors, and properly pronounced guilty thereof by the vote of thirty-five senators." It did not seem to enter the minds of the delegates that such a political party act of attainder did not hurt Johnson, but in its violation of the spirit at least of the constitutional principles of the United States it merely would go down to future generations as a condemnation on the heads of the more ruthless radical leaders who so misled their party. It is sometimes hard to be partizan and consistent at the same time!

Some attention was paid to foreign affairs in the sound statement of American policy, that "the doctrine of Great Britain and other European powers that because a man is once a subject he is always so, must be resisted at every hazard by the United States as a relic of feudal times, not authorized by the laws of nations, and at war with our national honor and independence." Two amendments were added in the form of additional planks offered by Carl Schurz declaring in substance that "foreign immigration . . . should be fostered and encouraged by liberal and just policy," and that "this convention declares itself in sympathy with all oppressed peoples struggling for their rights." A halting gesture of conciliation was held out to the South in the words: "We favor the removal of the disqualifications and restrictions imposed upon the late rebels in the same measure as the spirit of disloyalty will die out, and as may be consistent with the safety of the loyal people."

This was perhaps a belated recognition of the fact that the convention had adopted the name of National Union Republican party, thus showing its political succession in continuity from the Republicans of 1856 and 1860, and the Union men of the convention of 1864.

When the proper time had arrived, General John A. Logan took the floor and nominated Grant in the following neat little speech: "In the name of the loyal citizens, soldiers and sailors of this great republic of the United States of America; in the name of loyalty, of liberty, of humanity, of justice; in the name of the National Union Republican party; I nominate, as candidate for the chief magistracy of this nation, Ulysses S. Grant." When the enthusiasm had died down, and the roll of states had been called, General Hawley made this announcement: "Gentlemen of the convention, you have six hundred and fifty votes. You have given six hundred and fifty votes for Ulysses S. Grant."

The usual long-continued cheering followed, while a large full-length picture of Grant, painted on canvas, and containing the words "Match him," was lowered at the rear of the platform. A white dove was let loose and flew about the hall. Then a song was sung by "Chaplain" Lozier, "Chaplain" McCabe, and Major H. G. Lombard. It was written for the occasion by George F. Root and was entitled "We'll fight it out here on the old Union line." It was little better than doggerel, and is not worth repeating, but almost worthy of a Homer if compared with the senseless "jazz" piffle of to-day.

For some time there had been active popular discussion throughout the country of a person who should accompany, as candidate for Vice-President, the foreordained nomination of Grant. When the convention turned its attention to this office, there was a pronounced feeling that after the experience with Johnson it was necessary to choose a candidate who, in case of succession, would be reliable for party purposes—or who, in modern political parlance, would "stand hitched." A large number of names was presented, the most prominent being Benjamin F. Wade of Ohio, Reuben E. Fenton of New

York, Henry Wilson of Massachusetts, Schuyler Colfax of Indiana, Andrew G. Curtin of Pennsylvania, Hannibal Hamlin of Maine, James Speed of Kentucky, James Harlan of Iowa, and John A. J. Creswell of Maryland. Wade led at first, but on the fifth ballot Schuyler Colfax received a majority, and the nomination then was promptly made unanimous. A new National Committee was announced, with William Claflin of Massachusets as chairman. The convention then adjourned.

Grant issued his letter of acceptance on May 29, and in clear and dignified words stated his indorsement of the platform and his intention, if elected, to "administer all the laws in good faith, with economy, and with the view of giving peace, quiet and protection everywhere." He promised to follow "the will of the people" as new political issues might arise, and closed with this heartening and admirable paragraph: "Peace and universal prosperity—its sequence—with economy of administration, will lighten the burden of taxation, while it constantly reduces the national debt. Let us have peace."

Schuyler Colfax was one of the genial and popular men of his time. Of undoubted ability, he had been in Congress for thirteen years and now was serving his third term as speaker of the House of Representatives. Born in New York city in 1823, he was just forty-five years of age. Grant was but forty-six, so the Republicans, by nominating two comparatively young men, showed they were taking a new start and their party thus was preparing to change from a mere organization opposed to the extension of slavery, to one filled with a consciousness of the mission to strengthen and perpetuate in times of peace a strong national government, based upon the idea of a real national unity. This was good ground for successful political coöperation, especially when that unity meant sound finance, sound business, and vigorous economic and social expansion.

The Democratic party held its convention at Tammany Hall (of all places!) on July 4, and lasted for about a week. At once there appeared the strength of George H. Pendleton of Ohio, who had been the Vice-Presidential candidate with

McClellan four years before, and on account of his refinement was known as "Gentleman George." He now, however, had originated or taken up what was known as the "Ohio idea," against which the Republicans had launched their declarations in favor of sound money and no repudiation. Pendleton's plan was to pay the national bonds in greenbacks, or legal tender, then much depreciated, the resulting loss to the moneyed interests and resulting inflation through the issue of more notes being especially (as always) pleasing to the debtor class, then large in the Northwest of that day. If the debt were paid or refunded in gold, said Pendleton, then the Eastern capitalists would be favored at the expense of the taxpayers, forgetting that these same Easterners also paid the majority of the taxes. The same heresy is rather well known at the later time of McNary-Haugen bills and other legislative and political monstrosities. Pendleton also was shrewd enough to adopt the demagogic cry: "The same currency for the bondholder and the plowholder."

Pendleton's followers wrote the Democratic platform, in spite of the opposition of delegates from the more conservative East. It declared for the payment of the United States bonds in "lawful money," meaning depreciated greenbacks; "one currency for the government and the people, the laborer and the office-holder, the pensioner and the soldier, the producer and the bondholder"; the taxation of government bonds; tariff for revenue; and condemned the reconstruction acts of the Republican Congress. This required only a majority vote, but the two thirds vote for a nomination prevented that honor going to Pendleton. Chase, "lusting for the office of President," as Godkin wrote, had hoped the Democrats might turn to him, and even Andrew Johnson was "willing." The convention struggled for many ballots and then on the twenty-second ballot Ohio suddenly swung to Horatio Seymour, the permanent chairman of the convention. Seymour protested, but there was a stampede and he received all the votes and was nominated. The soft-money crowd had the platform, and the sound-money element the candidate. It is possible that, with a different platform and candidate, the Democrats might have given more trouble to the Republicans to beat them. Many of the old original members of the Republican party, especially the followers of Lincoln, were becoming more and more disgusted with the radical leadership, and the mistaken policies of reconstruction and negro suffrage were showing their sad and tragic results. But Seymour had been at least lukewarm in his support of the Federal Government during the war, and had a decided taint of a "Copperhead." This, added to the Democratic soft-money platform, was too much for these Republicans, and they returned whole-heartedly, for the most part, to their support of Grant and Colfax. Also, the business interests took part in the campaign and used their influence, as might be expected, against the Democratic nominees.

Henry Adams says[4] that "at least four-fifths of the American people . . . united in the election of General Grant to the Presidency, and probably had been more or less affected in their choice by the parallel they felt between Grant and Washington. Nothing could be more obvious. Grant represented order. He was a great soldier, and the soldier always represented order. He might be as partizan as he pleased, but a general who had organized and commanded half a million or a million men in the field, must know how to administer. . . . No doubt the confusion, especially in the old slave states and in the currency, was considerable, but the general disposition was good, and every one had echoed the famous phrase: 'Let us have peace.' "

It was during this campaign that the famous Ku Klux Klan first made itself felt. It comprised the best of the population at the South, at first, who were alarmed by negro suffrage and its effects on the Government, for, as E. L. Godkin said at the time, "Worse instructors for men emerging from slavery and coming for the first time face to face with the problems of free life than the radical agitators who have undertaken the political guidance of the blacks it would be hard to meet with."[5] It is estimated that the order contained over half a million men at

[4] "Education of Henry Adams," 260.
[5] Quoted in Rhodes, "History of the United States," VI, 181.

this time, and its activity was great in scaring off the negroes from the polls. No doubt there was violence on both sides, and the state of feeling in the North, uninformed as to the true status of affairs in the South, entirely ignorant of real conditions, offered good material for the demagogic exhortations of the radicals and professional office-seekers. "Ben" Butler, cheap and demagogic as usual, went over to the greenback crowd, even carrying Thaddeus Stevens with him, but he still remained allied with the Republican party.

When the voting took place in November, Grant was elected, as was expected, but not by the overwhelming majority anticipated. Already there were defections enough from the Republican party of those who did not support the radical plan of reconstruction, to portend trouble in the future. Grant carried twenty-six states and received 214 electoral votes, while Seymour carried eight, with 80 votes. The popular vote was, 3,012,833 for Grant; 2,703,249 for Seymour. Three Southern states, Virginia, Mississippi, and Texas were still "unreconstructed" and took no part in the election. Grant carried North Carolina, South Carolina, Tennessee, Florida, Alabama, and Arkansas; Georgia and Louisiana went for Seymour, in spite of the negro vote. The Ku Klux Klan evidently was effective, and the radicals swore vengeance. Seymour also carried New York, New Jersey, and Oregon by small majorities. It was curious that the vote in New York was 429,883 Republican, and 439,883 Democrat, thus giving Seymour exactly 10,000 majority. At this time the Tammany Tweed ring was in complete control of New York city, and common report had it that this exact majority was engineered by the Tammany officials in order to save certain election bets which had been made by the "faithful."

It is evident that Grant's personal popularity was the basis of coöperation for the Republicans, for the two sound-money states of New York and New Jersey went for Seymour, by fair or foul means, and Ohio and Indiana, where soft money and greenbacks were most popular at the time, went for Grant.

When the count of the electoral vote took place in Congress

on February 10, 1869, Ben Butler raised a most acrimonious and bitter discussion in fighting the count of the vote of Georgia. When the houses separated for deliberation according to the Twenty-second Joint Rule, the Representatives first decided against Georgia, and the Senate in favor of counting. When they reassembled in joint session Wade, who was presiding over the Senate, announced that on a technical point the objection of the House of Representatives was not in order, and that the result would be announced both with and without the vote of Georgia, since Grant was elected in either case. Ben Butler now objected in most offensive and insolent manner, attempting to browbeat Wade and the Senate into doing as he desired and throw out the vote of Georgia. After order was restored, the vote was announced according to Wade's plan, and it is a satisfaction to know that the contemptible Butler did not carry his point. Stevens had died the year before, and Butler now was aspiring to the radical leadership.

Grant was inaugurated on March 4, 1869. His inaugural address was clear and straightforward in its statement of a policy of sound money and enforcement of all laws without fear or favor. He stated that he felt the responsibilities of his new office, but would "accept them without fear." He added that "Laws are to govern all alike—those opposed as well as those who favor them. I know no method to secure the repeal of bad or obnoxious laws so effective as their stringent execution." He gave great satisfaction to the business and commercial interests, as well as to all citizens who believed in an honest financial policy for the Government, by saying that "to protect the national honor, every dollar of government indebtedness should be paid in gold, unless otherwise expressly stipulated in the contract." Grant thus deserves the thanks of posterity for standing four-square on the subject of national finances, and this should always be borne in mind when an attempt is made to assess the value of his administrations. Finally, he took a strong stand in favor of the ratification of the proposed Fifteenth Amendment to the national Constitution passed by Congress a few days before on February 27, 1869, which would prevent the disfranchisement of any person on account of "race, color or previous condition of servitude." Its practical effect would be to enfranchise the negroes throughout the United States, and it was looked upon with grave misgivings by the more thoughtful people—misgivings which since that time have been proved well founded. The ratification soon was accepted by the necessary number of states, and declared in force on March 30, 1870.

Aside from this, Grant was hardly a successful President. Henry Adams tersely sums up the cause of his many failures by remarking, "Grant avowed from the start a policy of drift; and a policy of drift attaches only barnacles." [6] These barnacles consisted in a horde of grafters, place-hunters, and more or less disreputable demagogues. Grant was thoroughly honest himself, but dull and unimaginative. Selfish politicians stressed to their profit that first rule of political organization, gratitude. Grant was always grateful to his friends, and stood by them through thick and thin, even though the public in general were convinced of their rascality and general worthlessness. For his obtuseness and sublime indifference to public opinion he must take the blame, for the responsibility of office was his.

Grant's cabinet appointments caused him much difficulty, and public restlessness from the beginning. Three final appointments were first class in every particular, those of Hamilton Fish as secretary of state, a man of unusual ability and, as it proved, success in that office; Jacob D. Cox of Ohio as secretary of the interior, and Judge E. Rockwood Hoar of Massachusetts as attorney-general. Grant now did exactly what Harding and Coolidge have done forty-five years later and first chose a big business man for secretary of the treasury. This was the late Alexander T. Stewart of New York, a successful merchant of that city and reputed one of the richest men in the country. This appointment aroused a great outcry, and after-events in Grant's administration have caused later students of the period to accept the complaints as valid; but there

[6] "Education of Henry Adams," 267.

is no reason to believe otherwise than that Mr. Stewart would have made a head of the Treasury Department comparable to that of the able and successful Mr. Mellon. The appointment was promptly confirmed by the Senate, but within two or three days thereafter it was discovered that Mr. Stewart was ineligible, due to the fact that the law of 1789 which established the Treasury Department provided that no one appointed secretary should be "directly or indirectly concerned or interested in carrying on the business of trade or commerce." Grant desired this law modified, but Sumner objected, and finally, to save any further difficulty, George S. Boutwell of Massachusetts was appointed to the office. He was honest, sincere, but with no especial experience to qualify him for the position and its responsibilities. He gave an honest but undistinguished administration of the office.

The appointment as secretary of war of General John A. Rawlins, Grant's former chief of staff and continually his most intimate friend and adviser, had a far greater significance than has usually been appreciated. This is brought out and much of Grant's strange and inconsistent career explained by a very important book entitled the "Life of John A. Rawlins," by the late General James Harrison Wilson, published in 1916. In this work it is convincingly shown that in the years of Grant's career, from the beginning of the Civil War until his assumption of the Presidency, Rawlins was the power behind the throne—a man whom Grant trusted absolutely, and whose sound good judgment and keen insight into men and events was the balancing and even inspiring force in the more prominent leader's life. Rawlins now was in the last stages of tuberculosis, and death removed him six months later, in September, 1869. Rawlins was succeeded by William W. Belknap of Iowa, who later was compelled to resign under charges of official corruption. This was the turning point in Grant's career. Instead of Rawlins' sound judgment, unselfish devotion, and driving influence came other and less worthy advisers and friends. They knew what they wanted, and how to get it—from Grant or otherwise. They well-nigh wrecked his administration and carried it finally to the depths of disgrace and even degradation.

Adolph E. Borie of Pennsylvania was named secretary of the navy. Rhodes tartly says that his "only distinction was that of being a rich man of Philadelphia and a personal friend of Grant's. . . . Only unbounded confidence in the President enabled the country to swallow this appointment." John A. J. Creswell of Maryland was appointed postmaster-general. He was a man of fair ability, rather extreme in his support of the radical wing of the Republican party, and his administration of the office was without special incident, when considered in connection with the rather hectic temperature of the times.

Grant soon began to make political mistakes and his difficulties rapidly thickened. Under the influence of Butler and his associates he undertook the armed support of the Republican party and its more or less legal governments in the Southern states, under the guise of enforcing the Fourteenth Amendment. He totally failed to understand conditions in the ex-Confederate states, and by his support made possible the continuance of "Carpet-Bag" and "Scalawag" domination. He next aroused the opposition of Senator Sumner of Massachusetts by his attempt to force through his pet policy of the annexation of San Domingo, and the controversy soon degenerated into a bitter personal quarrel, hardly dignified when the high official rank of the two contestants is remembered.

During the year 1870 Grant lost two of his ablest and best cabinet members, largely on account of the bitter opposition of the spoilsmen and grafters who were the curse of his administration. Attorney-General Hoar was removed in the attempt to thereby purchase favorable votes for the San Domingo annexation. Jacob D. Cox, secretary of the interior, ran foul of the grafters by opposing schemes to obtain mining lands in the West, and by undertaking to introduce civil-service reform in the administration of his department. He also began to disturb the complacency of the corrupt Indian agents, who were a very stench in the nostrils of decent people. In order to test his sup-

[1] "History of the United States," VI, 238.

Photograph by Brown Brothers

REPUBLICAN CONVENTION AT PHILADELPHIA, 1872, AT WHICH GRANT WAS NOMINATED FOR PRESIDENT

port by Grant and the administration, as against this opposition, Cox offered his resignation and Grant promptly accepted it. This was practically an invitation to the spoilsmen to do their worst and they proceeded to accept it.

A bill was passed by Congress in 1871 empowering the President to make rules for the selection of civil servants. Grant at first seemed favorable, and appointed George William Curtis as chairman of the advisory commission. Of course, the spoilsmen were rampant against the law, and Grant soon went over entirely to their side and made little or no attempt to enforce it. Curtis resigned in disgust. More sinister still was the fact that Jay Gould and James Fiske, Jr., the latter a vain and showy financial adventurer, used Grant's influence to cause the United States Treasury to withhold gold from the market at the time that they were bidding it up in an attempt to "corner" the supply. Grant's brother-in-law, Abel Rathbone Corbin, was the more or less conscious tool for their manipulation, and the result was the celebrated panic of "Black Friday" in New York city on September 24, 1869, in which many speculators were ruined as well as many other more deserving people.

General George Gordon Meade, in a private letter to a friend while associated with Grant in the campaign before Richmond, had made a shrewd and sound judgment of the man. Writing to Henry A. Cram of New York, under date of "Headquarters of the Army of the Potomac, November 20, 1864,"[8] Meade said: "Grant is not a mighty genius, but he is a good soldier, of great force of character, honest and upright, of pure purposes, I think, without political aspirations, certainly not influenced by them. His prominent quality is unflinching tenacity of purpose, which blinds him to opposition and obstacles—certainly a great quality in a commander, when controlled by judgment, but a dangerous one otherwise. Grant is not without his faults and weaknesses. Among these is a want of sensibility, and almost too confident and sanguine disposition, and particularly a simple and guileless disposition, which is apt to put him, unknown to himself, under the influ-

[8] "Life and Letters of General G. G. Meade," II, 246.

ence of those who should not influence him, and desire to do so only for their own purposes."

Grant's lack of sensibility was shown at this later time in his refusal to hear the complaints and charges of corruption and graft when brought to his attention by the best elements in the Republican party; by his unblushing acceptance of handsome gifts not only of cigars, in the use of which he was inveterate, but even of horses and jewelry, and even gifts from those individuals against whom frequent charges of questionable practices were continually being brought. He showed his obstinacy in his attempt to control elections and the administration of the governments of the Southern states, as already mentioned, and this against the open protests of many of the best people in the North, who were more and more becoming aware of what really was taking place in the South in spite of the radical attempts to gloss it over and hush it up.

Congress participated in the same enforcement policy, passing the Enforcement Act of May 31, 1870, which revived the Civil Rights Act of 1866 and attempted to enforce the Fourteenth and Fifteenth Amendments. It extended the jurisdiction of the United States courts, since the Southern whites prevented the state courts from acting to protect the freedmen. Following this came the congressional elections in the fall of 1870, which showed decided Democratic gains. The Republican majority in the next Congress was reduced from 97 to 35, and the states of North Carolina and Alabama went under Democratic control. The radical Republicans met these reverses by passing on February 28, 1871, during the "lame duck" session of the old Congress (the Forty-first), an act which instituted a rigorous system of Federal supervision over the elections of congressmen.

The Forty-second Congress, whose session began in March, 1871, passed, upon Grant's recommendation, the Ku Klux Act of April 20, 1871, which strengthened the hands of the national judiciary for handling any election conspiracy and allowed the President to suspend the writ of *habeas corpus* and to use military forces to suppress any rioting or other unlawful acts of violence. Although the joint select committee of the two houses of Congress which was appointed to investigate the insurrectionary states later made a lengthy and exhaustive report, which showed that the Ku Klux Klan was only a local and sporadic movement by now, yet Grant enforced the law with extreme rigor in nine counties of South Carolina by virtue of a proclamation of October 17, 1871.[6] All of this policy was bitterly opposed by the more conservative Republicans as well as the Democrats, and led directly to the revolt in the Republican party known as the "Liberal Republican" movement, its nomination of Horace Greeley in 1872 for the Presidency, and the indorsement of the nomination by the Democrats.

Meanwhile, and much to the credit of Grant and his administration, Hamilton Fish had succeeded in bringing to a close our difficulties and controversies with Great Britain due to her unfriendly governmental acts during the Civil War and her share in the responsibility for the depredations committed by the *Alabama* and other Confederate vessels. The treaty of Washington was negotiated, and signed on May 8, 1871, and provided for the Geneva arbitration tribunal and the settlement of the Northwest boundary and fishery disputes. This removed the most dangerous causes of friction between the two countries and has done much to cement the natural friendship and bonds of relationship which exist between the two peoples.

But as Grant's administration grew toward a close, it was seen that the great popular expectations with which he had begun his Presidential service had been disappointed. The Ku Klux Act showed the failure of the radical policy of Southern reconstruction, for, with well-nigh unlimited political power for five years, they had been unable to pacify the South and bring back normal life, much less any friendly or coöperative relations between the white and negro races. Added to this was the already mentioned attempt to annex San Domingo, which had alienated such strong old-line Republicans as Sumner and Greeley. Then there was the final scandal of the manipulation

[6] Richardson, "Messages and Papers," VII, 136–8.

of political offices and appointments for private and partizan purposes to an extent of shameful recklessness never known before. It may be said that the standard of public and official life in national affairs had reached the depth of its greatest shame. Revolt was the inevitable result.

The beginning of serious opposition began in the state of Missouri, where that honest and intrepid individualist, Carl Schurz, now United States senator from the state, led a movement of "Liberal Republicans" who desired reform, especially in the policy of the Government toward the South. These Republicans nominated B. Gratz Brown for governor and elected him with Democratic aid. The movement rapidly spread to other states, and kept pace with the increasing dissatisfaction with the administration at Washington. It was brought to a head by a convention at Jefferson City, Missouri, on January 24, 1872, at which most of the counties of the state were represented. After definitely assuming the name of Liberal Republican, it formally invited all Republicans throughout the country who were dissatisfied with the conduct of national affairs and desired a reform of them, to meet in a national convention at Cincinnati on the first Wednesday in the following May, 1872. A number of Republicans of prominence and influence gave their adhesion to the movement, and for a time it looked as though the defeat of Grant was both possible and probable. Such men as Charles Francis Adams, Edward Atkinson, Samuel Bowles, William Cullen Bryant, Jacob D. Cox, Andrew G. Curtin, Murat Halstead, Horace Greeley, Judge Stanley Matthews, Joseph Pulitzer, Senator Reuben E. Fenton (of New York), Lyman Trumbull, Whitelaw Reid, and Austin Blair (of Michigan) gave their approval, and some of the strongest and ablest of the daily papers gave steady support. Among the many names mentioned for the Presidential nomination by the new wing of the Republican party the most outstanding were Charles Francis Adams and Lyman Trumbull, both men of undoubted ability and likely to attract the loyalty and win the confidence of thoughtful people. It early was seen that the tariff would be the most difficult question to handle, as there were both free trade and high protection elements in the Liberal Republican ranks.

The Liberal Republican convention met at Cincinnati on May 1, 1872, in pursuance of the call of the Jefferson City convention. It was more of a mass meeting than a convention, in this respect corresponding to the Philadelphia convention of 1856, but it lacked the unifying force of the great anti-slavery crusade which made the latter the beginning of a new political organization. Judge Stanley Matthews was made temporary chairman and Carl Schurz was chosen permanent president. Rhodes thinks this was the great and outstanding tactical mistake, as there was left no one person who could dominate the convention from the floor, and parliamentary leadership soon was seen to be sadly lacking.

There was hope that the Democrats would indorse the candidate, hence everything was done to promote unity and avoid disputes. This tendency was carried too far, resulting in a silly plank in the platform that left the tariff question "to the people in their congressional districts and to the decisions of Congress thereon, wholly free from executive interference or dictation." Aside from this the platform was a sound, able and clear-cut demand for reform. A bitter attack was made upon Grant for his shortcomings, and it opposed any reopening of the questions settled by the Thirteenth, Fourteenth, and Fifteenth Amendments; demanded "the immediate and absolute removal of all disabilities imposed on account of the rebellion"; a thorough reform of the civil service; the maintenance of the public credit, and a "speedy return to specie payments."

Horace Greeley was nominated for President on the sixth ballot, and B. Gratz Brown for Vice-President. Stanwood says that "the work of the convention was received by Republicans throughout the country with a shout of derision." [10] The nomination of Greeley made defeat inevitable. Although undoubted in honesty and courage, his erratic, excitable, and unstable nature made him impossible to contemplate as a President of the United States. He was one of the most brilliant polemical

[10] "History of the Presidency," 345.

writers this country ever has known, but he had incurred many enmities thereby, and lack of confidence in his executive ability was the finishing touch. Lord Charnwood, in his brilliant life of Lincoln, describes Greeley as "a vigorous writer whose omniscience was unabated by the variation of his own opinion." It is probable that, had the convention nominated either Trumbull or Charles Francis Adams, especially the latter, Grant might have been defeated. Just before sailing for Europe a few weeks before the convention, Adams had written his disinclination to become the nominee, but practically stated his willingness if the nomination came to him with the wholehearted support of the people. He would have carried great weight with the people, and have been a strong candidate in spite of the openly expressed opposition of many Democrats. This probably was the dominating influence that finally caused the convention to decide against him, and lack of leadership, as mentioned above, caused the movement to drift toward the energetic and spectacular Greeley.

The Democratic convention met in Baltimore on July 9 and in a helpless and halting manner ratified the Liberal Republican candidates and platform. There was opposition, but a feeling seemed to prevail that the leaders already had gone too far in committing themselves to the Liberal Republicans to withdraw at this late date. It seemed as though the stars in their courses were working for Grant, and this child of good political fortune, in spite of his own mistakes and failures, profited by the mistakes of his opponents, and his reëlection hardly was in doubt for a moment after Greeley's nomination. In fact, many of the leaders in the Liberal Republican cause lost all enthusiasm and interest in the campaign, or dropped out of the movement altogether. In spite of this, Greeley entered actively into the campaign and evidently believed he was going to be elected.

The regular or National Union Republican convention met at Philadelphia on June 5, and finished all its business and adjourned on the second day. The sessions were held in the Academy of Music, the largest convention hall in the city, which also was connected with another large building, Horticultural Hall, by means of a passageway, and the latter building was used for committee meetings and other purposes. The Academy was so profusely decorated with American flags and bunting that but little daylight could enter, making necessary its lighting by gas, which made the building hot and the air close.[11]

The convention was called to order by William Claflin of Massachusetts, the chairman of the National Committee. Morton McMichael, a journalist and former mayor of Philadelphia, was made temporary chairman, and made a clever address in which he stated that "the malcontents who recently met at Chicago were without a constituency; the Democrats who are soon to meet at Baltimore will be without a principle. The former, having no motive in common but personal disappointment, attempted a fusion of repelling elements, which has resulted in explosion; the latter, degraded from the high estate they once occupied, propose an abandonment of their identity, which means death. Unlike the first, you are the authentic exponents of a great national organization, based upon principles . . . unlike the last, your object is to preserve, not to destroy." This sentence, though partizan, sums up the strength of the Republican party and the weakness of its opponents.

While waiting for the report of the committee on permanent organization, numerous speeches were made, among others by John A. Logan, by the aged Gerrit Smith, the abolitionist and friend of John Brown; by Senator Oliver P. Morton of Indiana, who was seated while he spoke, due to illness, and by James L. Orr of South Carolina. Three colored delegates from the South followed these speakers and were loudly cheered.

The convention was permanently organized by the choice of Judge Thomas Settle of North Carolina, a Democrat before the war and an ex-Confederate, who had become a Republican in 1865 and was a judge of the state supreme court.

[11] John Tweedy, "History of the Republican National Conventions," 114.

The nomination of Grant then was made, his name being presented by Shelby M. Cullom of Illinois in a brief speech which was received with great enthusiasm. "A scene of the wildest excitement followed this speech. The spacious Academy was crowded with thousands of spectators in every part, and on the stage, in the parquet, and in tier upon tier of galleries, arose deafening, prolonged, tremendous cheers, swelling from pit to dome. A perfect wilderness of hats, caps and handkerchiefs waved to and fro in a surging mass as three times three reverberated from thousands of voices. The band appeared to catch the prevailing enthusiasm and waved their instruments as though they had been flags. Amid cries of 'Music! Music!' they struck up 'Hail to the Chief.' As the majestic stream of music came floating down from the balcony, a life-size equestrian portrait of General Grant came down, as if by magic, filling the entire space of the back scene, and the enthusiasm knew no bounds." [12] The nomination was seconded by Stewart L. Woodford of New York and M. D. Boruck of California and the convention at once began balloting. When this was completed, it was announced that the total number of votes was 752—of which Ulysses S. Grant had received 752.

Renewed cheering followed this announcement, and then the band played a "Grant Campaign Song," the verse of which was sung by a man standing among the instruments, and the chorus by a large number of men. The concluding lines of the latter ran:

> The sons of freedom in their might
>   Have come from hill and plain
> To make the brave Ulysses
>   Our President again.

This was followed by "John Brown's Body," "Rally Round the Flag," "Yankee Doodle," and "The Red, White and Blue." The last song was sung by Lyman B. Church of Montana, who also had sung it at the Wigwam in Chicago at the time of Lincoln's nomination.

The name of Vice-President Schuyler Colfax was pre-

[12] John Tweedy, "History of the Republican National Conventions," 120.

sented for renomination, and also that of Senator Henry Wilson of Massachusetts. On the first ballot the results were—Wilson, 399½; Colfax, 308½; Horace Maynard of Tennessee, 26; Edmund J. Davis of Texas, 16; scattering, 2. The nomination of Wilson then was made unanimous.

Wilson was born in Farmington, New Hampshire, on February 16, 1812. His original name was Jeremiah Jones Colbaith, which he had changed by legislative enactment when he became of age. He was the son of a farm laborer, was apprenticed to a farmer for eleven years from the age of ten, and later worked as a shoemaker in Natick, Massachusetts. During his apprenticeship it is said he received not more than twelve months of schooling, but read more than a thousand books. He was a former anti-slavery Whig, a Free Soiler, and a life-long abolitionist. He had been in the United States Senate since 1855, and had taken an active part in the formation of the Republican party. It has been tartly said of him and his senatorial colleague from Massachusetts, Charles Sumner, that Sumner was all intellect and no emotions, while Wilson was all emotions and no intellect. While grossly exaggerated, this statement has a decided element of truth.

It is matter for wonder at the present day that Colfax failed to receive a renomination. There seems to have been no dissatisfaction with him, he was popular, and had discharged his duties with care and ability. Tweedy says that a year before this, Colfax had written to a friend saying that he had decided not to be a candidate again. This caused doubt to arise in the minds of his friends and injured his chances before the convention.[13] Stanwood gives a somewhat different story.[14] He says that Colfax had in some way given offense to certain newspaper correspondents at Washington and they determined to do everything in their power to prevent his renomination. They were aided in this by the presentation of Wilson's name by the Republicans of Massachusetts, and considering the closeness of the vote in the convention it is probable that these corre-

[13] "History of the Republican National Conventions," 123.
[14] "History of the Presidency," 345.

spondents succeeded in their attempt to get their revenge upon Mr. Colfax. It was, after all, very fortunate that he was not reëlected to the office of Vice-President, for his connection with the Crédit Mobilier scandals, although unknown at this time, would have been a terrible blow to the Grant administrations.

The platform was reported by the committee and adopted by the convention between the balloting for the Presidential and Vice-Presidential candidates. It may be summarized as follows:

The opening plank comprised a *résumé* of the achievements of the Republican party, stating among other things that "it suppressed a gigantic rebellion, emancipated four millions of slaves, decreed the equal citizenship of all, and established universal suffrage. Exhibiting unparalleled magnanimity, it criminally punished no man for political offenses, and warmly welcomed all who proved loyalty by obeying the laws and dealing justly with their neighbors. . . . A uniform national currency has been provided, repudiation frowned down, the national credit sustained under the most extraordinary burdens, and new bonds negotiated at lower rates. . . . Despite annual large reductions of the rates of taxation, the public debt has been reduced during General Grant's presidency at the rate of a hundred millions a year."

The resolutions then went on to advocate the following: "The recent amendments to the national Constitution should be cordially sustained." "Complete liberty and exact equality in the enjoyment of all civil, political, and public rights should be established and effectually maintained throughout the Union by efficient and appropriate state and federal legislation." "Any system of the civil service under which the subordinate positions of the government are considered rewards for mere party zeal is fatally demoralizing, and we therefore favor a reform of the system by laws which shall abolish the evils of patronage and make honesty, efficiency, and fidelity the essential qualifications for public positions, without practically creating a life-tenure of office." After this masterpiece of enigmatic statement a declaration was made "that revenue, except so much as may be derived from a tax upon tobacco and liquors, should be raised by duties upon importations, the details of which should be so adjusted as to aid in securing remunerative wages to labor, and promote the industries, prosperity and growth of the whole country." Another enigmatic statement, which might be interpreted at liberty, was that "the Republican party recognizes the duty of so shaping legislation as to secure full protection and the amplest field for capital, and labor, the creator of capital, the largest opportunities and a just share of the mutual profits of these two great servants of civilization." It is significant that such a subject should be included at this time.

The attacks of the Liberal Republicans were squarely met by the statement that "Congress and the President have only fulfilled an imperative duty in their measures for the suppression of violent and treasonable organizations in certain lately rebellious regions, and for the protection of the ballot-box; and therefore they are entitled to the thanks of the nation." "Repudiation of the public debt, in any form or disguise," was denounced as "a national crime." "The action of Congress in extending amnesty to those lately in rebellion" was also "heartily approved."

The President was indorsed in strong words that stated "the modest patriotism, the earnest purpose, the sound judgment, the practical wisdom, the incorruptible integrity, and the illustrious services of Ulysses S. Grant have commended him to the heart of the American people, and with him at our head we start today upon a new march to victory." A plank was added, after the nomination of Henry Wilson, in which he too was indorsed and commended. Altogether, the platform was sound and clear-cut upon financial matters, and apologetic upon many weaknesses that the discerning and patriotic citizens might at once detect. The convention soon after adjourned, showing that unity and discipline which had been so badly lacking in the gatherings of its opponents.

Tweedy says [15] that when Judge Settle and the committee

[15] "History of the Republican National Conventions," 131–2

appointed by the convention went to Washington to notify Grant of his nomination, they were received by the President in his private parlor at the White House on June 10. Settle, after a few formal words, handed Grant an official letter, informing him of his nomination, which the latter took and, bowing, said, "Well, gentlemen, at present I am not prepared to fully respond to your letter, but will do so soon." After several brief speeches of congratulation had been made by different members of the committee, they withdrew. Later, on the same day, Grant's letter was received by them. It was a commonplace expression of thanks, and promised "the same zeal and devotion to the good of the whole people for the future of my official life as shown in the past."

Politicians in both parties, not to mention the new and ephemeral one, were at first entirely at sea with regard to the extent of disaffection in the Republican party, and the amount of loyalty that the Democrats would show in support of their old and bitter enemy. The campaign soon developed into one of bitter personalities, in which the erratic Greeley offered a fine target for the shafts of his critical opponents. Thomas Nast, in his great caricatures of Greeley in the "Harper's Weekly" cartoons, depicted him with relentless skill, especially featuring his whiskers and his white high hat, which had been accepted by many of his followers as a sort of campaign emblem. In his letter of acceptance of the nomination, dated May 29, Greeley had said: "If elected I shall be the president not of a party, but of the whole people. I accept your nomination in the confident trust that the masses of our countrymen, North and South, are eager to clasp hands across the bloody chasm which has so long divided them, forgetting that they have been enemies in the joyous consciousness that they are, and must henceforth, remain brethren."

This was seized upon by Nast to depict Greeley ("Harper's Weekly," August 3, 1872) shaking hands with a Southern desperado, the foot of the latter upon the prostrate murdered form of a United States soldier. There thus had come into fashion the sad but effective method of political demagoguery known as "waving the bloody shirt," used with such telling effect by radical and other Republican politicians for the next two decades, which consisted in rousing in the North and West the old hatreds of the Civil War as well as the newer reconstruction period. It was based mainly upon passion and unreasoning hatred, but was tragically effective, not only in arousing the patriotic prejudices of the Unionists and other anti-slavery people who had stood by Lincoln and the Federal Government in the trying days of treason and secession, but also the narrow, selfish, and unthinking. So great was the fear of the so-called "Southern brigadiers," that even the best of the people of the North often were fairly swept off their feet. This plan of campaign was especially effective against Greeley, staunch Union man and Republican as he had been, due to his indorsement by the Democrats. A man of such ability and standing as Julius C. Burrows of Michigan used this method in a campaign speech, as follows: "I do not want Greeley for President, because I believe he is politically dishonest; because he is a secessionist. If Horace Greeley should, perchance, be elected President of the United States, I believe that before two years have passed away General Grant will be called to put down another rebellion. The followers of Horace Greeley at the South say the 'lost cause' is not lost, but that it will yet be revived and successful. I do not like the followers of Horace Greeley because they comprise the old rebel-Democratic party. Austin Blair says we must not go about 'rattling the dry bones of soldiers before the people.' What say the fathers, mothers, sisters, and brothers of men who laid down their lives on Southern battlefields? Lyman Trumbull says we must 'stop yelling about the horrors of Andersonville.' What! must the mother whose son, shut up in that horrible pen and reduced to a living skeleton, crawled to the dead line, and, while reaching his bony fingers across it to pick up a crumb of bread, was shot like a dog,—must she forget the horrors of Andersonville?" [16]

[16] Quoted in W. D. Orcutt, "Burrows of Michigan and the Republican Party," I, 142.

The feeling of the average person of thought and common sense was well summed up by James A. Garfield in a private letter at the time, in which he said confidentially: "In my interior view of the case, I would say Grant was not fit to be nominated and Greeley is not fit to be elected." [17]

Garfield was a staunch Republican and a party man of undoubted loyalty, but while unwavering in his support of Grant for these reasons, he could see his shortcomings, and also the added necessity of supporting him due to lack of confidence in the executive ability and intellectual balance of Greeley, no matter how honest and able the latter might be. The Republican managers stressed these defects in Greeley, the dubious character of some of his political supporters, and "played up" the old popularity of Grant the soldier and his rugged personal honesty. Public opinion gradually accepted this basis of political coöperation and turned toward the reëlection of Grant as at worst a necessary evil.

But Greeley did not despair, although the October elections showed Republican victories in Pennsylvania and Ohio, and a legislature of the same party in Indiana, where, due to personal popularity, Thomas A. Hendricks was elected governor by a small majority of 1148. Departing from the usual custom of Presidential candidates, he stumped the country, drawing enormous crowds, and impressing them by his able and statesmanlike speeches, which were of a very high order of excellence. This caused him to increase in hope of success, and Colonel A. K. McClure of "The Philadelphia Times," wrote: "I never saw a happier face than that of Greeley when I met him, as he was . . . entirely confident of success, and in a very kind and facetious way he reminded me that I had underestimated his strength with the people. When opportunity came in conversation I suggested to him, that a man who was elected President by a combination of opposing political interests would have very grave and complicated duties to perform, and that he should especially avoid any cabinet complications."

John Bigelow wrote: "Greeley, I think, is destined to learn

[17] T. C. Smith, "James A. Garfield," I, 495.

the differences between notoriety and popularity, and to discover in the course of this canvass from his own experience that it is possible to have one without the other. He may learn, too, that a man may have popularity of a certain sort without being desired for a president. . . . Greeley is an interesting curiosity, which every one likes to see and to show, and in whom we all feel a certain kind of natural pride, but I do not think any one can seriously believe in his fitness for any administrative position whatever. If they do, they know as little of him as he knows of himself."

Bigelow also voiced the general popular apprehension by writing: "It is not so much Greeley's eccentricities, nor his ill manners, nor his vanity, that I am afraid of, as the circumstances under which the Democratic and Secession parties have been converted to his support. . . . It is certain that the worst rogues in the country have formed in the Greeley procession, for it includes the New York city ring (Tammany), and all the secessionists; and it is difficult to believe that, with or without Greeley's knowledge, the Devil does not bear the Cross."[18]

Of course, Greeley's followers took up the cudgels for their candidate, and bitter personal attacks were made upon Grant. But the result was a foregone conclusion. When the election took place on November 5 it was found that Greeley's defeat was overwhelming. Thirty-seven states now formed the Union, and all states voted, for the first time since 1860. Furthermore, the states also chose Presidential electors by popular vote. Grant carried every Northern and Western state, with 272 electoral votes, while only 66 were to go for Greeley, being those of the six states of Georgia, Kentucky, Maryland, Missouri, Tennessee, and Texas. The popular vote was: Grant and Wilson, 3,597,132; Greeley and Brown, 2,834,125.

The Liberal Republican movement was one of the most honest, sincere, and unselfish movements in our political history. It was ended at this election, but not without an element of tragedy. Greeley, with his sensitive and high-strung nature,

[18] Quoted in Don C. Seitz, "Horace Greeley," 380–81.

was cut to the quick by the campaign of vituperation and ridicule. After nursing his wife, to whom he was tenderly devoted, she died on October 30. After a fortnight of anxiety in her behalf he had said to a friend: "I am a broken old man [he was sixty-one]; I have not slept one hour in twenty-four for a month; if she lasts, poor soul, another week, I shall go before her." Mrs. Greeley's death was followed by the terrible defeat of November 5, which caused all his hopes and ambitions to fall like a house of cards. But on the seventh appeared a card in "The New York Tribune," stating that he resumed the editorship of the paper. His last editorial appeared on the eighth, and about that time he learned of a movement among the stockholders of the "Tribune" to deprive him of his position. The accumulation of sorrows was too great even for his heroic and energetic nature. He broke down, went into brain fever, and his reason left him. He died in a private sanatorium at Pleasantville, New York, on November 29, 1872. "There was an immediate and nation-wide revulsion of feeling. Horace Greeley had done so much for liberty, so much for human welfare, had done it so tirelessly, so unselfishly, and at such sacrifice, that all the land went into mourning over the man it had lately covered with odium. There were no enemies left." [19]

The rigid convention or usage of our Constitution, under which a Presidential elector is morally bound to vote for the nominee of his party, caused an embarrassing situation to arise in the case of the Greeley electors. Their candidate died before the time appointed for them to meet at their respective state capitals and cast their votes. While most of them solved their difficulty by voting for other men, B. Gratz Brown and Thomas A. Hendricks receiving the major support, yet three of them were so bound by their traditions that they actually cast their votes for Greeley, a dead man. It is difficult to imagine a more extreme case of subserviency to precedent. When the votes were counted by Congress on February 12, 1873, the three Greeley votes were thrown out, since the candidate was dead,

[19] D. C. Seitz, "Horace Greeley," 403.

Courtesy of Harper & Brothers

CLASPING HANDS OVER THE BLOODLESS (SAR)C(H)ASM, 1872

A cartoon by Thomas Nast in the Richard Croker days

as also were the votes of Arkansas and Louisiana, due to irregularities in the certification of the returns. Had they been counted, Grant and Wilson would have received 286 votes.

The radicals now were at the height of their power. They had swept the country, and even the Liberal Republican-Democratic platform had accepted the results of the war and the three subsequent constitutional amendments. They had control of both houses of Congress, and it seemed that organized political opposition was at an end. Reconstruction on the basis of negro suffrage had won a victory on the surface, at least, and the Republican party seemed at last to be a national one when viewed from the standpoint of Grant's nation-wide triumph. In the country as a whole it had polled 56 per cent. of the entire vote, the largest proportion cast by the Republicans up to that time.

Grant was inaugurated for his second term on March 4, 1873. His address was a dull and uninspiring statement of his views, without any sign of appreciation of the basis of truth in the charges that had been brought against his administration by many of the best men in the Republican party, irrespective of whether or not they had supported Greeley. No greater proof of his utterly callous and self-satisfied disposition could have been given. He showed that he considered his political triumph as a complete vindication by saying in concluding his address: "Throughout the war, and from my candidacy for my present office in 1868 to the close of the last Presidential campaign, I have been the subject of abuse and slander scarcely ever equaled in political history, which today I feel that I can afford to disregard in view of your verdict, which I gratefully accept as my vindication." [20]

The second administration of Grant was even more unsuccessful than the first. There was much less unity of purpose, and the President was more erratic and uncertain in his direction than ever. Also, the scandals, long deep-seated and existent with ever-growing menace, came to a head with results that were the most disgraceful in our history. The Forty-third

[20] Richardson, "Messages and Papers," VII, 221–3.

Congress probably was abler than the preceding, and even possibly less dishonest and corrupt. It also was aware that its constituencies which it severally represented were more alert and suspicious than before, due to the wholesale charges during the preceding campaign. James G. Blaine was its brilliant speaker, and the notorious but able "Ben" Butler was prominent as a Grant leader upon the floor. Garfield, now coming to the front with greater influence than ever before, was the sign of a coming day of change.

For some time before the inauguration of Grant there had been rumors of a railroad scandal in which prominent Republicans were supposed to be involved. While for a time they had died down as merely a campaign charge, yet they persisted, and finally two investigating committees were appointed, the Poland committee of the House of Representatives and the Wilson committee of the Senate. Blaine, who himself was accused, had asked for an investigation. There rapidly followed disclosures which, under the name of the Crédit Mobilier frauds, shook the National Government to its foundations.

The Crédit Mobilier was a corporation chartered in the state of Pennsylvania in 1863, for construction purposes. It passed into new hands in 1867, its stock was increased, and its stockholders were also those of the new Union Pacific Railroad. By this means all the profits from the contracts for the construction of the railroad were gained by the controlling stockholders of the railroad. In other words, "it meant that a group of men controlling the Union Pacific had found a way of transferring to themselves in the capacity of a construction company a large part of the road's securities and among them large issues of stock." [21] Since the United States Government had made large donations of bonds and public lands in aid of the construction of this great national work of internal improvement, there was danger of congressional or other interference. To obviate this, Oakes Ames, a wealthy member of the House of Representatives who was heavily interested in the Union Pacific Railroad, joined with others in secretly dis-

[21] J. S. Bassett, "History of the United States," 650.

tributing at par a large amount of Crédit Mobilier stock among members of Congress in places "where it would do the most good." This was at much below its true value. In less than a year the dividends soared to about 340 per cent. The investigation showed that many of the most prominent men in various parts of the Government were implicated. Vice-President Colfax was involved, but not impeached, as his term of office soon would expire. His career was wrecked. The Poland committee recommended the expulsion from Congress of Ames and Representative James Brooks of New York. The House changed this to censure, and both men died within three months. The Wilson committee recommended the expulsion of Senator James W. Patterson of New Hampshire. Since he had only five more days of his term of office, no action was taken and he was allowed to go in disgrace. Vice-President Wilson was somewhat involved, but permitted to escape any hostile action, as were many others who were guilty at least of impropriety, if not of downright wrong-doing. The whole scandal caused deep popular distrust and paved the way for Republican downfall in the next congressional elections.

Popular feeling had been further aroused by the action of the Forty-second Congress, which, on the day before the expiration of its term, had voted to itself an increase of pay from $5000 to $7500, making it retroactive, so that each member was to receive $5000 in back pay. This was advocated by Butler and opposed by such men as Garfield. Although the salaries of the President, Vice-President, cabinet officers, and judges of the Supreme Court also were included, and there was no valid objection to a proper increase in the meager remuneration of the public servants, yet the back pay for the congressmen caused an outburst of popular passion, and the "salary grab," as it was called, caused the defeat of many members in the election of 1874. When the new or Forty-third Congress assembled in December, 1873, it promptly repealed the salary increase of congressmen and restored the pay to $5000. The salaries of the President, Vice-President, and justices remained at the advanced figure. Fortunately, they were prevented from being reduced, by constitutional limitation, and remained at the more equitable figure.

In 1874 was disclosed the scandal of the Sanborn contracts, by means of which John D. Sanborn, a henchman of Butler, had procured by contract the right to collect overdue internal revenue claims at a commission of 50 per cent. His profits were shown by congressional investigation to amount to about $213,-000, and it is probable that a large part of this was used for political purposes in Massachusetts. William A. Richardson, who had succeeded Boutwell as secretary of the treasury in 1873, resigned in order to escape a vote of censure by Congress.

A financial panic came in the fall of 1873, when the public was astounded to learn that the prominent and important banking house of Jay Cooke & Company had failed on September 18. Of the highest financial standing, it had become involved by an attempt to finance the Northern Pacific Railroad. This was rapidly followed by other failures, until the financial panic became widespread and most serious in its consequences. The overexpansion of railroad building was one of the main causes. The New York Stock Exchange was closed for eight days, an event unprecedented in its history, and following the panic came real economic depression and suffering on the part of industrial classes in particular, and especially in Pennsylvania and the middle West. In order to meet governmental needs and to alleviate the stringency in currency, Secretary Richardson began, on his own account, to reissue greenbacks until the amount reissued reached $26,000,000 by January, 1874, and the total of greenbacks outstanding reached that of $382,000,000. Congress passed, in April, 1874, a bill further to inflate the currency by the issue of $12,000,000 greenbacks, by fixing the maximum amount of these at $400,000,000. Grant, after some hesitation, wisely vetoed this "Inflation Bill," and was sustained by the Senate. This action on his part did much to reinstate him in popular esteem among more intelligent citizens. But greater enmity was aroused among the soft-money men of the West, which was but little alleviated by the passage of a compromise bill in June which provided that the amount

Courtesy of Harper & Brothers

THE FIRST APPEARANCE OF THE REPUBLICAN ELEPHANT, NOVEMBER, 1874

A cartoon by Thomas Nast in the Richard Croker days

of greenbacks should stand permanently at $382,000,000, the figure to which they had been reissued by the inflation policy of Secretary Richardson.

All these difficulties and scandals led to the great Republican defeat in the congressional elections of 1874, which far exceeded anything that the radicals had feared or the Democrats had hoped. In the Forty-fourth Congress the House of Representatives had stood: 195 Republicans, 88 Democrats, and 4 Liberals. In the Forty-fifth Congress it would be 108 Republicans, 168 Democrats, and 14 Liberals and independents. Pennsylvania, Ohio, Indiana, and Massachusetts all went Democratic on state elections. For the first time since 1858 the Democrats clearly had carried the country. It was the beginning of the end of radical domination, although the latter had waved the "bloody shirt," sounded "Southern outrages," and done their best to rally the Union-loving people behind them. The period which had begun with the death of Lincoln was about to come to an end.

Unfortunately, the Republican party still had to stand further humiliation and disgrace at the hands of Grant and his conscienceless followers—or manipulators. Two more scandals came to the front that merely accentuated the radical disgrace. Secretary Richardson had been succeeded in the Treasury Department by the high-minded and able reformer, Benjamin H. Bristow of Kentucky, in the year 1874. The same year Marshall Jewell of Connecticut succeeded James W. Marshall of Virginia, who recently had taken the portfolio of John A. J. Creswell of Maryland as postmaster-general. He too was of reforming tendencies, and these two men soon gave a finer tone to the administration. Bristow, in the process of reforming and cleaning up his department, unearthed a scandal in the internal revenue office at St. Louis, where one John McDonald, in collusion with a group of distillers known as the Whisky Ring, had defrauded the Government of large sums of money annually. Bristow caused the prosecution of the conspirators, and McDonald was sent to the penitentiary. He had handsomely entertained Grant and given him expensive presents, out of all proportion to his visible means of support, when the President visited St. Louis in 1874. It soon was found that Grant's private secretary, Orville H. Babcock, had been implicated with the ring and possibly had shared in its profits. When Babcock was put on trial, Grant not only retained him in office but waived immunity and testified in his favor. Babcock was acquitted, but the public was not convinced of his innocence, and finally Grant was forced to let him go.

Still worse was the evidence that William W. Belknap, the secretary of war, had been, with Mrs. Belknap, directly involved in the levying of graft upon the Indian agent at Fort Sill, Indian Territory. The House of Representatives unanimously voted impeachment on March 2, 1876, but Belknap resigned and Grant accepted his resignation, with the evident purpose of escaping impeachment proceedings. Grant may have been loyal to his friends, but he also was, perhaps unconsciously and in his dogged stubbornness and denseness of perception, disloyal to the country he was charged with administering in its highest office. To add to his derelictions, he now began to show decided coolness to Bristow and Jewell, so that they resigned and were succeeded respectively by Lot M. Morrill of Maine and James N. Tyner of Indiana. Alphonso Taft of Ohio, and then James Donald Cameron of Pennsylvania, successively followed Belknap in the War Department during the same year. Taft, who was the father of William Howard Taft, was moved to the position of attorney-general to succeed Edwards Pierrepont of New York.

In writing to a friend in April, 1875, Garfield made the pregnant comment: "I think Grant has done more than all predecessors to let down and degrade the position of cabinet officer. It has come to be understood that a man is chosen . . . because he is a special friend of the president rather than because he is a strong representative man. . . . Bristow, Fish and Jewell are about all of the present cabinet that show any personal manliness. The rest seem to be so happy over their elevation that their chief anxiety is to retain their places." [22]

[22] Quoted in T. C. Smith, "Garfield," I, 585.

It now was time for the Republicans of all kinds and classes to begin to "take stock" with regard to the approaching Presidential campaign of 1876. The period of their unbroken supremacy in national affairs was gone. In spite of the seeming disintegration of the Democratic party at the election of 1872, it had come back into greater power than for twelve years, and was strongly to dispute control with the Republicans to the extent that for the next twenty-two years, there were only four in which the latter had control of all parts of the Federal Government. The Republican party meanwhile did not poll a clear majority of the popular vote at any one of the current Presidential elections, and lost those of 1884 and 1892. The Republicans were strong enough to prevent Democratic control of all parts of the National Government until 1892, but were not strong enough to dominate it themselves.[23]

The possible explanation lies in the suspicion that had grown in the minds of many intelligent people that many of the Republican leaders were attempting to make spoils and political plunder the cohesive force and the basis upon which the rank and file of the voters might coöperate. They at first had been fooled by the appeal to their Union prejudices, by the legitimate historical prestige of the Republican party which had been growing up, the tradition of Lincoln leadership, and the original great personal popularity of Grant. Added to this, and always to be relied upon, was the soldier vote, already being organized into the Grand Army of the Republic, and assiduously cultivated by practical politicians, many of whom were themselves veterans. The country to-day is not yet free from the effects of pension raids upon the Treasury which were just about to begin, and which soon were extended to almost a popular debauch and scandal.

But as always happens in this country of ours, at the point when matters seemed to have reached their worst the solid common sense and integrity of our people asserted themselves, a newer element of leaders gradually came to the front, newer issues emerged, and the real process of reunion and of healing

[23] A. N. Holcombe, "Political Parties of To-day," 185.

the wounds of the Civil War steadily and happily began to develop. The old-line politicians of the radical school contained many who never learned and never forgot anything, and they made a desperate fight for continued control. The fight was a long and fierce one, but change, though slow, was sure, and out of it came the active, aggressive reorganized party of the days of McKinley and Roosevelt. It now is necessary to trace the steps that led up to Rutherford B. Hayes, and his sound and profoundly able administration that accomplished so much in the stabilization of national affairs, and made possible the later rehabilitation of the Republican party.

Chapter X

THE ELECTION OF 1876 AND THE DISPUTED COUNT

CONDITIONS looked dark for the Republican party as it began to prepare for the campaign of 1876. As usual, it could rely upon a modicum of Democratic mistakes and the adherence of large numbers of loyal and patriotic people, but the administration of Grant, just closing, was a heavy encumbrance and one from which it would be difficult to break free. Even so staunch a part man as Garfield confided to his diary on January 7, 1875: "The Vice-President [Wilson] told me today that Grant was more unpopular than Andrew Johnson was in his darkest days, that he is struggling for a third term, in short, that he is the millstone around the neck of our party that would sink it. . . . I rode home from the House with Blaine and found him not so extreme but in nearly the same opinion of our prospects. That such a party should meet such a fate is lamentable. But far worse is the aspect of the cause for which the war was fought. The most extreme passions abound in the two parties and I cannot foresee the end."[1]

It must not be supposed that all the political corruption in the country was in the Republican party or at Washington, D. C. This was a period of low political, personal, and financial morality, and the decadence in popular honesty and integrity was widespread. In the years 1869 to 1871 came the gigantic corruption of Tammany and the Tweed Ring in New York city from which the reputation and prestige of Tammany, through the country at large, has never yet recovered. During all these later years this organization was

[1] T. C. Smith, "Garfield," I, 520.

helped on in its degradation, it is true, by other scandals that have smirched the Wigwam from time to time. In 1871 the governor of Nebraska was removed from office for embezzlement. Bribery was disclosed in the election of United States senators in Kansas. In 1872 General Robert C. Schenck, United States minister at London, became involved in a disgraceful mining speculation.

In April, 1876, the Republicans received another blow when James G. Blaine, one of the most brilliant and popular of their leaders, was accused by various newspapers of having received what Professor Dunning calls "substantial favors" from the Union Pacific Railroad and other land-grant companies in 1871, at which time he was speaker of the House of Representatives. Blaine was one of the most prominent candidates for the Republican nomination in 1876, and he and his friends explained the charges as an attempt of his enemies even in his own party, such as the New York leaders Conkling, Dorsey, and Cornell, to injure his prospects. This was the famous scandal of the "Mulligan Letters." These showed, it was claimed, that Blaine had engaged in dubious speculation in the stock of a railroad in Arkansas, and then "had been extricated from a dangerous financial situation by the interposition of three other railroads, which took the stock off his hands at figures wholly unwarranted by its market value."[2] It was found that correspondence with regard to these transactions was in the possession of a man named Mulligan. Blaine got hold of these letters and refused to produce them. However, under the pressure of attacks and investigation by a congressional committee, he arose in the House of Representatives on June 5, 1876, showed the package of letters, and then *himself read them* to that body. But he never let them get out of his possession. He closed the speech with a theatrical plea in self-defense and made a profound impression. Garfield wrote: "I have never witnessed so dramatic a scene since I have been in the House. It may give Blaine the nomination. The feeling tonight is that it will,

[2] T. C. Smith, "Garfield," I, 599.

though I am not so sure of his election as I would be glad to be."[3]

The after-effects upon the Republican party and national politics were so great that this was an event of prime importance in American history. It left a taint upon the reputation of Blaine which probably had much to do with preventing his nomination either in 1876 or 1880, and causing his defeat by Cleveland in 1884. As Professor Dunning well summed up the matter, "The facts developed put Mr. Blaine under grave suspicion of just that sort of questionable wealth-getting, if nothing worse, which had ruined his colleagues in the Crédit Mobilier."[4] One's judgment of the whole affair must finally depend upon one's confidence in Blaine himself. He read the letters, it is true, but *he* read them, and they were afterward sequestered. If they contained nothing incriminating, why did he refuse to give them to the House investigating committee? If a person trusts Blaine, he accepts the letters as Blaine read them. If a person does not trust Blaine, he refuses to do so. Says James Ford Rhodes: "Blaine's speech of June 5 is not the speech of an innocent man; but no more adroit and powerful plea from an avaricious man, who had made money illicitly, can be imagined. It convinced many men of the highest honor and the majority of the Republican party that he had been wrongfully accused. But for the verdict of history, a cold statement in dollars and cents showing what had become of his . . . bonds would have been more to the point than his impassioned rhetoric and fervid declamation."[5] Soon after this Blaine became ill, and before his recovery he was appointed by the governor of Maine to the United States Senate to succeed Senator Lot M. Morrill, who had become secretary of the treasury in succession to Bristow. This removed him from the jurisdiction of the House of Representatives, and the investigating committee never made any report.

[3] T. C. Smith, "Garfield," I, 600.
[4] W. A. Dunning, "Reconstruction Political and Economic," 292–3.
[5] "History of the United States," VII, 205.

Grant, invulnerable in his own self-esteem, probably wanted a third term, and of course his henchmen were enthusiastically in favor of it. But at the opening of Congress in December, 1875, the House of Representatives had passed a resolution by the vote of 234 to 18, which included nearly half of the Republican membership, that declared against a third term as "unwise, unpatriotic, and fraught with peril to our free institutions." While this declaration was of doubtful truth when considered as an abstract proposition, yet it undoubtedly was a statement of fact when considered in connection with Ulysses S. Grant.

As one of the first moves in the political strategy of the campaign, certain of the old Liberal Republican leaders and others of reforming tendencies, and coming from seventeen different states, met at the Fifth Avenue Hotel in New York city on May 15, 1876. The meeting was presided over by Theodore D. Woolsey of Connecticut, and Henry Cabot Lodge of Massachusetts was one of the secretaries. They issued a clearly worded address to the public, said to have been prepared by Carl Schurz, in which, without naming any one, they let it be known specifically that neither Blaine, Conkling of New York, nor Morton of Indiana would be acceptable to them. It is probable that ex-Secretary Bristow would have been most pleasing to them, but they did not name any one as their candidate. There is no question that, failing a third term for Grant, the radicals would prefer either Roscoe Conkling—the vain, sensitive, aggressive, high-handed, ruthless, and able senator from New York, who came close to being Grant's spokesman in the Senate—or else that other "rock-ribbed" regular, Senator Oliver P. Morton, also a man of ability, who just missed being a statesman. The organization of more or less respectable spoilsmen who made up the Grant contingent would have supported either one to a man, and there seems to have been an idea in Grant's mind that, failing either one of these, he should be glad to see Hamilton Fish chosen as the standard-bearer. This is much to Grant's credit, and also to the discretion and self-restraint of Secretary Fish. The Ohio Re-

From "As I Knew Them" by permission of Harper & Brothers

"THE PLUMED KNIGHT" AS PUCK SAW HIM

publicans now began to urge Governor Hayes, then serving his third term as state executive, while Governor John F. Hartranft of Pennsylvania and Marshall Jewell of Connecticut, postmaster-general, also had a following.

The national convention met at Cincinnati, Ohio, on June 14 in Exposition Hall. This building was a large structure, in appearance somewhat like the Wigwam in Chicago in 1860, but with different interior arrangements for seating the delegates and spectators. It had a capacity of about 10,000 people.[6] The convention was called to order by ex-Governor Edwin D. Morgan, the chairman of the National Committee, and Theodore M. Pomeroy of New York was chosen temporary chairman. George William Curtis read an address from the Republican Reform Club of New York city, which, in no uncertain terms, demanded honesty in administration, reform in the civil service, and the resumption of specie payments—in other words, a sound financial policy. Edward McPherson of Pennsylvania was chosen permanent president and the platform was adopted, after some contest over minor points, as reported by the Committee on Resolutions, of which General Joseph R. Hawley of Connecticut was chairman. It was well written and, the perilous situation of the party being considered, very clear and honest in its statements.

It was, in summary, as follows: "The United States of America is a nation, not a league. By the combined workings of the national and state governments, under their respective constitutions, the rights of every citizen are secured, at home and abroad, and the common welfare promoted." "The permanent pacification of the Southern section of the Union, and the complete protection of all its citizens in the free enjoyment of all their rights, is a duty to which the Republican party stand sacredly pledged." Since the first act of Congress that was signed by President Grant pledged the "redemption of the United States notes in coin," this promise was to be fulfilled "by a continuous and steady progress to specie pay-

[6] Tweedy, "History of the Republican National Conventions," 137–8.

ments." The spoils system was deftly handled in the plank which stated that "senators and representatives, who may be judges and accusers, should not dictate appointments to office. The invariable rule in appointments should have reference to the honesty, fidelity, and capacity of the appointees, giving to the party in power those places where harmony and vigor of administration require its policy to be represented, but permitting all others to be filled by persons selected with sole reference to the efficiency of the public service, and the right of all citizens to share in the honor of rendering faithful service to the country." Added to this was the statement that "we rejoice in the quickened conscience of the people concerning political affairs, and will hold all public officers to a rigid responsibility, and engage that the prosecution and punishment of all who betray official trusts shall be swift, thorough, and unsparing." One can well imagine how the Grant henchmen put their tongues in their cheeks or "winked the other eye" when they voted for this; and Hayes's experience when later he undertook loyally to carry this out was both a revelation to them, and also a cause of bitter opposition to him, their party's President.

An admirable plank stated that the "public-school system of the several states is a bulwark of the American republic and, with a view to its security and permanence, we recommend an amendment to the Constitution of the United States forbidding the application of any public funds or property for the benefit of any schools or institutions under sectarian control." Other statements reaffirmed "opposition to further grants of the public land to corporations and monopolies"; stated that it was "the right and duty of Congress to prohibit and extirpate, in the territories, that relic of barbarism, polygamy"; and "sincerely deprecated all sectional feeling and tendencies."

The convention could not refrain from "waving the bloody shirt," but did so in the course of a bitter and direct attack upon the Democratic party, which was cleverly phrased. "We charge the Democratic party with being the same in character and spirit as when it sympathized with treason; with making its control of the House of Representatives the triumph and opportunity of the nation's recent foes; with reasserting and applauding in the national capital the sentiments of unrepentant rebellion; with sending Union soldiers to the rear, and promoting Confederate soldiers to the front; with deliberately proposing to repudiate the plighted faith of the government; with being equally false and imbecile upon the overshadowing financial questions; with thwarting the ends of justice by its partizan mismanagement and obstruction of investigation; with proving itself, through the period of its ascendancy in the lower House of Congress, utterly incompetent to administer the government; and we warn the country against trusting a party thus alike unworthy, recreant, and incapable." President Grant, it was finally stated, "deserves the continued hearty gratitude of the American people for his patriotism and his eminent services, in war and in peace."

The various candidates were then placed before the convention by nominating speeches, among which that of Robert G. Ingersoll of Illinois in favor of Blaine became very famous. He stated the many requirements of the Republicans from their candidate, and added: "They demand a man whose political reputation is spotless as a star; but they do not demand that their candidate shall have a certificate of moral character signed by the Confederate congress." He went on:

"The people will call for the man who has preserved in Congress what their soldiers won upon the field . . . for the man who has torn from the throat of treason the tongue of slander; the man who has snatched the mask of Democracy from the hideous face of the rebellion; the man who, like the intellectual athlete, hath stood in the arena of debate challenging all comers, and who up to the present moment is a total stranger to defeat.

"Like an armed warrior, like a plumed knight, James G. Blaine marched down the halls of the American congress and threw his shining lance full and fair against the brazen forehead of every traitor to his country and every maligner of his fair reputation. For the Republican party to desert that gallant man now is as though an army should desert their general upon the field of battle. James G. Blaine is now and has been for years the bearer of the sacred standard of the Republican party. I call it sacred because no human being can stand beneath its folds without becoming and without remaining free.

"In the name of the great republic, the only republic that ever existed upon the face of the earth; in the name of all her defenders and of all her supporters; in the name of all her soldiers living; in the name of her soldiers that died upon the field of battle; in the name of those that perished in the skeleton clutch of famine at Andersonville and Libby, whose sufferings he so vividly remembers, Illinois—Illinois nominates . . . that prince of parliamentarians, that leader of leaders, James G. Blaine."

The theatrical and emotional effect can well be imagined, and it is possible that had the balloting begun soon after, Blaine might have received the nomination. As it happened, other speeches had to follow, and by that time evening was drawing on. It was announced that the hall could not be lighted for an evening session, so adjournment was taken until the next morning.

The nominations were made on the third day. On the first ballot the results stood: Total number of votes cast, 754, necessary to a choice, 378. Blaine, 285; Morton, 124; Bristow, 113; Conkling, 99; Hayes, 61; Hartranft, 58; Jewell, 11; Wheeler, 3. Five more ballots followed without any choice. During the progress of the second ballot a delegate from Pennsylvania questioned the report of the ballot as 58 for Hartranft, stating that two of the delegates had voted for Blaine, and he demanded that these two votes be counted for him, although the delegation had been instructed to vote as a unit. Great excitement followed, but Mr. McPherson, the president of the convention, ruled that the votes should be announced as cast, thus giving the two votes for Blaine. On an appeal, his decision was sustained by the convention by the vote of 395 to 354. The unit rule was thus broken, and after a

Photograph by Brown Brothers

JAMES G. BLAINE

similar experience four years later at the Chicago convention, it was finally relinquished by the Republican party. This was a decided step toward real popular rule of the party, which became most important during later years.

Hayes was the only one to gain on every ballot, and with the casting of the fifth the vote of Michigan, 22 in all, which had been divided hitherto, was cast solidly for him. At the close of the sixth ballot attempts were made to take a recess for conference purposes, and there was much excitement as well as confusion. When the seventh ballot was being cast, William Cumback took the platform and withdrew Morton's name and cast the 25 votes of Indiana for Hayes. John M. Harlan withdrew Bristow's name and cast the 34 votes of Kentucky for Hayes. When New York was called, Mr. Pomeroy withdrew Conkling's name and 61 votes from that state also went to Hayes, as did 28 of the Pennsylvania votes when Hartranft's name was withdrawn. The ballot then resulted: Whole number of votes, 756; necessary to a choice, 379. Hayes, 384; Blaine, 351; Bristow, 21. This gave Hayes the nomination by five votes, and on the motion of William P. Frye of Maine it was made unanimous.

Blaine evidently was defeated by the taint of scandal, which, popular as he otherwise was, would be too great for him to carry to a successful election. Bristow might have received the nomination were it not for the fact that he came from Kentucky, a state that had strong southern leanings and from which he probably could not get its electoral vote. Again, Grant had shown veiled hostility to him, and the radicals did not forget his part in clearing out the spoilsmen. Hayes was a clean, able, upright man of the finest character and reputation, upon whom all could unite, and he was the logical compromise.

Several names were presented for Vice-President. As the balloting proceeded, it was seen that William A. Wheeler of New York probably would be the choice of the convention, whereupon a delegate moved that the name of one of the candidates, Marshall Jewell, be withdrawn and Mr. Wheeler be nominated by acclamation. This motion was carried and the convention soon after adjourned.

Rutherford Birchard Hayes was born in Delaware, Ohio, on October 4, 1822. He graduated from Kenyon College and studied law at Harvard University. He had a fine record as lawyer, public citizen, and as a gallant and able soldier during the Civil War, where he rose to the rank of brigadier-general in 1864 and brevet major-general in 1865. He was in the House of Representatives for three terms, and at the time of this nomination was serving his third term as governor of Ohio. He made a strong stand for sound money at a time when the "Ohio idea" of soft money and inflation was at its zenith, and he won on it. He was a high-class man and a gentleman in every particular, and the convention made a happy choice in his nomination.

William Almon Wheeler also had long and honorable public service. He was born in Malone, New York, on June 30, 1819, studied at the University of Vermont, and became a lawyer. He was active in politics as a Whig, and supported Frémont in 1856. He was serving his fifth term in Congress when he was nominated. Altogether the ticket was an excellent one, and was well calculated to meet the demands of the reforming elements who had desired to work within the Republican party for improvement in political morals and administration.

The Democratic convention met at St. Louis on June 28, and the nomination of Samuel J. Tilden of New York was a foregone conclusion before it was called to order. Thomas A. Hendricks of Indiana was given second place on the ticket, and thus a definite bid was made for the necessary electoral votes of two doubtful states. These candidates were men of ability and integrity, so that no matter which ticket was successful, it was evident that a new day of higher standards of public service would follow the mistakes of the honest but inept Grant. The Democratic platform was ably written, and declared for the finality of the three war amendments, for reunion of the hearts of the people of the whole Union, for reform in administration and the civil service, for retrenchment in public expenditures, and for sound currency. When one considers the character of the make-up of the Democratic party at this time, it will be seen that even had Tilden become President, this excellent program would in large part have gone by the board, due to the ineptitude of the Democratic leadership at large.

One plank was especially dangerous for the Republicans, for it powerfully summed up the scandals and shortcomings of the Grant administrations. It is quoted in part here, for it shows what a load Hayes had necessarily to carry, and is a tribute to his success both as a candidate and, in spite of the doubtful title to the office, most assuredly to his success as an able, and hitherto often unappreciated President. "The annals of this republic show the disgrace and censure of a Vice-President; a late Speaker of the House of Representatives marketing his rulings as a presiding officer; three senators profiting secretly by their votes as law-makers; five chairmen of the leading committees of the House of Representatives exposed in jobbery; a late secretary of the treasury forcing balances in the public accounts; a late attorney-general misappropriating public funds; a secretary of the navy enriched or enriching friends by percentages levied off the profits of contractors with his department; an ambassador to England censured in a dishonorable speculation; the President's private secretary barely escaping conviction upon trial for guilty complicity in frauds upon the revenue; a secretary of war impeached for high crimes and misdemeanors." Certain of these charges were denied in whole or in part by leading Republicans, but at best the record was ghastly, and it well supports the judgment that it would have been far better for Grant himself and his future reputation, if not for the welfare of the country as well, if he never had been elected President. The fact that the Republican party survived this record, and entirely restored itself in the estimation of the major part of the thoughtful and intelligent people of the United States, is a great tribute to its newly developing leaders and its essential soundness in the rank and file of its members. Its record both before and since that time has been such that it can afford to hide nothing, but tell the truth and stand upon its entire history. And the Democrats have too many skeletons in their own family closet to be unwary in their bandying of charges, or in "pointing with pride." Most assuredly when we consider the present state of political and party life, just fifty years later, we can congratulate ourselves upon the undoubted progress that has been made in the country at large toward higher standards of public and private honor, and morals as well.

It is a matter of interest that a new party, known as the Independent National or Greenback party, was organized and this year ran for President Peter Cooper of New York, and Samuel F. Cary of Ohio for Vice-President. It declared for fiat money as "the best circulating medium ever devised," and showed about as much knowledge of sound principles of economics as the free-silver followers of William J. Bryan of twenty years later, or the advocates of the McNary-Haugen Agricultural Bill in 1927. It received only 81,737 votes at the November election, but served to keep financial heresy alive and ready to influence the people at a later day.

Hayes, in his letter of acceptance, put the contest on a high plane. He attacked the spoils system, urged the cause of civil-service reform, pledged himself not to accept a renomination, took a strong stand in favor of a "judicious system of preparation" for the resumption of specie payments, and expressed his desire to "wipe out forever the distinction between North and South in our common country." It made a great impression upon the country and did much to hearten the reforming elements, who in large part rallied around him. It is true the Republican party necessarily must be upon the defensive, not only because it was the party in power, but also on account of the delinquencies of the Grant administrations. On the other hand, Blaine had done much to continue the sectional bitterness so characteristic of the political struggles of this period by his speech in Congress during the preceding

January. He aroused a bitter controversy during the consideration of the bill to remove all remaining disabilities under the Fourteenth Amendment by moving to exclude Jefferson Davis, whom he charged with responsibility for Andersonville. This at once was taken up by the Southerners and a bitter debate followed, with "waving the bloody shirt" by the radicals. Hayes's kindly and conciliatory language could not do away with this feature of the campaign, especially since he himself urged that the necessity be stressed of the danger to the country of a solid South and rebel rule. All this was good politics but bad policy.

On the other hand, Tilden's letter of acceptance was decidedly disappointing, and was considered halting and evasive. Tilden had been an able politician and governor of New York, and as a private citizen had done much to clear out the corrupt Democratic Tammany and Tweed Ring. But he had coöperated with Tweed in party politics, and "Harper's Weekly" pointed out (July 15, 1876) that "during all Tweed's ascendancy and control in the Democratic party of the state, Mr. Tilden, as Democratic chairman, gave the weight of his name and official action to Tweed's nominations." [7] Furthermore, the Republicans charged, and with show of circumstantial evidence at least, that Mr. Tilden had evaded payments of his income tax during the year 1862. And there is no question that large sums of money were being spent, and "Tilden's barrel" became the theme of Republican orators on the stump and of Nast's brilliant and effective cartoons. The fact that Tilden was known in some sections as "Slippery Sam" had a most damaging effect. Says Rhodes:[8] "Hayes's personal character was a tower of strength on the Republican side but Tilden was vulnerable." Zachariah Chandler managed the Republican campaign with great skill, and, according to the reprehensible but unquestioned practice of the times, levied assessments upon office-holders for campaign funds. The poli-

[7] Quoted in the brilliant and scholarly "Life of R. B. Hayes," by Charles Richard Williams, I, 418 (note), which also contains an able and extended account of the whole campaign and disputed election.

[8] "History of the United States," VII, 221.

ticians of both sides were careful to see that the "sinews of war" were ruthlessly collected.

The greatest excitement was in the so-called doubtful states, especially those of the middle and middle-western groups, while the South was wrought up to a tremendous pitch of excitement with the idea of getting rid of the radicals and carpet-baggers, especially in the three "unredeemed" states of Florida, Louisiana, and South Carolina. Undoubtedly there was violence and intimidation on both sides, especially in the "bulldozed" parishes of Louisiana. The elections in the "October states" showed that the contest would be close, for Ohio went Republican by only 6636 and Indiana went Democratic by 5084.

The election on November 7 was quiet and without undue excitement in the North and West. When the election returns began to come in it became certain that Tilden had carried the doubtful states of New York (32,742 plurality), New Jersey (2445), Connecticut (2900), and apparently the solid South, which would give him 203 electoral votes to 166 for Hayes. The newspapers in general announced his election on the morning of the eighth, but "The New York Herald" and "The New York Times" doubted it, and soon began to claim in later editions that Florida, Louisiana, and South Carolina had gone for Hayes, which would thus give him 185 electoral votes to Tilden's 184, and elect him. The excitement became intense. That night the Republican National Committee also began to claim Hayes's election. The state of South Carolina seemed sure for Hayes, while the other two were under the control of the Republican canvassing boards which had the power to throw out returns where there were charges of intimidation or fraud; and there was no question that the latter had existed. The possibilities now were grasped by the people, and the politicians in particular. Grant, who now rose admirably to the occasion, gave orders that the military should preserve order and said in his despatch: "See that the proper and legal boards of canvassers are unmolested in the performance of their duties. Should there be any grounds of suspicion of a fraudulent count on either side, it should be reported and denounced at once. No man worthy of the office of President should be willing to hold it if counted in or placed there by fraud. Either party can afford to be disappointed in the result. The country cannot afford to have the result tainted by the suspicion of illegal or false returns." [9]

A number of politicians from both parties now went South to the disputed states to look after party interests, many of them being requested to do so by Grant himself, and by Abram S. Hewitt, the chairman of the Democratic National Committee. New Orleans was the special center of interest, and among those in that city to represent the Republican party were such men as John Sherman, Stanley Matthews and James A. Garfield of Ohio; William D. Kelley of Pennsylvania, and Eugene Hale of Maine. Among the Democrats were John M. Palmer and Lyman Trumbull of Illinois, Samuel J. Randall, A. G. Curtin, and William Bigler of Pennsylvania; J. R. Doolittle of Wisconsin, F. R. Coudert of New York, George W. Julian of Indiana, W. G. Sumner of Connecticut, and Henry Watterson of Kentucky. The presence of a number of former Republican names in this list shows the results of radical extremeness in driving some of the ablest and best of the early Republicans out of the party.

As already stated, it soon was seen that Hayes probably had carried South Carolina, but two sets of returns were sent from that state to Washington for the electoral count by Congress. The Republicans claimed Florida by 85 majority for Hayes, the Democrats claimed it by 90 for Tilden. While Louisiana had shown over 6000 majority for Tilden, the returning board threw out the "bulldozed" parishes and declared the state had gone for Hayes by 3437 majority. Said John Sherman some years later:[10] "The returning board . . . proceeded to perform its duty under the law, at each session the Republican and Democratic visitors were present, and I neither know of nor have ever heard of any act being done or

[9] Blaine, "Twenty Years of Congress," II, 581–2.
[10] "Recollections," I, 556–7.

testimony taken by the board except in the presence of committees of the two bodies of visitors. The proceedings of the returning board were reported for each body of visitors and for the returning board, and all the evidence taken was not only delivered in the presence of the two visiting bodies, but was reported to the President and was published by Congress. Whatever opinions may be expressed as to the correctness of the findings of the returning board, there can be no doubt that its proceedings were open, fair and impartial." Sherman speaks as an eye-witness.

To add to the troubles, the Democrats began to claim that one of the three Republican electors in Oregon was constitutionally ineligible through being a postmaster, hence all the votes cast for him were void and the Tilden elector chosen in his place. Two sets of returns came also from this state, and the change of one vote would be enough to defeat Hayes and elect Tilden, even though the three Southern states in dispute might have gone Republican. It should be noted that the Democratic returns had the certificate of the Democratic governor, and it was upon the gubernatorial certificate that special emphasis had been placed by the Republicans in connection with the three states of the South. Assuredly the whole contest was one of most dangerous complications and implications, and there was no law to deal with the problem.

The Constitution of the United States says:[11] "The president of the Senate shall, in the presence of the Senate and House of Representatives, open all the certificates, and the votes shall then be counted." But it neglected to say *by whom.* The Twenty-second Joint Rule, which became law on February 8, 1865, had provided that when there was a dispute as to the counting of the votes, each house should consider the matter separately, and no vote could be decided except by concurrent vote of both. But this only added to the confusion, for the Republicans controlled the Senate and the Democrats controlled the House. But there was even then doubt whether the rule still was in force.

[11] Art. II, sec. I, clause 3.

Moderate men of both parties now exerted themselves to find some solution, and as a result both houses appointed committees of seven men to act jointly and devise some plan. Finally, a bill for an electoral commission was reported and passed during the latter part of January which was of a compromise character and provided each step in the counting of the votes. First of all, the vote of no state was to be *rejected* without the concurrent action of both houses. If there were a dispute as to which of two returns was the correct one, the matter should be referred to a joint committee, or electoral commission, the composition of which should be five senators, five representatives, and five justices of the Supreme Court. This meant that there would be three Republicans and two Democrats from the Senate, and three Democrats and two Republicans from the House. Four of the justices were designated, and two each of these were Republicans and Democrats. These four should choose a fifth, who would have a deciding vote between the seven designated Republican and seven designated Democratic members, and it was understood that this one would be Justice David Davis of Illinois, an independent in politics. The bill was just in process of passage when, with strange fatuity, the Democratic legislature of Illinois chose Davis to succeed Logan as United States senator, and he at once accepted, doubtless glad to be relieved of such crushing responsibility. While ranked as an independent, Davis was known to have Democratic leanings, and that party would have had the advantage, if advantage lay anywhere. It was the Illinois legislature that finally made almost certain the choice of Hayes, for the remaining justices were Republicans, and the man chosen by the four justices was Joseph P. Bradley. It is greatly to the credit of the Democrats in Congress that they went ahead and passed the act, although aware of the potential make-up of the commission, now to be composed of eight Republicans and seven Democrats.

The members of the commission as finally appointed were: Senators Edmunds, Morton, and Frelinghuysen (Republicans), and Thurman and Bayard (Democrats); Representatives Payne, Hunton, Abbott (Democrats), and Garfield and George F. Hoar (Republicans); Justices Bradley, Miller, and Strong (Republicans), and Clifford and Field (Democrats). Justice Clifford was made president of the commission when it organized on January 31, 1877.

Congress began the count on February 1, and as the votes of Florida, Louisiana, South Carolina, and Oregon were objected to, they were successively referred to the electoral commission. At once the question arose, should the certificates be accepted as given by the governor of a state, or other legally qualified authority, or should the commission go behind the returns? If they did the latter, where should the investigation stop? If the first plan of procedure were adopted, the Republicans would get the votes of the three Southern states, all of which were certified by the governors. But then Tilden would get the one from Oregon, for the governor of that state was a Democrat and had certified the Democratic vote, while the Republicans were certified by the secretary of state to the governor, since by the laws of the state of Oregon the secretary of state was the canvassing officer. It seemed that no matter on which horn of the dilemma the Republican cause was hung, Tilden would be declared elected.

It is due to William M. Evarts, one of the greatest lawyers of his time and one of the counsel for the Republicans, that a point was made which won the case for Hayes. John W. Burgess, in a brilliant analysis of the argument, gives this point as follows:[12] "The Republicans took their stand at the outset upon the principle that Congress could not go behind the returns of the state canvassing board or officer, in counting the electoral vote from any state. They contended that in the election of the President and Vice-President, the Constitution had separated the procedure into two distinct parts, and had assigned the first part to the control of the separate states exclusively, and the second part to the control of Congress exclusively; that up to the completion of the election of the electors the exclusive control of the

[12] "Reconstruction and the Constitution," 292–3.

states respectively extended, but that all control after that point had been reached was in Congress, and that Congress had no power whatever, under the Constitution, to revise, interfere with, or examine into, that part assigned by the Constitution to the states respectively, and, on the other hand, that Congress was bound to disregard any act of the states, or of any of the officers or agents of the states, in that part assigned exclusively by the Constitution to its own control. There is no question that this was all sound constitutional law and that the Democrats would have to abandon entirely their old state's rights doctrine and go over to the most extreme nationalism in order to combat it.

"It did not appear to them necessary in order to win their case. One single electoral vote from any one of the four states, from which double returns had been received, would elect Tilden and Hendricks. It did not seem to them that the line between the powers of the states and those of Congress over the election of the President and Vice-President could under the existing facts be drawn anywhere without giving them at least this one vote. If the returns as certified by the governors and the state canvassing officer, officers, or boards, of these four states should be received and counted they would have this one vote from Oregon. If, on the other hand, the popular vote for the electors as it came into the hands of the state canvassing officers or boards was to be received and counted, then they would have the electoral votes of at least Louisiana, Florida, or South Carolina, and perhaps of all of them. . . .

"But the Republicans contended that the line between state control and congressional control was to be drawn between the governor's certification and the report of the state canvassing officer, officers, or board to the governor of the result of the vote for the electors. The certification issued by the governor, they held, was ordered by congressional law and was under congressional control, even when the state canvassing officer, officers, or board should join with the governor in the certification of the persons chosen electors. The report of the vote for the electors by the state canvassing officer, officers, or board to the governor was thus the final act under state control, in the election of the electors. This was unquestionably sound constitutional law. But it would give all the electoral votes from all four of the states, from which double returns had been received, to Hayes and Wheeler, and would elect them by one vote."

The counsel for both sides before the commission was unusually able and consisted of Evarts, Stanley Matthews, E. W. Stoughton, and Samuel Shellabarger for the Republicans. Those representing the Democrats were Jeremiah S. Black, Charles O'Conor, Matthew H. Carpenter, J. A. Campbell, Montgomery Blair, Ashbel Green, George Hoadley, R. T. Merrick, A. P. Morse, Lyman Trumbull, and William C. Whitney. As the decision was made on each vote, it invariably was given to Hayes and Wheeler by the partizan vote of eight to seven, and finally the last of the disputed votes was counted in their favor on February 28, four days before the end of Grant's term of office. When the Democrats saw how things were going, there were various objections made in the joint session of Congress to the votes of Vermont, followed by objections to those of Virginia and Wisconsin. This gave rise to disorderly proceedings in the House of Representatives, but Samuel J. Randall, the Democratic speaker, by strong rulings and even arbitrary procedure, squelched them, and was backed therein by the best elements of his party. It is greatly to his and their credit that they stood by their bargain, even though events were going against them. Finally, at ten minutes past four on the morning of March 2, Hayes and Wheeler were declared elected and the all-night final joint session was adjourned. Hayes took the oath of office on Saturday evening, March 3, at the White House, due to the fact that the fourth would fall on a Sunday, and Grant's term thus would expire before the public and formal inaugural exercises on March 5.

This peaceful conclusion was greatly assisted by an informal conference held in the rooms of Mr. Evarts at

Wormeley's Hotel, Washington, on February 26. While Mr. Hayes had no part in it directly or indirectly, it was known that he would be conciliatory toward the South and would withdraw the troops still in garrison in the states under carpet-bag control. The Southern Democrats were here assured of this fact, and since this assurance was what they had been driving at by their filibustering and disorderly tactics in Congress, they finally withdrew their opposition and permitted the results of the electoral count to be announced.[13] They did not so much care who had control of the National Government, so long as they were permitted to run their own state governments without outside interference.

During all this time Hayes had preserved a dignified silence and Tilden made no effort to defend his interests, aside from spending much time in drawing up a list of precedents for elections and for the casting of the electoral votes. He seemed to go into eclipse, and much disgusted his Democratic followers, who felt that he had more or less deserted them.

Of course, there has been much contention concerning the rights and wrongs of this election. It is interesting to note that the biographer of Hayes, the late Charles Richard Williams, himself a Democrat and a scholar of great ability, has this to say: "Without elaboration or argument, the writer desires to say that, as a result of his prolonged study of the conditions and contentions of the time, he is thoroughly convinced that in the final arbitrament essential justice and right prevailed, and that the best interests of the country in all its parts were served. He ventures the prediction that more and more this will come to be the judgment of impartial historians." [14] This is a fair statement of the case. The eight to seven partizan vote of the members of the electoral commission is no proof either of unfairness or corruption. The fact that these men on both sides were Republicans or Democrats meant that they had a

[13] See Dunning, "Reconstruction Political and Economic," 339–40.
[14] "Life of Hayes," I, 491.

certain bent of mind which undoubtedly would influence and form the basis for their judgment, just as it does for the justices of the Supreme Court. Their high character and reputation for integrity and honesty precludes any charge or taint of corruption.

It may be added that in all probability the extent of corruption in buying, selling, and counting of votes was so great on both sides that no one ever will know who rightfully was elected. The people evidently felt that, come what may, at least they had the sounder man for President, for they did not forget that it was the upright Hayes against "Slippery Sam." Whether or not Tilden deserved this name, at least it expresses worlds of meaning. The whole episode was a sad and unfortunate incident in American history. But it has also its good side. The self-restraint and common sense of the American people, under the most exciting circumstances, is cause for the greatest and most patriotic pride. It is a sufficient answer to the pacifists and others of to-day who insist that armed military preparedness inevitably means conflict. At this time there were at least two million trained soldiers, veterans of the Civil War who had fought on both sides and still were well within the military age, and yet there was not one breath of a serious suggestion of armed conflict. There never could be a greater tribute to the essentially peaceful character of the American people than the statement of this fact.

It is a matter of interest that an attempt had been made in May, 1874, to amend the Constitution of the United States, in order to provide thereafter for a new method of voting for electors for President and Vice-President. Senator Morton of Indiana especially was urgent for its adoption, and had he succeeded in carrying it through to a successful conclusion, it is possible the Hayes-Tilden contested election never would have taken place. In brief, the plan was to have each voter in every state vote for two electors at large from the entire state, corresponding to the two senators, and also for one elector from each congressional district. This would mean that every voter would vote for *three* electors only, whether residing in the state of Delaware or Nevada, where the number of electors is three, or in New York or Pennsylvania, where the electoral vote is much larger. It would mean a nearer approach to equality for the citizens, and also cause the result of an election to approach more closely to the popular will. Even at the present day such a reform would be a great step in the right direction. It has the added merit that it would still retain the electoral votes as a buffer against wholesale ballot-box stuffing in any one state, in order to balance the popular vote in a number of others, which easily could happen in case we abolished the Electoral College entirely.[15]

In closing the chapter, it should be stated that according to the Republican count the vote in November had been: Hayes, 4,033,768; Tilden, 4,285,992—a Democratic popular plurality of 252,224. According to the Democratic count, the vote was: Tilden, 4,300,590; Hayes, 4,036,298—a Democratic plurality of 264,292. Thus it will be seen that Tilden had at least a plurality of over a quarter of a million votes. Both counts agreed in giving the Greenback party 81,737, and the Prohibitionists, whose candidates were Green Clay Smith of Kentucky and G. T. Stewart of Ohio, 9522.[16]

[15] See Stanwood, "History of the Presidency," 358–60, for a full account of the plan.

[16] These figures are taken from Stanwood, "History of the Presidency," 383.

Chapter XI

RUTHERFORD B. HAYES AND THE REËSTABLISHMENT OF HONESTY AND STABILITY

THE inauguration of President Hayes took place on March 5, 1877, and was accomplished quietly and with dignity. The inaugural address did much to strengthen the good impression that Hayes already had made upon the people, and in it he spoke in a friendly and conciliatory way to the South, making the significant statement that "I am sincerely anxious to use every legitimate influence in favor of honest and efficient local *self*-government as the true resource of those states for the promotion of the contentment and prosperity of their citizens." He added that it was his desire to "forever wipe out in our political affairs the color line and the distinction between North and South, to the end that we may have not merely a united North or a united South, but a united country." Then followed an urgent plea for "the paramount necessity of reform in our civil service . . . a change in the system of appointment itself; a reform that shall be thorough, radical, and complete; a return to the principles and practices of the founders of the government. They neither expected nor desired from public officers any partizan service. They meant that public officers should owe their whole service to the government and to the people." He then made the weighty and sound statement that served as a real keynote to his whole administration. "He serves his party best who serves the country best." There was also a plea for the early resumption of specie payments as part of a policy of sound currency and financial policy.[1]

President Hayes appointed one of the ablest cabinets that

[1] Richardson, "Messages and Papers," VII, 442–7.

Photograph by Brown Brothers

RUTHERFORD B. HAYES

ever has advised any President. In William M. Evarts, the secretary of state; John Sherman, secretary of the treasury, and Carl Schurz, secretary of the interior, were three outstanding men of our history. Richard W. Thompson of Indiana, the secretary of the navy, was a politician appointed for political purposes at the urgent solicitation of Senator Morton, but he gave a good administration of his office. Charles Devens of Massachusetts, the attorney-general; George W. McCrary of Iowa, the secretary of war, and David McK. Key, the postmaster-general, were all men of sound ability and integrity. Key had been in the Confederate army and had voted for Tilden. This appointment, meant as a tender of friendship toward the South, was not adequately appreciated by that section, and served to arouse the enmity and opposition of the Northern extremists, acting as a veritable red rag to a bull toward the radicals, who vigorously began to "wave the bloody shirt."

Their enmity was more thoroughly aroused by Hayes's next move—that of withdrawing the troops from the South, which had been placed there for political purposes. He also recognized Wade Hampton, Democrat, as governor of South Carolina, and when the troops were withdrawn from Louisiana the carpet-bag government of the notorious Packard fell and the Democrats took control. Hayes recognized this change, in spite of the charge brought upon the floors of Congress, in which movement Blaine was a leader, that if Packard was not elected, then Hayes was not elected. To those who insisted that the national Republicans should continue their control of Louisiana even with the use of troops Blaine gave the name "Stalwarts," and this term gradually superseded the name "radical," which happily disappeared from common use for that element of the party which had originated in the opposition to Lincoln, and had composed in large part the followers of Grant.

This action of Hayes marked the downfall of the radical policy of reconstruction of the South by means of negro enfranchisement. It also was the beginning of the end, for the time at least, of the negro vote in the Southern states, one of the most mistaken policies ever undertaken by the American people. It is well known now that Lincoln never intended wholesale negro enfranchisement, but was willing to go only to the extent of giving the vote to a few of the more intelligent or educated members of the race, or to those who also might be owners of property. Suddenly placing the duty of the ballot upon a people who were just emerged from slavery, without any preparation for the responsibility, was totally unfair to them, as well as to the white race. To raise ignorant and intellectually helpless recent slaves to a position of domination and rule over their former masters was a ghastly travesty on government and justice, and the tragic results were just exactly what might have been expected. Political liberty, as history shows, is a thing to be earned, and the negro race has found it out at a sad cost. When Hayes withdrew the Federal troops and the Southern whites came into power, popular passion was at its worst, and had its usual deplorable effects. The negro lost political rights, but soon gained economic rights in place of them. Only after fifty years are the effects now slowly disappearing, and the negro is gradually earning, in the South, the political rights which it is necessary for him to prove are justly his. Radical reconstruction only set back this accomplishment and made it a thousandfold more difficult of attainment.

Hayes came into office under the most difficult circumstances due to the contest over the election. Literally millions of people believed that Tilden rightfully was entitled to the place, but as Rhodes well says:[2] "Hayes had no choice but to abide by the decision [of the Electoral Commission]. Duty to his country and to his party . . . required his acceptance of the office, and there is no reason for thinking that he had any doubts regarding his proper course. His legal title was perfect, but his moral title was unsound, and it added to the difficulty of his situation that the opposition, the Democrats, had a majority in the House of Representatives. None but a determined optimist could have predicted anything but failure for an administration beginning under such conditions." The Democrats

[2] "Historical Essays," 245–6.

also secured control of the Senate in 1879, and by that time the "stalwart" members of his own party, as well as those partizans who were avid for office and power, were aroused to bitter opposition by his attempts to introduce civil-service reform and the merit system in appointments, in spite of the lack of congressional action or even sympathy. But courageously and without a moment's hesitation Rutherford B. Hayes went ahead and did what he thought was right, and what succeeding years have proved was right, and his administration cannot be called "a failure," certainly from the standpoint of sound statesmanship, whatever may have been the contemporary political handicaps and seeming lack of success. He paved the way for much of the reform and administrative and financial progress of the next two decades.

Hayes was compelled to call Congress in special session due to the failure of the preceding Congress to pass the necessary appropriations for the support of the United States army because it had been employed to sustain Republican governments in certain Southern states. As soon as the Forty-fifth Congress met, the Democrats made an attempt to impugn the title of Hayes to the Presidential office. A resolution was introduced by Clarkson N. Potter of New York to appoint a committee to make an investigation into the election, and this was passed after a struggle lasting four days. During the course of the investigation certain cipher telegrams were brought before the committee which were finally deciphered sufficiently to show that an attempt had been made by certain of Tilden's followers to buy enough electoral votes to make certain his election. Thomas Brackett Reed of Maine, who was serving his first term in Congress, was a minority member of this committee and by his merciless cross-examination showed the sinister and weighty character of the evidence. While there were both majority and minority reports of the committee, as might have been expected, yet the majority had to admit that Tilden's friends had shown "mistaken zeal . . . without authority on his part," and no formal debate or further action took place upon the matter. This seemed to end any hostile moves of this character against Hayes and his title to office, and it is rather significant that in the year 1880 the Democrats made no real attempt to run Tilden again for the Presidency, to secure that "vindication" that should have been so easy in a triumphal election, if there were clear popular belief that he, an entirely innocent man, had been egregiously cheated out of office.

Hayes had a difficult problem to meet of an entirely new character in our history, caused by the great railroad strikes in July, 1877. When violence and bloodshed became rampant he did not hesitate, but sent troops on the call of the governors of West Virginia, Maryland, Pennsylvania, and Illinois, and, in addition, to Indiana and Missouri on the call of the United States marshals. This was the first time that any such labor troubles ever had arisen in the United States, and was a forecast of what has most unhappily arisen to greater prominence since that time, due in large part to two things—the increasing industrialization of the country, and the hordes of foreign immigrants since admitted without proper weeding out of the undesirables or their proper instruction in the principles of American law and government. Had a policy of restriction of immigration, similar to that of forty-five years later, then been introduced by the statesmen of the day, millions to-day would be rising up and calling blessed not only Hayes but also the leaders of both parties of that time. The President's action, however, as was usually the case, caused a steady growth in appreciation of him among the thoughtful American citizenship, whatever the cheap politicians in both parties might think of him.

Hayes showed that he meant what he said about civil service by removing from office Chester A. Arthur, collector of the port of New York, and A. B. Cornell, naval officer at the same place. Their protector, Senator Roscoe Conkling, stalwart leader of New York, bitterly fought the move and attempted to prevent the appointment of any successors. This downright challenge to senatorial patronage and the spoils system was bitterly resented, and only fifteen months later—when the better element in the party got behind Hayes, and John Sherman even threatened to resign—were Hayes's appointees to the places, namely, Edwin A. Merritt and Silas W. Burt, confirmed. The final struggle lasted for seven hours in the Senate.[3] Hayes also reappointed the able and efficient postmaster of New York city, Thomas L. James, and loyally supported him in this center of stalwart strength. He strongly backed Schurz in his efforts to conduct the affairs of the Department of the Interior on a merit basis.

The partizans and spoilsmen were enraged, and Congress definitely ignored all Hayes's recommendations for a law to reform the civil service or for appropriations to support the Civil-Service Commission. When the politicians went to the White House to protest to the President against his policy, he coolly read the Republican platform to them, and they retired, baffled and disgusted. Any advance in reform of this type was entirely due to the brave and courageous efforts of Hayes and his cabinet, with only lukewarm support from public opinion and the press. There was required the terrible tragedy of Garfield's assassination to awaken the country and Congress to the dangers of the situation, and bring about the real beginning of a better day, the fruits of which have not yet been brought to perfection, even fifty years later.

John Sherman had been the author and prime mover, while in the United States Senate, of the bill to resume specie payments on January 1, 1879, and which had become a law on January 14, 1875. In spite of efforts to prevent the accomplishment of this purpose, the Republicans had in general stood by the law, and the platform of 1876, as already shown, had contained an indorsement of this principle. Hayes stressed the need of resumption in his inaugural message, and it is due to him, with the cordial assistance and able financial strategy of Sherman as secretary of the treasury, that the law was carried out and resumption accomplished on January 1, 1879. The beneficial effect on business and finance throughout the country, with its reflex effect on international trade and finance, can well be imagined. Sherman also skilfully refunded $845,-

[3] John Sherman, "Recollections," 679–85.

000,000 of the public debt at a lower rate of interest. This was an achievement alone sufficient to make Hayes's administration memorable, and did much to stabilize the economic welfare of the country and prepare it not alone for the remarkable expansion of the next few years, but also to withstand the economic reverses that came during the last decade of the nineteenth century. There was much opposition to all this throughout the country, and also in both parties in Congress, especially among the Democrats, who all through this period were the party of soft money and bad financial policy. The taint persisted until that party was entirely given over to financial heresy at the time of the Bryan campaign in 1896.

One great mistake of the times resulted from the passage by the House of Representatives in November, 1877, of a bill introduced by Richard P. Bland, a Democrat from Missouri, providing for the free coinage of silver dollars of 412½ grains. When the Bland bill reached the Senate, and to prevent its passage in that form, Senator Allison of Iowa, in conference with Secretary Sherman (who mistakenly thought some such unsound measure necessary to obviate something worse), caused a compromise measure to be adopted which provided that the secretary of the treasury be required to purchase per month not less than two million and not more than four million dollars' worth of silver for coining into silver dollars. It also stipulated that the amount of money invested in bullion should not at any time be in excess of $5,000,000. Hayes most courageously vetoed the bill on February 20, 1878, sending in a strong and able message,[4] but Congress passed it over his veto by a decided majority. In spite of all the statesmanlike work of the Hayes administration with regard to finance, this was the beginning of a policy that was to cause serious economic trouble, leading finally to real distress. That Hayes clearly foresaw this is shown by the closing sentence of his veto message, in which he said: "A currency worth less than it purports to be worth will in the end defraud not only creditors, but all who are engaged in legitimate business, and none

[4] Text found in Richardson, "Messages and Papers," VII, 486–8.

more surely than those who are dependent on their daily labor for their daily bread." A sinister element in the whole affair was the fact that the Senate was under Republican control, and enough Republicans deserted their President and joined with the Democrats to pass the Bland bill over his veto. Rhodes soundly observes that the improvement in business conditions following resumption of specie payments, and the clean and efficient administration of Hayes, made possible the Republican success in the election of 1880. The family life of Mr. and Mrs. Hayes was all that could be desired, and the White House, on its domestic as well as its political side, was a stimulating example to the whole country.

Hayes and his administration stand out in strong contrast with the rather cheap policy followed both by the opponents in his party and by the Democrats in both houses of Congress. The stalwarts were playing a selfish game, doing anything to carry through their own ideas and nothing to coöperate with the remainder of the party. Hayes might have played "politics" to his own practical success, but it is doubtful if he thereby would have added to his own reputation as a statesman. The old radicals were not at all reconciled to their defeat in the Cincinnati convention of 1876, but already were preparing for another attempt to nominate Grant for a third term in 1880. Their animosity to Hayes should have been soothed by his reiterated statement that he would not be a candidate to succeed himself, a policy that resulted, as so often is the case when an executive forswears reëlection, in the opposite effect, so that the rank and file lost interest in him and were busily engaged in laying plans to influence the choice of the next occupant of the office, in the hope of grateful favors to follow.

The Democrats were even more foolish, especially those from the South who, at the very time when Hayes was defying large and powerful elements in his own party by withdrawing the troops and showing conciliation toward them, undertook by the Potter investigation to question his title to his office. Said Garfield to them on the floor of the House of Representatives: "The people whom I try to represent . . .

feel that their efforts at pacification have not been met with in the spirit in which they were offered, and that if this sort of proceeding goes forward, you not only cripple the President in his efforts to bring about that pacification, but you cripple every man who attempts to sustain him." [5]

The Democrats also tried by factious opposition and by attaching riders to appropriation bills to prevent the Federal control of Congressional and Presidential elections, which was a part of the reconstruction policy of the Grant *régime*. They announced that if Hayes vetoed these bills, then Congress would pass no appropriations, and the Government break down. Garfield, who at this time was the Republican minority leader in the House of Representatives, observed that "the Democrats are so fearful of interfering with state rights that they are unwilling the general government shall protect them from yellow fever, unless they can degrade the nation in comparison with the state. This they shall not do with my consent." [6] Hayes again met this opposition courageously, and vetoed seven bills; but in 1879, when the Democrats had gained control of the Senate as well as the House of Representatives, he was compelled to sign an appropriation bill with a rider prohibiting the use of troops by United States marshals.

The record of Hayes stands for itself. He brought new life and a spirit of efficiency into the executive department of the Government, raised anew the standard of personal and official honesty and integrity, stabilized the financial affairs of the Government, and contributed toward the economic soundness of the condition of the people at large. He also took the first great and necessary steps toward conciliation and reëstablishing, in truth as well as in name, the American Union. Garfield's tragic administration was to be too short to estimate his real capacity. Cleveland the Democrat was far above the average of our national executives. But it is a fair statement that Hayes was the best President we had from Lincoln to McKinley.

[5] T. C. Smith, "Garfield," II, 665.
[6] T. C. Smith, "Garfield," II, 674.

Chapter XII

THE GARFIELD TRAGEDY AND THE SUCCESSION OF ARTHUR

For a year before the convention of 1880 there was much talk of candidates, especially since Hayes had removed himself from the contest by his statement in his letter of acceptance of the nomination in 1877. Blaine was early in the field, rounding up delegates, and of course this meant that his inveterate enemy, Roscoe Conkling, would take measures against him. The vain and ruthless senator from New York never had forgiven the sarcastic personal attack made upon him by Blaine in the House of Representatives on April 30, 1866. Blaine used the following scorching language in describing the New Yorker: "His haughty disdain, his grandiloquent swell, his majestic, super-eminent, overpowering, turkey-gobbler strut has been so crushing to myself and all the members of this house, that I know it was an act of the greatest temerity for me to venture upon a controversy with him. But, sir, I know who is responsible for all this. . . . That gifted and satirical writer, Theodore Tilton [wrote] a little jocose satire, a part of which was the statement that the mantle of the late Winter Davis had fallen upon the member from New York. The gentleman took it seriously and it has given his strut additional pomposity. The resemblance is great. It is striking. Hyperion to a satyr, Thersites to Hercules, mud to marble, dunghill to diamond, a singed cat to a Bengal tiger, a whining puppy to a roaring lion. Shade of the mighty Davis, forgive the almost profanation of that jocose satire!" [1] Blaine forgot that the calling of names is like children making faces, and

[1] Quoted in Rhodes, "History of the United States," VII, 211 (note).

about as effective in argument, the result being merely Conkling's undying enmity, which cost him dear, much as Conkling may have deserved the characterization.

Grant had just returned from a tour around the world, and his trip from San Francisco, where he landed, was a continual popular ovation, no doubt sincere and spontaneous at first, but helped on by his followers, who felt that with his great personal popularity the mistakes of his Presidency might be forgotten and they could ride back to power on his shoulders. Conkling was most active in this movement, as were J. Donald Cameron of Pennsylvania and John A. Logan of Illinois. In making him their candidate, the stalwarts, as they now should be called, argued that Hayes's policy had given the entire control of the South, electoral votes and all, to the Democrats, who would prevent the negroes from voting and thus cast a solid block of votes for any Northern Democrat who would coöperate with these "traitorous" elements. To prevent this, it was necessary to nominate a great popular hero like Grant, who might carry every Northern and Western state and, when elected, vigorously use the power of the National Government, military and civil, to provide a way for the negro to vote and thus break the "solid South." Also, the deserving stalwarts, in many cases deprived of office by the "snivel service reform" of Hayes and his reformers, would come back into their own. Already delegates were being lined up for Grant, and he would make a strong contender against the brilliant and popular Blaine, who, although himself a leading stalwart, was weaned from their ranks by the feud with Conkling and his opposition to their idol, Grant. These latter were using most ruthless methods to corral delegates and instruct them, by fair means or foul, for their candidate.

Ohio put forth a very worthy and acceptable candidate in the person of John Sherman, and the latter induced James A. Garfield to go to the convention as one of his managers. In general, Sherman of course had the support of the Hayes men, although some of the reformers were for Senator George F. Edmunds of Vermont. It became evident, as the time for the convention approached, that the delegates would be so divided among a number of candidates that no one would start off on the balloting with anything like a majority, consequently a compromise candidate was probable, and this was the hope of the followers of Sherman, Edmunds, and others.

The name of James A. Garfield often was mentioned, for he had had a brilliant career as soldier, congressman, and educator, was exceedingly popular, and was known as an able man with an exceedingly lovable and attractive personality. Garfield himself took little or no part in this movement, for he confided to his diary, on February 5, 1879: "I am receiving a large number of letters from various parts of the country in regard to the presidency. While I am not indifferent to the good opinion of men who think me fit for that high place, I am still wholly disinclined to believe that any result will come out of it other than some general talk. I have so long and so often seen the evil effects of the presidential fever upon my associates and friends that I am determined it shall not seize upon me, for in almost every case it impairs if it does not destroy the usefulness of its victim." [2] Garfield's able and judicious biographer, Theodore C. Smith, says of the question of Garfield as a candidate: "All the evidence in existence shows that Garfield was not even a receptive candidate for the Presidency, but tended to view the 'dark horse' movement with disquiet if not actual alarm. He seems to have felt regarding it about as he did toward the Ohio governorship—that he did not want it, and was not a candidate for it, but could not absolutely say in advance that he would not take it, since it was conceivable that his party might really need him in that position to carry the state." He went to Chicago sincerely desirous of securing the nomination for his friend Sherman, and only under the most dramatic circumstances was he himself chosen to lead the Republican party.

The hotels in Chicago for some days prior to the meeting of the convention were packed with delegates, politicians, and hangers-on, excitedly discussing the prospects of the various

[2] T. C. Smith, "Garfield," II, 947.

candidates, and the political pot was boiling at a savage rate. John Tweedy, who was present, gives a vivid account of the hall, meetings, and various events.[3] The convention contained among its delegates some of the ablest men in the party of their day, and was a mixture of politicians of an age now passing away, combined with those who were to have the greatest influence during the next thirty or forty years. Among the latter were Levi P. Morton and Thomas C. Platt of New York; Matthew S. Quay, Christopher L. Magee, and James A. Beaver of Pennsylvania; Benjamin Harrison of Indiana; D. B. Henderson and J. S. Clarkson of Iowa; Eugene Hale and William P. Frye of Maine; George F. Hoar and Henry Cabot Lodge of Massachusetts; William J. Sewell of New Jersey; James A Gary and Lloyd Lowndes of Maryland. The convention met in Exhibition Hall, a large building said to seat about 15,000, which stood near the lake and not far from the site of the later Auditorium Hotel. In this same building both Blaine and Cleveland were nominated in 1884, but it was soon after taken down. Galleries ran around three sides of it, and the platform was at the remaining end. The latter was very large and would seat several hundred people. It was reserved for invited guests, and many ladies were among them. The front of the main floor was reserved for delegates, with the alternates sitting just behind them. A railing with several gates divided these two bodies, but the street entrances were side by side. The New York, Ohio, Indiana, and Illinois delegates were seated near the center. This gave the choice position to the Grant followers, while those Ohio men who were for Sherman also were in an advantageous situation.

The convention was called to order on Wednesday, June 2, 1880, at twelve o'clock noon by J. Donald Cameron, chairman of the National Committee. George F. Hoar of Massachusetts was made temporary chairman as the prearranged result of an agreement between the Grant and Blaine forces. They were willing to unite upon him due to his character and his reputation for fairness, and to the additional fact that he was known

[3] "History of the Republican National Conventions," 167–200.

to favor the nomination of Senator Edmunds. In his Autobiography,[4] published some years later, Senator Hoar gives in full an account of the whole transaction which is of supreme interest. It appears that a few days before the time appointed for the meeting of the convention it was rumored that Cameron, with the other Grant leaders, had evolved a scheme that would make the nomination of Grant almost certain, by the use of prearranged steam-roller methods. Any one who knew Cameron, Conkling, and Logan was certain that the rumor was a fact. They were utterly ruthless, high-handed and remorseless where their political objectives were concerned, and they had behind them about 308 absolutely certain votes of delegates for Grant. The state conventions of New York, Pennsylvania, and Illinois, and possibly several others, had instructed their delegations to vote as a unit for him. But there were 19 delegates from New York, 26 from Pennsylvania, and 18 from Illinois who were for other candidates. If the unit rule should be enforced these 63 votes would have to go to Grant, which, as later was shown in the actual balloting, would give just 13 votes short of the necessary number to nominate. There is no question that these easily could have been secured from the floating votes at times cast for Grant or other candidates during the long-drawn-out process of balloting, and hence the stalwart conspirators could have captured the nomination for their favorite.

Hoar says Cameron was pledged, when he called the convention to order as national chairman, to hold that the unit rule must apply to the voting for temporary chairman. When this was properly carried through, then the temporary chairman was to hold to the same rule when the permanent president was chosen, and this last man was to continue the ruling throughout the convention.

The National Committee met in Chicago about a day before the convention was to open, and fortunately the majority of its members were not Grant men. Cameron was asked point-blank whether or not he had made the above pledge. He re-

[4] Vol. I, 388–401.

fused to answer. A motion then was made that the chairman be instructed, after calling the convention to order, to receive the votes of the individual delegates without regard to instructions of the majority of the delegations. Cameron refused to put this motion, saying it was beyond the powers of the committee. A long discussion followed, with intimations that Cameron might be removed from the chairmanship of the committee unless he put the motion. The committee adjourned over until the next day, and the Grant men then approached Strong of Illinois, who already had been appointed sergeant-at-arms by the committee and was a Grant supporter, to find if he would refuse to recognize any successor to Cameron as entitled to call the convention to order and would execute the orders of Cameron until a temporary chairman was chosen. Strong hesitated and, after conferring with several men, declined to accede to the proposed plan as being illegal. Cameron therefore backed down and gave the assurance desired. As part of the bargain, the choice of Hoar was agreed upon, and thus the danger averted of an uproar and possible disruption of the convention. It was later thought best to do away with any chances of a further contest, and Mr. Hoar was also made permanent president. He filled the onerous and difficult duties of his office with great fairness and success, having a most excited and at times unruly convention to control.

The first great struggle came over a motion, made by Conkling, that every member of the convention be bound to support its nominee, no matter who he might be. This motion has appeared at other times and in other places and, as a means of impugning the integrity or good faith of independent members, and handcuffing them to any political monstrosity, is the last refuge of the demagogues—especially such a one as Conkling was, in spite of his undoubted ability. The motion, of course, was carried and by the vote of 716 to 3. Conkling at once further moved to expel the opposing three from the convention. The negative votes were those of Campbell, Moore, and McCormick, all of West Virginia, who stood up and said they intended to support the nominee of the convention, but did not think the resolution wise. A heated discussion now arose, when Garfield took the floor and stood by the freedom of conviction of each individual, although protesting his own loyalty to the convention. Finally Conkling was compelled to withdraw his motion in defeat, but not until he had attempted to browbeat Mr. Hoar, the presiding officer.

This event was of vast importance. It arraigned Garfield and Conkling as rival floor leaders of the convention, and opened that bitter struggle that helped toward the assassination of the former a little more than a year later. Conkling, as Rhodes points out,[5] was playing the part of the demagogue with studied effect. He was stopping at the Grand Pacific Hotel and courted publicity. He swaggered around with his "turkey-cock strut" which Blaine had so well if indiscreetly described, and his entrance into the convention would take place, by intent, after it was called to order. This was in order to attract the most attention and receive the applause of his followers among the delegates and the mob of onlookers. During the proceedings he was high-handed as a czar, had the manner of a present-day traffic policeman, and steadily estranged the delegates by his insolent and dictatorial manner. In contrast, Garfield was all fairness, kindness, and affability. This was not a pose but the true nature of the man.

The convention was in such a high pitch of excitement during most of the time that the disorderly and childish scenes which so often disgrace the proceedings, even at a later time, of what should be a most dignified and important assembly were here enacted. Robert Ingersoll on one occasion waved a woman's red shawl. Delegates paraded around the hall whooping and yelling and generally making fools of themselves. A woman jumped up on the rail behind the president and tried to make a speech, swinging her parasol around, while a man sitting beneath her raised his umbrella to protect himself.[6] On one occasion, while Conkling was making a speech, which was often the case, Garfield, who rapidly was becoming the favorite

[5] "History of the United States," VIII, 116–7.
[6] Rhodes, "History of the United States," VIII, 118–19.

of the convention, happened to enter—his enemies said by plan—and the crowds cheered him to the echo, drowning out Conkling in the midst of his "oration," for, able speaker that he was, he usually "orated" on all occasions.

In order to do away with all uncertainty, the Committee on Rules, of which Garfield was the chairman, brought in a provision definitely abolishing the unit rule. It provided that when the vote of any state should be announced by the chairman of the delegation, if any exception should be taken to the announcement, "the president of the convention shall direct the roll of members of such delegation to be called, and the result recorded in accordance with the votes individually given." There was a minority report against it, but it was defeated without a division. An amendment also was adopted directing the National Committee to prepare a method for the election of delegates to the convention of 1884. This was a final blow at the unit rule and a step toward greater popular control of the party.

The platform was reported on Saturday, the fourth day (June 5), and adopted. It was a statement by the Republican party of its administration "at the end of twenty years since the federal government was first committed to its charge," and contained the usual summary of achievements and also the usual attack upon the Democratic party for "the habitual sacrifice of patriotism and justice to a supreme and insatiable lust of office and patronage." Nationalism was upheld in the sound statement that "some powers are denied to the nation, while others are denied to the states; but the boundary between the powers delegated and those reserved is to be determined by the national, and not by the state tribunals." The excellent and praiseworthy American plank of 1876, in favor of the public schools, was repeated, with the recommendation "that the Constitution be so amended as to . . . forbid the appropriation of public funds to the support of sectarian schools." It especially was stated that this should apply to "the legislature of each state." There were the usual declarations against "further grant of the public domain" to "any railway or other

From "As I Knew Them" by permission of Harper & Brothers

ROSCOE CONKLING'S "TURKEY GOBBLER STRUT"

corporation"; against polygamy; also that "the duties levied for the purpose of revenue should so discriminate as to favor American labor"; for the restriction of Chinese immigration; and in praise of President Hayes due to his "efficient, just and courteous discharge of the public business and . . . his interposition between the people and proposed partisan laws." There might well have been the additional statement that the main hope of Republican success at the polls was the prestige of his fine and honest administration.

It will be noted that there was no mention of the burning question of that time—civil-service reform. A delegate from Massachusetts, Mr. James M. Barker, offered an additional plank stating that the Republican party "adopts the declaration of President Hayes, that the reform of the civil service should be thorough, radical, and complete. To this end it demands the coöperation of the legislative with the executive department of the government, and that Congress shall so legislate that fitness, ascertained by proper practical tests, shall admit to the public service." After some haggling, this was finally adopted and the whole platform accepted. It was to mean something concrete this time, for Hayes had paved the way, and Garfield's death made imperative the enactment of a proper civil-service law.

On that same Saturday, at an evening session, the nominating speeches were made, the most telling being those of Conkling when he proposed the name of Grant, and of Garfield in proposing Sherman. Conkling made one of the great speeches of political history, at least so far as its effects were concerned, and it can be compared in this regard with the celebrated Ingersoll speech proposing Blaine in 1876. In a most dramatic way he began by repeating the verse:

> And when asked what state he hails from,
> Our sole reply shall be—
> He comes from Appomattox,
> And its famous apple-tree.

Conkling swept the convention with him, and then Garfield had the exceedingly difficult task of following, when there had been a storm of applause lasting twenty-five minutes. Hoar says:[7] "One of the greatest oratorical triumphs I ever witnessed was obtained by Garfield. . . . There was nothing stimulant or romantic in the plain wisdom of John Sherman." He began quietly by remarking: "I have witnessed the extraordinary scene of this convention with deep solicitude. Nothing touches my heart more quickly than a tribute of honor to a great and noble character. But as I sat in my seat and witnessed this demonstration, this assemblage seemed to me a human ocean in a tempest. I have seen the sea lashed into fury and tossed into spray, and its grandeur moves the soul of the dullest man; but I remember it is not the billows, but the calm level of the sea from which all heights and depths are measured. . . . Not here, in this brilliant circle; but by four millions of Republican firesides. . . *there* God prepares the verdict which will determine the wisdom of our work tonight." As Hoar points out, Conkling, by his overbearing disposition and sneering sarcasm, made it difficult for any person who had differed with him at the beginning to come over to him at the end. He lost ground continually; and, in fact, this convention was to prove the beginning of the end of his political career. Garfield conciliated at every step, and when in the course of his speech just quoted he said, "And now, gentlemen of the convention, what do we want?" a voice of one of the delegates called out, "We want Garfield." Garfield hurriedly went on in his plea for Sherman. The convention adjourned over until Monday morning and the excitement and suspense of that intervening Sunday well can be imagined.

The first ballot, on Monday morning, resulted as follows: U. S. Grant, Illinois, 304; James G. Blaine, Maine, 284; John Sherman, Ohio, 93; George F. Edmunds, Vermont, 33; Elihu B. Washburne, Illinois, 31; William Windon, Minnesota, 10. Then followed a long-drawn-out struggle until the final result on the thirty-sixth ballot on Tuesday, the sixth day of the convention. On the thirty-third ballot Mr. Garfield still had only one vote. On the thirty-fourth he received 17 and at once rose

[7] "Autobiography," I, 393–5.

to a question of order. Said Garfield: "I challenge the correctness of the announcement. The announcement contains votes for me. No man has a right, without the consent of the person voted for, to announce that person's name, and vote for him, in this convention. Such consent I have not given—" Hoar, who was presiding, interrupted Garfield in the middle of a sentence. He was fearful he might say something that would make his nomination impossible, or his acceptance impossible if his nomination were made. Said Hoar: "The gentleman from Ohio is not stating a question of order. He will resume his seat. No person having received a majority of the votes cast, another ballot will be taken. The clerk will call the roll." The thirty-fifth ballot showed a total of 50 for Garfield, while Grant received 313; Blaine, 257; Sherman, 99; Edmunds, 11; Washburne, 23; Windom, 3. The thirty-sixth ballot then was taken and Garfield received 399 votes and was nominated. All the votes but 42 of those previously for Blaine were transferred to him. On this last ballot Grant still received 306; Blaine, 42; Sherman, 3; Washburne, 5.

On motion of Conkling, who did not mention the choice of the convention, seconded by Logan, Beaver, Hale, Harrison of Indiana, and others, the vote was made unanimous. Garfield sat motionless. It is reported that he seemed stunned by surprise. Said Shelby M. Cullom:[8] "I remember vividly the form and features of Garfield in that convention. I see him placing Sherman in nomination, probably not realizing at the time that he was in nomination himself. I see him taking an active part in all the debates, and as I look back now I do not think I ever saw a man so affected as General Garfield was when it was announced that he was the nominee of the Republican party for the Presidency of the United States. Seemingly he almost utterly collapsed. He sank into his seat, overcome. He was taken out of the convention and to a room in the Grand Pacific [Hotel], where I met him a very few minutes afterwards."

The usual cheers, excitement, marching around the hall followed, and then came at once the question of the choice of

[8] "Fifty Years of Public Service," 124.

a running-mate. The 306 stalwarts had stood by Grant to the end, and so at once an attempt was made to placate them. A recess was taken from 2:30 P.M. until 5 P.M. Tweedy says:[9] "Soon after the recess of the convention began, and when a large part of the spectators and delegates had left, while crossing the floor of the hall, I saw Chester A. Arthur approaching from the opposite side. Just then William Dennison of the Ohio delegation, war governor of Ohio and later postmaster-general in President Lincoln's cabinet, seeing Mr. Arthur, hurried toward him and said: 'Arthur, New York must name the candidate for Vice-President.' Mr. Arthur, evidently feeling very sore over Grant's defeat, walked on, scarcely making a reply." It is said that Garfield desired Levi P. Morton of New York, but he declined on the advice of Boutwell. The stalwarts then recommended Arthur, who was nominated. Conkling condemned Arthur's action, saying that Garfield could not possibly be elected.[10]

When the convention reassembled after the recess, a number of the Blaine and other followers refused to support Arthur, but he was nominated on the first ballot. It was as follows: Arthur, 468; Washburne, 199; Jewell, 43; Maynard (Tennessee), 30; Davis (Texas), 20; Bruce (Mississippi; a negro), 8; Alcorn (Mississippi), 4; Settle (Florida), 2; Woodford (New York), 1. After the usual motion to make the nomination unanimous, the convention adjourned.

James Abram Garfield was born at Orange, Cuyahoga county, Ohio, on November 19, 1831. As a boy he worked hard at various occupations, since his mother was left a widow with several small children. For some weeks he was driver on the towpath of a canal, but this was a mere interlude in his other occupations. He graduated from Hiram College, Ohio, in 1854 and from Williams College in 1856, working his way through. He was an instructor and later president of Hiram College, a member of the Ohio state senate 1859-61, and enlisted at the beginning of the Civil War. He had an honorable and brilliant

[9] "History of the Republican National Conventions," 199.
[10] D. S. Alexander, "History of the State of New York," III, 442-6.

service, being promoted major-general in 1863. He was elected to Congress the same year and served in the House of Representatives until 1880. He had recently been elected United States senator from Ohio when he was nominated for President, at about the age of forty-eight years and a half.

The nomination of Garfield was received with enthusiasm, not to mention satisfaction, throughout the country, with the exception of the stalwarts, who were unreconciled. Conkling made a few speeches in the subsequent campaign, without once mentioning Garfield's name. Says Hoar:[11] "Garfield was a man of indefatigable industry and vast information. He seemed constantly possessed by an intelligent curiosity in regard to all subjects. He had a tenacious memory. Its stores were always ready at hand for use on all occasions. There has been no man in public life in my time, except Charles Sumner, who was always so glad to render any service in his power to literature and science. . . . During Garfield's service in the House he was the leader of its best thought. Everything he did and said manifested the serious, reverent love of excellence. He was ever grave, earnest, addressing himself only to the reason and conscience of his auditors. You will search his speeches in vain for an appeal to a base motive or an evil passion. He was remarkably independent in forming his judgments and inflexible in adhering to them on all great essential occasions."

There were bitter attacks upon him for his alleged disloyalty to Sherman in using his candidacy for the purpose of furthering his own. Says T. C. Smith on this subject:[12] "In view of the contents of his diary and letters during the period culminating in the balloting, this theory can scarcely be considered tenable. He certainly did nothing knowingly to foster his own chances, if his most confidential utterances are not to be dismissed as elaborate hypocrisy. And the strongest argument against this theory is found in Garfield's whole career and deep-founded habits of mind regarding methods of political advancement." The final answer to the allegation is the fact that

[11] "Autobiography," I, 403–4.
[12] "Life of Garfield," II, 987.

Sherman himself absolved Garfield from all such charges and cordially supported him for the election.[13] He did believe, however, that certain members of the Ohio delegation, as well as other friends, had not stood by him properly and loyally.

The nomination of Chester Alan Arthur was received with coldness or downright opposition. Arthur's only service under the National Government had been as collector of the port of New York, from which he had been summarily removed by President Hayes, with the consequent struggle and defeat of Conkling. He was born at Fairfield, Vermont, October 5, 1830, and was thus over forty-nine years old, and a year older than Garfield. He graduated at Union College, Schenectady, New York, in 1848, taught school, practised law in New York city, and was appointed on the governor's staff in 1861, being inspector-general and quartermaster-general of the New York troops in 1862. Grant had appointed him collector of the port in 1871. Fortunately, the popularity of the head of the ticket was sufficient to "carry the ticket," as the politicians say, and Arthur did not prove too much of a drag during the campaign. He later surprised people by his dignity, fairness, and ability when called upon to succeed Garfield at the tragedy of the latter's death.

After the convention adjourned, the committee on notification assembled in the club-room of the Grand Pacific Hotel at Chicago, on Tuesday, June 8, and at eleven in the evening formally notified Garfield of his nomination. Mr. Hoar made the speech, to which Garfield replied briefly in very modest and unassuming terms, which were a disappointment to some of the emotional Republicans. "I assure you," said he, "that the information you have officially given me brings the sense of a very grave responsibility, and especially so in view of the fact that I was a member of your body, a fact that could not have existed with propriety had I the slightest expectation that my name would be connected with the nomination for the office. I have felt with you great solicitude concerning the situation of our party during the struggle; but believing that you are cor-

[13] "Recollections," II, 775–8.

rect in assuring me that substantial unity had been reached in the conclusion, it gave me a gratification far greater than any personal pleasure your announcement can bring. I accept the trust committed to my hands." President Hayes was especially pleased with the nomination, for he knew Garfield well and had relied upon him as Republican minority floor leader in the House of Representatives. He wrote in his diary: "Garfield's nomination at Chicago was the best that was possible. It is altogether good. He is the ideal candidate because he is the ideal self-made man." [14] Having been closely allied to the Hayes administration, as Garfield was, his choice by the convention was in a sense an indorsement of it, and a vindication of all the best that Hayes was and that he had stood for. He may be called an accident, and at least he was a "dark horse." But he was, according to the best judgment of his contemporaries and of historians since that time, eminently worthy of the honor and responsibility.

The Greenback convention met at Chicago on June 9 and nominated James B. Weaver of Iowa, of later "Populist" fame, and B. J. Chambers of Texas. The Prohibitionists held their convention at Cleveland, Ohio, on June 17 and nominated General Neal Dow of Maine, the great and courageous temperance leader, and with him as a running-mate, A. M. Thompson of Ohio. The last convention was that of the Democrats, which met at Cincinnati on June 22. It is said that about one third of the delegates would have been glad to nominate Tilden, but he sent a letter in which he "renounced" the nomination, whatever that may mean, on the score of health, and the convention doubtless was glad to take him at his word. Had there been a popular feeling that he was the deeply wronged man that some of his partizans claimed, he would have been nominated in spite of this and by acclamation. The fact that the Democratic party turned elsewhere is the greatest justification of Hayes and the work of the electoral commission.

The Democrats nominated, on the second ballot, General Winfield S. Hancock, a man of irreproachable integrity, for-

[14] C. R. Williams, "Hayes," II, 239.

merly a major-general in the Civil War, and often spoken of as one of the great heroes of Gettysburg. This nomination enabled them to meet the war record of Garfield. The other prominent contenders for the honor were Thomas F. Bayard of Delaware, Henry B. Payne of Ohio, Allen G. Thurman of Ohio, Stephen J. Field of California, William R. Morrison of Illinois, Thomas A. Hendricks of Indiana and Samuel J. Randall of Pennsylvania. For Vice-President the choice was William H. English of Indiana, a man of good reputation and ability. The platform was short, and after stating opposition to centralization of government, sumptuary laws, and Chinese immigration, it advocated home rule, honest money, a "tariff for revenue only," and declared itself the friend of labor. But it also declared that the issue of the "great fraud of 1876-7" was the predominant one, which "precedes and dwarfs every other" and "imposes a more sacred duty upon the people of the Union than ever addressed the conscience of a nation of freemen."

In spite of this attempt to make an issue of the disputed election, the whole thing fell absolutely flat. Knowing that their own candidate bore an unblemished reputation, the Democrats entered upon one of the most disgraceful and contemptible campaigns against the private character of General Garfield. They accused him of immorality, which his biographer, Professor Theodore C. Smith, is able summarily to dispose of, and few right-minded people believed it at the time. Also, he was attacked on account of the Crédit Mobilier, the number "329" being "painted, chalked, and printed everywhere, on sidewalks, doors, and dead-walls, and in the opposition newspapers; that being the number of dollars he was alleged to have received as a Crédit Mobilier dividend."[15] A forged letter in Garfield's supposed handwriting, to a mythical person named Morey, expressed sentiments on Chinese immigration intended to arouse opposition on the Pacific coast. "In this case, as in earlier ones, Garfield's reluctance to make a personal statement simply played into the hands of his enemies,

[15] Stanwood, "History of the Presidency," 416.

who promptly claimed that his denial was under compulsion." [16] It is probable that the Democratic campaign of vilification and personalities disgusted the rank and file of the people, and by it the Democrats threw away whatever chances they had of winning, and these were thought excellent.

Garfield had the hard task of harmonizing a discordant party. He was in danger of falling down between the bitterly opposing wings of Blaine on one side, and Conkling, Grant, and Logan on the other, while opposed to both of them likewise were the independents, reformers, and many Hayes men generally. As showing the bitter feeling of the times, an eyewitness has told the writer of a chance meeting one day during the campaign, on Fifth Avenue, New York, between General McClellan, of Civil War fame, and James G. Blaine. The conversation turned to the recent Republican convention and nomination, and McClellan remarked, "Well, Blaine, you did not get it, did you?" "No," answered Blaine, "but I put Grant to sleep!"

In the first place, when the question came of a choice of chairman of the Republican National Committee to manage the campaign, Garfield merely recommended to them four names, those of W. E. Chandler, Eugene Hale, R. C. McComins, and Marshall Jewell, adding that he recommended the appointment of Thomas C. Platt as secretary "on account of his knowledge of New York politics." The committee chose Jewell, and to placate the stalwarts, a regular machine politician, S. W. Dorsey, was made secretary. Dorsey's type may be imagined when he was preferred over "Tom" Platt!

The stalwarts and spoilsmen, the 306 followers of Grant in the recent convention, were afraid that Garfield might prove another Hayes when it came to dividing the patronage and political favors, and it was felt imperative to give them some sort of assurance of recognition which at the same time would not anger or alienate the reformers and Hayes men. Garfield did this by saying, in his formal letter of acceptance: "To select wisely from our vast population those who are best fitted

[16] T. C. Smith, "Garfield," II, 1041.

for the many offices to be filled, requires an acquaintance far beyond the range of any one man. The Executive, therefore, should seek and receive the information and assistance of those whose knowledge of the communities in which the duties are to be performed best qualifies them to aid in making the wisest choice." This caused disappointment among the independents, but few of them left his support. On the other hand, it did not pacify the stalwarts. Garfield made a trip to New York for conference purposes, but Conkling did not see him. A conference with the leaders was held at the Fifth Avenue Hotel. Garfield asked Levi P. Morton, a stalwart, to act as chairman of the campaign committee on finance, and Morton accepted. It was afterward charged that Garfield made definite promises to the stalwarts at this conference concerning the patronage, but while he was conciliatory and friendly, it is evident that such was not the case.[17]

On September 13 the state of Maine was carried by a Democrat-Greenback fusion, and efforts were redoubled to bring about party harmony. On the twenty-eighth of September Grant, Conkling, and Logan called to see Garfield at the latter's farm at Mentor, Ohio, but only a species of lukewarm friendship seemed to result, and in a subsequent Republican meeting in New York Conkling barely referred to Garfield. On October 12 the Republicans carried both Ohio and Indiana in the state elections, so there was a feeling of encouragement, but every one knew the November election would be close.

The Republicans cleverly took advantage of the declaration in the Democratic platform that favored a tariff for revenue only. This was helped by the blunt statement of Hancock, in an interview, that "the tariff question is a local question." The changes were rung on the difference between a tariff for revenue and one for protection, and business and labor were aroused to active endeavor in Garfield's behalf. On his above-mentioned trip to New York and his way back,

[17] For a judicial and scholarly discussion of this and other campaign disputes and incidents see T. C. Smith, "Garfield," II, chapter XXVI.

Garfield made numerous speeches, and also conducted a "front-porch campaign" from his home at Mentor, speaking to numerous delegations who visited him. This was a new departure in campaign policy and Garfield showed great courage and initiative in carrying it through, for the other Presidents or Presidential candidates who had regularly "gone on the stump," so to speak—Winfield Scott, Andrew Johnson, and Horace Greeley—had all suffered defeat. There was little "waving of the bloody shirt," happy to say, and the South and the negroes were not a leading issue for the first time in forty years, or since the campaign of Harrison and Tyler in 1840. This was a fortunate omen and marked a real change in conditions since the Civil War.

Garfield carried the election on November 3 by a small national plurality of less than 10,000, but won 214 electoral votes to Hancock's 155. Hancock carried the "solid South," where the Republican votes significantly fell off as much as one half in some states. He also had the old "border states," with California (by 78 votes and the loss of one of the electoral votes of the state), Nevada (by 81 votes), New Jersey (by 2010 votes) and West Virginia. Garfield carried the Northern and Western states, but Colorado by only 3203, Connecticut by 2661, and Oregon by 671. The total popular vote was: Garfield, 4,454,416; Hancock, 4,444,952; Weaver, 308,578; Dow, 10,305. The independents and reformers undoubtedly supported Garfield, as did many others who were disgusted by the disgraceful Democratic campaign lies. The tariff also helped, while Garfield himself, in a private letter to Sherman, said "the distrust of the solid South, and of adverse financial legislation, have been the chief factors in the contest. I think also that the country wanted to rebuke the attempt of the Democrats to narrow the issue to the low level of personal abuse." [18] These were the three Republican bases of national popular coöperation. The Democrats based everything on the personality of their candidate.

[18] J. Sherman, "Recollections," II, 789.

Garfield soon turned his attention to his prospective cabinet. He first offered the position of secretary of state to Blaine, who accepted it. While at first acquaintance and for a long time afterward Garfield had shown an innate suspicion of Blaine,[19] which had taken years to wear off, yet they now were intimate friends and worked most cordially together. There was much talk of a movement to continue Sherman in the Treasury Department, where he had made such a brilliant record, but Garfield himself told Sherman that Blaine objected, on the grounds that it would seem unfriendly discrimination against the other members of Hayes's cabinet. Sherman agreed, and a rival withdrawing from the contest in Ohio, he was chosen to succeed Garfield in the United States Senate.[20] It is probable that Blaine's enmity to Hayes and his administration was the cause of his opposition to Sherman. The appointment of Blaine of course angered Conkling and the stalwarts, and they virtually made the demand that Levi P. Morton succeed Sherman. Garfield steadily refused, putting William Windom of Minnesota in the Treasury Department. Thomas L. James, a New York stalwart, was made postmaster-general, and Morton was given the ministry to France, but this attempt to satisfy Conkling and his followers was of no avail. Wayne MacVeagh of Pennsylvania was made attorney-general, Samuel J. Kirkwood of Iowa secretary of the interior, Robert T. Lincoln of Illinois secretary of war, and William H. Hunt of Louisiana secretary of the navy. Several men declined appointments, including William B. Allison of Iowa, to whom he offered the Treasury, and John Hay, as secretary to the President; but as finally formed the cabinet was sound and satisfactory, even brilliant in several places. There were, of course, charges, especially on the part of the stalwarts, that Blaine had dictated the choice of the various members, but with the possible exception of the refusal to continue Sherman this was not the case. The correspondence between the two men, as printed and

[19] T. C. Smith, "Garfield," I, 440, 957.
[20] J. Sherman, "Recollections," II, 802–3.

judicially explained in Professor T. C. Smith's biography of Garfield, effectually disproves that.[21]

Conkling soon showed himself ready to declare war on Garfield. The latter made strenuous efforts, almost pitiful in their sincerity and good intent, to come to terms with his antagonist. He had been warned of Conkling by Sherman, who told him in a private letter of January 23, 1881, just what to expect. Said he:[22] "I know him well, and while I concede his ability as a party leader and debater, I think him greatly overrated in other respects. His egotism is unbounded. He is sensible to criticism and ridicule. He never interests himself in anything but personal antagonisms, he never rises above a custom-house or a post-office. As an able Republican and the recognized leader of a great state where bosses seem to be necessary, he is entitled to consideration and full recognition but, if you ever yield to him so that he thinks you fear him, he becomes overbearing. He treats his New York friends like lackeys. Your great office will enable you, without loss of self-respect, to make advances to him to do what seems best and proper to conciliate him. . . . If that fails, then the only way is to give him blow for blow. President Hayes could have crushed him but would not. If Conkling opens on you as he did on Hayes you ought without delay or hesitation to do what Jackson did with his senatorial enemies, strike them back through their friends. The Executive always has power to command the respect even if it cannot win the favor of members of Congress." This letter is especially important in the light of what followed. Garfield evidently took the lesson to heart.

Garfield was inaugurated on March 4, 1881, with the usual pomp and ceremony. His inaugural address had been written under great pressure and he himself stated that he wrote the last sentence at 2:30 A.M. on the morning of inauguration day. It was in plain and common-sense language and without any emotional or imaginative passages. The most

[21] Vol. II, 1080–81, 1095, 1098–9, 1100.
[22] Given in T. C. Smith, "Garfield," II, 1081–2.

significant points were as follows: He discussed the racial question in the South in temperate words and stated that "under our institutions there was no middle ground for the negro race between slavery and equal citizenship. There can be no permanent disfranchised peasantry in the United States." He acknowledged the peril of an uneducated electorate, adding that "to the South this question is of supreme importance. But the responsibility for the existence of slavery did not rest upon the South alone. The nation itself is responsible for the extension of the suffrage, and is under special obligations to aid in removing the illiteracy which it has added to the voting population." He took his stand for sound money and hinted at bimetallism. He was most specific on the subject of civil-service reform, and thereby added to the wrath against him of the stalwarts and the spoilsmen. "The civil service can never be placed on a satisfactory basis until it is regulated by law. . . . I shall at the proper time ask Congress to fix the tenure of the minor offices of the several executive departments and prescribe the grounds upon which removal shall be made during the terms for which incumbents have been appointed." [23]

The fight with Conkling was not long in coming. On March 20 Conkling had a conference with Garfield by invitation, and the latter evidently at once raised the question of dividing the New York offices between stalwarts and independents. Conkling also evidently refused and "would accept nothing but submission to his wishes," in the words of Professor Smith.[24] Garfield now made a bold and theatrical stroke. On March 24 he sent to the Senate, now meeting in special session for the purpose of ratifying appointments, a group of appointments such as had not been anticipated by any one. Among others, he removed Merritt, the reform collector of the port of New York, and nominated him for

[23] Richardson, "Messages and Papers," VIII, 6–12.

[24] See his excellent and lucid account of the Garfield-Conkling struggle, especially on pages 1104, 1106, 1134–6, 1141, in Vol. II of his "Garfield."

consul-general to London. To fill Merritt's place he nominated Judge W. H. Robertson, leader of the New York independents. Other nominations showed the President's independence of Blaine, Grant, or any other influence. Professor Smith well says (page 1106): "It was in the highest degree aggressive, almost ruthless, and it challenged opposition from all quarters, from civil-service reformers as well as from spoilsmen. It violated at one blow as many different political conventions as it well could." The fight at once broke loose. Garfield was obdurate, and the struggle lasted for weeks, amid great popular excitement and interest, as well may be imagined. Efforts at compromise were repeatedly made by different people of different factions. Garfield refused. He was willing to negotiate only on the terms that the independents, now beginning to be called "half-breeds" in contrast to the stalwarts, should have a division in New York appointments. Even Vice-President Arthur and Postmaster-General James formally protested. Conkling was fighting the political battle of his life. Finally, although the New York state senate had, on March 24, passed a resolution favoring the confirmation by the United States Senate of the Robertson appointment, much to the general surprise Conkling and Platt on May 16 tendered their resignations as senators as a protest, and sent a letter of explanation to the governor of New York. They evidently expected vindication before the people by their triumphant reëlection by the New York legislature. After the withdrawal of the New York senators, the Senate ratified the appointment of Robertson and adjourned on May 24.

But the climax of the struggle was yet to be reached, and in a way to make the gods laugh! After a struggle in the New York legislature, that body failed to reëlect Conkling and Platt, but chose Warner Miller and E. G. Lapham to fill their places! This was the virtual end of Conkling's political career. Platt went into retirement for a time. He had merely won the sobriquet of "Me Too" at the hands of humorists and cartoonists of the time. But he later returned to political power and became a dominating force in New York and national politics until he met his master in the honest and able statesman but adept politician, Theodore Roosevelt.

Garfield had been quick to sense the humorous aspect of his great victory. He wrote in his journal, under date of May 16: "At twelve Senators Conkling and Platt tendered their resignation as senators, a very weak attempt at the heroic. If I do not mistake, it will be received with guffaws of laughter. They appeal to a legislature which they think is already secured. Even in this they may fail. They have wounded the self-love of their brother senators and may lose by it. . . . Their letter to Governor Cornell giving their reasons for resigning . . . is a weak attempt at masquerading as injured innocents and civil-service reformers. They are neither. I go on without disturbance. Having done all I fairly could to avoid a fight I will fight to the end." [25] Garfield had taken well to heart the sage advice of John Sherman. And the world did guffaw!

Professor Smith sums up the contest and its results as follows: "Whatever tactical shortcomings Garfield may have displayed, he proved beyond question that he had the power of deciding on a policy, the ability to hold absolutely firm to it and the will power to compel the Senate to yield to his determination. When it is realized that every member of his party in the Senate sympathized with Conkling and Platt on their right to be 'consulted,' it is not too much to say that no President ever won a more striking personal triumph."[26] And Garfield also had achieved something that may show its effects in the years yet to come. In this later day of rivalry between the President and the Senate, a rivalry which has been growing for the past twenty-five years with ever-increasing significance, he showed the way for the President to win the final and inevitable victory, by shortening the contest. This is inevitable if present political tendencies continue, for the President more and more has come to represent the people as the one great nation-wide representative institution.

[25] Quoted in Smith, "Garfield," II, 1134-5.
[26] "Garfield," II, 1141.

One of the first problems that met the new administration was that of the near maturity of a large number of 5 and 6 per cent. United States bonds. Through the firm, sound, and almost brilliant financial policy of William Windom, secretary of the treasury, ably advised by Attorney-General MacVeagh, new 3½ per cent. bonds to the amount of $250,000,000 were sold, much to Garfield's satisfaction. It was one of the bright and successful achievements of his all too short administration, and he strongly supported and advised during the whole process of financial negotiations. An entirely different activity was that of Postmaster-General James, who, at Garfield's direction, undertook an investigation into the contracts for carrying the mails. This unearthed great dishonesty and graft in the department and showed that, in spite of the best endeavors of Hayes and his cabinet, corruption had been at work. These celebrated frauds, known as the "Star Route frauds," showed the complicity of the second assistant postmaster-general, Thomas W. Brady, a hold-over from the administration of Grant, and ex-Senator Dorsey of Arkansas, late secretary of the Republican National Committee. Their method was to secure contracts by the lowest bids, then add large amounts, out of all proportion to the original bid, for "more frequent service" or "expedited service." There was proved widespread collusion, and certain of the guilty ones showed signs of fight. Brady, after threats, published in retaliation a letter of Garfield, written during the campaign to Jay A. Hubbell, in which he had indorsed the levying of campaign contributions upon office-holders, an iniquitous practice common to all peoples and all parties at the time. Garfield never swerved from his duty, and only three days before his assassination complained that the prosecutions were too slow. Sending for officials, he directed them to speed up the proceedings.

Garfield also was deeply interested in Blaine's celebrated plans for bringing the United States into closer touch with the Latin-American countries, a policy that later developed into the Pan American Union. But all the time he was harried and his life nearly dogged out of him by the disgraceful and persistent, not to mention impudent, demands and manipulations of the office-seekers. The conflict with Conkling led to the greatest bitterness of feeling everywhere, as might be expected, and there is no doubt that this led directly to Garfield's death. One day, during the short term of his life in the White House, he came out of the private office of the President, closed the door, and going up to one of his children said in a weary and harassed way: "When I am gone, always be fair to the President. He is the last person in the country to know what the people really want and think. Not a person comes to see me but he has some axe to grind or some personal favor to ask."

On the morning of July 2, 1881, as Garfield was passing through the old Pennsylvania Railroad station, at Sixth and B Streets in Washington, D. C., accompanied by Blaine, and about to take the train to go to Williamstown, Massachusetts, to attend a reunion of his class, Charles J. Guiteau, a disappointed and disgruntled office-seeker, fired two shots point-blank at him with a pistol, both of them taking effect. Garfield was carried to the White House, and later moved to Elberon, near Long Branch, New Jersey, where he improved slightly under the refreshing effects of the sea air. After lingering in agony, he died on September 19, the anniversary of the battle of Chickamauga, where he had so heroically distinguished himself in 1863. His courage, heroism, and sweet consideration for others, with his patient and Christian resignation to what he evidently from the first thought inevitable, aroused the affectionate interest and admiration of all the people without exception. His death was a real national sorrow.

Senator Hoar, twenty years later, made this estimate of Garfield:[27] "I do not believe he would have been a tool or servant in the presidency. He would have mastered for himself the great subjects to be dealt with in our foreign policy, as well as in domestic administration and legislation. His will

[27] "Autobiography," I, 400.

would, in my opinion, if he had been spared to us, have been the dominant will in our government for eight fortunate and happy years. Next to the assassination of Lincoln, his death was the greatest national misfortune ever caused to this country by the loss of a single life."

After a trial that was carried on to a great length, amounting almost to a scandal, Guiteau was condemned and executed by hanging on June 30, 1882. As in the more recent malodorous Sacco-Vanzetti case, the defense made every effort, and nothing was overlooked in the attempt to secure the acquittal of the accused. They even had the bad taste to ask President Arthur for a reprieve.

Arthur at once took the oath of office following Garfield's death, and there was great popular apprehension that the whole administration would now be handed over to the stalwarts. He had actively intervened on Conkling's side in the struggle with Garfield, and later had even gone to Albany, New York, in the endeavor to procure the reëlection of Conkling and Platt, following their resignations. But he surprised every one by assuming at once an attitude of dignity and judicial fairness. He seemed to drop the ideas and attitude of a mere politician and make statesmanship his real ambition. He must have been shocked and deeply impressed by the assassination of his predecessor, and responsibility, as so often in the world's history, begat a sobering effect. He gave an administration which, if not distinguished, was eminently satisfactory.

The members of Garfield's cabinet at once handed in their resignations when Arthur succeeded him, but the latter requested them to remain in office until Congress met. However, Windom left the Treasury in October and was succeeded by Charles J. Folger of New York, a stalwart who had been urged on Garfield for the appointment when he refused to give it to Morton, and whom he had considered for other positions. Blaine left in December and was succeeded by Frederick T. Frelinghuysen of New Jersey.

When Congress met in December, Arthur, in his first annual message, made a long discussion of civil service and merit tests, and gave a somewhat reserved and unenthusiastic indorsement of the cause, but with the statement of his desire for some such legislation as should deal conservatively with the question. Republican reverses at the polls in 1882, with the warning given by the murder of Garfield, gave such point to the devoted and unselfish agitation of the reforming elements, that finally Congress passed the Pendleton act, which became law on January 16, 1883. This was a landmark of progress in American history. It provided for examinations to determine appointments, and that there should be no other recommendation than as to residence and moral character. The President was authorized to extend the act from time to time to such branches of the service as he might choose. Also, campaign contributions from officers and employees were forbidden. This act was introduced by a Democrat, Senator George H. Pendleton of Ohio, was passed practically as a non-partizan measure, and was signed by a Republican President. Arthur showed his sympathy with it by appointing as the first chairman of the commission in whose hands was the enforcement of the law no less a person than Dorman B. Eaton, one of the pioneers in the work for the enactment of such a measure. From that time the growth in civil-service reform has been fairly steady, until to-day it is accepted as one of the most fundamental and important of all governmental policies, and happily is being extended to municipalities and other local areas of government.

A new subject of political disagreement and contest now loomed up—that of the tariff. The loss of the House of Representatives by the Republicans in the election of 1882, when the Democrats secured a majority of 77, awakened them to the need for changes in the schedules, especially since there was a large treasury surplus and the reforming elements had now turned their attention to this subject. A tariff commission had been appointed in 1882, and although the protectionists got control of it, it actually recommended an average reduction of about 20 per cent. In order to forestall greater reductions at Democratic hands the Republicans put through the House of

Courtesy of Harper & Brothers

THE REPUBLICAN PACHYDERM, ALIVE AND KICKING, NOVEMBER, 1880

Representatives a moderate revenue bill. But the Senate further lowered rates and attached this measure as an amendment to an internal revenue bill that recently had passed the lower house. A bitter struggle followed, which finally resulted, after conference and a great deal of parliamentary manipulation, in the moderate reductions of 1883.

Another act of importance was the Chinese Exclusion Act of May 6, 1882, which suspended the immigration of skilled and unskilled Chinese labor for ten years. This was the real beginning of immigration restriction in the United States, which not only was later strengthened with regard to the Chinese, but also gradually was extended to include people of other nations. But it was the second decade of the twentieth century before strict and rational immigration restriction became a settled policy of the country. There also was passed the Edmunds act a short time before this, which abolished polygamy in the territory of Utah and other parts of the West and provided ample and efficient means for enforcement. When the Forty-eighth Congress met, the Democrats controlled the House of Representatives. In fact, the House of Representatives of the Forty-seventh Congress, elected in 1880, was the only one controlled by the Republicans between 1872 and 1888. Most of the legislation during the Arthur and first Cleveland administrations was more or less of a non-partizan character, due to the divided party control of the National Government, and the more or less disintegrated character of both parties in its leadership. Now that the "cohesive power of public plunder" was being removed, both parties had gradually to substitute other means of coöperative force. For the most part personalities served this purpose, and the campaign of 1884 was destined in large part to be fought on low grounds.

The Republicans now were to experience a time of eclipse, with a transition period to new and at last younger leadership. The generation of the Civil War times was passing away and a newer one coming to the front. Due to the fact that the Republican party was much sounder and more reliable than the Democratic party upon the subjects of finance and trade, as well as more consistent in every way, with the added prestige of the Civil War days, and also the added series of Democratic vagaries and mistakes, the party not only was able to survive the time of Democratic ascendancy, but emerged stronger than ever.

This was cleverly summed up in a telling manner by Julius C. Burrows in a campaign speech of the times. Said he:[28] "It is one of the peculiarities of modern Democracy that the principles it avowed yesterday it repudiates today. The cause it espouses today it will abandon tomorrow. Indeed, it may well be questioned whether as a party it has any fixed and abiding convictions. Its history for the last twenty-five years is a history of vacillation, insincerity and folly. In 1872 it demanded a speedy return to specie payments; in 1876 it denounced the resumption act and demanded its repeal. In 1868 it demanded the payment of the interest-bearing obligations of the government in irredeemable paper; in 1872 it denounced repudiation in every form and guise. In 1868 it demanded the abolition of all instrumentalities designed to secure negro supremacy; in 1872 it recognized the equality of all men before the law, of whatever race or color. From 1860 to 1865 it wielded its party power to obstruct the successful prosecution of the war for the Union; in 1882 it proclaimed itself the chief instrument in accomplishing its successful results. In 1868 it publicly thanked Andrew Johnson for exercising the veto power in resisting the aggressions of Congress; in 1880 it declared that the use of the veto power insults the people and imperils their institutions. In 1860 it drove labor to the shambles and sold it at public auction; in 1880 it declared itself the friend of the laboringmen. In 1868 it was for a Democrat for President; in 1872 it enlisted under the banner of a Republican. In war it followed the leadership of a peace general; in peace it supported a general who was for war. One of your own number, the distinguished gentleman from Texas, Mr. Upson, has fitly characterized the course of the Democratic party as follows: 'It can

[28] W. D. Orcutt, "Burrows of Michigan and the Republican Party," I, 203–5.

succeed,' he says, 'if the Democratic party will be true to its time-honored principles, true to itself, shake off its spell of vacillation and lethargy, cease its cowardly trimming at every doubting whisper, quit dodging at every flitting shadow, stop tweedling every political crank, and drag itself from the meshes of that dragnet policy thrown out to catch the followers of every new-fangled ism and popular whim.' And so the Democratic party, for a quarter of a century, without chart or compass, has been cruising in every sea, intent upon and anxious only to avail itself of any breeze from any quarter that might fill its sails and carry it into political power. I thank God that I belong to a party that in storm or sunshine has kept steadily on its course."

While Arthur did not seek the nomination in 1884, yet he let it be known that he would not be averse to having it. Certainly it was only natural that a man, after succeeding to an office by accident and making a success of its administration, should desire a vote of popular confidence and the possession of the office in his own right, so to speak. And Arthur really had made a success as President. Says Rhodes: "Arthur was fundamentally a gentleman and was simply his better self during his occupancy of the Presidency."[29] On the other hand, he was a stalwart who had profited, no matter how innocently, by the death of the "half-breed" chief. The Republican party was shot through with rivalries and the enmities of factions. Prospects appeared dark, for the Democrats swept New York state in 1882 and elected Grover Cleveland governor by 192,854 majority over Folger, Arthur's secretary of the treasury. The handwriting on the wall had become plain.

[29] "History of the United States," VIII, 206.

Chapter XIII

A PERIOD OF REPUBLICAN ECLIPSE

Signs were not wanting of a change in the whole aspect of national politics, leading to a more direct popular control of the parties. In the year 1883 the Republican National Committee took up a problem, often played with since and never yet courageously handled—as handled it must be. The problem is to do away with the crying shame of phantom Republican organizations in Southern states being fully represented in the national conventions, and their having as much influence there as those states in the North and West that supply all the electoral votes when it comes to the final elections. The committee drew up several plans looking toward a more equitable arrangement, but each proposal was rejected, and the convention of 1884 was held upon the basis of former conventions of the party. One thing had been definitely gained at the convention of 1880, however, and that was the abolition of the unit rule.

When the leaders began to look around for available candidates, it was decided by many of them that Arthur would not do. It was doubtful if he could carry his own state of New York, and in view of the solid South, the necessity for carrying that state now was imperative for the Republicans. Against this latter they must pit themselves for many years to come, and even to-day (1927) have not escaped from this necessity. This is a clear legacy of evil left by the radicals of 1865 to 1876. Blaine had a host of followers in every part of the North and West, and was the most popular candidate with the rank and file of the people, both politicians and voters, although many shook their heads when they remembered the past charges against him and fully appreciated his vulnerability. He himself made it clear that he would not work for the nomination, but would accept it if it came to him. He stressed the fact that no money must be spent in his behalf. He stated that he did not want the nomination "unless it be the unbought, unbiased will of the nominating power. I enjoin this upon you with special emphasis. . . . This is not merely a question of conscience and principle with me, but has become almost a superstition. Nomination procured by objectionable means would not merely be unwelcome to me, but would prove disastrous." [1] Blaine also was a shrewd enough politician to know that the Democrats probably would nominate Cleveland, who easily could carry New York and would be elected. He himself would have liked to have General William T. Sherman run, and again use the "war hero" to arouse enthusiasm and serve as a convenient basis of coöperation. But Sherman emphatically and absolutely refused, in the most peremptory terms. John Sherman, his brother, again had a following, and was willing but not desirous. General John A. Logan, a conspicuous soldier of the Civil War and practical politician since that time, had a large following but was not of the prominence of Sherman, nor were the independent elements friendly toward him. Again the independents, soon to be known under the new name of "Mugwumps," favored Senator Edmunds, and his nomination might have carried the Republican party to victory. It soon became clear that Blaine was the leading candidate, but the matter of doubt consisted in the question, Could the various members of the opposition unite upon some available man and beat him? Grant had suffered great business reverses, was not in good health, and was withdrawing from politics. The stalwarts gradually were disintegrating, but their animosities still slumbered when it came to various individuals. Interesting to say, Thomas C. Platt had bobbed up serenely and went to the convention as the supporter of Blaine. And the stalwarts, or at least many of them, still remembered that Blaine had been among the first of their number, and had given them their appellation.

[1] E. Stanwood, "Blaine," 269–70.

The convention met in the Exposition Building, Chicago, at noon on Tuesday, June 3, 1884, pursuant to the call of the National Committee, which also had designated ex-Senator Powell Clayton of Arkansas to be temporary chairman. The convention was called to order by the chairman of the National Committee, Dwight M. Sabin of Minnesota, who had been chosen to fill the vacancy created by the death of Marshall Jewell in February, 1883. Mr. Sabin proposed the name of Mr. Clayton for temporary chairman, when the young Henry Cabot Lodge of Massachusetts arose and said that while the committee might make such a suggestion, yet it was also the right of the convention to choose some one else who would strengthen the party throughout the country. He then nominated John R. Lynch, a colored man from Mississippi. This nomination was supported by Theodore Roosevelt and George William Curtis, and was carried by the vote of—Lynch, 424; Clayton, 384. This action was looked upon as a revolt against machine domination.

This speech of Theodore Roosevelt in favor of Lynch was his first appearance in national politics, which he was so to dominate twenty years later, and to its great and everlasting good, so a description of his appearance at this time, as given by "The New York Times," is especially interesting.[2] "Up from the midst of the Empire State delegates rose a slight, almost boyish figure. It was that of an active, nervous, light-haired, gray-eyed man who had just thrown off a straw hat and scrambled to his perch on the chair, with juvenile activity. Everybody knew the man, for there is not a state headquarters which he had not visited in his canvass for Edmunds, and scarce an influential delegate with whom he has not conversed in a straightforward, manly way, carrying conviction even when he could not convert. It was Theodore Roosevelt, of New York, the leader of the younger Republicans, and he was greeted with a rousing burst of applause as he stood waiting to speak. When he spoke it was not the

[2] Quoted in Joseph Bucklin Bishop, "Theodore Roosevelt and His Time," I, 34.

voice of a youth, but of a man—and a positive, practical man. His sensible speech was in delightful contrast with the plausible apologies of the men who had endeavored to excuse the outrage which the National Committee had committed."

In general, the convention was harmonious as well as leisurely, taking four days to complete its work. The list of delegates showed the transition character of politics at that time, as mentioned above. Among them were Theodore Roosevelt, the young politician from New York, along with Andrew D. White, George William Curtis, William H. Robinson, Benjamin B. Odell, Thomas C. Platt, and James W. Wadsworth. Also, Galusha A. Grow of Pennsylvania; Shelby M. Cullom of Illinois; Benjamin Harrison of Indiana; William McKinley, Joseph B. Foraker, and Mark Hanna of Ohio; Julius C. Burrows and Russell A. Alger of Michigan; Cushman K. Davis of Minnesota; Thomas R. Bard of California; William O. Bradley of Kentucky; James A. Gary and George L. Wellington of Maryland; George F. Hoar, John D. Long, Henry Cabot Lodge, and Edward L. Pierce of Massachusetts; John M. Thurston of Nebraska; William Walter Phelps, William J. Sewell, J. Franklin Fort, and John I. Blair of New Jersey; and Redfield Proctor of Vermont.

On the second day of the convention a resolution was introduced by S. W. Hawkins of Tennessee which resolved "that it is the sense of this convention, that every member of it is bound in honor to support its nominee, whoever that nominee may be; and that no man should hold a seat here who is not willing so to agree." At once bitter opposition was voiced to it, especially by Edward L. Pierce and George William Curtis on the grounds of its binding of the consciences of the free individual and against the Declaration of Independence. They might have added that it was an absolute denial of the principles of representative government which should obtain in political parties, as agencies of government, just as in governments themselves. It soon was withdrawn, not even coming to a vote—a testimony to the advancement toward popular government made during the four years since Roscoe Conkling had attempted, and with nearer approach to success, to put through an almost identical resolution.

On the third day the Committee on Resolutions, of which William McKinley was chairman, reported the platform, the most important features of which follow: A strong declaration was made for the policy of levying duties upon foreign imports—not for revenue only but "to afford security to our diversified industries, and protection to the rights and wages of the laborers, to the end that active and intelligent labor, as well as capital, may have its just reward, and the laboring man his full share in the national prosperity." It protested "against the so-called economical system which would degrade our labor to the foreign standard," and pledged a revision of the tariff "not by vicious and indiscriminate process of horizontal reduction but by such methods as will relieve the taxpayer without injuring the laborer or the great productive interests of the country." A readjustment of the duties upon wool was specifically mentioned, "in order that such industry shall have full and adequate protection." This had a twofold object—to catch not only labor but also the farmer. Other statements favored international bimetallism; "such legislation as will fully and efficiently carry out the constitutional power of congress over interstate commerce"; the "principle of the public regulation of railway corporations"; a national bureau of labor; enforcement of the eight-hour law in federal employment; restriction of Chinese immigration; and denounced the importation of contract labor.

Additional important planks were those which favored the further extension of the Civil-Service Law; "a policy which shall keep us from entangling alliances with foreign nations"; and "the restoration of our navy to its old-time strength and efficiency." Of course, there were the usual planks sympathizing with the Southern Republicans and attempting, though in a faint and half-hearted way, to rouse the smoldering embers of sectionalism. It will at once be noted how new issues of economics, labor, and a strong move toward nationalism and international independence were coming to the front. Those

Photograph by Brown Brothers

THOMAS B. REED

who drew up the platform had a keen and prophetic eye for the future and were laying deep the foundations of later Republican success under McKinley himself, the chairman of the committee, followed by Roosevelt. In fact, upon the basis of the political coöperation of labor and capital, with a deft handling of the agricultural question, has been built up the strong and dominating Republican party of the present day.

That same evening (Thursday) nominating speeches were made, presenting the names of various candidates to the convention, and this consumed so much time that adjournment was taken at 1:45 A.M. on Friday until eleven o'clock of the same morning. The result of the first ballot was: James G. Blaine of Maine, 334½; Chester A. Arthur, New York, 278; George F. Edmunds, Vermont, 93; John A. Logan, Illinois, 63½; John Sherman, Ohio, 30; Joseph R. Hawley, Connecticut, 13; Robert T. Lincoln, Illinois, 4; William T. Sherman, Missouri, 2. On the second and third ballots there was little change, with the exception of steady though small gains for Blaine, the others remaining stationary or marking slight losses. After the third ballot there was a motion to take a recess, but this was voted down. Foraker of Ohio then moved that the rules of the convention be suspended and that Blaine be nominated by acclamation. This was opposed by Roosevelt and others, and Foraker withdrew his motion.

During this time a number of delegates, led by Mark Hanna and Roosevelt, tried to persuade the Edmunds men to unite on John Sherman as a compromise but failed. In spite of the refusal of General Sherman to be a candidate, Hoar and George William Curtis then attempted to swing the convention to him, but were met with the steady objection to him on account of the religion of his wife, which caused them to desist from their attempt. The fourth ballot now was taken, and in the midst of it Cullom announced that he had a telegram from Logan, withdrawing his name. The major part of this strength went to Blaine and he received a total of 541 votes and was nominated. The other candidates received—Arthur, 207; Edmunds, 41; Logan, 7; Hawley, 15; Lincoln, 2. At once a telegram from President Arthur was read by the chairman, pledging earnest support to Blaine. At an evening session the convention soon nominated John A. Logan of Illinois for the Vice-Presidency and adjourned.

James Gillespie Blaine was one of the most brilliant and popular men of his day. He was born at West Brownsville, Pennsylvania, on January 31, 1830. He later moved to Maine. He was a member of the first Republican national convention in 1856 and later was in the Maine legislature. He was a member of the House of Representatives from 1863 to 1876; speaker, 1869 to 1875; senator, 1876 to 1881, and had served less than a year as secretary of state. There was no question of his brilliancy and statesmanship; but, as shown above, his integrity had been seriously questioned.

John Alexander Logan was born in Jackson county, Illinois, February 9, 1826. He served in the Mexican War, later became a lawyer, and as a Democrat served in the legislature in both 1852 and 1856. He was a Presidential elector in the latter year on the Buchanan ticket. He served in Congress, as a Douglas Democrat, from 1859 to 1861, entered the Union army, and after a fine record rose to the rank of major-general. He had now become a Republican, and as such again served in the House of Representatives from 1867 to 1871. He was United States senator from Illinois from 1871 to 1877, and was again elected to the same office in 1879, being in that position when nominated by the convention. He was of the radical school, was a high-handed machine politician, and his nomination was not calculated to arouse the enthusiasm of the independents or reformers, already disgruntled over the nomination of Blaine.

In fact, the independents received the news of the ticket with dismay, and a secession soon developed that threatened to become as great as that of 1872, but proved to be more extensive among the leaders than among the rank and file of the party. Now become definitely known as "Mugwumps," the independents either bolted the ticket or refused to vote at all. The name Mugwump is said to have had an Algonquin Indian origin, and to mean chief or leader. It seems to have had no particular importance until this time, when it was used first of all as a term of reproach for the independents, and probably first by "The New York Sun," but was promptly accepted by them as a title of honor. It is occasionally used to-day to mean an independent in politics, but has been superseded by the politician's slang reproach of "goo-goo," or goody-goody, or else by that of progressive or liberal.

The Democrats were at once awake to this potential Republican defection, and knew that Governor Grover Cleveland of New York had a high reputation with the reforming elements of the country, who looked upon him as honest, sincere, courageous, and a reformer himself. Furthermore, he had carried New York by an enormous plurality for those days, and was not in the good graces of Tammany Hall, which rightly was anathema to all sincere lovers of good government. The Democratic convention met at Chicago on July 8 and nominated Cleveland on the second ballot. The platform was long, verbose, and dull. The party evidently put all their trust in the personality of their candidate, and the hope that his running-mate, Hendricks, could help to carry the doubtful state of Indiana.

The campaign was one of personalities almost entirely. Blaine was very vulnerable, as before pointed out, and the Republicans attempted to turn away attention from their own man by attacks on Cleveland. Unfortunately, these took the form of bitter criticism of his private morals, which was bravely and courageously met by Cleveland by the instruction to his managers to tell everything, in order that his indiscretions, which had been the basis of these charges, should be fully known. This policy on his part did much to rally the Mugwumps around him, and a secession of prominent men of independent proclivities followed. The nomination of Blaine caused a serious crisis in the career of the young Roosevelt. After long hesitation he decided not only to stand by Blaine but even to canvass actively for him. As he later said,[3] "Mr.

[3] "Autobiography," 86.

Blaine was clearly the choice of the rank and file of the party; his nomination was won in fair and aboveboard fashion, because the rank and file of the party stood back of him; and I supported him to the best of my ability in the ensuing campaign."

The Greenback party held its convention at Indianapolis on May 28 and appropriately nominated that prince of calculating demagogues, Benjamin F. Butler of Massachusetts, now happily out of the Republican party, where his machine had almost disrupted the party in his own state and driven many decent citizens away. Alanson M. West of Mississippi was his running-mate. The Prohibitionists met at Pittsburgh, July 23, and nominated for President and Vice-President unusually able candidates in John P. St. John of Kansas and William Daniel of Maryland. Their party came into greater prominence due to the fact that many independents, driven away from the Republican ticket by their dislike for Blaine, voted for St. John.

Carl Schurz, George William Curtis, and others took an active part in the Democratic canvass. Especially to offset Schurz's speeches in the "October state" of Ohio, Blaine made a stumping tour, where he roused intense enthusiasm through his brilliant and statesmanlike speeches. The state went Republican by about 11,000 plurality at the October election, and Blaine continued his tour through the Northwest and with the same success. On his return to New York he was present at a gathering of clergymen of all denominations at the Fifth Avenue Hotel on October 29. About a thousand were present, and Blaine was given a great ovation and resolutions of indorsement were passed in his honor. Among the addresses was one by the Rev. Dr. Samuel Dickinson Burchard, a Presbyterian minister of New York city, who closed with the statement, "We are Republicans and don't propose to leave our party and identify ourselves with the party whose antecedents have been rum, Romanism and rebellion." This alliterative statement was at once taken up and used by the Democrats with terrific effect. Blaine had not said these words. It is doubtful if he even had noticed them; but they were pinned to his name and evidently cost him thousands of votes. The friendship for Blaine of the Irish had been a constant worry to the Democrats, but this statement of Burchard's gave them just the whip they desired, and with it they drove back many of the Irish into their former party.

A Republican leader who was present on the above occasion told the writer he remembers the whole affair well—how Blaine looked, Dr. Burchard's speech, and that gentleman himself, and all with the greatest clearness, but he has no recollection whatever of the celebrated words having been said. Said they must have been, or they would at once have been denied; but they made no impression until caught by the reporters and exploited by them. Blaine tried to stem the tide by disavowing any religious prejudice, but it was too late.

The strength of the Democratic party was mainly in the solid South, and the cities and other thickly populated sections of the North where many foreigners had settled, especially the Irish. Blaine had hoped to break in on the Irish vote, but lost all chance of that.

The election took place on November 4, 1884, and the vote was so close that it was several days before the final result was known. Mr. Cleveland carried all the Southern states, as was expected, also New York (by 1149 votes in a total of 1,167,169 cast in the state), New Jersey (by 4358), Connecticut (by 1276), and Indiana (by 6527). He had a total of 4,874,986 popular votes and 219 electoral votes. Blaine carried the usual Republican states in the North and West, with the exception of the above four, and received 4,851,981 popular votes, and 182 electoral votes. This gave the Democrats a popular plurality of only 23,005. The Greenback party had a total vote of 175,370 and the Prohibitionists, 150,369. It is interesting to note that their votes in New York were: Greenback, 16,994, and Prohibitionist, 25,016.

The Mugwumps were loud in their boastings that they had caused Blaine's defeat, and undoubtedly they had contributed toward it. But the best historical judgment of to-day would seem to be of the opinion that the Prohibitionists had about as much to do with it. The writer feels sure that many old-line Republicans, who never had failed to vote the national ticket before, could not take Blaine and for the first time voted Prohibitionist. In such a close election a few hundreds or thousands of such people easily could turn the tide. The late Senator Hoar, usually cautious and conservative in his statements, had the following to say in his autobiography, published twenty years later:[4] "I suppose it would hardly be denied now by persons acquainted with the details of the management of the Democratic campaign, at any rate I have heard the fact admitted by several very distinguished Democrats, members of the Senate of the United States, that the plurality of the vote of New York was really cast for Mr. Blaine, and that he was unjustly deprived of election by the fraud at Long Island City by which votes cast for the Butler electoral ticket were counted for Cleveland." A change of 1200 votes would have given the state to Blaine and elected him, so if this be true it entirely reverses any Democratic charge anent 1876, and with this real parallel: that the people at large were satisfied, after all, that the better man had won.

Grover Cleveland was inaugurated President on March 4, 1885, and instituted the first Democratic administration since James Buchanan. In spite of radical and partizan fears to the contrary, the country did not go to the dogs, although the Republicans soon found many grounds for legitimate criticism. Mr. Cleveland was far better than his party, as the Mugwumps truthfully had pointed out during the campaign, but he was not able to run the entire administration alone. He changed the Democratic party from one of mere protest, as it had been since 1860, into an aggressive force with a definite program of tariff reform, on the basis of revenue only, and of sound money. But these were exactly the two things which were most disputed by both leaders and rank and file. Added to this was the sharp difference of opinion over the civil service. As long as Cleveland was able to dominate by his own per-

[4] Vol. I, 408.

sonality, there was a semblance of Democratic unity. He was not a skilful politician though a good administrator, with the real instincts of a statesman. Consequently, he was unable to hold his party together; but after an internecine struggle lasting the better part of twelve years the Democrats split to pieces in 1896, giving sixteen years of almost unbroken Republican domination and striking success in national affairs.

Opposed to Cleveland on the patronage and civil-service reform questions were Arthur P. Gorman of Maryland and David Bennett Hill of New York, the latter the friend and ally of Tammany Hall. His low-tariff views were opposed by Samuel J. Randall of Pennsylvania, with strong support in New York, New Jersey, New England, and other manufacturing centers. His sound-money views alienated many Democrats in the West and South. The Republicans were united in favor of some protective tariff of a greater or less degree, and in general they far better supported, in the rank and file, both civil-service reform and sound money. Hence they won out in the end as the sounder and better party. But the story of the next twelve years is a weary one of contention and parliamentary struggle by both sides to carry through some form of constructive legislation, with a policy of administration that would appeal to the average American citizen.

When Cleveland became President there were about 5000 officials who were appointed by the President, and approximately 49,000 fourth class postmasters to be appointed by the postmaster-general. Cleveland of course was besieged by a horde of "deserving Democrats," as Bryan later designated them, and followed a policy of standing by the classified service already under the Civil-Service Act, but he made many "removals for partisanship" in the unclassified service as noted above. He removed possibly two thirds of those in the latter, much to the disgust of the more idealistic of the Mugwumps and other reformers. It is probable he did the best he could, but the independents had learned their lesson and were now more inclined to remain loyal Republicans and fight for reform within the party lines, which, after all, is in most cases the sound and successful method of political procedure if ever party government is to be a success anywhere in the world.

In his first annual message Cleveland proposed the enactment of a tariff for revenue only. There was a Republican Senate and a Democratic House of Representatives, the latter presided over by John G. Carlisle of Kentucky as speaker. A tariff bill was brought in, the Morrison bill; but Randall, who had been deposed from Democratic leadership, was able to swing thirty-five Democrats to unite with the Republicans and defeat the bill. The election of the year 1886, which followed this Democratic fiasco, reduced the majority of that party in the House of Representatives from 40 to 12. Cleveland found that his party would do nothing in Congress, so he appealed to the country over their heads in his celebrated annual message of 1887, which was devoted entirely to the tariff and urged that "it is a condition that confronts us, not a theory." This was followed by the introduction of a moderate protective measure, the famous Mills bill, by the chairman of the Committee of Ways and Means, Roger Q. Mills. After long debate and acrimonious discussion, it passed the House of Representatives by the majority of 13. The main leadership of the opposition was taken by one of the ablest Republicans of his time, now just coming into great prominence—namely, Thomas B. Reed of Maine. He was known for his wit and his sense of humor, and remarked that Mills, when asked to explain the features of his bill, "finds it necessary to fly into a passion, finds it necessary to go off into a defense of his own virtue." [5] The bill was not even given any consideration by the Senate, which went ahead on its own lines of tariff legislation. Of course, all this legislative activity was merely meant for election purposes, but Cleveland had succeeded in making the tariff a clear-cut issue for the campaign of 1888.

The Republicans accepted this gleefully. At first it seemed as though Blaine's popularity with the people at large was such that the nomination would go to him in 1888 by acclamation. But he evidently was convinced that on account of

[5] S. W. McCall, "Life of Thomas B. Reed," 160.

his health it would be inadvisable to undergo the worry and strain of another campaign. Furthermore, he probably was loath to meet the personal attacks that inevitably would be leveled at him. He was traveling abroad, and sent a letter from Florence, Italy, under date of January 25, 1888, in which he made the formal announcement that due to "considerations entirely personal to myself" his name would not be presented to the national convention. The effect was much the same as followed the celebrated message of withdrawal made public by President Coolidge on August 2, 1927. At first Blaine's dismayed followers insisted upon forcing the nomination upon him, and there was even more reason for his subsequent acceptance than might be anticipated from a person in the position of Mr. Coolidge. But gradually it dawned upon the minds of his friends that Blaine meant exactly what he said, although he was compelled to issue several further statements to prevent his nomination—some of them even during the sessions of the convention itself. As time went on and his withdrawal brought forth a host of new contenders for the nomination, there always remained in the background the fear, or hope, as it might be, that there would be a sudden stampede for Blaine. The story of the convention must have a knowledge of this feeling as a necessary background, in order that its proceedings may be understood. In spite of all this, as Senator Hoar insists, there was "but little of the eager antagonisms that had characterized the preceding conventions. The Republican party had been sobered a good deal by four years of adversity." [6] There is frequent mention in the writings of the times of the high caliber, balance, and common sense of the members of the convention, which would seem to show the correctness of the appraisement by Senator Hoar.

The Republican national convention met on Tuesday, June 19, 1888, in the Auditorium at Chicago. It was called to order by B. F. Jones, chairman of the National Committee, and prayer was offered by Rev. Frank W. Gunsaulus. John M. Thurston of Nebraska was chosen temporary chairman. John

[6] "Autobiography," I, 409.

C. Frémont, the first Republican candidate for President, was called to the platform and gave a brief address. He was followed in an address by the negro leader of the time, Frederick Douglass. The convention was not only deliberate in its proceedings, taking six days and only adjourning on Monday, June 25, after an adjournment over Sunday (twenty-fourth); it also was deliberative. Having been out of power for three years, the delegates felt the seriousness of the occasion and also the opportunity to win a victory and return to power if no vital mistakes were made. Among its members were such well-known personages as Frank Hiscock, Warner Miller, Thomas C. Platt, and Chauncey M. Depew of New York, who formed the "big four" delegates-at-large from that state; W. J. Sewell, John W. Griggs, and John I. Blair of New Jersey; Joseph B. Foraker, William McKinley, Myron T. Herrick, and Mark Hanna of Ohio; Matthew S. Quay of Pennsylvania; D. B. Henderson, J. S. Clarkson, J. P. Dolliver, and W. P. Hepburn of Iowa; William O. Bradley of Kentucky, George F. Hoar and Samuel W. McCall of Massachusetts; James A. Gary and George L. Wellington of Maryland; William M. Stewart and John P. Jones of Nevada; John M. Thurston of Nebraska; John C. Spooner of Wisconsin; Redfield Proctor and H. C. Ide of Vermont; Jacob H. Gallinger of New Hampshire.

On Thursday, June 21, the Committee on Resolutions, through its chairman, William McKinley, reported the platform. It showed the beginnings of the present foolish practice of drawing the pronouncements out to a silly length and was mainly characterized by its stressing of economic issues. It seized the opportunity given by the Democrats, and wisely made protection the main issue of the campaign. Its words were: "We are uncompromisingly in favor of the American system of protection. We protest against its destruction, as proposed by the President and his party. They serve the interests of Europe; we will support the interest of America. We accept the issue, and confidently appeal to the people for their judgment. The protective system must be maintained. Its abandonment has always been followed by disaster to all interests, except those of the usurer and the sheriff. . . . We condemn the proposition of the Democratic party to place wool on the free list, and we insist that the duties thereon shall be adjusted and maintained so as to furnish full and adequate protection to that industry."

The Republican party would effect all needed reduction by lowering the internal revenue duties on tobacco, spirits used in mechanical arts, etc., "and by such revision of the tariff laws as will tend to check imports of such articles as are produced by our people, the production of which gives employment to our labor, and release from import duties those articles of foreign production, except luxuries, the like of which cannot be produced at home. If there shall still remain a larger revenue than is requisite for the wants of the government, we favor the entire repeal of internal taxes, rather than the surrender of any part of our protective system, at the joint behest of the whiskey trusts and the agents of foreign manufacturers."

Other planks, after this important pronouncement, declared hostility to the introduction of foreign contract labor and to Chinese labor; and to "all combinations of capital, organized in trusts or otherwise, to control arbitrarily the condition of trade among our citizens." There was indorsement of "the policy of appropriating the public lands of the United States to be homesteads for American citizens"; the admission of the territories as new states; the rehabilitation of our American merchant marine; the "early rebuilding of our navy"; "the construction of coast fortifications and modern ordnance"; and of "necessary works of national importance in the improvement of harbors and the channels of internal, coastwise, and foreign commerce."

Other planks declared the party to be "in favor of the use of both gold and silver as money, and condemned the policy of the Democratic administration in its efforts to demonetize silver"; that "the conduct of foreign affairs by the present administration has been distinguished by its inefficiency and cowardice." Respects were carefully paid to the Mugwumps by stating that "the men who abandoned the Republican party in 1884, and continue to adhere to the Democratic party, have deserted not only the cause of honest government, of sound finance, of freedom, of purity of the ballot, but especially have deserted the cause of reform in the civil service. We will not fail to keep our pledges because they have broken theirs, nor because their candidate has broken his." The pledge in the platform of 1884 to support and extend the Civil-Service Law was then repeated verbatim. But a sinister plank, under the guise of gratitude and patriotic pride, opened the way for the wholesale pension scandals of the next forty years, and continuing even to the present day, by which patriotism has become commercialized and alms-giving made a political virtue. It stated that the laws should "provide against the possibility that any man who honorably wore the federal uniform shall become the inmate of an alms-house or dependent upon private charity." This carefully brushed aside all considerations of how the "wearer of the federal uniform" had behaved himself since that early time!

In order to catch the Irish vote if possible, and detach it from the Democratic party, the convention cheapened itself to the almost incredible extent of abandoning the American policy of non-interference in the affairs of other and especially European nations by a supremely silly plank that expressed the earnest "hope that we may soon congratulate our fellow-citizens of Irish birth upon the peaceful recovery of home rule for Ireland"! This was the official recognition by a great American party of the hyphenate, who was to arise in an entirely different and unexpected form to involve the welfare and happiness of the country about thirty years later. In these days of Bolshevism and Sacco-Vanzetti agitation, the country has learned a little better, and its loyal citizens of foreign birth are no longer insulted by thus being singled out by American party organizations—for the Democrats have sinned far more in this regard than the Republicans, in their wildest moments, ever thought of doing. Fortunately for the latter, and for the country as well, they have since had the leadership and example of Theodore Roosevelt and all he stood for in the line of sound and single-minded patriotism.

Just before the convention finally adjourned, a resolution was offered from the floor and adopted with but one opposing vote, and which declared that "The first concern of all good government is the virtue and sobriety of the people, and the purity of their homes. The Republican party cordially sympathizes with all wise and well-directed efforts for the promotion of temperance and morality." There evidently was a lingering and natural hope that former Republicans who had wandered into the Mugwump and Prohibition ranks might be induced to return. Most of them finally did, and the few yet remaining outside were brought back in large part by the Bryan financial heresies of eight years later.

The balloting for the nomination for President began on Friday, June 22, and lasted over until Monday, the twenty-fifth, when Benjamin Harrison of Indiana was nominated on the eighth ballot. Rhodes well sums up the political situation in the convention at the beginning of the balloting by saying: "The contest was really John Sherman against the field, with Blaine's friends in the background ready to spring his nomination on the convention at any time. . . . Of all the candidates Sherman was the best fitted man for the presidency and he had a capable manager in Mark Hanna and loyal support from McKinley. . . . The reason why he was not nominated was because he had antagonized New York State or rather the influential men in the delegation, chief of whom was Thomas C. Platt. If he could have secured New York, that large addition to his vote together with the votes certain to be influenced by the action of the Empire State would have nominated him." [7]

The first ballot resulted as follows: John Sherman, Ohio, 229; Walter Q. Gresham, Indiana, 111; Chauncey M. Depew, New York, 99; Russell A. Alger, Michigan, 84; Benjamin Harrison, Indiana, 80; William B. Allison, Iowa, 72; James

[7] History of the United States, VIII, 310–11.

G. Blaine, Maine, 35; John J. Ingalls, Kansas, 28; Jeremiah M. Rusk, Wisconsin, 25; William Walter Phelps, New Jersey, 25; E. H. Fitler, Pennsylvania, 24; Joseph R. Hawley, Connecticut, 13; Robert T. Lincoln, Illinois, 3; William McKinley, Ohio, 2; whole number of votes, 830; necessary for a choice, 416. Stanwood gives the following excellent analysis of the votes:[8] "The votes were divided among thirteen candidates [fourteen], and even on the fourth trial the number had been reduced only to ten. How greatly the votes were scattered may be seen from the statement that, on the first vote for a candidate, Senator Sherman received more or less support from twenty-three states and territories, Judge Gresham from twenty-three, Mr. Harrison from twenty-three, Mr. Alger from twenty, Mr. Allison from nineteen, Mr. Depew from sixteen, and Mr. Blaine from thirteen. Only nine states of the Union gave a solid vote to any candidate, and five of the nine presented 'favorite sons' as candidates." During the course of the fourth ballot McKinley arose and said he could not with honor longer remain silent. That votes were being cast for him, but he was for Sherman. He demanded that no one cast a further ballot for him.

Mr. Depew had withdrawn his name after the third ballot, and Senator Hoar [9] tells of a conference that occurred which had a marked effect on the results of the fourth ballot, when Harrison's vote jumped from 94 to 217. It appears that a caucus was held during a recess of the convention at which were present representatives or delegates from New York, Illinois, Wisconsin, Pennsylvania, Massachusetts, Iowa, California, and Missouri. Among them were Platt, Miller, Hiscock, Spooner, Clarkson, Quay, and Senator Hoar himself, who made an earnest plea for a concentration upon Allison of Iowa. This was agreed to, but just before the convention resumed its sitting the New York delegates came to the others who had been in the conference and said that they must withdraw from the agreement; that Depew, who had withdrawn

[8] "History of the Presidency," 478–9.
[9] "Autobiography," 410–13.

his own name, was unwilling to support Allison and "submit to such an unreasonable and socialistic sentiment" as that of the Northwest, where the main strength of Allison already lay, so as to permit it to "dictate a candidate for the Republican party." Therefore, the other three members of the "big four" from New York could not vote for Allison. It will be remembered that Depew was then president of the New York Central & Hudson River Railroad, hence would naturally be especially sensitive to the radical and populistic ideas already becoming rife in certain parts of the West. Most of the votes in the proposed agreement now went to Harrison, and he was nominated on the eighth ballot, when he received 544 votes, to 118 for Sherman, 59 for Gresham, 100 for Alger, and with a few scattering. Hoar adds: "I think no other person ever came so near the Presidency of the United States [as Allison] and missed it." Blaine also sent the message during the convention, "Take Harrison."

Harrison was the grandson of William Henry Harrison, the old Whig President in 1841. He was born at North Bend, Ohio, on August 20, 1833. He graduated from Miami University in 1852, studied law, and practised in Indianapolis. After holding a local office he served in the Civil War, where he arose to the rank of brevet brigadier-general in 1865. He was the unsuccessful candidate for governor of Indiana on the Republican ticket in 1876, and was United States senator from 1881-87.

Senator Hoar gives the following sound estimate of Harrison: [10] "I had become very intimate with him, and had learned to respect him very highly as an able, upright and wise man, although he developed, as President, an ability which I think his most intimate friends had not known before. . . . He was a wise, pure, upright and able President, and an eloquent orator, capable of uttering great truths in a great way, and able to bring them home to the understanding and conviction of his countrymen. He lacked what gave Mr. Blaine so great a

[10] "Autobiography," 413–14.

charm, the quality of an agreeable and gracious manner. He had little tact in dealing with individuals. . . . Blaine would refuse a request in a way that would seem like doing a favor. Harrison would grant a request in a way which seemed as if he were denying it. An eminent Western senator said to me once what, of course, was a great exaggeration, that if Harrison were to address an audience of ten thousand men, he would capture them all. But if each one of them were presented to him in private, he would make him his enemy."

The nomination of Harrison was immediately made unanimous, and was promptly followed by the nomination for Vice-President of Levi P. Morton of New York on the first ballot, in which he received 592 votes, while 119 went to William Walter Phelps of New Jersey, 103 to William O. Bradley of Kentucky, and a few scattered. After also making Morton's nomination unanimous, the convention adjourned.

Levi Parsons Morton was born at Shoreham, Vermont, May 16, 1824. He became a merchant in Boston and later removed to New York, where he rose to be a leading banker, business man, and Republican politician. He was minister to France, 1881-85. While the Republicans evidently looked to the two doubtful states of Indiana and New York in their choice of candidates, they evidently relied also upon specific economic issues, of which the most important was the tariff, and on this basis of coöperation aroused the interest of the people and, as will be seen, carried the campaign to a successful conclusion.

As had been expected, the Democrats held their convention at St. Louis on June 5 and nominated Grover Cleveland by acclamation. Vice-President Hendricks had died in office, so Allen G. Thurman of Ohio was nominated in his place. The Democrats perforce must make Cleveland and his administration the issue, with tariff for revenue as the outstanding policy to be followed if successful. The Prohibitionists nominated Clinton B. Fisk of New Jersey and John A. Brooks of Missouri. The Greenback party had about disappeared, and a new or radical Labor party arose in its place. It nominated Alson

J. Streeter of Illinois and Samuel Evans of Texas. It was in favor of government ownership of railroads, some form of the single tax, attacked the banks, and included other like projects which even then had become the stock in trade for most radicals of an unsound economic training or belief. These two parties had little influence on current politics.

The campaign which followed was one marked for the most part by calm argument and deep discussion. Harrison conducted a front-porch campaign from his home in Indianapolis, making short and happy speeches which were very effective as campaign material. He stressed the fact that there should be no personalities, but a discussion of measures and issues. This had a very favorable effect upon the country following the campaign of defamation waged in 1884. Both sides raised and spent much money, the main onus of this policy resting upon the Republicans due to the publication of a letter written by W. W. Dudley, treasurer of the National Committee, and sent to party leaders in Indiana, which said: "Divide the floaters into blocks of five and put a trusted man with the necessary funds in charge of these five, and make him responsible that none get away and that all vote our ticket." Matthew S. Quay of Pennsylvania, prince of manipulators, was chairman of the National Committee. But Rhodes thinks that "the popular mind exaggerated the amount of money used in the actual purchase of votes; indeed an electorate of over eleven millions is too large to warrant much buying by the National Committees save in the doubtful States. The legitimate expenses of a presidential campaign, meetings, speeches, travelling expenses, bands and processions generally consume a large part of what the National Committee could raise." [11]

Probably the most important incident of the campaign was a tactless mistake made by the British minister, Sir Lionel Sackville-West, who was trapped by a person going under the name of Charles F. Murchison of Pomona, California, into expressing an opinion upon the merits of the respective candi-

[11] "History of the United States," VIII, 322-3.

dates. He hinted that, everything considered, Cleveland's election would be more to the interest of Great Britain. This evidently was a trick perpetrated by some morally obtuse Republican, for although the letter was marked private, it was published and made a great sensation. The Republicans were quick to say that this letter showed that the low-tariff policy of Cleveland would help the British and other foreigners, and at the expense of American labor and industry. Cleveland at once directed his secretary of state to make representations at London, which should have led to the immediate recall of Sackville-West. Lord Salisbury, totally misunderstanding the serious character of the offense, delayed and asked further particulars. Cleveland at once dismissed the British minister, and the court at London was so displeased that no minister was sent in Sackville-West's place until after the close of Cleveland's administration. Political clubs, and an educational campaign involving the use of tons of literature, were added features of the contest.

Since Pennsylvania, Ohio, and Indiana had placed their elections at the regular November season, there were no longer any "October states," but it soon was realized that the vote would be close. Cleveland would carry the solid South, and Harrison the usual Republican states of the North and West. As in 1884, the four doubtful states of New York, New Jersey, Connecticut, and Indiana were the main battle-ground and held the balance of power. All interests were centered there, and strenuous efforts were made by both parties to carry them. The Republicans had the advantage of the manufacturing and industrial interests, while the Democrats had that of the large foreign vote.

When the election took place in November each party carried two of the doubtful states, New Jersey and Connecticut (by 336 votes) going to Cleveland, and New York and Indiana (by 2348) to Harrison. Harrison, therefore, was elected. It was charged and believed that Tammany by a deal "sold" Cleveland, whom it disliked, in exchange for its Democratic candidate for governor of the state, David Bennett Hill.

Harrison received 13,002 plurality in the state, while Hill was elected by 1489. The electoral vote was: Harrison, 233; Cleveland, 168. On the other hand, the popular vote was: Harrison, 5,439,853; Cleveland, 5,540,329; thus giving the latter a Democratic plurality of 110,476, with a large electoral majority to his Republican opponent—a curious result possible under our system of indirect election of the President. The other parties cast votes—Fisk, Prohibitionist, 249,506; Streeter, Labor, 146,935.

Before turning our attention to the events of Harrison's administration three important laws of this period, essentially non-partizan in their character and enactment, should be mentioned. Due in large part to the initiative of a Republican, Senator Shelby M. Cullom of Illinois, the Interstate Commerce Act of 1887 was passed and became law on February 4. This established the powerful Interstate Commerce Commission and definitely undertook the regulation of railroads and railroad rates, since extended so broadly with regard to all common carriers and of the greatest importance in our economic life. Of an entirely different type, but also due to a Republican senator, Edmunds of Vermont, was the Electoral Count Act of February 3, 1887. This wisely provided against a repetition of the contest of 1876 by placing the final determination of the regularity of the returns from any disputed state upon the executive of the state itself. Meanwhile, a third law, the Presidential Succession Act, was approved January 18, 1886, and provided for the succession to office as *acting President,* following the death or incapacity of the President and Vice-President, of the seven members of the President's cabinet then created, in the order of the establishment of their departments by law. All of this legislation, while partly in the way of locking the stable after the stealing of the horse, yet made a decided step in advance along the line of efficient administration of the Government.

Benjamin Harrison was inaugurated President on March 4, 1889. As might have been expected from him, the inaugural address was dignified, well written, and had a decided literary flavor. It was perhaps of too great length, especially on a rainy day, but Harrison undertook to give an historical sketch of American government on this approximate anniversary of the beginning of Washington's first administration, and thus to mark the rounding out of a century of national administration under the Constitution. Also, he reindorsed, so to speak, the main planks in the platform upon which he had been elected and stressed other important matters. Among these, he stated, "I look hopefully to the continuance of our protective system and to the consequent development of manufacturing and mining enterprises in the states hitherto wholly given to agriculture as a potent influence in the perfect unification of our people." He later on added the significant clause: "I have altogether rejected the suggestion of a special executive policy for any section of our country. It is the duty of the Executive to administer and enforce in the methods and by the instrumentalities pointed out and provided by the Constitution all the laws enacted by Congress." His remarks upon the all-absorbing topic of the civil service were sound but somewhat evasive, in the opinion of the sincere and enthusiastic reformers of the time. "The civil list is so large that a personal knowledge of any large number of applicants is impossible. The President must rely upon the representation of others, and these are often made inconsiderately and without any just sense of responsibility. . . . Honest party service will certainly not be esteemed by me a disqualification for public office, but it will in no case be allowed to serve as a shield of official negligence, incompetency, or delinquency. . . . Persistent importunity will not, therefore, be the best support of an application for office. Heads of departments, bureaus, and all other public officers having any duty connected therewith will be expected to enforce the civil-service law fully and without evasion. Beyond this obvious duty I hope to do something more to advance the reform of the civil service. The ideal, or even my own ideal, I shall probably not attain." What proved a significant reference was made to ballot abuses in the states and the possibility of a need for congressional action to control the state elections. This was followed by the introduction of the unfortunate "force bill" of a short time later.[12]

The cabinet was evidently a series of "personal appointments" by Harrison, for it contained in large part men who were not of outstanding prominence, with the exceptions of Blaine and Windom. In other words, it was able but undistinguished. Blaine had taken so large a share in the influences that had brought about the nomination of Harrison that the tender to him of the office of secretary of state was inevitable. He was eminently fitted for the place, had served for nine months in that office under Garfield, and in that short time had given signs of great and successful ability. The offer and acceptance were made in the best and most cordial friendship, and popular prophecies of immediate personal friction, due to the strong individual peculiarities of the two men, were entirely disappointed for some time, although there was some friction as the time approached for the 1892 election. Harrison, not Blaine, ran the administration while the latter was in office. Windom had begun a very successful administration of the Treasury under Garfield, and his appointment was an excellent one and gave confidence to the various elements of the people. The other appointments were those of Redfield Proctor of Vermont, secretary of war; John W. Noble of Missouri, secretary of the interior; William H. H. Miller of Indiana, who was Harrison's law partner, attorney-general; Benjamin F. Tracy of New York, secretary of the navy; John Wanamaker of Pennsylvania, postmaster-general; and for the recently established new Department of Agriculture, ex-Governor Jeremiah M. Rusk of Wisconsin. Many of the reformers, in newspapers and otherwise, were quick to impute improper motives to Harrison in the appointment of John Wanamaker, who, as was commonly known at the time, had been a generous contributor to the Republican campaign fund. This gratuitous insult to the character and intentions of two perfectly honest, upright, and high-minded American citizens fell of its

[12] The whole message may be found in Richardson, "Messages and Papers," IX, 5-14.

own weight, and was merely another instance of that most unfortunate characteristic of reformers and other idealists which has its expression in a sinister lack of confidence in any one but themselves. This has brought the name of "reform" into unjust and undeserved disrepute and suspicion. Thomas C. Platt let it be known that he was much disappointed by the failure of Harrison to make him secretary of the treasury. Harrison denied that any such promise or understanding had been entered into, and the country was mercifully preserved from any such misfortune—not to mention the Republican party.

Harrison met the same difficulties with the civil service that had dogged the progress of Cleveland. He incurred the bitter enmity of the reformers by permitting J. S. Clarkson of Iowa, his appointee as first assistant postmaster-general, to make a clean sweep in large numbers of post-office appointments. Public opposition became so great that Clarkson finally resigned in September, 1890, having made a total of 32,335 changes in offices of the fourth class. His work thus was done. Harrison also made a very bad appointment in "Corporal" Tanner to the office of commissioner of pensions. Tanner opened the gates so wide to members of the Grand Army and others that the pension list became a disgrace to the nation. He too, finally, had to relinquish office. On the other hand, Harrison appointed the young Theodore Roosevelt on the Civil-Service Commission, and with the loyal coöperation of his colleagues the latter was able to make great extensions of the service and great improvements in administration of the law. The bitter opposition of the Civil-Service Reform League toward Harrison cooled considerably toward the end of his administration, and Rhodes gives it as his mature judgment that there was little to choose between the successes and failures of the Cleveland and Harrison administrations.[13]

The Fifty-first Congress, which assembled in its first session on Monday, December 2, 1889, was the result in large

[13] See Rhodes, "History of the United States," VIII, 330–38 for a fair and non-partizan account of the whole subject.

part of the preceding Presidential election, and was Republican in both branches. Thus the party, for the first time since 1875, had control of both the legislative and executive departments of the Government. There was a sharp contest in the House of Representatives over the election of speaker, the leading candidates being McKinley, Reed, and Henderson of Iowa. Reed finally won in the caucus after a lively fight, being in great part successful through the efforts in his behalf of Henry Cabot Lodge of Massachusetts. He was promptly elected by the vote of 166 to 154 for Carlisle. He appointed McKinley chairman of the Committee on Ways and Means; and his own chairmanship of the Committee on Rules, as customary in the House of Representatives at that time, made his leadership predominant. The small Republican majority of about 12 was further reduced to 11 by the death of a member. With such a small margin, and the balance of power over the country so close, conflict was inevitable and it was not long in coming. The Democrats, when they desired to prevent the passage of legislation, would sit silent in their seats while the roll was called. Under the practice which had prevailed from the First Congress, of determining a quorum merely by a call of the roll, they thus were able to block all legislation by preventing a quorum being technically present. A series of fruitless roll-calls would then follow, and all to no effect.

Reed now decided to end this. He had carefully thought out a plan of procedure, intended once for all to break up this practice of obstruction; and if his party did not support him, to resign from the speakership and membership in the House.[14] On January 29, 1890, Mr. Dalzell reported from the Committee on Elections a contested case, awarding the seat to a Republican. Mr. Crisp of Georgia raised the question of a quorum and only 163 members answered, two less than a quorum. Every Republican would have to be on hand all the time and every day for potential votes if a quorum were thus

[14] See the clear and concise account of this parliamentary conflict in S. W. McCall, "Life of Reed," chapter XIII. I have drawn largely upon this in my own narrative.

to be preserved and any business transacted; or else complete surrender must be made to the Democrats and only compromise pieces of legislation passed, if any, by means of a nonpartizan bargain. Instead of ordering another roll-call, Reed quietly and crisply said: "The chair directs the clerk to record the names of the following members present and refusing to vote." He then named Carlisle and a number of Democratic leaders who were present when their names were called and who had refused to vote. The surprise and excitement well can be imagined. There followed an uproar that stopped all business for a time. Angry protests were made, and in the moments of silence Reed quietly continued to name other Democrats. These individuals hardly could be present to protest, and yet not to vote!

McCall [15] tells the story that one Democrat gravely rose and said: "I deny your right, Mr. Speaker, to count me as present and I desire to read from the parliamentary law on the subject." Reed was unperturbed and quietly replied in his characteristic drawl, "The chair is making a statement of fact that the gentleman from Kentucky is present. Does he deny it?" A hearty laugh relieved the tension. Reed waited until there was sufficient quiet to make a statement, and then gave his opinion that the Constitution intended that when a majority of the members were actually present there was a quorum for the transaction of business, whether they voted or not. "Inasmuch as the Constitution only provides for their attendance, that attendance is enough. If more was needed the Constitution would have provided for more."

Even greater disorder followed this statement, and "for three days the House was a perfect bedlam." During all this time every possible means of parliamentary obstruction known to man seems to have been used and Reed, who was perhaps the coolest man in the House, calmly ruled them out of order. The Republicans loyally stood by their speaker, and finally his decision was submitted to a vote of the House. His ruling was sustained by the solid vote of his party colleagues. "Thus was

[15] "Life of Reed," 167–8.

established the most important landmark in the parliamentary practice of the House. . . . Not merely did the Supreme Court subsequently sustain the constitutionality of Reed's ruling, but within a brief period, by the endorsement of his party antagonists, it was destined to become the settled law of the House. In the next two succeeding congresses the House was controlled by the Democrats and the ancient practice was reëstablished. At an important juncture they found themselves unable to procure a quorum from their own ranks. And as Reed had established the new precedent, so there came to him the distinction as leader of the opposition of forcing his antagonists to ratify it. . . . The deadlock was at last broken by the adoption of a rule providing that a member who was present might be counted for the purpose of making a quorum whether he voted or not." [16] This was on April 17, 1894.

Reed suffered the most bitter public attacks and reproaches throughout all this time, the name of "Czar" Reed being one of the mildest of his appellations. When it was seen that the Democrats inevitably must give in and adopt his ruling of five years before, "The New York Tribune," on April 15, 1894, said, in an editorial crisply entitled "Down on Their Knees": "Mr. Reed is entitled to feel some little satisfaction in the final surrender of the Democrats at Washington. His instincts are not cruel, and he will undoubtedly behave in this hour of his signal triumph with all the dignity, gentleness and modesty that distinguish him in every situation. . . . And now, after four years, the Democratic party gets down on its knees before him and begs his pardon—not quite decently, not with the penitence and remorse which, in all conscience, it ought to show; but abjectly enough and cringingly. Its motive is bad, as its motive always is. It does not do right for right's sake nor to make amends for the wrong it has done. But it acknowledges the compulsion which makes right the only thing it can do now, and that is something. There, at all events it is,— Crisp, Springer, Kilgo', sah, who kicked down the doo', sah;

[16] McCall, "Reed," 171–2.

the fiery McMillin, the boisterous Outhwaite—there they are, down on their knees with their heads in the dust, taking it all back!" This sarcastic and bitter editorial well illustrates the feelings of the times. On the other hand, Reed, as before stated, never lost his equanimity. The following, which had appeared in all the newspapers of the time, is typical:

"Speaker Tom Reed does not wish to be killed in Kentucky where such an occurrence is too common to give eclat to death:

House of Representatives
Washington, Feb. 23 [1890].

DEAR MR. CARRUTH—I shall not accept the invitation tendered me by the Blue Grass Club. The reason is very simple. I noticed that Jay F. Durham assured me, during the late 'disturbances', that if they had me in Kentucky they would 'kill me.' Knowing said Durham to be a journalist, his declarations to me import absolute verity. I do not wish to be killed, especially in Kentucky, where such an event is too common to attract attention. For a good man to die anywhere is of course, a gain, but I think I can make more by dying later and elsewhere.

Very truly,

T. B. REED."

Now that the Republicans had control of the Government, they made the mistake of overenthusiasm and carried through legislation of too extreme a character, so that this period of Harrison's administration is well named by Professor C. R. Lingley, in his book entitled "Since the Civil War," as that of "extreme Republicanism." Under the efficient parliamentary leadership of Reed and McKinley a new tariff bill, known since as "the McKinley bill," was introduced in the House of Representatives in April, 1890, passed that House in May, and the Senate in September. It was signed by the President on October 1. The already high tariff was increased on an average of 4 per cent. As in the later case of the Fordney-McCumber tariff of recent times, an attempt was made to secure the agricultural interests, and duties were laid on such products as cereals, flax, and potatoes. Also, duties were increased on wool and woolens. The duty on raw sugar was removed, but to satisfy the native producers a duty of one half cent a pound was levied on the refined product, and in addition a bounty of two cents a pound was to be paid on all sugar produced in the country during a period of fifteen years. Sugar was one of the most remunerative articles for revenue, so this arrangement was intended to reduce the unwieldy surplus. The duty on tin-plate also was largely increased.[17]

Blaine warned that the tariff was too high, and under his influence a reciprocity provision was included. Several treaties were negotiated under this act, but during Cleveland's second administration the provision was repealed and the treaties abrogated. As soon as the tariff went into effect, prices were markedly increased in retail trade, the cost of living went up, and great popular discontent was the result. By overdoing their opportunity for tariff reform the Republicans in their turn played right into the hands of the Democrats, who held that the election of 1888 had been a mandate for a tariff revision at the hands of its friends, which mandate the Republicans had violated. Their appeal was heard by the people, somewhat bewildered by this conflict of self-appointed experts, and the reverses of 1890 were the result.

A new turn was given to the currency question by the reappearance of the agitation for the free coinage of silver, which had slumbered more or less during the past ten or twelve years, with periods of fitful waking. It now was given new life and energy by the aid in Congress of the four new Western states that recently had been admitted—namely, North Dakota, South Dakota, Montana, and Washington. The Senate voted in favor of free coinage on June 17, 1890, by 42 to 25, but Speaker Reed, by his able and courageous, not to mention

[17] See C. S. Olcott, "Life of William McKinley," I, 158–80.

strong, leadership blocked such legislation in the House of Representatives. After some negotiations, the compromise known as the Sherman Silver Purchase Act was passed in July, 1890. The Westerners traded their votes for the tariff for Eastern votes for the new silver law. It provided that the secretary of the treasury must purchase 4,500,000 ounces of silver bullion each month, to be paid for by the issue of treasury notes, which were to be legal tender for debts and redeemable in gold or silver at the discretion of the secretary of the treasury. This of course went much further than the Bland act of 1878, for all discretion was taken away from the secretary.[18] Senator Sherman did not believe in the financial soundness of the measure, but supported it to prevent a worse one. Having been fed this bait, the silver interests were less satisfied than ever, and as silver bullion steadily decreased in price for a number of years in spite of the legislative attempts to prevent it, they finally succeeded in bringing the issue of unlimited free coinage of silver to the front as the main question to be decided in 1896, but long ere that time the evil effects of the Silver Purchase Act were seen and our national financial stability was almost wrecked. This came to a crisis under the succeeding administration of Cleveland.

Another act which was passed at this time bearing the name of John Sherman, and which has become even more famous, was the Anti-Trust Act of July 2, 1890. It was in answer to the popular fear of the new monopolies which were rapidly developing in finance and trade and threatened to control completely all the business of the country. The Republican platform of 1888 had taken cognizance of this feeling, and had declared the party opposition to "all combinations of capital, organized in trusts or otherwise, to control arbitrarily the condition of trade among our citizens." This feeling of apprehension so grew among the people that the party leaders felt it necessary to take some action. This resulted in the Sherman law which made illegal "every contract, combination in the form of trust or otherwise, or conspiracy, in restraint of trade

[18] See D. R. Dewey, "National Problems," 222–8.

or commerce," and made it a misdemeanor to infringe the law. Senators Edmunds and Hoar both claimed that the bill merely extended English common law principles to international and interstate commerce. The act seemed almost futile for some years to come, until during the first decade of the twentieth century a new interpretation and real effectiveness were given to it by measures taken under the initiative of the active and able Roosevelt.

Another act was attempted which, while possibly proper in intent and purpose, could not fail to arouse the bitter hostility of the South and undo in large part the work of conciliation between the sections which had been going on slowly but steadily under the wise policy inaugurated by the Hayes administration. This was the so-called "force bill." Mention already has been made of the reference to the subject in Harrison's inaugural address, and there probably was some party understanding before the matter was taken up in Congress. The Republicans could not become reconciled to the "solid South," for which they themselves were largely to blame due to the radical mistakes of twenty years before. Senator Hoar and Representative Henry Cabot Lodge were interested in getting some form of fair national election law through the two houses of Congress, and finally Lodge introduced in 1890 a bill which provided that Federal officials representing both parties should be appointed upon election boards in any part of the country upon the petition of 500 voters in any district. These officials could not only inspect and verify returns but also had power to pass upon the qualifications of voters and receive ballots refused by local officials. Senator Hoar says that its most important provisions were borrowed from the English election law of 1868.[19] Of course, while general in its provisions, it was aimed especially at the South, although it was claimed that many Northern Democrats sympathized with the objects of the bill. But the Southern members of Congress were not slow to make a great outcry against it, and a bitter fight was waged both inside and outside Congress. Furthermore, un-

[19] "Autobiography," II, 153.

doubtedly business men with financial and other trade interests in the "New South" that was now happily coming to the front were alarmed, and used pressure against it.[20] The bill passed the House of Representatives on July 2, 1890, but never passed the Senate. While there undoubtedly was much justice in the contention of the Northern leaders that the South could not continue to permit the Democrats to rule by means of dishonest elections, yet it took such wise leaders as McKinley and Roosevelt to realize that the best way to regain Republican respect and support among the whites of the South was to let sleeping dogs lie and improve the situation by means of local reform.

The congressional election of 1890 came within a few weeks after the McKinley tariff went into effect, and under the influence of the consequent and natural rise in retail prices. This angered and alienated the very people who most would benefit by it—namely, the laboring and industrial classes, as well as the salaried and professional classes, who always pay directly for benefits assessed upon any community for the interest of any narrow class. Likewise, the attempt was made to "protect" and thus secure the allegiance of the farmers, and it proved just as impossible in 1890 as it has since proved under the provisions of the Fordney-McCumber tariff of thirty years later. The election was a Republican *débâcle.* The slender but efficient majority in the House of Representatives was reduced to a minority of only 88, as against a strength of 236 Democrats and 8 "Farmers' Alliance." The party still retained control of the Senate in the new Fifty-second Congress, where there were 47 Republicans, 39 Democrats, and 2 of the Farmers' Alliance. This meant a renewal of the conflict and deadlock during the remainder of Harrison's administration which had been so fruitless in a legislative sense during the time of Cleveland's first administration.

The Democrats organized by electing Charles F. Crisp of Georgia to the office of speaker, while Reed ably led the minority. McKinley had not been reëlected, but was elected

[20] Dewey, "National Problems," 169–70.

governor of Ohio in 1891. Everything was done and action was taken by both parties with an eye single to the glory of the 1892 campaign. It was during this time that Harrison failed to take a sufficiently strong stand upon the issues of free silver and sound money and this later cost him dear, as evasion usually does. On the other hand, and much to the credit of Mr. Cleveland, he took a strong stand upon the same subjects. It enabled him to secure the nomination and election in 1892, but his party did not have the courage, loyalty, or possibly not sufficient intelligence, to stand by him; and the Democratic downfall of 1896, so richly deserved, was the just and proper result. It was but another proof of the old Mugwump contention that, with all his possible limitations, Cleveland was much better than his party.

As 1892 approached, the friends of Blaine became active again and seemed about as undiscouraged, as well as unfortunate, as the old Whig followers of Henry Clay of about fifty years before. Blaine promptly took himself out of the running, but his devoted friends continued to discuss his possible candidacy until it evidently aroused some coolness of feeling between the President and his brilliant secretary of state. This culminated in Blaine's resignation, just before the national convention, on June 4, 1892. Harrison at once accepted it and appointed in Blaine's place the able and scholarly John W. Foster of Indiana. Both Blaine and Harrison wrote rather "cool" notes. Senator Shelby M. Cullom says [21] of a conversation he had with Harrison at this time: "Harrison and Blaine had fallen out. Jealousy was probably at the bottom of their disaffection. Harrison did not treat Blaine with that degree of confidence and courtesy one would expect from the Chief Executive to the premier of his cabinet; while on the other hand Blaine hated Harrison and was plotting more or less against him while he was a member of the cabinet. The President talked very freely to me about Mr. Blaine. He declared that he had been doing the work of the state department himself for a year or more; that he had prepared every important

[21] "Fifty Years of Public Service," 252–3.

official document, and had the originals in his own handwriting in the desk before him. And yet, he said, Mr. Blaine, as secretary of state, was giving out accounts of what was being done in the state department, taking all the credit to himself." This is substantiated by the fact of Blaine's ill health, and his death about eight months later. If Blaine intended now to try for the nomination at the convention, it was too late, and Harrison's renomination was inevitable.

The Republican national convention met in Convention Hall, Industrial Exposition Building, Minneapolis, Minnesota, on June 7, 1892. Among its delegates were such prominent leaders of the time as Hiscock, Platt, Depew, and Miller, again the "big four" from New York; also Horace Porter, Elliott F. Shepard, William H. Robertson, James S. Sherman, and J. Sloat Fassett from the same state. From Pennsylvania were Matthew S. Quay and William Flinn; from Illinois, Shelby M. Cullom, Joseph G. Cannon, Richard J. Oglesby, and H. H. Kohlsaat; from Ohio, William McKinley, Joseph B. Foraker, and Charles Dick; from Indiana, Lew Wallace; from Iowa, James S. Clarkson; from Wisconsin, John C. Spooner and Isaac Stephenson; from Colorado, Henry M. Teller and Edward O. Wolcott; from Connecticut, Frank Brandegee; from Kansas, John J. Ingalls; from Kentucky, William O. Bradley; from Maine, Charles E. Littlefield; from Maryland, James A. Gary and Louis E. McComas; from Massachusetts, W. Murray Crane; from New Jersey, William J. Sewell, John I. Blair, Garrett A. Hobart, and David Baird; from Tennessee, H. Clay Evans.

The convention was called to order by James S. Clarkson of Iowa, which was not very pleasing to the civil-service reformers, but who at the time was chairman of the National Committee. He announced that the committee recommended for temporary chairman J. Sloat Fassett of New York. Mr. Fassett was elected and the remainder of the day was taken up with routine business. The next day William McKinley, now governor of Ohio, was chosen permanent president and made a strong tariff speech on taking the chair. McKinley easily was the favorite of the convention, a forecast of what was to happen four years later. On the third day the platform was reported by the Committee on Resolutions, of which Joseph B. Foraker was chairman. There had been a struggle in the committee over the currency plank due to the demand of the Western delegates that a declaration be made for free silver. Of course, this was opposed by those from the East, and the result was a compromise. It would seem that this convention at Minneapolis was in a sense a curtain-raiser for the more important one of 1896.

In general, the platform was a *résumé* of that of 1888, which for a long time seems to have stood in the minds of rock-ribbed, stand-pat Republicans as the ultimate test of party orthodoxy. Some leaders have not moved from it after nearly forty years. It "reaffirmed the American policy of protection" and maintained that "the prosperous condition of our country is largely due to the wise revenue legislation of the Republican congress." There was added the statement that "we believe that all articles which cannot be produced in the United States, except luxuries [which were not defined] should be admitted free of duty, and that on all imports coming into competition with the products of American labor there should be levied duties equal to the difference between wages abroad and at home." At least this was somewhat more specific than the present-day mirage concerning the "differences between cost of production at home and abroad," the determination of which would seem to be the main cause for sleeplessness on the part of the Tariff Commission in 1927. The resolutions also pointed "to the success of the Republican policy of reciprocity, under which our export trade has vastly increased, and new and enlarged markets have been opened for the products of our farms and workshops." The party thus was unrepentant, in spite of the defeat of 1890.

The currency platform is especially significant, and was compromised into the following terms: "The American people, from tradition and interest, favor bimetallism, and the Republican party demands the use of both gold and silver as standard money, with such restrictions and under such provisions, to be determined by legislation, as will secure the maintenance of the parity of values to the two metals, so that the purchasing and debt-paying power of the dollar, whether of silver, gold or paper, shall be at all times equal. The interests of the producers of the country, its farmers and its workingmen, demand that every dollar, paper or coin, issued by the government, shall be as good as any other." This masterpiece of evasion succeeded well in saying nothing important, and merely stated a few undisputed if valuable facts. But in the fluid and uncrystallized state of public opinion with regard to the financial and currency question, it probably was a matter of necessity for the party leaders to evade a strong stand if there were to be any basis for party coöperation. There was a faint echo of the "force bill" in the statement that the party would "never relax its efforts until the integrity of the ballot and the purity of elections shall be fully guaranteed and protected in every state." Civil-service reform was again indorsed. A sign of clear-sighted statesmanship was shown in the plank which favored "the construction of the Nicaragua Canal" as "of the highest importance to the American people."

Temperance was given a sympathetic plank favoring "all wise and legitimate efforts to lessen and prevent the evils of intemperance and promote morality," and there was a "pledge anew to the veteran soldiers of the republic a watchful care and recognition of their just claims upon a grateful people." Probably "Corporal" Tanner smiled with benign delight. The silly season was not quite over, as evidenced by sympathy "with the cause of home rule in Ireland," and protests against "the persecution of the Jews in Russia." It is doubtful if one in a thousand of the American people failed to feel exactly that way about Ireland and the Jews also, but this was no place to state the fact—and the plank was put there for entirely different purposes than mere altruistic feelings!

It was, of course, certain that the convention would renominate Harrison. Any President of any party, unless there are striking and unusual reasons for the contrary, can secure a renomination if he wants it. And of course, and naturally, Harrison wanted it. Nevertheless, there was an element of irreconcilables who desired to prevent Harrison's securing the prize. He had, says Rhodes, alienated such leaders as Quay and Platt, and Speaker Reed; and Blaine's son, Emmons, was on hand working hard for his father.[22] McKinley's friends also were alert, although the latter gave no countenance to their efforts. The balloting took place on the fourth day, following nomination speeches by E. O. Wolcott of Colorado, for Blaine, seconded among others by William H. Eustis of Minnesota and Warner Miller of New York. Harrison was nominated by Richard W. Thompson of Indiana, seconded by several, including Chauncey M. Depew of New York and John C. Spooner of Wisconsin. There was but one ballot: Benjamin Harrison, 535 1/6; James G. Blaine, 182 5/6; William McKinley, 182; Thomas B. Reed, 4; Robert T. Lincoln, 1. The nomination, of course, was then made unanimous. It is a matter of special interest that the votes for McKinley came from delegates from 25 different states. This was placing him in line for 1896. Whitelaw Reid of New York was nominated for Vice-President by acclamation. The name of Thomas B. Reed was presented, but withdrawn at the special request of his friends. After a resolution of thanks to McKinley for the "splendid, impartial and courteous way" in which he had presided, the convention adjourned.

The nomination of Whitelaw Reid was an excellent one. He was born near Xenia, Ohio, on October 27, 1837, graduated from Miami University in 1856, became a journalist, and was a most capable and successful war correspondent at the time of the Civil War. He later went to New York, became editorial writer on the "Tribune," and succeeded Horace Greeley as editor-in-chief of that paper in 1872. His brilliant career as a journalist was followed by that of diplomat, and he was finishing a most successful period of service as minister to France, to which President Harrison had appointed him in 1889, when thus honored by the Minneapolis convention.

[22] "History of the United States," VIII, 382-3.

David Bennett Hill of New York, by means of sharp politics characteristic of him and his Tammany allies, had attempted to secure the Democratic nomination, but the feeling for Cleveland, fortunately for the country, was too strong to be overcome. The Democracy could not in decency afford to "turn down" its only President since the time of Buchanan, and Cleveland was nominated at the Chicago convention of the party on the first ballot. Adlai E. Stevenson of Illinois was selected as his running-mate. The platform was, like the Republican, evasive on the currency question, with an undertone of bimetallism running through it. But Cleveland himself was the embodiment of sound-money principles, and platform statements on this and other subjects amounted to little. The real issue of the campaign was that of the Cleveland and Harrison administrations, with the McKinley tariff to give point to the latter. As both men had been tried out, there was little excitement, but the usual discussion of tariff, currency, monopolies, trusts, and other economic questions. This, while not exciting, was very educational, and its very direct results were to show in future years. "So unenthusiastic were the usual political leaders that Colonel Robert Ingersoll declared that each party would like to beat the other without electing its own candidate." [23] The Australian ballot was used in the majority of the states in this election, so that the purchase of votes was very much reduced. The minor parties were the People's party, or Populist, which nominated James B. Weaver of Iowa and James G. Field of Virginia; and the Prohibitionists, who nominated John Bidwell of California and J. B. Cranfill of Texas. Finally, a Socialist-Labor party nominated Simon Wing of Massachusetts and Charles H. Matchett of New York. The emergence of this party was a direct result of the heavy Continental European immigration which was causing immigrants to settle in the country faster than they could be absorbed.

The founding of the new Populist party, especially in the West, led to fusion in a number of the states of that section

[23] C. R. Lingley, "Since the Civil War," 265.

and the South. There was complete fusion between Democrats and Populists in Colorado, Kansas, Idaho, North Dakota, and Wyoming, and partial fusion in Nevada, Oregon, and Minnesota. There also was partial fusion between Republicans and Populists in Alabama and Louisiana. This series of fusions was of great immediate help to the political power of the Populist party, but meant its final downfall due to an inherent lack of public confidence. Four years later it was difficult to determine whether the Populists had swallowed the Democrats or the Democrats had swallowed the Populists. To a large number of old-line Democrats who believed in sound money and sane economic policies it was difficult to tell the difference between a Bryan Democrat and a Populist.

In spite of the high hopes of the party, the election in November was a veritable Republican Waterloo. Cleveland carried not only the usual solid South, but also Connecticut, New York, New Jersey, West Virginia, Indiana, Illinois, Wisconsin, and California, and split the vote of Michigan and Ohio, receiving five electors from the former state and one from the latter. The Populist fusion with the Democrats gave Weaver Colorado, Idaho, Kansas, Nevada, and one electoral vote each from North Dakota and Oregon. The total electoral vote was: Cleveland, 277; Harrison, 145; Weaver, 22. The popular vote was difficult to apportion, due to the fusion, and possibly the estimate of Stanwood[24] is the best—Cleveland, 5,556,543; Harrison, 5,175,582; Weaver, 1,040,886; Bidwell, 255,841; Wing, 21,532. It must be noted that a large number of votes credited to Weaver in reality belonged to Democrats who voted for the fusion tickets.

There is no question that, in spite of his integrity, honesty, and ability, Harrison was not popular, and had nothing of the theatrical about him to strike the popular imagination or arouse interest. But this was not the main cause of the overwhelming defeat. Senator Cullom hit the mark when he wrote to President Harrison a few days later: "I specially desire to say that the cause of the defeat does not lie at your door personally.

[24] "History of the Presidency," 517.

Any man in the country standing upon the doctrine of high protection would have been defeated. The people sat down upon the McKinley tariff bill two years ago, and they have never gotten up. They were thoroughly imbued with the feeling that the party did not do right in revising the tariff up instead of down. They beat us for it in '90 and now again." [25]

The Democrats were surprised by their own victory. For the first time since the days before the Civil War they had control not only of the Presidency but also of both the Senate and House of Representatives. Professor A. N. Holcombe makes a keen analysis of the results of this election. Says he: [26] "The Republican ticket received only 43 per cent. of the total [vote], the smallest proportion received at any presidential election since 1860. . . . The election of 1892 has usually been regarded as a great triumph for the Democratic party. It was certainly a great triumph for the Democratic candidate. . . . But the Democratic ticket received only 46 per cent. of the popular vote in 1892, whereas it had received around 49 per cent. at the two previous Cleveland campaigns. . . . More than 10 per cent. of those who went to the polls were unwilling to accept the leadership of either of the major party organizations."

Cleveland's second administration was a period of misfortune ending in almost complete demoralization of the Democratic party. This was not due primarily to Cleveland himself, but to the fact that his party by now had become a mere collection of mutually hostile elements, divided upon almost every subject but the enjoyment of the spoils of office. When he was inaugurated on March 4, 1893, he was face to face with a financial crisis in national affairs, due to the steady drain on the gold reserve by the Sherman Silver Purchase Act, and the necessity for meeting the demands of the European balance of trade. While the Treasury conditions were thus critical, an industrial panic loomed on the horizon. There was a real economic basis for the discontent of the West, and pro-

[25] See Cullom, "Fifty Years of Public Service," 259.
[26] "Political Parties of Today," 214–5.

tection of the industries of the East could not solve the difficulty of overproduction of agricultural products of the other section. There, all the ills of the situation were ascribed to the grasping dishonesty of the Eastern capitalists, and the cure was found in new political and agricultural organizations which too often were the innocent cat's-paws used by cheap politicians to pull their own political chestnuts out of the fire.

Cleveland called Congress to meet in special session on August 7, 1893, to repeal the Sherman Silver Purchase Act and relieve the pressure on the gold reserve. Samuel W. McCall wisely says:[27] "Undoubtedly the threat of radical reductions of the tariff had imposed caution on prudent manufacturers and caused them to prepare for possibly rough weather by taking in sail; but the condition of the currency was so menacing that it is difficult to believe that the tariff was the only or indeed the chief cause of the economic difficulties." The repeal was accomplished after a memorable debate, and was largely due to the insistence of Cleveland, which caused him to lose much popularity with his party, and to the strong support of the Republicans, who were led by Reed. John Sherman was the man who did most to carry it through the Senate. At this time the panic of 1893 was upon the country in full force. Banks failed throughout the nation. Railroads went into the hands of receivers. There was wide distress, unemployment, and general economic depression.

To add to this economic disturbance, Congress now went ahead to revise the tariff and thus further upset business and industry. William L. Wilson of West Virgina, the Democratic chairman of the Committee of Ways and Means, brought in a measure which was an honest attempt to carry out the Democratic platform pledges. It was not a radical change in rates, but made moderate reductions and increased the free list. It passed the House of Representatives with little difficulty on February 1, 1894, by a vote of 204 to 140—a vote slightly smaller than the total Democratic majority. But when it reached the Senate, that body, under the leadership of such

[27] "Life of Reed," 193.

real protectionists calling themselves Democrats as Senators Gorman of Maryland, Brice of Ohio, and James Smith of New Jersey, radically rewrote the whole measure and made just 634 changes, largely in the direction of much higher duties than those proposed in the Wilson bill. There was a long wrangle in conference committee between the representatives of the two houses, but Gorman stood firm and forced the House of Representatives to accept the Senate bill. During this period of the contest Cleveland exerted himself in an honest, if somewhat tactless, attempt to force the Senate to recede and stand by the Wilson bill as a sincere attempt to carry out the party platform. Wilson, therefore, read in the House of Representatives a letter from the President in which he truthfully spoke of the action of the Democrats in the Senate as an example of "party perfidy and party dishonor." This made the contest more of a personal one and did much further to disrupt the Democratic ranks. Cleveland was in a difficult position after the capitulation of the House of Representatives. He disliked the new Tariff Bill, since known as the Wilson-Gorman tariff, but thought it possibly less questionable than the McKinley bill. He therefore allowed it to become a law without his signature on August 27, 1894.

The Republicans were jubilant and rightly claimed that the Democratic party had deserted its position and come over to the tariff views of its opponents. The Wilson-Gorman bill practically removed the tariff from the list of Democratic issues for the next twelve years and did much to destroy what little unity was left in the party after the split over the currency and silver questions. Republicans could not fail to poke fun at their Democratic friends both inside and outside Congress. Thus Julius C. Burrows, now a Republican leader of the House of Representatives, in the course of the debate upon the Wilson bill remarked:[28] "I shall not pause to call attention to the many incongruities in this bill. . . . There is one criticism I would not venture to make, but as it comes from the Troy

[28] Quoted in Orcutt, "Burrows of Michigan and the Republican Party," I, 317.

Photograph by Brown Brothers

MARCUS ALONZO HANNA

Daily Times, I ask the clerk to read the following: "The framers of the Wilson bill having classified hydraulic hose, which is used exclusively for extinguishing fires among articles of wearing apparel, no doubt will remodel that extraordinary measure so as to include hydraulic rams and spinning-mules in the live-stock schedule.'" A provision for a 2 per cent. tax on incomes above $4000 a year was declared unconstitutional, as a direct tax, by the United States Supreme Court on May 20, 1895. This rendered nugatory the Democratic attempt to take care of the deficit due to the trade depression and general economic condition of the country.

Meanwhile, Cleveland was making heroic efforts to preserve the gold reserve, which was steadily depleted by greenbacks and other paper being presented at the Treasury for redemption in gold. At two different times in the year 1894 the secretary of the treasury sold issues of $50,000,000 in gold bonds, acting under the Resumption Act of 1875. This did not suffice to stop the drain, and the reserve had fallen to about $41,000,000 by February, 1895, in place of the $100,000,000 deemed the safe minimum by governmental financiers. Cleveland now went ahead and by a legitimate and statesmanlike assumption of power made a contract with J. P. Morgan and other bankers for the purchase of three and one half million ounces of gold bullion, to be paid for with United States bonds, and followed this by another sale of bonds to the extent of $100,000,000 in January, 1896. By this time these heroic measures had taken effect and the gold standard was preserved, much to the good fortune and financial solvency of the country, and to the credit of President Cleveland. It was during this same period that Cleveland added to the debt of gratitude the country always will owe him by manfully sending United States troops to Chicago to put down violence and enforce the laws of the United States, the disregard of which was brought about by the disastrous Pullman strike of June, 1894. His action with regard to the Venezuelan controversy with Great Britain was successful in the end, but possibly could have been couched in more tactful form and the same diplomatic results obtained without the grave danger of conflict with the Mother Country.

Like the Republicans in 1890, the Democrats had the misfortune of meeting the issues of a national congressional election in 1894, just a short time after the Wilson-Gorman tariff went into effect, and likewise they suffered a disastrous defeat. Their membership in the House of Representatives was reduced from 235 to 105; their plurality was changed from 94 to a Republican plurality of 142. Reed was chosen speaker again; and, since the President was a Democrat, he became in a sense the official head of his party in the country. The Republicans controlled the Senate by 12 votes. There was little accomplished in the line of legislation during the last years of the Cleveland administration, and every one was preparing for the great struggle for control which was destined to come in 1896 not only between the two parties but within the organizations of the parties themselves. In spite of the difficulties and divisions within the Republican party, the Democrats were in a far worse condition. Cleveland's administration had been a political failure, but historical writers are more and more coming to the conclusion that in spite of his undoubted limitations as a party leader, Grover Cleveland was acting upon principles of sound and wise statesmanship. It was his misfortune that his party lacked the ability and wisdom loyally to follow him. Both parties were looking around for leaders in the coming contest; and, fortunately for the Republicans, they had several men at hand both ready and capable to lead to victory. Also, the trying issues of tariff and currency were better understood by these men, as well as possibly by more of the rank and file of the party, so that although there was some hesitation and needless delay in taking a stand, the party finally was brought to take due advantage of its opportunities, and its triumphant control of the national administration for a succeeding period of sixteen years was the result.

Chapter XIV

WILLIAM McKINLEY AND REPUBLICAN TRIUMPH

As already stated, Thomas B. Reed as speaker of the House of Representatives was the official and rightful leader of his party in the year 1895. There were those who thought that he should receive the nomination in 1896, and among them were Theodore Roosevelt, a keen judge of men, and also Henry Cabot Lodge. There is no doubt that Reed was one of the ablest men of his time and generation, and would have made a President of outstanding statesmanship. But everything seemed to swing toward McKinley, and the movement for Reed failed. The sweeping Democratic defeat following the enactment of the Wilson-Gorman tariff, and the hard times of the Democratic years of administration, acted as a great justification of McKinley in the popular mind and there was great prejudice in his favor. Of a most attractive and winning personality, he achieved wide popularity over the country for his own sake. His able and deft handling of contentious questions, his great good humor and kindliness as presiding officer of the Minneapolis convention in 1892, had made him favorably known to the party leaders of the entire country. When there is added to this the fact of an able, adroit, and competent campaign manager in the person of Mark Hanna, there could be only one result of the struggle for the nomination.

Marcus Alonzo Hanna was one of the most remarkable men in American history. A business man, with long training and experience, he early became interested in public affairs, ranging from politics pure and simple to the civil-service reform movement. He was an active member of various political committees in Cleveland and the state of Ohio, and in the convention of 1888 was an active delegate who worked hard to nominate John Sherman. His old acquaintance and friendship with McKinley grew steadily, and their intimacy led to an odd action on the part of Hanna. Following the great Republican victory in the congressional campaign of 1894, he suddenly retired from business at the age of fifty-eight years, being hitherto known as a very successful operator in the iron and coal trades, and made politics his sole business. From January, 1895, he made his one great object in life the securing of the Presidential nomination for McKinley in 1896. He was actuated in this not only by his love and affection for McKinley the man, but also by the sincere belief which, as a business man, he had gradually formed. This belief was that a protective tariff was the salvation of the country in an economic sense and that McKinley, as the foremost leader of the tariff forces, was the one man to carry though the protective policy as head of the Government.

Hanna later was attacked as an unscrupulous "boodler," and was held up to scorn by his opponents, both in and outside the Republican party, as the incarnation of ruthless capitalism and actuated only by a mercenary and selfish love of power and wealth. Nothing could be farther from the truth. He was large-hearted, honest, sincere, generous, sympathetic with the cause of labor, and merely acted according to his lights and the ideas of his time. He was in reality what to-day might be known as an efficiency expert in politics, and reduced political management to a species of business administration. Added to this was an understanding of human nature and an ability to size up individuals, so necessary in political activity, and his natural shrewdness and common sense did the rest. His rapid rise to power was largely through sheer ability and not, as the host of his enemies said, by monetary purchase and by "ownership" of William McKinley.[1] Says C. S. Olcott, the biographer of McKinley: "The insinuation of the cartoons that McKinley

[1] C. S. Olcott, "Life of William McKinley," I, 298, *et seq.* See Herbert Croly, "Life of M. A. Hanna." Rhodes is interesting—"McKinley and Roosevelt Administrations," 1, 43—as that of a conservative Democrat.

was dominated by Hanna was . . . false. On the contrary, McKinley was at all times the chief and was so recognized by his able political manager. . . . The fact that the two men remained mutually loyal to the end is the best proof that their relations were on a proper basis and thoroughly understood, for McKinley was jealous of his reputation and would never have tolerated the slightest imputation that he was not his own master. The secret of this perfect understanding was the disinterested spirit of Mr. Hanna, who demanded nothing, received only what he ought to have, and in all requests and suggestions sought only the highest good of the country and of the administration of his friend." H. H. Kohlsaat, the intimate friend of both men, later wrote: "There is an impression that Mark Hanna controlled William McKinley. That is not so. His attitude was always that of a big, bashful boy toward a girl he loves. It was not the power that it brought Mr. Hanna that made him fight for McKinley's nomination and election; it was the love of a strong man for a friend who was worthy of that affection."

Twenty-five years ago this statement would have been laughed at. As a matter of fact, Mark Hanna came nearer being a national boss or irresponsible party leader than any other man in American history. But at the present time, and in the light of the more recent history of the past twenty years, opinion in general has changed in this country. In the first place, it is being realized that, due to his office, his power, and his influence as the national representative institution, the President of the United States himself comes nearest to being the national boss. In the second place, the friendships of such men as Cleveland Dodge and Woodrow Wilson, or Frank Stearns and Calvin Coolidge, have never roused any just criticism in responsible quarters, and the ties between Mark Hanna and William McKinley were of the same kind. Great Britain long ago appreciated the real value of the business man in active politics. America is coming slowly to it and, strange to say, only in this unofficial way. Of course, the essentially evil-minded among the loose-thinking radicals, knowing the undoubted evil influence that (what Roosevelt well dubbed) "predatory capital" often has wielded upon corrupt politicians, impute evil everywhere. But it is time that an intelligent public should discriminate, and the American people slowly are coming to realize this. Rhodes [2] quotes Senator Scott of West Virginia as saying: "I shall never forget one morning during the campaign of 1896 when Hanna handed me a New York paper containing a cartoon of himself pictured as a huge monster, clad in a suit covered over with the dollar marks, smoking an immense cigar, and trampling under foot women and children until their eyes protruded from the sockets and their skeleton forms writhed in agony. After I had looked at it for a moment he said to me, 'That hurts.'" Hanna later acquired great influence with organized labor, due to its confidence in him and his real sympathy for its legitimate endeavors. The National Civic Federation, which to-day is doing such a striking and beneficial work toward harmonizing capital and labor, in a united and patriotic program of economic amelioration, is largely the result of his organizing ability.

Hanna soon found that the bosses in the various states, due to their confident feeling that "a rag baby" could carry the campaign for the Republican party, were planning to manage the convention and the nomination for their own purposes. Also, there was a crop of "favorite sons" springing up who might easily have been used to kill each other off, as was neatly done with Leonard Wood and Frank O. Lowden in the convention of 1920 and doubtless will be tried again. Thomas C. Platt of New York was backing Levi P. Morton of that state. Quay of Pennsylvania characteristically was backing himself. Senator Allison of Iowa and Senator Cullom of Illinois also were among prospective or receptive candidates. Hanna now took up the gage of battle and, as a representative of the people, set out to break the power of the bosses and succeeded. First of all, he undertook to make deals with them, in frank and open business fashion, agreeing that if McKinley were nominated and elected by their support, they would be assured of the

[2] "McKinley and Roosevelt Administrations," 6.

patronage of their state or section. Hanna was inclined to agree, but McKinley promptly put his foot down and refused any such bargains. "Mark," said he, "there are some things that come too high. If I were to accept the nomination on these terms it would be worth nothing to me, and less to the people."[3]

Results soon crowned the systematic efforts of Hanna. Ohio first indorsed McKinley, then Kansas, Wisconsin, Oregon, Nebraska, North Dakota, Vermont, and Indiana in order. Illinois seemed hopeless from the McKinley viewpoint. Then "a young man, singularly capable of leadership, but hitherto unknown in politics, whose action was inspired, as was Mr. Hanna's, solely by the noble qualities of the candidate himself,"[4] took hold and by adroit and clever generalship caused the state convention to instruct for McKinley. This young man was Charles G. Dawes, now (1927) Vice-President of the United States. By the time the national convention met at St. Louis, Missouri, Hanna had control of enough delegates to make the nomination of McKinley potentially secure.

The next question to which he turned his attention was that of the platform. Both McKinley and Hanna desired to make the tariff the main issue, and even attempted to do this for some weeks after the convention had done its prescribed work and adjourned. They both were sincere bimetallists, and McKinley, as a good practical politician, thought that if the currency issue were kept in the background until after the convention had met and adjourned it might be possible to reconcile both the gold and silver wings of the party on a bimetallism plank and thus escape the danger of a party split. But Henry Cabot Lodge and other Eastern leaders more correctly gaged the situation, and due to their insistence a specific indorsement of "the existing gold standard" was adopted. Says Olcott:[5] "McKinley's friends, including such men as Hanna, Herrick, Fairbanks, Proctor, Merriam, and others, went to the convention a unit in favor of the gold standard. They were in com-

[3] C. S. Olcott, "McKinley," I, 360.
[4] C. S. Olcott, "McKinley," I, 309.
[5] "McKinley," I, 314.

plete control of the situation, and any statement that the gold plank was forced upon McKinley and his friends by Eastern politicians is manifestly untrue. To Mr. Fairbanks McKinley sent word, referring to this subject, 'Tell our friends at St. Louis they can't make the platform too strong for me.' " Where McKinley and Hanna really failed was in correctly gaging the strength of the silver sentiment, which forced the nomination of Bryan at the Democratic convention and brought about entirely new strategy for the conduct of the campaign.

The eleventh Republican national convention met in Exposition Hall, St. Louis, on June 16, 1896. Among the delegates were Henry M. Teller of Colorado, Richard J. Oglesby of Illinois; Charles W. Fairbanks, Lew Wallace, and Henry S. New of Indiana; W. P. Hepburn, D. B. Henderson, and J. S. Clarkson of Iowa; Charles E. Littlefield and Edwin C. Burleigh of Maine; George L. Wellington and James A. Gary of Maryland; Henry Cabot Lodge, W. Murray Crane, and Curtis Guild, Jr., of Massachusetts; Russell A. Alger of Michigan; William R. Merriam of Minnesota; John M. Thurston of Nebraska; William J. Sewell, Garret A. Hobart, Franklin Murphy, John Kean, and J. Franklin Fort of New Jersey; Thomas C. Platt, Warner Miller, Chauncey M. Depew, Timothy L. Woodruff, B. B. Odell, Jr., Frank S. Black, Frank Hiscock, and Sereno E. Payne of New York; Jeter C. Pritchard of North Carolina; Joseph B. Foraker, Charles H. Grosvenor, and Mark Hanna of Ohio; Daniel H. Hastings, Edwin S. Stuart, William Flinn, and M. S. Quay of Pennsylvania; H. Clay Evans of Tennessee; Redfield Proctor of Vermont; and Robert M. La Follette of Wisconsin. Charles W. Fairbanks was chosen temporary chairman, and on the next day John M. Thurston was elected permanent president. It was not till the third day that the Committee on Resolutions, of which Senator-elect Joseph B. Foraker of Ohio was chairman, made its report. The platform may be summed up in the following paragraphs: Reference first was made to "the matchless achievements of the thirty years of Republican rule," and in contrast to that were placed the "calamitous consequences of

HANNA—"In 1900 we will be against the DANGEROUS Trusts."

Photograph by Brown Brothers

HANNA—"IN 1900 WE WILL BE AGAINST DANGEROUS TRUSTS"

full and unrestricted Democratic control of the government." These latter were emotionally stated as "a record of unparalleled incapacity, dishonor, and disaster," which had "piled up the public debt by $262,000,000 in time of peace," while it had "precipitated panic, blighted industry and trade with prolonged depression, closed factories, reduced work and wages, halted enterprise, and crippled American production while stimulating foreign production for the American market." In sharp contrast to all this was placed the statement, "We renew and emphasize our allegiance to the policy of protection as the bulwark of American industrial independence and the foundation of American development and prosperity." This was amplified by adding: "We denounce the present Democratic tariff as sectional, injurious to the public credit, and destructive of business enterprise. . . . Protection and reciprocity are twin measures of Republican policy and go hand in hand. . . . To all our products—to those of the mine and the fields, as well as those of shop and factory; to hemp, to wool . . . we promise the most ample protection."

The currency question was handled in specific fashion, but without attempting to close the door entirely upon those who desired to "do something for silver." This was handled in the following words: "The Republican party is unreservedly for sound money. . . . We are unalterably opposed to every measure calculated to debase our currency or impair the credit of our country. We are, therefore, opposed to the free coinage of silver, except by international agreement with the leading commercial nations of the world, which we pledge ourselves to promote, and until such agreement can be obtained the existing gold standard must be preserved. All our silver and paper currency must be maintained at parity with gold."

There was the usual pledge of further pension favors for the soldiers with a mischievous statement that "wherever practicable they should be given the preference in the matter of employment," which doubtless meant "political" employment. "The massacres in Armenia" received a deserved, if inappropriate, condemnation; and there was strong reassertion of the

Monroe Doctrine with the odd statement that "we hopefully look forward to the eventual withdrawal of the European powers from this hemisphere, and to the ultimate union of all English-speaking parts of the continent by the free consent of its inhabitants." Verily this was another proof of an oversheltering Providence which has kept the American people from the logical consequences of their international sins of omission and commission! The Cuban patriots received a pat on the back. There was a further statement that "we . . . favor the continued enlargement of the navy and a complete system of harbor and seacoast defenses." There was an excellent plank advocating that "the immigration laws be thoroughly enforced, and so extended as to exclude from entrance to the United States those who can neither read nor write." The Civil-Service Law was to be "thoroughly and honestly enforced and extended wherever practicable." Finally came the pious platitudes that "we sympathize with all wise and legitimate efforts to lessen and prevent the evils of intemperance and promote morality"; and that "we favor the admission of women to wider spheres of usefulness, and welcome their cooperation in rescuing the country from Democratic and Populist mismanagement and misrule." Any person who to-day states that the prohibition and women's suffrage amendments were "put over on unsuspecting people" should be easily convinced of his mistake if he only would read the continuing series of planks in the platforms of the past thirty years which dealt with these subjects in many and varying, but continuing, forms.

As soon as the platform was read to the convention, Senator Henry M. Teller of Colorado, who was the outstanding advocate of silver in the convention, speaking in behalf of a minority of the Committee on Resolutions, offered a substitute plank advocating the "free, unrestricted and independent coinage of gold and silver at our mints at the ratio of sixteen parts of silver to one of gold." This was laid on the table by the convention by a vote of 818½ to 105½, and the financial plank as reported by the committee was then adopted separately, by a vote of 812½ to 110½. Senator Frank Cannon of Utah then read a carefully prepared protest, signed by a number of the silver advocates, after which 34 members of the convention, including four senators and two representatives in Congress, withdrew, being led by Senator Teller himself. The remainder of the platform was adopted by acclamation. After the withdrawal of the "silverites," the president of the convention remarked: "There seem to be enough delegates left to transact the business of the convention!" This was received with "a general uproar and laughter." Following this came the announcement of a new National Committee, and significantly the name of Marcus A. Hanna was announced as the new chairman. Nominating speeches were declared in order, and Senator Allison of Iowa was nominated by John N. Baldwin of that state, Speaker Reed by Henry Cabot Lodge, and Levi P. Morton by Chauncey M. Depew. Then Foraker made a speech placing McKinley's name before the convention. He was interrupted by cheering for twenty-five minutes when he mentioned the name in the midst of his speech. Governor Hastings of Pennsylvania nominated Matthew S. Quay, and the roll of states was called with the following result: Whole number of votes, 906; necessary for a choice, 453½; William McKinley, Ohio, 661½; Thomas B. Reed, Maine, 84½; Matthew S. Quay, Pennsylvania, 61½; Levi P. Morton, New York, 58; William B. Allison, Iowa, 35½; J. Donald Cameron, Pennsylvania, 1; blank, 4. The nomination of McKinley then was made unanimous. Hanna was called to the platform and made a brief speech in which he said that "what feeble effort I may have contributed to the result, I am here to lay the fruits of it at the feet of my party and upon the altar of my country."

The convention next turned to the nomination of a candidate for Vice-President. The name of Morgan G. Bulkeley of Connecticut was put forward by Samuel Fessenden of that state, and that of Garret A. Hobart of New Jersey by J. Franklin Fort of the same state. The names of several others were presented, after which one vote was taken—Hobart, 533½; Evans (Tennessee), 277½; Bulkeley, 39; Walker (Virginia), 24; Lippitt (Rhode Island), 8; Reed (Maine), 3; Depew (New

York), 3; Thurston (Nebraska), 2; Frederick D. Grant (New York), 2; Morton (New York), 1. The convention promptly adjourned after the announcement of the nomination of Mr. Hobart.

William McKinley was born at Niles, Ohio, on January 29, 1843. He served in the Civil War, reaching the rank of major, and was the last veteran of that war nominated for President. His career had been long and honorable in the public service, and his national prominence was accelerated by the fact that when he first entered Congress as the result of the election of 1876, his old military friend and adviser, Hayes, was just entering upon his term as President. He advised McKinley to make a special study of the tariff, the suggestion was followed, with the result of the steady rise of McKinley to a place of power and influence as the chairman of the Committee on Ways and Means.[6] The frequent mention of his name in the pages of this narrative already has made plain his growth to power and influence outside the halls of Congress.

Garret Augustus Hobart was born at Long Branch, in Monmouth county, New Jersey, on June 3, 1844. He graduated from Rutgers College, studied law, and was admitted to the bar. He was a very active and successful member of the New Jersey legislature for a number of years, and remained influential in the politics of his native state. His nomination was a good one, but undistinguished.

Hanna and the Republican leaders now thought the fight was over, and that, after the demoralization of the Democratic party due to its desertion of President Cleveland, any candidate of that party could be defeated. But when its convention met at Chicago on July 7 it was seen that it would declare for free silver and thus make that the paramount issue of the campaign. A bitter fight was precipitated, for the eastern Democrats had no intention of allowing the western radicals and Populists to capture the convention without a struggle to prevent it. In spite of their efforts, however, the platform contained a plank demanding "the free and unlimited coinage of

[6] Olcott, "McKinley," I, 113.

Photograph by Brown Brothers

WILLIAM MCKINLEY

both silver and gold at the present legal ratio of sixteen to one without waiting for the aid or consent of any other nation." Under the complete control of the radicals, who were smarting under the wrongs and economic depression of their section, they unfortunately accepted the faulty theories and unsound ideas of the most extreme members of that wing of the party. Although absolutely sincere, they advocated a set of measures that were either fallacious, or else the direct growth of the newly imported influence of European socialism. Their extreme and unbalanced position on many questions caused an unfortunate reaction against them and their wrongs, with the result that much of their difficulty has been totally misunderstood both by themselves and their opponents, and they have not received the proper and statesmanlike attention they deserve. From the Populism and Bryanism of free-silver days to the so-called "progressive" campaign of La Follette in 1924 and the McNary-Haugen mania of 1927 is not a far cry, except in time. The American people will awaken some day to the real importance of the question, and then approach its solution in a spirit of sympathy and understanding. Unsound economics and political nostrums will never do more than aggravate an already unfair situation. The movement had a large element of the emotional in it, and in its search for a leader one naturally would be found who could appeal to this element. Furthermore, free silver had become a sort of religion with these aroused and honest, if mistaken, people, who were deeply conscious of what they sincerely believed were their "wrongs." The Democratic conventions of thirty states had declared in clear and unequivocal language in favor of free silver. To them "gold was the symbol of cruel, snobbish plutocracy: silver of upright democracy. Gold deserted the country in its hour of need; silver remained at home to minister to the wants of the people."[7]

Under these conditions the membership of the convention was in a fit mood to be "stampeded," and the expected happened. A young man, thirty-six years of age, who was known only locally or as a member of Congress from Nebraska, was

[7] C. R. Lingley, "Since the Civil War," 352.

called upon to address the convention. This was William J. Bryan, and he showed himself an orator of masterly ability, although a thinker of the most superficial character. His main strength lay in his ability to voice discontent, although his mental limitations were such that he was unable to work out any adequate constructive remedy. He swept the convention off its feet by the great peroration—"Having behind us the producing masses of this nation and the world, supported by the commercial interests, the laboring interests, and the toilers everywhere, we will answer their demand for a gold standard by saying to them: You shall not press down upon the brow of labor this crown of thorns; you shall not crucify mankind upon a cross of gold!" Bryan's nomination soon followed, and Arthur Sewall, a business man of Maine, was nominated for Vice-President.

The question was, what would the gold Democrats do? Many of them bolted outright and supported McKinley. The Republican party numbers among its most prominent members to-day many who, as young men, were driven out of the Democratic party by the vagaries of Bryanism, as the tenets of the Chicago platform soon were called, and they never returned to it. Other Democrats met and made independent nominations in the persons of John M. Palmer of Illinois for President and that fine old soldier of the Mexican War and the Confederacy, General Simon B. Buckner of Kentucky, for Vice-President. The Populists nominated Bryan, since the Democrats had adopted the main tenets of the Populist party, and showed their political acumen by nominating Thomas Watson of Georgia for Vice-President, thus guaranteeing an inevitable split of electoral votes, in case of Democratic success, between Sewall and Watson and the probable election of a Vice-President by the United States Senate! The Prohibitionists split in two wings over the subject of free silver, and the "single plank" element nominated Joshua Levering of Maryland and Hale Johnson of Illinois. The seceding "broad-gagers" later nominated Charles E. Bentley of Nebraska and James H. Southgate of North Carolina. Finally, the Socialist-Labor party nominated

Charles H. Matchett of New York and Matthew Maguire of New Jersey. It was confidently expected that their party would win an overwhelming victory not later than 1925!

The Republicans had received the news of the St. Louis nominations with equanimity and pleasure. Roosevelt wrote to Lodge, under date of June 20, 1896: "I am dreadfully sorry and sore about Reed; but we must do all we can for McKinley, of course. He is an honorable man; and the platform is admirable; the only plank I don't like is the pension plank." [8] But they suddenly were awakened out of their complacency by the wave of free silver and radical hysteria that swept the whole country. At first McKinley failed to appreciate what this might portend. "Soon after the convention a number of friends were at Major McKinley's house in Canton discussing what would be the issues of the campaign. Among those present were Judge Day, Mr. Hanna, and Mr. Kohlsaat. Some one said, 'The money issue is the vital thing,' to which McKinley replied, 'I am a tariff man, standing on a tariff platform. This money matter is unduly prominent. In thirty days you won't hear anything about it.' Judge Day remarked, laconically, 'In my opinion, in thirty days you won't hear of anything else.' And so it proved." [9]

It is the writer's own belief that had the election taken place at any time before September 1 of 1896, Bryan would have been elected. The mob was beside itself with excitement and the unthinking were in the saddle. Bryan undertook to carry the war "into the enemy's country" and had his notification ceremony in Madison Square Garden, New York, but this proved a failure. He read his speech, and when it afterward was subjected to thoughtful analysis, the thinking people saw it would not hold together. The people of the South were in a quandary. For the first time since the foundation of the republic the plainer element of people in that section, earlier known as "poor white trash," and their descendants were in power in the Southern Democracy. Jacksonian Democracy in

[8] "Correspondence of Roosevelt and Lodge," I, 223.
[9] Olcott, "William McKinley," I, 321.

the South more than half a century before had failed to put the control of politics in the hands of the middle or lower classes. Party management had been aristocratic until the eighties and nineties of the past century. A new set of leaders, not to be compared in competence to the older generations that were passing away, had taken over the control. "Jeff" Davis of Arkansas, Josephus Daniels of North Carolina, and "Ben" Tillman of South Carolina were among those who now had come to the front, and they had gone "hell bent" for Bryan and free silver. The writer well remembers the situation in North Carolina during this campaign, where he was then attending the state university. Most of his friends throughout the state were Democrats, and while the major portions of them were opposed to all for which Bryan stood yet the majority voted for him, hoping that the *state* would go Democratic, but that he be overwhelmingly defeated throughout the nation. A few voted for Palmer and Buckner, and still fewer voted for McKinley and Hobart—the first Republican vote they ever had cast.

Hanna soon woke up to the task before him and rightly judged that a campaign of education was the only antidote. He had an unerring belief in the common sense of the American people, that all they needed was to be informed, and that they would "see through" the fallacies of Bryan, the apostle of discontent and the tribune of the morons. But this required organization and money. Hanna went at the job of supplying both and, with his genius for direction and his wonderful insight into men and affairs, he succeeded completely. Tons of literature were printed and distributed. Campaign buttons, banners, meetings, brass bands, all the theatrical paraphernalia were not forgotten. McKinley was advertised, in the words of Senator Dolliver of Iowa, as the "advance agent of prosperity." The American people, so to speak, went to school and studied economics. It is probable that the economic reforms in the laws of the next two decades, with the especial success of the Federal Reserve Act in 1913, were made possible by the work done at this time, and the gradual understanding and

Photograph by Brown Brothers

PRESIDENT MCKINLEY AND ADMIRAL DEWEY

consequent acceptance of the fundamental laws of economics and sound finance by the rank and file of the American people. Hanna did not hesitate to "assess" contributions from business, big and little, but he did it openly and upon the grounds of the necessity for its own safety, if not its actual existence. There was a great intellectual awakening of the people, and for once a clear-cut issue was presented to them. Many good people, sound in mind and reasoning, did support Bryan for various reasons of conviction, but for the most part they were more influenced by the fact of the existence of certain great evils than by the proper idea of the means to meet or alleviate them. But as so often in American history, emotionalism was defeated by reason and common sense, and as election day approached it "looked" more and more like a great Republican victory.

McKinley carried on a remarkable "front-porch" campaign, in which he addressed with telling effect thousands of people who came in delegations from all over the country. He had the spokesmen of the latter submit their addresses to him so that he could guide their line of thought for public consumption, and give adequate answers to the various questions that were bound to be thrust at him from far and wide. He delayed his letter of acceptance until August 26 to meet current issues. Bryan made a most remarkable canvass of the entire country, such as no man ever had attempted before, much less succeeded in accomplishing. He traveled 18,000 miles and made hundreds of speeches. Olcott says [10] Hanna caused 120,000,000 documents to be distributed throughout the country as an antidote and answer to the speeches of Bryan. Meetings were held by the thousand, and all parties were hard at work.

The election took place on November 3 and resulted in the overwhelming victory of the Republican ticket. Stanwood [11] states that about 13,936,957 citizens voted. McKinley carried the Eastern and middle Northwestern states, with the border states, and also California and Oregon, and received 271 elec-

[10] "McKinley," I, 324–5.
[11] "History of the Presidency," 566–9.

toral votes. Bryan carried the solid South and the Western mining states and received 176. The Populist help had much to do with this, for North Carolina went Republican on the state ticket, since there was no fusion between the Democrats and Populists for those offices. For Vice-President, Hobart received 271 electoral votes, Sewall 149, and Watson 27. The popular vote was: McKinley, 7,111,607; Bryan, 6,509,052, a plurality for the former of 602,555. Of the minor tickets, the votes were: Bryan and Watson (Populist), 222,583, where there was no fusion; Palmer, 134,645; Levering, 131,312; Bentley, 13,968; Matchett, 36,373. While Bryan was to play a prominent *rôle* in American politics for nearly thirty more years, free silver was virtually dead as an issue from this time forward, although there was an echo of its support in the congressional campaign of 1898 and the Presidential election of 1900.

McKinley was inaugurated on March 4, 1897, and the Republicans took complete control of the Government. They held the prospective new Congress, the Fifty-fifth, in both houses. The Senate would contain a membership of—Republicans, 46; Democrats, 34; Populists, 5; Independents, 3; Silver party, 2. In the House of Representatives there would be —Republicans, 202; Democrats, 130; Populists, 21; Silver party, 3; Fusion, 1. The new cabinet, as announced, received the indorsement of the country. It was of good average ability, although later to prove weak in one or two departments. John Sherman was made secretary of state. He was nearly 74 years of age. Since he was succeeded in the United States Senate by Hanna, through appointment of the governor of Ohio, upon whom pressure was brought to secure the result, the carping critics of the administration charged a corrupt bargain to place an old and senile man in an important department of the Government, in order to find a place in the Senate for Mark Hanna. Olcott shows [12] these charges to be entirely false. Sherman was one of the most able and distinguished members of the

[12] "McKinley," I, 327–36. See H. H. Kohlsaat, "From McKinley to Harding," 55–62.

Republican party, and his appointment was a natural attempt to give stability to the administration and inspire popular confidence. McKinley urged Hanna to accept a cabinet position, but the latter declined after due thought, since he did not want to appear to be accepting a mere reward. Nevertheless, McKinley urged acceptance of the position of postmaster-general as late as the middle of February, 1897, and only reluctantly turned elsewhere. The offer to Sherman had been made and accepted more than a month before. Sherman did break down under the strain due to the emergence of the complications leading to the Spanish War, and resigned on April 25, 1898. Meanwhile, he had found his work more and more taken over by the assistant secretary of state, William R. Day, who immediately succeeded him and thus caused querulous complaints from the elderly man and the expression of suspicion that he had been "used." The remainder of the cabinet were: Lyman J. Gage of Illinois, secretary of the treasury; Russell A. Alger of Michigan, secretary of war; Joseph McKenna of California, attorney-general; John D. Long of Massachusetts, secretary of the navy; Cornelius N. Bliss of New York, secretary of the interior; James A. Gary of Maryland, postmaster-general; James Wilson of Iowa, secretary of agriculture.

In his inaugural address McKinley placed the tariff as the first problem for the consideration of Congress and the people, adding that changes in the financial laws could be undertaken only when there was adequate revenue secured. He was bitterly attacked for this, but it soon became evident that he was acting upon principles of sound statesmanship. Although his party had absolute control of the House of Representatives, so far as "gold" legislation went, yet the nominal Republican majority in the Senate meant in reality that there was a serious division of the party upon the principles of gold and silver, and the silverites would probably have a fusion majority of eight or ten senators in favor of free coinage.[13] On the other hand, the Republicans would be apt to stand together on the old issue

[13] I have used the figures of Stanwood, "History of the Presidency," II, 29.

of the tariff, and McKinley desired to have this question, with its necessary further disturbance to business conditions, out of the way.

Almost immediately following the inauguration, McKinley called Congress in special session and it met on March 15. Reed was at once reëlected speaker, and by prearrangement he appointed certain designated members on the Committee on Ways and Means, with Nelson Dingley of Maine at its head. These men already had been diligently holding hearings and preparing a tariff bill which was practically ready for submission when Congress met. The report was made on the opening day, was at once formally referred to the new committee, and reported back to the House of Representatives within three days. Under the smooth working of the Reed machinery, with party unity and responsibility at a proper state of efficiency, reminding one of the excellence of parliamentary practice in Great Britain, the bill passed on March 31. The rates were somewhat lower than those of the McKinley bill of 1890, the Republican leaders showing a common sense view of their situation and not having forgotten their extreme action and the punishment for it on a previous occasion. Due to the high-tariff attitude of the silver men in the Senate, who showed a propensity to "out-Herod Herod," the duties were forced up and finally placed at a much higher figure than intended by the Republican leaders. On the other hand, they were by no means as extreme as had been feared by moderate or tariff-for-revenue advocates, and these accepted what they got with a feeling akin to relief. The bill finally passed the Senate in July and was signed by McKinley on the fourteenth of the month. The Dingley tariff remained in force for twelve years, being superseded only by the Payne-Aldrich tariff of 1909, which was made necessary by changes in economic conditions. Business felt relieved from uncertainty and, no matter what mistakes were made in the Dingley bill—and there were many—the country suddenly came into a feeling of confidence. It began to recover lost ground and actively to make up the deficiencies in various products, both raw and manufactured.

This also led to renewed trade, both domestic and foreign, and the revenues rapidly recovered, so that the Spanish War was financed with little difficulty and the "adequate revenue," mentioned by McKinley as necessary for fiscal legislation, was secured.

This prosperity also was made possible by the congressional elections of 1898. The Republican majority in the Fifty-sixth Congress was slightly less, but the number of silver advocates also was markedly decreased. On the other hand, no less than eight silverites lost their seats in the Senate as the result of senatorial elections by the state legislatures immediately following the popular election, and gold men took their places. McKinley now acted promptly. In his annual message of December 5, 1899, he spoke of the sound economic and business conditions of the country and the good condition in the United States Treasury "as the most fitting time to make adequate provision to insure the continuance of the gold standard and of public confidence in the ability and purpose of the government to meet all its obligations in the money which the civilized world recognizes as the best." Promptly following this, Representative Overstreet of Indiana presented a bill to make the standard of value consist in the gold dollar of "25.8 grains, nine-tenths fine." It passed the Representatives with expedition, but was long debated in the Senate, as might be expected, and finally became law on March 14, 1900. This ended the real struggle of over thirty years to secure a sound and honest currency.

Meanwhile the stability of the McKinley administration and the temper of Congress and the country were tested in a new and entirely unforeseen manner by the Spanish War in 1898. For thirty or more years affairs had dragged their weary and disgraceful way from one difficulty to another in the adjacent island of Cuba, due to Spanish incompetence and corruption of administration and the heroic efforts of the Cuban people to secure their independence. This naturally aroused deep interest and sympathy in the United States, both on grounds of altruism and emotionalism, as well as on those of business and economic conditions, which were continually suffering under the disturbance of a near-by conflict. This situation was brought to a sudden head, after the long years of wearying conflict, by an impudent and indiscreet letter of de Lome, the Spanish minister to this country, who spoke of McKinley in disparaging terms. The publication of this letter was followed within a week by the shocking news that the battleship *Maine* had been blown up in Havana harbor on the night of February 15, 1898. The country showed great restraint under the circumstances, which was buttressed and encouraged by the calm and steady policy of McKinley. He appointed a commission which, after due study and investigation, reported that the cause of destruction had been an exterior explosion. Public opinion now became rampant, and this had its natural reflex in Congress. The President fought for peace till the last moment, and then sent in a message to Congress on April 11 in which he reviewed the course of negotiations with Spain and their unsatisfactory termination. War was now inevitable and the declaration came on April 25.

McKinley had acted admirably during this time, and shown great poise and ability. He made two mistakes, however—first, in not inviting Spain, a hitherto friendly power, to take part in the investigation of the *Maine* disaster, and in the second place, in making no real preparation for hostilities should they come. The great "preparedness" work of Theodore Roosevelt and Leonard Wood had to come years later, in order to awaken the American people to the need of at least a minimum military preparation for national safety. The President realized this too late.[14] The difficulties and delays, the sacrifice of the health and safety of the young men who responded to the call to arms, the breakdown of the War Department under Secretary Alger and the consequent disgrace to the administration and the country—all were the direct result. But both President and people pulled themselves together and retrieved themselves completely. On March 9 Congress had placed an appropriation of $50,000,000 in the hands of the President to be used at his

[14] See H. H. Kohlsaat, "McKinley to Harding," 66–7.

discretion for purposes of national defense. The Navy Department, in part under the inspiration of the assistant secretary, Theodore Roosevelt, had its fleets ready to strike, and the overwhelming victory of Dewey in Manila Bay on May 1 immediately followed. The Spanish fleet was destroyed off Santiago on July 3 by the fleet under Admiral Sampson. The land forces, sometimes badly led, showed fine spirit and dashing bravery, and won victories on land both in Cuba and Porto Rico. Whatever failures were made by politicians, both at home and in the army, the regular soldiers in general showed their old ability, and newer men such as Wood and Roosevelt won great and deserved fame. McKinley stood by Alger after the breakdown of his administration of the War Department, in order to give him a fair chance, and only when pressure and criticism threatened to become dangerous for his entire administration did the President supersede him and put the able and efficient Elihu Root at the head of the department in July, 1899, practically a year after the war was over. An average politician was thus superseded by a great statesman.

The American people were now for the first time beginning to awaken to the importance of our international relations. Under the impelling force of national danger, and to increase the defense line of the country, the Hawaiian Islands were annexed by joint resolution of Congress, approved by McKinley on July 7, 1898. This was a sound act of statesmanship, and greatly lessened the vulnerability of the country on the Pacific Ocean. Our arms had been so uniformly successful within a few months after the beginning of the war that indirect negotiations for the resumption of peace soon were begun through the mediation of M. Jules Cambon, the French ambassador, on July 26. Following this, a protocol was signed by William R. Day, who had succeeded Sherman as secretary of state, and M. Cambon on August 12. The President appointed as commissioners to negotiate with Spain in Paris three United States senators, Cushman K. Davis, William P. Frye, and George Gray, with Whitelaw Reid, and as chairman, William R. Day, who resigned his office and was succeeded by John Hay.

Negotiations were begun directly at Paris on October 1, and McKinley remained at Washington, keeping a close touch with the negotiations on one hand and with the state of public opinion on the other. Dewey's victory had placed the problem of the Philippine Islands at our doors. It was an entirely unforeseen development of the war. H. H. Kohlsaat says that he visited McKinley a short time after the battle of Manila. "McKinley said: 'When we received the cable from Admiral Dewey telling of the taking of the Philippines I looked up their location on the globe. I could not have told where those darned islands were within 2000 miles!' Some months later he said: 'If old Dewey had just sailed away when he smashed the Spanish fleet, what a lot of trouble he would have saved us.' "[15] While the matter was discussed in both official and private circles, the American people gradually came to the conclusion that it would be not only unwise but a neglect of duty to hand the islands back to Spain. On the other hand, the Filipinos were totally incapable of self-government, even under our "protectorate," so McKinley, who had an uncanny appreciation of the public feeling which could be likened to that of Jefferson or Lincoln, finally came to the conclusion that we must annex these islands. On December 10 the treaty with Spain was signed, and that country ceded to us Porto Rico, Guam, and the Philippines, and relinquished sovereignty over Cuba. We in return paid her $20,000,000. The American people accepted, for the most part, these new accessions with great reluctance, and only because they did not know what else to do. The treaty was ratified by the Senate after a struggle on February 6, 1899, the event being precipitated in the last moments by the news of the insurrection of the Philippine revolutionists against the American forces on February 4. In spite of a natural hesitation to overthrow any set of people, no matter how incompetent, who proclaimed their desire for independence, the American people did not falter, but led by the wise and sound policy of McKinley and the Republican leaders they raised and equipped

[15] "From McKinley to Harding," 68.

Photograph by Brown Brothers

NATIONAL REPUBLICAN CONVENTION IN PHILADELPHIA, JUNE, 1900. THEODORE ROOSEVELT, TOM PLATT, AND BENJAMIN ODELL ARE IN THE PICTURE

the necessary forces, sent them to the Philippines, and put down the rebellion.

Of course, this aroused tremendous opposition which ran athwart party lines, a number of life-long Republicans being allied with the Anti-Imperialist League of Boston and other organizations that bitterly opposed the United States' going beyond its old borders for the annexation of territory. The retort was, What else could we do? and this pointed question was finally answered by the American people under the stress of necessity and according to the lines that had been perceived by the insight of McKinley. Nevertheless, the Democrats decided to make this issue of "imperialism" the paramount question for the campaign of 1900, allowing free silver discreetly to drop to the rear. Bryan seized upon the issue as entirely to his liking. When the treaty had come before the Senate he had used all his powers of personal influence and persuasion to secure its adoption, for he always posed as a man of peace. His favorite lecture on "The Prince of Peace" was formed with great sincerity and delivered to admiring throngs of more or less intelligent people with great gusto, and also with legitimate financial returns to the orator.

For almost the first time in our history there was no real contest in 1900 for the nominations of the two great political parties. The Democratic party being the "party in opposition," it naturally would look to an eloquent and expert voice in the expression of its discontent, and William J. Bryan fulfilled that duty to perfection. Furthermore, it was a real tribute to his personal honesty and sincerity, not to mention his personal charm, that he held in almost undiminished degree the loyalty of his followers. This he was able to do, though later to a much less extent, for the remaining twenty-five years of his life, a remarkable record of sincere and personal devotion that is much to his credit. This fact probably will be his greatest title to fame, as future generations more and more realize the essentially fallacious nature of many of the measures he advocated.

That Mr. Bryan would receive the nomination again in

1900, therefore, went without question. Of course, it was the same with the Republicans. McKinley had made such an outstanding success of the administration of his office, that the rank and file of the party were overwhelmingly in his favor. The leaders perceived this, and also were very fond of the man himself, who had such a winning personality and kindly and sincere disposition. Mr. Hobart died on November 21, 1899, so the only question before the party was the choice of a candidate for Vice-President. Theodore Roosevelt had gained great applause for his striking services during the Spanish War and now was the popular and exceedingly successful governor of New York. He was prominently mentioned for the place, but had let it be known in the decided fashion characteristic of him that he did not desire the nomination for Vice-President, but wished to be reëlected to his present office.

The twelfth national convention of the Republican party met in Convention Hall, Philadelphia, Pennsylvania, on Tuesday, June 19, 1900. It was called to order by Senator Hanna, as chairman of the National Committee, who presented as temporary chairman Senator E. O. Wolcott of Colorado. The membership of this convention showed the usual disappearance of old leaders, who were gradually weeded out by age, death, and political misfortune, and the appearance of many new names, still prominent in party ranks after the lapse of more than twenty-five years. The rolls contained the names of E. O. Wolcott of Colorado; Frank B. Brandegee of Connecticut; Joseph G. Cannon, Charles S. Deneen, and Frank O. Lowden of Illinois; Charles W. Fairbanks and Albert J. Beveridge of Indiana; Leslie M. Shaw and Lafayette Young of Iowa; W. O. Bradley of Kentucky; Louis E. McComas and Phillips L. Goldsborough of Maryland; Henry Cabot Lodge and Samuel W. McCall of Massachusetts; Cushman K. Davis and Knute Nelson of Minnesota; Thomas H. Carter of Montana; John M. Thurston of Nebraska; Jacob H. Gallinger of New Hampshire; William J. Sewell, Foster M. Voorhees, and Franklin Murphy of New Jersey; Thomas C. Platt, Chauncey M. Depew, Theodore Roosevelt, B. B. Odell, Jr., Cornelius N. Bliss,

Francis V. Greene, Frank S. Black, and Sereno E. Payne of New York; Jeter C. Pritchard of North Carolina; Porter McCumber of North Dakota; J. B. Foraker, Charles H. Grosvenor, Charles Dick, and Charles P. Taft of Ohio; M. S. Quay, Boies Penrose, and William Flinn of Pennsylvania; Isaac Stephenson of Wisconsin; and Francis E. Warren of Wyoming.

Henry Cabot Lodge was chosen permanent chairman, following the presentation to the convention of thirteen survivors of the first national convention in 1856. They were Joseph R. Hawley of Connecticut; S. Woodward and George Schneider, Illinois; Jacob Russell, Maryland; D. F. Appleton, New York; Rush R. Sloane and B. D. Brinkerhoff, Ohio; John Jacobs, Walter Laing, G. W. Holstein, Edgar M. Levy, Jacob Wyand, Pennsylvania; George H. Bell, Rhode Island.[16] An effort was made, led by Senator Quay of Pennsylvania, to base representation in future conventions upon the number of Republican votes polled. This of course was merely another just attempt to cut down the phantom representation from the Southern states, but it was bitterly opposed and the proposal dropped. Senator Charles W. Fairbanks of Indiana, chairman of the Committee on Resolutions, presented the platform, which was unanimously agreed to without debate. It was not of great importance, for the record of the McKinley administration and the personality of the President were a sufficient "platform" for popular judgment. In fact, popular coöperation in the campaign of 1900 was easier to secure for the Republican party than at any previous election.

The most important features of the platform may be summarized in a few words. It stated that the Republican party, in 1896, had "promised to restore prosperity by means of two legislative measures—a protective tariff and a law making gold the standard of value." This had been fulfilled, with the result that there now was "prosperity more general and more abundant than we have ever known." After this statement of actual fact, it further was added that the American people

[16] F. Curtis, "The Republican Party," II, 389.

"have conducted, and in victory concluded, a war for liberty and human rights. No thought of national aggrandizement tarnished the high purpose with which American standards were unfurled. It was a war unsought and patiently resisted, but when it came, the American government was ready." The resolutions then gave a personal indorsement to McKinley by saying: "Walking untried paths and facing unforeseen responsibilities, President McKinley has been in every situation the true American patriot and the upright statesman, clear in vision, strong in judgment, firm in action, always inspiring and deserving the confidence of his countrymen."

The specific statements of policy then followed. "We renew our allegiance to the principle of the gold standard. . . . We declare our steadfast opposition to the free and unlimited coinage of silver." "We condemn all conspiracies and combinations intended to restrict business, to create monopolies, to limit production or to control prices; and favor such legislation as will effectively restrain and prevent all such abuses, protect and promote competition, and secure the rights of producers, laborers and all who are engaged in industry and commerce." This passage was especially significant as showing the gathering opposition to the power of "big business" and the popular feeling that some method of control of the aggregations of great wealth must be attempted. It was to have its results in the enlightened administration of Roosevelt.

The resolutions repeated the "faith in the policy of protection to American labor" and the "associated policy of reciprocity," with further restriction of immigration. Also there should be "legislation which will enable us to recover our former place among the trade-carrying fleets of the world." A bad plank, as usual, was that dealing with pensions, which were steadily becoming a greater national scandal and reproach. It stated: "The pension laws . . . should be liberal, and should be liberally administered, and preference should be given wherever practicable with respect to employment in the public service to soldiers and sailors and to their widows and orphans." This was followed by the statement that the

Photograph by Brown Brothers

"HE'S GOOD ENOUGH FOR ME"

A Davenport cartoon used in the campaign of 1904

party had maintained the efficiency of the civil service, but right at this point was the weakest record of the McKinley administration. Certain offices had been withdrawn from the classified service and consequently there was great and justified criticism on the part of the Civil-Service Reform League. Happily, this retrocession was canceled under the vigorous and enlightened administration of Roosevelt, soon to come, and the service placed far in advance of anything that had been attempted by any party or administration up to that time. There were declarations in favor of "a permanent improvement of the roads and highways"; "adequate national legislation to reclaim the arid lands of the United States"; in favor of "the construction, ownership, control, and protection of an isthmian canal by the government of the United States," and an indorsement of the Monroe Doctrine.

The issues arising out of the recent war were fairly and honestly met. "In accepting by the treaty of Paris the just responsibility of our victories in the Spanish War, the President and the Senate won the undoubted approval of the American people." The Government must maintain its authority, but "the largest measure of self-government consistent with their welfare and our duties shall be secured to them [the Spanish possessions] by law." This was a statement of sound and statesmanlike policy.

Following the adoption of the platform a new National Committee was chosen, with Mark Hanna as chairman and Cornelius N. Bliss of New York as treasurer. On the third day, nominations for President and Vice-President were to be made. McKinley was placed in nomination by Foraker, who had performed that service in 1896, and the most important seconding speech was made by Theodore Roosevelt. The call of the roll of the states was made and McKinley received every one of the 926 votes.

Then came the nomination for Vice-President. The name of Theodore Roosevelt was placed before the convention by Lafayette Young of Iowa, followed by several others in seconding speeches, including Chauncey M. Depew. His was the only name presented, and the vote was announced as 925 for Roosevelt, one delegate, Roosevelt himself, not voting. Both the nominations of McKinley and Roosevelt were received with demonstrations of cordial approval. This was one of the most happy, united, and enthusiastic Republican conventions ever held, and the ticket was one of the strongest ever placed before the American people.

The nomination of Roosevelt came about as the result of such pressure, popular and political, that he could not withstand it. Roosevelt himself says in his "Autobiography"[17] that Senator Platt and the New York machine leaders were very anxious to get him out of the governorship, chiefly because of the opposition of the big corporations to him. They enlisted the aid of Quay of Pennsylvania and other bosses from various states. Hanna did not want Roosevelt, but had no definite candidate, his earlier suggestions having proved impossible for some reason or other. Elihu Root, Senator Allison, Cornelius N. Bliss, Senator Fairbanks, John D. Long—all were considered but declined, or proved not to be available. Platt and Quay took advantage of this situation and used Roosevelt's great popularity throughout the country, which was reflected among the delegates, to bring about his nomination, and succeeded.

It is well to tell the story in Roosevelt's own words. "My supporters in New York state did not wish me nominated for Vice-President because they wished me to continue as governor; but in every other state all the people who admired me were bound that I should be nominated as Vice-President. These people were almost all desirous of seeing Mr. McKinley renominated as President, but they became angry at Senator Hanna's opposition to me as Vice-President. He in his turn suddenly became aware that if he persisted he might find that in their anger these men would oppose Mr. McKinley's renomination, and although they could not have prevented the

[17] 308–9. See also Olcott, "McKinley," II, 267–284; J. B. Bishop, "Roosevelt and His Time," I, 134–41; H. H. Kohlsaat, "From McKinley to Harding," 85–88.

nomination, such opposition would have been a serious blow in the campaign which was to follow. Senator Hanna, therefore, began to waver. Meanwhile a meeting of the New York delegation was called. Most of the delegates were under the control of Senator Platt. The senator notified me that if I refused to accept the nomination for Vice-President I would be beaten for the nomination for governor. I answered that I would accept the challenge, that we would have a straight-out fight on the proposition, and that I would begin it at once by telling the assembled delegates of the threat, and giving fair warning that I intended to fight for the governorship nomination, and, moreover, that I intended to get it. This brought Senator Platt to terms. . . . I supposed that this closed the incident, and that no further effort would be made to nominate me for the Vice-Presidency. On the contrary, the effect was directly the reverse. The upset of the New York machine increased the feeling of the delegates from other states that it was necessary to draft me for the nomination. By next day Senator Hanna himself concluded that this was a necessity, and acquiesced in the movement. As New York was already committed against me, and as I was not willing that there should be any chance of supposing that the New Yorkers had nominated me to get rid of me, the result was that I was nominated and seconded from outside states. No other candidate was placed in the field."

The Democrats met at Kansas City, Missouri, on July 4 and nominated Bryan, as was expected. They also placed former Vice-President Adlai E. Stevenson on the ticket with him. The platform was drawn out to wearying length of querulous complaint, and declared "the burning issue of imperialism" as the "paramount issue of the campaign." There also was the demand for "the immediate restoration of the free and unlimited coinage of silver and gold at the present legal ratio of 16 to 1, without waiting for the aid or consent of any other nation." The "trust question" also came in for a large amount of wordy and emotional discussion. The whole campaign thus was to be another direct judgment of the people between the two personalities of McKinley and Bryan; with "imperialism," silver, and the radical policies of the Democrats as side issues. The Social-Democrats nominated Eugene V. Debs of Illinois and Job Harriman of California; the "middle-of-the-road" Populists, who did not believe in fusion with the Democrats, nominated Wharton Barker of Pennsylvania and Ignatius Donnelley of Minnesota; the Prohibitionists nominated John G. Woolley of Illinois and Henry B. Metcalf of Rhode Island; and the Socialist-Labor party nominated Joseph Malloney of Massachusetts and Valentine Remmel of Pennsylvania.

McKinley, in his speech and letter of acceptance, made a straight-out statement of his policy, defended the handling of the Philippine question, and stated "there must be no scuttle policy." He shrewdly added, "the Republican party . . . broke the shackles of 4,000,000 slaves and made them free and to the party of Lincoln has come another supreme opportunity which it has bravely met in the liberation of 10,000,000 of the human family from the yoke of imperialism." This was a deft turning of the argument back upon Bryan and his Democratic followers.

It generally was supposed that there would be a Republican sweep, and such in reality was the case, but Senator Hanna refused to take any chances. He went upon the stump himself, showing new and unexpected power as a speaker. But the outstanding campaigner, even exceeding the effectiveness of Bryan himself, was Roosevelt. He swept across the country and crowds came to hear him. Bryan always could get the crowds to hear him, but they did not follow this up by voting for him. Roosevelt got not only the crowds but also their votes.

The election took place on November 6, 1900, and was held in forty-five states. Bryan carried only the solid South, including Kentucky and Missouri, and the four additional states of Colorado, Idaho, Montana, and Nevada. He even lost his own state of Nebraska. McKinley received 292 electoral votes to 155 for Bryan. The popular vote was: McKinley,

7,219,525; Bryan, 6,358,737; Woolley, 209,157; Debs, 94,864; Malloney, 33,432; Barker, 50,599.

Professor A. N. Holcombe points out [18] the important fact that from 1900 dates the revival of the old Democratic tradition under the leadership of Bryan, while the Republicans were forming a new tradition, a revival of the principles of Hamilton, and which is dominant in its party belief to-day. Mr. Bryan, in his attack upon "imperialism," went back to the teachings of Thomas Jefferson, and made the attempt to extend to backward and uneducated people the strict and unmodified application of the underlying principles of the Declaration of Independence—a thing that Jefferson himself never attempted to do. The present writer believes that Woodrow Wilson and his "self-determination" of the years 1917 to 1920 were the logical sequence. In the first case, the defeat of Bryan made impossible the carrying of so-called idealism to the point of the absurd. In later years, Wilson was already in power, and the unhappy results of his mistaken policy and diplomacy are the misfortune of many peoples in the world to-day. Both Bryan and Wilson overlooked the fact that self-determination is an ideal to be worked for, not a principle of practical politics to be applied alike to all races and people of the world and without exception. Every person who believes in democracy wishes that it might be so applied, but many know that it cannot, and that the only practical and workable principle at present is that government exists for the benefit of the governed.

Hamilton had taught the doctrines of sound business economics, the protection of property rightly gained, and strong nationalism. This might have been pushed to a dangerous extreme but for the leadership of Roosevelt, now coming to the front. Professor Holcombe says further:[19] "The effect of the new Republican tradition upon the unity of the party would have been more serious if Theodore Roosevelt had not become its official leader. . . . With less grace than Bryan,

[18] "Political Parties of Today," 249–54.
[19] "Political Parties of Today," 254–5.

but with even greater vigor, Roosevelt impressed the stamp of his dynamic personality upon the conscience of his time. He brought the Ten Commandments into the political arena, and thereby prevented the new Republican tradition from destroying the old Republican spirit. A more substantial cause of dissension within the Republican party was the mutual jealousy on the part of the two principal interests which constituted the bulk of its strength, the manufacturers and 'business men' of the Northeast, and the grain growers of the old and new Northwest."

Within these few lines we find summed up the underlying history of the Republican party from 1900 until the present day. The industrial and business East wants a high protective tariff, and has persuaded the agricultural West that the same policy of protection would apply to them. The latter has suffered continually from "hard times," and yet has always seemed to be impervious to the fact that it is practically impossible, under present conditions in the United States, to protect the farming interests by a high tariff. It is the play of these two forces, often cut athwart and disturbed by other issues ranging from railroad rates to prohibition and the League of Nations, that has deferred the inevitable day of some solution or compromise beneficial to both interests. This must come some time—if not in the immediate future, surely at some later day.

Meanwhile, the Republicans entered upon their new lease of power with well-justified feelings of elation and success. McKinley was inaugurated on March 4, 1901. Roosevelt quietly took office, and the country went on its way rejoicing. Kohlsaat tells the story [20] that some one asked Senator Platt if he were going to the inaugural exercises. "Yes," he replied; "I am going to Washington to see Theodore Roosevelt take the veil." Roosevelt himself thought it was the end of his public career. He had written to Edward S. Martin on November 22, 1900:[21] "I do not expect to go any further in

[20] "From McKinley to Harding," 89.
[21] J. B. Bishop, "Theodore Roosevelt and His Time," I, 140.

politics. Heaven knows there is no reason to expect that a man of so many and so loudly and not always wisely expressed convictions on so many different subjects should go so far! But I have had a first-class run for my money, and I honestly think I have accomplished a certain amount." Platt and his fellow-bosses were joyful, but their joy was to be short-lived.

McKinley during the last year or so of his administration had appointed commissions to study and handle Philippine affairs, headed successively by such able men as Jacob Gould Schurman and William Howard Taft. Under the administration of Leonard Wood, Tasker H. Bliss, Hugh L. Scott, and other army officers Cuba was literally "cleaned up" and proper sanitary methods installed, the island was pacified, patroled, and reduced to some semblance of law and order, and later given over to the control of its own people—a sufficient proof of the unselfish character of the Republican policy begun at the close of the Spanish War. John Hay handled the tangled skein of our relations in China with brilliant effect, and succeeded in bringing about the adoption of the "open-door" policy by other great powers. While our rights and the protection of our citizens were upheld with dignity and restraint at the time of the Boxer troubles, there yet was no diminution of the friendly attitude of our Government toward the Chinese people.

McKinley himself showed signs of an appreciation of the agrarian and other difficulties in this country, due to a continuance of the unmodified policy of a high protective tariff, and in his speech at the Buffalo Exposition on September 5, 1901, he advocated closer relations with other nations of the world, both in friendship and trade. "The period of exclusiveness is past. The expansion of our trade and commerce is the pressing problem. Commercial wars are unprofitable. A policy of good-will and friendly trade relations will prevent reprisals. Reciprocity treaties are in harmony with the spirit of the times; measures of retaliation are not. If, perchance, some of our tariffs are no longer needed for revenue or to encourage and protect some of our industries at home, why should they not be employed to extend and promote our markets abroad?"

What finally he had in mind can never be known. The very next day he was shot by an anarchist, and died on September 14, after a week of lingering and painful illness. Theodore Roosevelt at once took the oath of office and became President. McKinley was a conscientious Christian gentleman who made a great President because of his honesty and his integrity, his rare insight shown in estimating and choosing men, and his great power of both understanding and leading public opinion. Possibly he was not a great statesman, but assuredly he was a great politician, using that much-abused word only in the best sense of the term. His death came at the height of his power and success, and he left behind him a record of great achievement. With him may be said to have ended the last vestiges of real Civil War politics. A new era had dawned, and with it had come a man to lead the people in a new direction, but with the hand of a master.

Chapter XV

THEODORE ROOSEVELT

"Tom" Platt of New York, and the bosses allied with him, who had listened to the word of the big corporations that told of their dislike of Theodore Roosevelt, had the grimmest joke played upon them that fate could have imagined. It was a well-deserved nemesis, and the American people were quick to sense the fact. These servants of unrestrained privilege had shelved Roosevelt and kindly but sardonically kicked him up-stairs, only to find him upon their hands as President of the United States—and a President who knew his own mind and the mind of the people. What followed was their own undoing, wherever they had transgressed the bounds of justice, but at the hands of a man who knew how far to go in reforming evils without wrecking prosperity or the fair rights of legitimate business enterprise. What he stood for and in large part accomplished by his brilliant service as President was a "square deal" for all the people.

Theodore Roosevelt was born in New York city on October 27, 1858. He graduated from Harvard University in 1880 and made a special study of history, writing several clever studies in the field of American biography and naval history and western expansion. As a member of the New York legislature, civil-service commissioner at Washington, D. C., police commissioner of the city of New York, and as assistant secretary of the navy under McKinley, he had made a clean and enviable record of honesty and efficiency, with a driving force and keen insight into persons and things that rapidly extended his influence. His service in the Spanish War was brilliant, if not extensive, and he followed this with a masterful administration of the affairs of the state as governor of New York. As mentioned above, his efficiency and incorruptible stand for the rights and welfare of all the people had aroused the apprehensions, if not the opposition and hatred, of the selfish elements in big business and big politics, and they shelved him, but to their own undoing.

Roosevelt immediately took the oath of office when President McKinley died and announced that he would make it his aim "to continue absolutely unbroken the policy of President McKinley for the peace, prosperity and honor of our beloved country." He was thoroughly sincere in this statement, but the inherent differences in personality and temperament between the two men made inevitable certain changes in stress, if not in policy. He retained the members of the former cabinet until process of time made certain changes necessary. Roosevelt was farsighted and keen in his sizing-up of men and affairs, and his mind worked with incredible swiftness. Many a time he was attacked as being impulsive, when he already had thought his way through some foreseen problem and was ready to act upon a well-formed judgment. He also had the reputation of being domineering; but those who worked in close touch with him all state that he was always open to reason and advice, would confer with his subordinates, and be much influenced by their counsels. If he trusted a man, he trusted him completely and gave him free rein. If once he had reason to suspect him, he was at his heels all the time. He was exceedingly fortunate in his choice of secretary of state—John Hay continuing until death in 1905, and Elihu Root succeeding him. These two men are outstanding in the quality of their public service. Roosevelt once remarked to a friend that of the two he preferred Root; that Hay was able, but too much of a "yes, yes" man, while Root had an opinion of his own and would fight for it. This remark was also typical of Roosevelt.

In his first annual message he much disturbed business by stating his belief that great aggregations of capital should be brought under control by government supervision, which he always distinguished from direction. He desired laws in the interest of the public providing for publicity and uniformity in the affairs of corporations doing a monopolistic or quasi-public business, also the creation of a department of commerce and labor with a cabinet member at the head. He continued with speeches and writings in which he caught the ear of the people, and impressed them by his sound common sense and his moderation. He followed this up with court proceedings leading to the Northern Securities case, which resulted in the decision of 1904 by which the Supreme Court [1] put real life into the Sherman Anti-Trust Act. The court declared that the Northern Securities Company, which had been organized to purchase and control a majority of the stock of the two lines of railway, the Great Northern Railway Company and the Northern Pacific Railway Company, was a combination in restraint of trade and therefore illegal under the above act. It also enjoined any attempt on the part of the holding company to control the affairs of either one of the two railroads. With regard to the power of the Federal Government, it stated, "so long as Congress keeps within the limits of its authority as defined by the Constitution, infringing no rights recognized or secured by that instrument, its regulations of interstate and international commerce, whether founded in wisdom or not, must be submitted to by all."

Roosevelt also took the position that organized labor must be just as subordinate to the law as were corporations. He fearlessly held the balance true as between labor and capital, and thus gained the confidence and loyalty of the entire people with but minor exceptions. His action in settling the long-drawn-out anthracite coal strike of 1902, in which he forced both sides to come together and make a settlement to be based upon arbitration by a commission to be appointed by him, was a remarkable public service. He threatened to seize the mines and operate them, and, although this would have involved almost insurmountable difficulties, everybody knew he intended to keep his word and attempt it, and not merely to make an

[1] 193 U. S. 197.

empty threat. The National Civic Federation, of which Senator Hanna then was president, had a large part in assisting President Roosevelt to bring this settlement about by continued conferences and appeals to John Mitchell, president of the Mine Workers' Union, and also to J. Pierpont Morgan and other representatives of both labor and capital.

Mr. Marcus M. Marks of New York city, who was active in these negotiations, informs the writer that "the way having thus been cleared, two members of the National Civic Federation went to Washington to present the plan to President Roosevelt. They had no appointments, but knowing the President, took the chance of obtaining a conference with him. Upon arrival, a telephone call to the White House stating their mission brought prompt assurance of a welcome. The hour then spent with the President was a revelation of real democracy. Two plain citizens holding neither office nor title could so easily reach the head of the nation without ceremony! The President and his wife were together; there was no officer or secretary in attendance; such an informal heart-to-heart meeting with the most influential ruler in the world thrilled the committeemen. They told their story and made their suggestions to an eager listener. In response, the President frankly stated that all his efforts to bring about a settlement of the strike through the intervention of important public officials had failed. He realized the gravity of the crisis and heartily approved the plan proposed.[2] The committee returned to New York at once to make their last efforts with the various interests. Two days later Mr. Morgan and Mr. Mitchell answered President Roosevelt's summons to appear in Washington, and they agreed to the settlement of the coal strike by commission."

[2] Under date of New York, February 19, 1926, Mr. Marks wrote the present writer in addition: "Professor Jeremiah W. Jenks and I were the two men who went to see President Roosevelt. At the end of our conference he said to me: 'If you can close up this proposition, for God's sake don't lose a moment's time. Root has failed, Governor Odell has failed and all my efforts have failed. You can save us from having a revolution in this country.' On my return the machinery was set in motion and within a few days Morgan and Mitchell were on their way to Washington in response to President Roosevelt's request, with the result that you know."

Probably the most outstanding event in his first administration was Roosevelt's handling of the Panama canal matter. In January, 1903, Congress passed an act authorizing the construction of a trans-isthmian canal, and negotiations were opened with the French company which already had extensive rights and had made partial construction at Panama, and also with the Government of the United States of Colombia. The latter held off, evidently due to the desire of certain officials to secure special financial and other private favors, with the result that a revolution broke out in Panama on November 4, 1904. Roosevelt, when there was assurance of the success of the revolution, promptly recognized the new Government and the independence of Panama, and other nations followed suit. He then went ahead and negotiated a treaty by which the rights to construct a canal were purchased and its control and fortification secured. An additional treaty with Great Britain, the Hay-Pauncefote treaty, cleared the way from complications with the only other great power directly interested. This great success and happy solution of a long-standing international difficulty were at once seized upon by Roosevelt's enemies and used as a matter of reproach. It is now becoming recognized that probably the only mistake Roosevelt made was that of too quick recognition of the new republic of Panama, when a few days' delay would have sealed the lips of all unreasonable and carping critics, without any consequent danger to the international relations of the United States. The charges that the Roosevelt administration had connived at and fomented the revolution have fallen down completely by lack of any authentic evidence, the mere circumstantial evidence being furnished by the fertile imaginations of those well-meaning citizens who think the only way they can prove their own moral integrity is by impugning that of their own country.

As the campaign of 1904 approached, it was early seen that Roosevelt was destined to be the first man who, as Vice-President, should succeed to the office of President, and then be nominated and reëlected to the office "in his own right." Mr. Coolidge is the only man who has since equaled the record. Of the two wings of the Republican party, the conservative or business element, now dubbed "stand-pat" as the result of a phrase used by Mark Hanna in an address, was not pleased with Roosevelt's attitude toward big business and desired a change provided a sound and conservative friend might be secured as Democratic candidate. Mark Hanna himself might have attempted to secure the nomination of the party, but he and his friends became aware of the overwhelming popularity of Roosevelt and his unbounded strength with the people and this, added to the ill health of Hanna, caused them to withdraw their opposition. The western or agricultural wing of the party had great confidence in Roosevelt, and the fact that business and trade were generally good caused economic discontent to be at a minimum.

Roosevelt pushed the civil service further than any predecessor. While a good party man who believed sincerely in party organization and the necessity of "regularity" if any practical results were to follow along the line of good government, nevertheless he let it be known without any doubt that he intended to require efficiency and honesty in the administration of all offices, so far as it lay in his power to secure it. At the beginning of his administration he wrote to an Illinois political leader: "I want it thoroughly understood that no Presidential appointee has a prescriptive right to hold office. I intend to consult only the public welfare in making appointments. As long as a man proves himself fit and efficient his position is safe. When he shows himself unfit and inefficient he will be removed." [3] In the light of this attitude toward the spoils system, the friendly attitude of the party workers of the "old school" may be attributed to their appreciation of the fact that Roosevelt had the backing of public opinion, and that was, as always, an all-powerful influence. Senator Cullom well says [4] that "as President, Colonel Roosevelt was not popular with senators generally." It was the same old jealousy of the Senate in its relations with the executive department,

[3] J. B. Bishop, "Theodore Roosevelt and His Time," I, 155.
[4] "Fifty Years of Public Service," 294.

but Roosevelt usually won out in his contests with that body, just as did Wilson during his first administration and until public opinion had turned against him. In both cases it was due to appreciation of the possibilities of Presidential leadership when backed by public opinion, as already stressed in this work.

The Republican national convention of 1904 met on Tuesday, June 21, in the Coliseum at Chicago, Illinois, and lasted for three days. It was called to order by Henry C. Payne of Wisconsin, vice-chairman of the National Committee, since Chairman Hanna had died the preceding February. In order to appreciate the gradual assumption of power by new leadership, it is only necessary to read on the roll the following names of delegates: E. O. Wolcott of Colorado; Frank B. Brandegee and Charles S. Mellen of Connecticut; Shelby M. Cullom, Joseph G. Cannon, and Frank O. Lowden of Illinois; Charles W. Fairbanks, Albert J. Beveridge, and James P. Goodrich of Indiana; William B. Allison, J. P. Dolliver, and A. B. Cummins of Iowa; William O. Bradley and Richard P. Ernst of Kentucky; L. E. McComas and Phillips L. Goldsborough of Maryland; Henry Cabot Lodge, W. Murray Crane, and John D. Long of Massachusetts; Knute Nelson and Moses E. Clapp of Minnesota; Thomas H. Carter of Montana; Jacob H. Gallinger of New Hampshire; Franklin Murphy, John Kean, John F. Dryden, and David Baird of New Jersey; Thomas C. Platt, Chauncey M. Depew, B. B. Odell, Jr., Frank S. Black, T. L. Woodruff, Cornelius N. Bliss, Elihu Root, Edward H. Harriman, Sereno E. Payne, and J. Sloat Fassett of New York; Myron T. Herrick, Charles Dick, and Joseph B. Foraker of Ohio; Porter J. McCumber of North Dakota; S. W. Pennypacker, William Flinn, and George T. Oliver of Pennsylvania; Henry Clay Evans of Tennessee; W. P. Dillingham of Vermont; John C. Spooner of Wisconsin; F. E. Warren of Wyoming.

It was announced that Elihu Root had been selected for temporary chairman, and this nomination was unanimously agreed to. Joseph G. Cannon was chosen permanent president, and the proceedings of the convention went ahead with great smoothness and despatch, for practically all important matters had been arranged before the convention ever met. Henry Cabot Lodge as chairman of the Committee on Resolutions presented the platform, which was promptly and unanimously adopted. It was rather lengthy but well written. There were certain significant planks which should be mentioned, for they showed without any evasion exactly what the country would have the right to expect if Roosevelt should be reëlected, and his administration loyally attempted to carry out the main provisions. It was stated that "Laws enacted by the Republican party which the Democratic party failed to enforce, and which were intended for the protection of the public against the unjust discrimination or the illegal encroachment of vast aggregations of capital, have been fearlessly enforced by a Republican President, and new laws insuring reasonable publicity as to the operations of great corporations and providing additional remedies for the prevention of discrimination in freight rates have been passed by a Republican congress." With this plank went a later one of equal importance: "Combinations of capital and labor are the results of the economic movement of the age, but neither must be permitted to infringe upon the rights and interests of the people. Such combinations, when lawfully formed for lawful purposes, are alike entitled to the protection of the laws, but both are subject to the laws, and neither can be permitted to break them."

The protective tariff was strongly indorsed with the additional statement, so characteristic of the present day, that "the measure of protection should always at least equal the difference in the cost of production at home and abroad." There was the true boast that "in the Philippines we have suppressed insurrection, established order, and given to life and property a security never known there before. We have organized civil government [and] made it effective and strong in administration." There followed the statements that "the maintenance of the gold standard, established by the Republican party, cannot safely be committed to the Democratic party"; "we favor legislation which will encourage and build up the American merchant marine"; "a navy powerful enough to defend the United States against any attack"; that the Civil-Service Law "be thoroughly and honestly enforced"; that there be a "liberal administration of the pension laws"; "the peaceful settlement of international differences by arbitration." President Roosevelt was given a handsome indorsement, in extended phrases, ending with the statement: "In the enforcement of the laws he has shown not only courage, but the wisdom that understands that to permit laws to be violated or disregarded opens the door to anarchy, while the just enforcement of the law is the soundest conservatism. He has held firmly to the fundamental American doctrine that all men must obey the law; that there must be no distinction between rich and poor, between strong and weak; but that justice and equal protection under the law must be secured to every citizen without regard to race, creed, or condition."

According to prearrangement, Frank S. Black of New York placed the name of Roosevelt before the convention and it was seconded by Senator Beveridge of Indiana and a number of others. The roll of states was called and the chair announced that the total number of votes was 994, and that all had been cast for Theodore Roosevelt. Immediately following this announcement and the usual noisy demonstrations came the nomination of Charles W. Fairbanks of Indiana for Vice-President. His name was placed before the convention by Senator J. P. Dolliver of Iowa and seconded by Senator Chauncey M. Depew and others. Fairbanks also was nominated by acclamation. This most harmonious convention then adjourned.

Charles Warren Fairbanks was born on a farm in Union county, Ohio, on May 11, 1852. He graduated at Ohio Wesleyan College in 1872. After studying law he was admitted to the bar and practised in Indianapolis, Indiana, being active in politics, and later was elected to the United States Senate. He was a man of sound ability, of conservative tendencies, and thus satisfied the most stand-pat elements of the party who were not altogether satisfied with Mr. Roosevelt's somewhat radical beliefs. He was an able but unimaginative speaker, and did good service on the stump in various Republican campaigns. Had necessity called, he would have made a safe but mediocre President.

Due to two previous failures on the part of Mr. Bryan and his followers to bring success to the Democratic party, the more conservative elements gained control and decided to meet the "radicalism" of Roosevelt with an attempt to capture the vote of big business and the sound-money East. Strange to say, they succeeded in holding Bryan and his element of the party at least to a pretense of loyalty, but there was little enthusiasm for the nomination of Judge Alton B. Parker of New York and the aged Henry G. Davis of West Virginia. Judge Parker was a man of good ability, of delightful personality, and at least local prominence in the greatest state from the point of population. The platform was a hodge-podge of conservatism and Bryan radicalism, intended to catch the widely differing elements of the party, but without success. Roosevelt was too strong with all elements of the people to be checked in his triumphant progress.

The Prohibitionists nominated Silas C. Swallow of Pennsylvania and George W. Carroll of Texas; the Socialists nominated Eugene V. Debs of Indiana and Benjamin Hanford of New York; the Socialist-Labor party nominated Charles H. Corregan of New York and William W. Cox of Illinois; and the old Populist party, now on its last legs, put forward Thomas E. Watson of Georgia and Thomas H. Tibbles of Nebraska.

The campaign was a singularly lethargic one, with little excitement until the last few days, when Judge Parker insinuated that Mr. George B. Cortelyou, the chairman of the Republican National Committee, who was managing the campaign for Roosevelt, was using his knowledge gained as recent secretary of commerce and labor in Roosevelt's cabinet in order to levy contributions upon large corporations and big business generally. Roosevelt promptly denounced such charges as a "wicked falsehood." Although they were reiterated by partizan newspapers and on the stump, they played but little part in the campaign. In a last desperate attempt to stem the adverse tide, Judge Parker went on the stump and made speeches throughout several doubtful states. It was all to no purpose, and Roosevelt and Fairbanks were elected with a great Republican sweep. There was the strange spectacle of a rather conservative Republican party, at least in the main part of its leadership, with a moderate radical as its candidate. On the other hand, the predominantly radical Democratic party had a conservative candidate. No wonder there was only one issue, Theodore Roosevelt—and the Republicans monopolized that!

Late on the evening of November 8, 1904, when it became certain that he was reëlected by an overwhelming majority, Roosevelt issued the following statement, which arose to dog him later on, and aroused a great deal of useless discussion: "I am deeply sensitive of the honor done me by the American people in thus expressing their confidence in what I have done and have tried to do. I appreciate to the full the solemn responsibility that confidence imposes upon me, and I shall do all that in my power lies not to forfeit it. On the 4th of March next I shall have served three and a half years, and that three and a half years constitutes my first term. The wise custom which limits the President to two terms regards the substance and not the form, and under no circumstances will I be a candidate for or accept another nomination."

The popular vote at the election was: Roosevelt, 7,628,785; Parker, 5,084,442; Swallow, 258,950; Debs, 402,895; Corregan, 33,490; Watson, 114,546. The Republican plurality was 2,544,343. The electoral vote was: Roosevelt, 336; Parker, 140. This was the greatest popular plurality and the greater number of electoral votes ever given up to that time. Roosevelt carried all the Northern and Western states, the border states of Delaware, Missouri, and West Virginia, and the state of Maryland by just 50 votes, though he lost all the electoral votes from that state except one. The Democrats raised the cry of "nigger" in the last-named state, and frightened many people into voting the Parker ticket. The Booker Washington incident, in which Roosevelt had invited the great negro leader to lunch at the White House, was used in a clever but demagogic way. As part of the advertising campaign of the Republican party, there were spread abroad large posters with a cartoon by Homer Davenport picturing "Uncle Sam," with hand upon the shoulder of Roosevelt, saying, "He's good enough for me!" The Democrats matched this with another poster picturing Roosevelt with his hand upon a large "buck" negro and saying, "He's good enough for me!" Such claptrap was effective, as on many occasions before, especially in Maryland.

Roosevelt was inaugurated on March 4, 1905, with great pomp and enthusiasm, and now felt that he was President in his own right. It is to this period that one must look to see him at his best, for he dominated his administration as truly as Andrew Jackson did his seventy-five years before, but with a leadership as great, and statesmanship far exceeding anything ever shown by that Democratic leader. A personal friend wrote him at this time, urging him to take up the tariff and revise it downward, since the Dingley rates had become outgrown, certain lines of manufacture were over-protected, and trouble was certain to come. Roosevelt replied that the friend was correct in his judgment with regard to the tariff situation, but he thought it unwise to attempt the revision; that it would be possible for him, under present conditions, to carry through the major part of his program for the reform of business, and various other matters of social and economic betterment, but if he attempted the tariff, he could carry through such a bill only after a desperate fight, if at all, and meanwhile he would jeopardize his other reform legislation as already indicated; that he thought it better to undertake what he knew to be possible, rather than to bank upon an uncertainty. There is no doubt that Roosevelt showed good judgment in this, but it also is interesting as showing that he foresaw the tariff fight and the needed legislation along that line which

Photograph from Brown Brothers

THEODORE ROOSEVELT

were to wreck Mr. Taft and his administration. It has been well said [5] that "the old order which was incarnated in Hanna had not then passed away, but it was passing. . . . An entirely new type of man was President, who had no knowledge of the Civil War excepting that gained from books and from his family associations both with the North and with the South. When McKinley and Hanna died, the old dynasty fell." McKinley, by his appointment of old Confederate soldiers such as Joseph Wheeler and Fitzhugh Lee to the command of United States troops in the Spanish War had done the greatest service to the cause of unity and patriotism in wiping away the remains of the old sectionalism. The policy of hands-off preserved toward the South in political matters showed its results in the carrying of the border states at the 1904 election. But the "old order" was not willing to give up as yet. The stand-pat element made its effort anew to control the party, as we shall see, during the Taft administration, with results disastrous to the party and to the country. Meanwhile, Roosevelt was at the helm, and his opponents could only bide their time and wait.

It was during the time of the campaign of 1904, just described, that there was held on July 6, at Jackson, Michigan, the celebration of the fiftieth anniversary of the foundation of the Republican party. John Hay made the principal address on this occasion, and naturally it was an enthusiastic glorification of the "grand old party," in which Hay himself had taken so large a part. William Roscoe Thayer afterward remarked:[6] "The laudation of the Republican party, to which Hay attributed almost every beneficent act in fifty years, except possibly the introduction of antiseptic surgery, must have tickled Hay's sense of humor in the writing, as it surely fed the satisfaction of the thousands who heard it. Underneath the exuberance of encomium there is still an honest outline of the services of the party." The reading of this graceful

[5] Charles G. Washburne, "Theodore Roosevelt," 54.
[6] "Life of John Hay," II, 381.

speech amply repays the student of politics, even though its "exuberance" may be a trifle wearying.

Roosevelt's masterly handling of foreign affairs, ably assisted as he was by John Hay and Elihu Root, ranks among the greatest of his triumphs and places him at the forefront of our Presidents. It was during his first administration that he checked the career of Emperor William of Germany in his aggressive attitude toward Venezuela, and did it in such a deft but successful way that few people, except those initiated in international diplomacy, realized the magnitude of his personal and national success. His brilliantly conceived and executed plan of sending the battleship fleet around the world was of striking effect in the cause of peace, little as his pacifist opponents suspected it. It took courage and daring of the most marked kind to conceive of and carry through to a successful completion the intervention at the time of the Russo-Japanese War, and the treaty of Portsmouth, in 1905. Charged as he was with the most aggressive ideas of militarism, he accomplished more in the cause of peace than any man of his time or age. An enthusiastic advocate of preparedness against war, he brought the army and navy of the United States to the height of effectiveness, and the impetus he gave stood us in good stead some ten years later when we were precipitated into a great world conflict. A continuation of his wise policies under his successors would have changed the whole course of history and saved countless lives and countless treasure. But it would be too much to expect an administration such as that of Roosevelt to be immediately equaled, no matter how earnest or devoted his successors might be.

In the line of domestic legislation we have the important measures dealing further with economic conditions. As a result of the election of 1904 the Republicans controlled both houses of Congress. In the Senate there were 57 Republicans, 32 Democrats, and one vacancy; in the house of Representatives, 249 Republicans and 137 Democrats. The great problem for Roosevelt was to hold his party together, and then carry out the promises in the platform upon which he had been elected. That he succeeded in large part in doing so was of course due, as always, to his skill as a party leader and to his strength with the people of the country.

Under Roosevelt's direction and encouragement the United States commissioner of corporations investigated the activities of the Standard Oil Company, the so-called "beef trust," the American Tobacco Company, the American Sugar Refining Company, and various railroad and other corporations or establishments of "big business." As a result, suits were brought, many holding corporations were dissolved, and a healthful and sanitary sunlight of publicity was turned upon monopolies in general. Further legislation was carried through Congress and placed upon the statute-books, such as the Pure Food and Drugs Act of 1906, and the Hepburn act of the same year. The latter act vastly increased the power of the Interstate Commerce Commission, placing express and sleeping-car companies under its jurisdiction and giving it rate-making powers.

A storm of disapproval and even bitter personal attacks upon Roosevelt failed to shake him in his policy, and it is interesting to note that one of the few indorsements from a man in big business came from the late Judge Elbert H. Gary, known to fame as the president of the United States Steel Corporation. Under date of March 15, 1907, he wrote to President Roosevelt a letter of indorsement, in which he said: "I think the attitude of the present administration, as frequently stated in your utterances, is exactly what this country needs. I do not intend to be a hypocrite. If any company in which I am interested is wrong, it must get right. All of us must be measured by the standard of right. The application of this principle, from which as President I think you have never deviated, is building for you a monument which will be permanent and will be the lasting pride of all your friends. It is embodied in the sentiment expressed by you: A square deal for all. I do not hesitate to say that your influence as President of this great republic has been of great benefit to me personally and I feel equally certain that it is beginning to have a good effect upon others who have been reluctant to see their faults." [7] Roosevelt's helpful attitude toward business and finance at the time of the panic of 1907, the responsibility for which unjustly was laid entirely at his door by his big-business critics; his hard and successful work in advocacy of conservation of natural resources, and the betterment of country life; his advocacy of employer's liability laws—all showed his character as a statesman of real constructive ability.

As the time approached for the election of 1908 it became a very important question as to whom the Republicans would nominate. This was especially important, due to the fact that it would show whether the progressive or the stand-pat elements of the party would control, for in his successor the country would see the continuation or the reversal of the Roosevelt policies. Roosevelt himself was well aware of this, and looked around for a man who could be relied upon to follow in his footsteps. He thought he had found such a man in his able and popular, as well as personally attractive, secretary of war, William Howard Taft of Ohio. Judge Taft was born in the city of Cincinnati, Ohio, on September 15, 1857. He graduated from Yale University, studied law, and later settled in his native city. He held various offices, and was made solicitor-general of the United States by President Harrison, and a Federal judge of the sixth judicial circuit. President McKinley sent him to the Philippines as chairman of the Second Philippine Commission in 1900, and he became the first American governor-general by the appointment of President Roosevelt in 1901. His brilliant work in ending military government and substituting civil administration, his clever handling of the various weighty problems that arose in connection with both national and international relations, caused his appointment as secretary of war in the Roosevelt cabinet. The friendship between the President and his secretary was of

[7] Quoted in "The Life of Elbert H. Gary—the Story of Steel," by Ida M. Tarbell, 193.

old standing, and they were seemingly very congenial and united in their viewpoints.

Roosevelt used all his influence as President, and, as might be expected, with success, and when the national convention met it was a foregone conclusion that Taft would win the nomination. He had said to H. H. Kohlsaat, in 1907, that if he had the power of a dictator he would appoint Elihu Root as President and Secretary Taft as Chief Justice of the Supreme Court. Later he wisely said with his usual acute judgment, "Root would make the best President, but Taft the best candidate." [8] It evidently was Roosevelt's idea to choose a moderate, not too much identified with either wing of the party, hence he went to work for Taft with all the energy and devotion to an object so characteristic of the man. There is no question that the stand-pat element would have preferred Speaker Joseph G. Cannon, a man of great ability and popularity, or, failing him, to unite upon Vice-President Fairbanks. The power of the administration was too great, however, and the fortunes of these men, as well as those of various favorite sons, soon diminished to insignificance. Roosevelt kept up his work for Taft until the very day of the meeting of the convention, and then was fearful there would be a stampede for him at the time of the national gathering.

The fourteenth national Republican convention met at the Coliseum, in Chicago, Illinois, on Tuesday, June 16, 1908. It was called to order by Harry S. New of Indiana, chairman of the National Committee, who had succeeded George B. Cortelyou in that office when the latter had resigned to reënter Roosevelt's cabinet, as postmaster-general. Cortelyou later was advanced to the position of secretary of the treasury in 1907 upon the retirement of Leslie M. Shaw of Iowa, who himself had succeeded Lyman J. Gage in 1901. It is of interest to note on the roll of delegates the names of Hubert Work of Colorado; Henry A. du Pont and Preston Lea of Delaware; Shelby M. Cullom, Charles S. Deneen, and William B. McKinley of Illinois; Albert J. Beveridge, James A. Hemenway,

[8] Kohlsaat, "From McKinley to Harding," 161.

James P. Goodrich, and George Ade of Indiana; Lafayette Young of Iowa; Charles Curtis of Kansas; George A. Pearre and Phillips L. Goldsborough of Maryland; Henry Cabot Lodge, W. Murray Crane, and John D. Long of Massachusetts; Frank B. Kellogg of Minnesota; Herbert S. Hadley of Missouri; Jacob H. Gallinger of New Hampshire; J. Franklin Fort, John Kean, Frank O. Briggs, David Baird, and Thomas N. McCarter of New Jersey; Stewart L. Woodford, Seth Low, T. L. Woodruff, Ezra P. Prentice, Chauncey M. Depew, Job E. Hedges, Herbert Parsons, William L. Ward, and Benjamin B. Odell, Jr., of New York; Myron T. Herrick, Charles P. Taft, Arthur L. Vorys, J. Warren Keifer, Theodore E. Burton, and Harry M. Daugherty of Ohio; C. W. Fulton of Oregon, Edwin S. Stuart, Boies Penrose, Israel W. Durham, and David Martin of Pennsylvania; Coe J. Crawford of South Dakota; H. Clay Evans of Tennessee; George Sutherland and Reed Smoot of Utah; William P. Dillingham and Frank L. Greene of Vermont; C. B. Slemp of Virginia, R. A. Ballinger of Washington; Isaac Stephenson and Henry A. Cooper of Wisconsin; Francis E. Warren and Frank W. Mondell of Wyoming.

Mr. New announced that the National Committee had recommended Senator Julius C. Burrows of Michigan as temporary chairman, and he was at once elected. Henry Cabot Lodge was chosen permanent president and made an address in which he referred to Roosevelt in glowing terms. At once the applause of the delegates was taken up by the galleries, and there was evidently an attempt to stampede the convention, the demonstration lasting for forty-six minutes.[9] Mr. Lodge had referred to Roosevelt as "the best abused and most popular man in the United States to-day," and this statement was recognized as a fact and used by the Roosevelt partizans accordingly. Quiet was finally restored, for the convention, acting under orders of Roosevelt and the political leaders, had in large part come together to nominate Taft and meant to fulfil their duty. Another vigorous attempt was made, under the

[9] See E. Stanwood, "History of the Presidency," II, 170.

leadership of James F. Burke of Pennsylvania, to reform the method of representation in future conventions, and failed as before, but not until a lengthy discussion had been made, and the vote in its favor was large and influential. Albert J. Hopkins of Illinois presented the platform, as chairman of the Committee on Resolutions. There was a minority report at the hands of Henry A. Cooper of Wisconsin, who represented the partizans of Governor La Follette of that state, and for whom the Roosevelt policies were not sufficiently radical. Mr. Cooper's resolutions, the three most important advocating the publication of campaign expenses by candidates, the physical valuation of railroads, and the election of senators by direct vote of the people, were defeated by enormous majorities. The platform as reported by the committee then was adopted by acclamation.

These resolutions had now grown to the inordinate length so characteristic of to-day. It is to be hoped that at some time in the near future, and before platforms become so long that they are disregarded entirely, political leaders in national conventions will have the statesmanship to see the advisability, generally recognized everywhere, of issuing a short, pointed, and specific statement of principles or policies, in such brief form that they can be read in a few minutes. Any further elaboration could later be made by the statements of the candidates, for these latter are becoming more and more important as political leadership is taking its rightful place of influence in party strategy. The platform of 1908 may be summarized in fairly brief form.

President Roosevelt was given a most thorough and hearty indorsement, "The highest aspirations of the American people have found a voice." His "great accomplishments" were listed as "a brave and impartial enforcement of the law, the prosecution of illegal trusts and monopolies, the exposure and punishment of evildoers in the public service, the more effective regulation of the rates and service of the great transportation lines, the complete overthrow of preferences, rebates, and discriminations, the arbitration of labor disputes, the amelioration of the condition of wage-workers everywhere, the conservation of the natural resources of the country, the forward step in the improvement of the inland waterways, and always the earnest support and defense of every wholesome safeguard which has made more secure the guarantees of life, liberty, and property." The convention then went on record by declaring its "unfaltering adherence to the policies thus inaugurated, and pledge[ing] their continuance under a Republican administration of the government . . . the Republican party declares for the principle that in the development and enjoyment of wealth so great and blessings so benign there shall be equal opportunity for all."

One of the most important and, as it proved, possibly the most significant of passages was that dealing with the tariff, now rapidly becoming, as Roosevelt and others had foreseen years before, a dominant issue. "The Republican party declares unequivocally for a revision of the tariff by a special session of Congress immediately following the inauguration of the next President. . . . In all tariff legislation the true principle of protection is best maintained by the imposition of such duties as will equal the difference between the cost of production at home and abroad, together with a reasonable profit to American industries." This statement, with the sentiments publicly and privately expressed by political leaders and reinforced later by the statements of Mr. Taft, the party candidate, was popularly accepted as a promise to revise the tariff schedules downward, and a large proportion of the voters specifically voted for the Republican candidates with this idea and expectation. Other planks favored the establishment of postal savings banks; the extension of rural free delivery; measures for good roads and other aids to the prosperity and welfare of the agricultural population; conservation of natural resources; the old bugbear and disgrace, "a liberal administration of all pension laws"; and that "the civil-service laws, enacted, extended, and enforced by the Republican party, shall continue to be maintained and obeyed."

There were two exceedingly clever pieces of political writ-

Photograph by Brown Brothers

PITTSBURGH MARCHING CLUB IN PARADE AT CHICAGO CONVENTION, 1908

ing embodied in the platform, one an attack upon the Democratic party and the second including in this an attack likewise upon the menace of socialism, growing with the increase of our foreign immigration, especially from Continental Europe, and its infiltration of the ideas of decayed and unprosperous peoples among our own citizenship. The first plank stated "in principle the difference between Democracy and Republicanism is that one stands for vacillation and timidity in government, the other for strength and purpose; one stands for obstruction, the other for construction; one promises, the other performs; one finds fault, the other finds work." This statement was accepted as true by the overwhelming majority of our thoughtful people, so long as the policies of Roosevelt were accepted and acted upon by the Republican party. The second plank supplemented this. "The trend of Democracy is toward socialism, while the Republican party stands for wise and regulated individualism. Socialism would destroy wealth, Republicanism would prevent its abuse. Socialism would give to each an equal right to take; Republicanism would give to each an equal right to earn. Socialism would offer an equality of possession, which would soon leave no one anything to possess; Republicanism would give equality of opportunity, which would assure to each his share of a constantly increasing sum of possessions." If a person should desire to procure a summary of the remarkable accomplishments of Roosevelt as President of the United States, let him read through the nine printed pages, in small type, which contain the entire platform as presented in Edward Stanwood's book on a "History of the Presidency." [10] This is all the more remarkable when it is remembered that there was steady and covert opposition to him throughout on the part of the stand-pat elements, which he was able to overcome, but which promptly proved too great a force for his successor to meet.

The names of Cannon, Fairbanks, Hughes, Taft, Foraker, and La Follette were placed before the convention in nominating speeches, and at the close a man held up a large portrait of

[10] II, 170–9.

Roosevelt which caused long applause, even after the sergeant-at-arms required him to take the portrait down. Then a man in the gallery unfolded a large flag with the portrait of Roosevelt, and the applause became greater than ever, leading to a definite attempt to stampede the convention. This second attempt was prevented by Senator Lodge, who ordered the roll of states to be called, even though the pandemonium continued. The name of Massachusetts had been reached before the reporters could hear sufficiently to count the vote. It was found that Taft's nomination was assured by that time, and quiet was restored.[11] Roosevelt himself was exceedingly afraid of a stampede of the convention in his favor, and did not feel relieved until the news came to him over the wire to the White House that Taft was safely nominated. He thanked Lodge, his intimate friend, most sincerely for the part he had taken by his masterly handling of the convention proceedings. He wrote to Mrs. Lodge on June 19, 1908: "I wish to send you just a line, primarily to say how admirably I think Cabot handled the peculiarly delicate and difficult work at Chicago. In point of judgment, taste and power it would be literally impossible to better either his words or his actions. He was in a peculiar sense the guardian not only of the national interests, but of my own personal honor; and to do his full duty as guardian it was necessary for him effectively to thwart the movements not merely of my foes but of the multitude of well-meaning friends who did not think deeply or who were not of very sensitive fiber. It was absolutely necessary that any stampede should be prevented, and that I should not be nominated; for now that it is over we can confess to one another that it would have been well-nigh impossible for me to refuse further the nomination, and perhaps ruin the party thereby, if the nomination had actually been made, and yet if I had accepted, my power for useful service would have forever been lessened, because nothing could have prevented the wide diffusion of the suspicion that I had not really meant what I had said, that my

[11] J. B. Bishop, "Theodore Roosevelt and His Time," II, 88–95; Stanwood, "History of the Presidency," II, 180.

actions did not really square with the highest and finest code of ethics." On June 24 he wrote to Lodge himself, "You rendered a great public service, and you also rendered me a personal service." These facts should be borne in mind when we reach a discussion of the contest for the nomination in 1912, and Roosevelt was unfairly charged by his opponents, with whom even Mr. Taft at that time was joined, as being merely selfish and self-seeking.

When the vote of the delegates was announced, it was: Whole number voting, 979; necessary to a choice, 490; William Howard Taft, Ohio, 702; Philander C. Knox, Pennsylvania, 68; Charles E. Hughes, New York, 67; Joseph G. Cannon, Illinois, 58; Charles W. Fairbanks, Indiana, 40; Robert M. La Follette, Wisconsin, 25; Joseph B. Foraker, Ohio, 16; Theodore Roosevelt, New York, 3. The three votes for Roosevelt came from Pennsylvania. The nomination of Taft was immediately made unanimous.

Efforts were made to induce Mr. Fairbanks to accept a renomination for Vice-President, but he declined, as did also Governor Hughes of New York. In order to satisfy the standpat element, the name of Representative James S. Sherman of New York, a strong member of that wing, was united upon as most available. There was one ballot for the nomination for the second place on the ticket, and that resulted: James S. Sherman, New York, 816; Franklin Murphy, New Jersey, 77; Curtis Guild, Jr., Massachusetts, 75; George L. Sheldon, Nebraska, 16; Charles W. Fairbanks, Indiana, 1. The nomination of Mr. Sherman promptly was made unanimous and the convention adjourned.

Mr. Sherman was born in Utica, New York, on October 25, 1855. He graduated from Hamilton College, studied and practised law, and was also prominent in business and banking circles. He was mayor of Utica in 1884, and had represented the Utica district in Congress for twenty years before his election to the Vice-Presidency. He was a man of ability, honesty, and great fairness, but was given over entirely to advocacy of the principles of the most conservative, stand-pat character.

Mr. Taft chose as the chairman of the National Committee, and to manage his campaign, Mr. Frank H. Hitchcock of Massachusetts, a politician of great ability, who also had managed the pre-convention campaign for Mr. Taft and with great success.

The Democrats had a hard problem before them when they met at Denver, Colorado, on July 7. Bryan had suffered two defeats as leader of the radicals, and Parker, as leader of the conservative wing, had fared even worse in 1904. But Bryan still had dominating influence in the party, so he finally was chosen to make the campaign a third time, John W. Kern of Indiana being selected as his running-mate. The platform was a condemnation of the Republican party as the partner of the trusts and big business, from whom big business was able to purchase for money the right to encroach upon popular rights. It had a specific promise to enact laws prohibiting contributions to campaign funds by corporations, and also to make public before elections all contributions by individuals. While there were numerous other promises, good, bad, and indifferent, the real issue before the people could not fail to be that of the indorsement or repudiation of the Roosevelt administrations. The Republicans had specifically identified themselves with Roosevelt progressivism, and the Democratic claims could only look like a weak imitation, especially when personified by such a man as Mr. Bryan. It was in this way that the majority of the people finally made judgment, as the Taft victory at the polls soon was to testify. As a basis of national coöperation, the Republicans never had a better person or issue than Theodore Roosevelt.

The minor parties made their usual nominations and issued their platforms. Their main work in American history has been that of propaganda, good or bad as the case may be, and they undoubtedly have performed a service of great value to the country. It is of course a matter of argument whether or not they might have turned their energies in some cases to a more profitable mode of patriotic service. The Prohibitionists nominated Eugene W. Chafin of Illinois and Aaron S. Watkins of

Photographs by Brown Brothers

UP-TO-DATE CAMPAIGN METHODS, NEW YORK, 1908

Ohio; the Socialists nominated Eugene Debs of Indiana and Benjamin Hanford of New York; the Socialist-Labor party nominated August Gilhaus of New York and Donald L. Munro of Virginia; the dying but not yet entirely deceased Populist party nominated Thomas E. Watson of Georgia and Samuel W. Williams of Indiana; and the hand-picked party of Mr. William Randolph Hearst and his satellites, the Independence party, nominated Thomas L. Hisgen of Massachusetts and John Temple Graves of Georgia.

The campaign opened with the expression of intention on the part of both Taft and Bryan not to go on the stump, but to use more of a front-porch method of reaching the people, found so useful a decade or more before by both Harrison and McKinley. The notification ceremonies were made much of, in order to arouse enthusiasm by great party demonstrations. But Bryan could not be restrained, and went on the stump the latter part of August, speaking constantly throughout the country until the close of the campaign. Mr. Hitchcock organized one of the most efficient campaigns seen up to this time. He held Mr. Taft back until a month later than the stumping of Mr. Bryan began, but then changed his policy, and the Republican candidate made wide tours speaking constantly and frequently. This method of campaign has been used frequently since, but never has appealed to the American people as a fitting and dignified way for a candidate for the chief magistracy of the republic to become known. On the other hand, there has been the influence of the "party leadership" idea of the office, so that it is not yet certain what the final developments may be. The recent invention and development of broadcasting by means of the radio may offer the final solution and extend the front-porch method into a wide use for the purpose of reaching all the people.

There could be little doubt of the final result of this conflict, but the Republican leaders took no chances. Mr. Roosevelt threw all the weight of his great influence toward Mr. Taft, and this was a power in itself. The election day was November 3, and Taft and Sherman were overwhelmingly victorious. They received 321 electoral votes to 162 for Mr. Bryan, who carried only the solid South, Nebraska, and Nevada, with the border states of Kentucky and Oklahoma. Taft carried all the remainder, including Delaware, Missouri (by 629 votes), and Maryland (by 605 votes, but receiving only 2 of the state's 8 electoral votes). The popular vote was: Taft, 7,677,788; Bryan, 6,407,982; Chafin, 252,511; Debs, 420,890; Gilhaus, 14,021; Watson, 29,146; Hisgen, 83,651. "In the country as a whole, judging by the popular vote in the Taft campaign of 1908, the Republicans had gained slightly since 1896, and their strategic position seemed better consolidated. In the Northeast and on the Pacific coast they seemed firmly established in power, and in the other sections of the North and West they had gained much of the ground lost in 1896. In the upper South also they were in a better position than ever before. Only in the lower South did their future seem hopeless." [12] But the party was facing the period of its greatest defeats, and a time of misfortune that was to break its hold on national power for all practical purposes for the space of eight years—from 1910 until 1918. There soon developed a complete schism between the conservatives, or stand-pat elements, on one side, and the progressives on the other. Mr. Taft and the Republican leaders with whom he worked were in large part responsible for this. And Mr. Roosevelt was not responsible, at least for its beginning, for the progressive movement was in existence and a strong aggressive Republican force long before he became identified with it.

[12] A. N. Holcombe, "Political Parties of Today," 246.

Chapter XVI

THE PROGRESSIVE MOVEMENT AND PARTY DEFEAT

Mr. Roosevelt was jubilant when he received the reports of Mr. Taft's great victory at the polls. In the light of the recent Chicago platform and his long experience of Mr. Taft as a co-worker, he had no misgivings. While the differences which led to such a tragic break of friendship between the two men did not become public for about two years, yet people "on the inside" soon were aware of a cooling of the earlier cordiality. Captain Archibald W. Butt, who was the personal aide to Roosevelt, wrote under date of February 14, 1909: "He feels very deeply the fact that Mr. Taft seems determined to sever all the ties which have bound them together in the past. He was the only one who did not foresee this, and I think he will be bitterly disappointed when he sees many of his policies reversed. He was so cocksure that Mr. Taft would continue all his policies, and I fear that a general reversal will be nearer the line he will follow. It will be a dangerous thing for him to do, for it will relieve Mr. Roosevelt of all responsibility of breaking the bonds and afford him every excuse to make the race in another four years if there is any demand for him from the people." [1] It was natural for Mr. Taft, who was a man of great ability and strength of character, to desire to "paddle his own canoe," to use the homely old phrase, and also it was natural for Roosevelt to feel a sense of loneliness and loss when he approached the time to give up the power he had wielded so strongly and efficiently for over seven years. Also it was probable and natural that the home influence of Mr.

[1] L. F. Abbott, "The Letters of Archie Butt," 338.

Taft's own family was being used to spur him on toward an assertion of personal independence.

Captain Butt made further acute observations, as under date of February 21, 1909, when he described a conversation with another person on the inside track: "I was talking with Alfred Henry Lewis yesterday and he made this pertinent remark: . . . 'Taft, I believe, is going to turn the government over to the men whom Roosevelt will regard as the enemy; I know that the old crowd is licking its chops and looking forward to seven fat years after the seven lean years which are just now drawing to a close. A reversal of policy means a return to Roosevelt when he comes out of Africa, and on concluding his tour of Europe, if he will come to the states again by way of San Francisco, and make a zig-zag trip across the country, nothing in the world can prevent his renomination. His unpopularity in Congress is as nothing. He has not got as much respect for the Senate as a dog has for a marriage license, and every time he swats either House, it is so much popularity from the people.' This is not my prediction, but the words of Lewis, who was even more picturesque in his language than I have given it." And on February 24, just three days later, Butt returned to the subject: "We Americans are poor bunglers as intriguers, and the less one intrigues for place the better off he is, in my judgment. My only fear is that this is a forerunner of what may be expected later on. It looks a little like the old weak days of McKinley. The Ohio school of politics breeds a peculiar genius and corruption always flourishes under it. I think I see the government drifting into the control of those whom Mr. Roosevelt would regard as the 'enemy.' The old crowd, especially as typified by the rich senators, such as Aldrich, Wetmore, Depew, are already 'licking their chops and looking forward to seven fat years after the seven lean years just about to close.' I have no fear of Mr. Taft, but only of Mr. Taft's amiability and doctrine of expediency." [2] Captain Butt and Alfred Henry Lewis were wrong in only one particular. The fat years came after the "seven

[2] L. F. Abbott, "Letters of Archie Butt," 352, 358.

lean years," but there were only four of them when the followers of Roosevelt bolted, and the party of both sides went down to defeat.

We have only to add the testimony of H. H. Kohlsaat. "The rift in the relations between President Taft and ex-President Roosevelt was apparent when Mr. Taft finished his inaugural address on March 4, 1909. Close observers wondered why Roosevelt broke all precedent by going to the Pennsylvania depot direct from the Senate chamber instead of riding back to the White House and receiving along with Taft the plaudits and cheers of the spectators who braved the blizzard to cheer the incoming and outgoing President. I remember one of the Chicago Record Herald staff saying, it may have been cold outside, but Theodore must have been hot inside about something to forego the cheers of Pennsylvania Avenue. The report that he was in a hurry to sail for Africa hardly held water, as half or three-quarters of an hour delay in reaching New York would make little difference in his plans. He could have taken the next train, as they run hourly between Washington and New York." [3] The desire of Roosevelt to get away, as now is well known, is easily explained by the undoubted fact that he wished to give Taft a free hand and not arouse ill feeling or jealousy in his followers by sharing any plaudits with him in this his hour of just triumph; but it does not explain the fact that there was some sign of strained relations between two formerly intimate friends, and this was noticed at the time.

Taft, as already indicated, was inaugurated on March 4, 1909, and the weather was so cold and disagreeable that the oath had to be administered in the Senate chamber instead of the usual platform on the east front of the capitol. As previously arranged, Mr. Roosevelt left at once to sail from New York for a hunting trip to Africa, and would not return for two years. There was therefore no opportunity for the friends of Mr. Taft to charge interference, as Roosevelt gave his successor the freest kind of a hand. He left in a blaze of glory.

[3] "From McKinley to Harding," 166.

An editorial in the "Outlook," under date of July 25, 1908, although written nearly eight months before his retirement from office, had correctly summed up the prevailing public opinion of this time. "We believe, then, that when Mr. Roosevelt lays down the cares, the duties, and the joys of office next March to enter upon his well-earned if somewhat vigorous vacation in the wilds of Africa, he will retire with the hatred of a few unprincipled men whose characters he has exposed and whose lawless practices he has made more dangerous and difficult; with a steadily diminishing hostility from a larger number who have neither comprehended his character nor the times and the country in which they were living; but with the confidence and affection of the overwhelming majority of the plain people, regardless of party affiliations."

It is proper to quote Captain Butt once more, who went with Roosevelt on a trip to Kentucky just a few weeks before the expiration of his Presidential term. "I watched the upturned faces in every crowd he addressed or yelled 'Good luck!' to, and there was always that unmistakable look of personal affection in the individual face as he appeared, and as he swept his eyes over the throng there was set up instantly, it seemed to me, a personal hand between him and every man or woman present. It was not the look which comes from admiration, and curiosity seemed to be absent entirely. It was purely one of affection. It made me think of a remark I heard Ambassador Bryce make only a few days ago: 'Nobody likes him now but the people.' "[4]

When President Taft announced his cabinet, it was found that he had retained only two men from Roosevelt's administration. These were George Von L. Meyer of Massachusetts, who was moved from the position of postmaster-general to that of secretary of the navy, and James Wilson of Iowa, who continued to hold the office of secretary of agriculture which he had filled so acceptably since the time of his appointment by McKinley in 1897. He served until the end of Mr. Taft's administration, making sixteen years in his office, the longest that

[4] L. F. Abbott, "Letters of Archie Butt," 337.

any person ever has held a cabinet position in American history. For secretary of state Mr. Taft chose Philander C. Knox of Pennsylvania, who had performed brilliant service as attorney-general during the years 1901 to 1904 in the administrations of both McKinley and Roosevelt and then had become senator from Pennsylvania. He belonged to the moderate school of Republicanism, as regards the extreme conservatives and radicals, and this was a fitting appointment. The rest of the cabinet were personal appointees of President Taft, or those men who were not distinctly party leaders. Franklin MacVeagh of Illinois became secretary of the treasury; Jacob M. Dickinson of Tennessee, secretary of war; Richard A. Ballinger of Washington, secretary of the interior; George W. Wickersham, attorney-general; Frank H. Hitchcock of Massachusetts, who had managed Mr. Taft's campaigns both for nomination and election, now became postmaster-general; and Charles Nagel of Missouri, secretary of commerce and labor. Mr. MacVeagh and Mr. Dickinson were former Cleveland Democrats, and all except Meyer and Wilson were lawyers.[5]

President Taft at once carried out the platform promise by calling the Sixty-first Congress in special session to meet on March 15, 1909. The Republicans had control of both houses with a vote of 61 to 32 in the Senate, and 219 to 172 in the House of Representatives. The latter body at once reelected Joseph G. Cannon of Illinois speaker, one of the ablest and most popular men who ever has held that office. He first was elected to the office in 1903, thereby succeeding D. B. Henderson of Iowa, who had followed Reed in 1899. Familiarly known as "Uncle Joe," he was one of the most efficient presiding officers that Congress ever had, but unfortunately he had aligned himself completely with the stand-pat wing of the party, and even at this last election to the speakership there were mutterings of autocratic power by the progressive or Roosevelt wing. As in 1897, there already had been drawn up a bill to revise the tariff at the hands of the destined Committee on Ways and Means, of which Sereno E. Payne of New York

[5] F. A. Ogg, "National Progress," 20–1.

was chairman. He reported the bill with great promptness, and the debate began. The fact should be stressed, as mentioned above, that there was a definite understanding among most Republicans, especially those of the Roosevelt or progressive wing, that there was to be a downward revision "at the hands of the friends of the tariff." The Payne bill did reduce schedules in a number of cases, and was an honest attempt to carry out platform understandings if not definite promises. Under the strong hand of Speaker Cannon and the rigid discipline of the Republican House organization, the bill was passed on April 9 by a vote of 217 to 161. When it reached the Senate, there was a very different story. That body also was well organized, and the overwhelming Republican majority was under the strict control of the old "stand-pat" element, with Senator Nelson W. Aldrich of Rhode Island, an unusually able parliamentarian and expert upon tariff questions, at the head of the Finance Committee. With the help of other Senate leaders of his way of thinking, to whom Roosevelt continually had referred as the "enemy," there was a general revision upward of the rates, which led to a bitter struggle of eleven weeks of debate. The more progressive among the Republican senators, including such men as Beveridge of Indiana, Joseph L. Bristow of Kansas, Cummins and Dolliver of Iowa, and La Follette of Wisconsin, with the help of others of a more or less Roosevelt stamp, strongly opposed this, but were voted down. The bill passed the Senate on July 8 by a vote of 45 to 34.

And now Mr. Taft came to the front with his ideas of the office of President. He held most strictly to the "literary" theory of the Constitution—that the President should hold back and allow the legislative department to prepare laws, which were to be accepted by the executive unless palpably unconstitutional in his opinion or surely against the public welfare. But when the tariff went to conference between the Senate and House of Representatives, Mr. Taft suddenly woke up to what was happening and made an effort to bring about the enactment of a tariff more in accordance with the platform understandings than the Senate desired. He made some progress and reduced a few rates, also securing the abolition of the duty on hides. The bill then was passed and was signed by the President on August 5, 1909. The ominous fact stood out that there were 20 negative Republican votes in the House of Representatives and 7 in the Senate. Following this, Mr. Taft made a speech at Winona, Minnesota, in which he defended Congress and the leaders and spoke of the tariff as the best the country ever had.[6] He thus allied himself completely, in the estimation of a large number of the Roosevelt followers, with the stand-pat, reactionary element of the party. And as later was proved, Mr. Roosevelt had done his work with such thoroughness that the stand-pat element was in the minority, little as the old leaders realized it, or wanted to realize it.

The writer always has thought that the Payne-Aldrich tariff was the turning point in President Taft's administration. Had he been a Roosevelt, with all the brilliant powers of leadership and popular control that his great predecessor had continually shown, he might have vetoed the law, appealed to the people, and his hold on the American people would have been second only to that of Roosevelt himself. In all probability he would have been able finally to defeat the stand-pat and old guard leaders in both Senate and House of Representatives, and nothing could have prevented his triumphant reëlection in 1912, helped most enthusiastically, as he would have been, by Roosevelt himself. The Republican party also would have enjoyed a veritable rebirth and change to modern conditions such as it has only partially secured at the present time, and which must come sooner or later if it is to continue its long life of usefulness. It must not become radical, but it must become thoroughly progressive in a real sense. This does not mean the erratic and superficial pretense of progressivism sponsored by the La Follette group of recent years, but a real liberalism that is based on conservative traditions. It is the liberal-conservative or the conservative-liberal who really constructs in politics and government, and Roosevelt was able to

[6] For more detailed account of this tariff, see C. R. Lingley, "Since the Civil War," 479–83; F. A. Ogg, "National Progress," 27–39.

make this suitable combination to a degree that stamped him as a great statesman as well as political leader.

But President Taft was not by character and training the man to undertake such a heroic but necessary part in political leadership. One of the most lovable and popular men in recent American history, he was essentially a judge by temperament. A fine administrator under the direction of others of a more vigorous and daring personality, he was not a politician, but a good illustration of the "round peg in the square hole." His elevation in later years to the Chief Justiceship in the Supreme Court was the proper and correct recognition of his peculiar abilities. His kindly and generous disposition made it too hard for him to give the necessary "no" to selfish or designing political interests. Furthermore, Mr. Roosevelt believed that the President was the steward of the people, and that the executive power was "limited only by specific restrictions and prohibitions appearing in the Constitution or imposed by Congress under its Constitutional powers." [7] Mr. Taft, as already stated, believed in a strict interpretation of these constitutional powers by the President,[8] and failed to appreciate what the people now expected of him as a party leader. He had to take the blame of the selfish and headstrong action of the stand-pat leaders both in and out of Congress, and a party split was inevitable.[9]

The Roosevelt wing of the party now felt that Taft had deserted them, and that their enemies had gotten control of the organization. A revolt against Speaker Cannon soon developed. It came in March, 1910, when the "insurgent" Republicans, led by George W. Norris of Nebraska, now (1927) senator from that state, joined with the Democrats and took away from Cannon most of the dictatorial powers which had lasted since the time of Speaker Reed. They placed them in the hands of the leading members of the two parties, but especially in the enlarged Committee on Rules, which was no longer sub-

[7] "Autobiography," 282.

[8] See Mr. Taft's book, "Our Chief Magistrate and His Powers," *passim.*

[9] See W. S. Myers, "American Democracy Today," Chapter IV, entitled "Presidential Leadership," for a more detailed discussion of this whole problem.

ject to the appointment of the speaker himself and thus dominated by him, but its membership was made subject to the choice of the entire House.[10] Aside from this, the Republican majority in Congress was large enough to put through quite a program of excellent legislation, for which Mr. Taft also deserves great credit. Mr. Cannon, brave old fighter that he was, was willing to resign the speakership, but his party rallied around him and by a large vote showed their desire that he continue in office.

Among the measures of the Taft administration may be mentioned laws establishing a system of postal savings banks; requiring safety appliances on railroads; establishing a bureau of mines; extending the powers of the Interstate Commerce Commission by the Mann-Elkins act; and requiring the publication of the names and amounts of campaign contributions and the expenditures of political committees. Also, with the urgent support of President Taft, Congress in both houses passed by a necessary vote the amendment to the United States Constitution, adopted in 1913, and now known as the Sixteenth, which gave Congress the power to levy a direct tax on incomes. The next Congress, with the recommendation of Taft but under bipartizan action due to the Democratic control of the House of Representatives, passed what later became known as the Seventeenth Amendment, which also was ratified in 1913. It provided for the direct election of United States senators by the people. All this legislative activity was toward greater popular rights, as well as greater popular participation in government. Mr. Taft was by no means an extreme "stand-patter" himself, although he was ranked with that wing of the party in the popular estimation.

A most unfortunate episode, from the standpoint of Mr. Taft and the welfare of his administration, was the Ballinger-Pinchot controversy. It confirmed the popular impression that he had fallen completely under the control of selfish and reactionary interests. Richard A. Ballinger, secretary of the interior, had brought in a report in December, 1909, which was

[10] W. S. Myers, "American Democracy Today," 82–3.

made the basis of a large part of the scientific conservation legislation that was passed during the ensuing three years. On the other hand, he had reversed the policy of Roosevelt and opened to private ownership large amounts of public land which contained various water-power and mining properties. Gifford Pinchot, close friend of Roosevelt and Chief Forester, openly attacked this act on the part of Secretary Ballinger and asserted that the property was being grabbed by a trust. An employee of the Interior Department, L. R. Glavis, charged the same thing with regard to public lands in Alaska. A popular outcry was made, but, following a congressional investigation, Ballinger was completely exonerated. But meanwhile both Pinchot and Glavis had been dismissed from office. Popular prejudice against Ballinger was so great that he was compelled to resign in March, 1911, and Walter L. Fisher of Illinois was appointed to the head of the Interior Department in his place. By this time progressive Republican feeling had been so aroused against President Taft that the whole matter was looked upon as only another illustration of the old adage that a man should be judged by the company he keeps, and that Mr. Taft's company was decidedly reactionary and stand-pat.

It was in the midst of this clamor and opposition to the administration that Theodore Roosevelt returned home and was received in New York city on June 18, 1910, with a tremendous popular welcome. He had been absent over a year, during which time he had been cut off from world affairs for months in the wilds of Africa, and then had traveled across Europe, where his reception had been one of the greatest ever received by an American. In fact, actually it was the greatest, from the intellectual standpoint and that of private worth; for both Grant, and Wilson at a later time, were the beneficiaries of emotion and mob psychology in a way that was absent to a great degree in the case of Roosevelt. Furthermore, a great deal of the honor paid to Wilson was due to his occupancy of the office of President of the United States. He personified a great country from which many blessings were flowing, and from which more were anticipated!

Of course, Roosevelt was besieged by his followers with the plea that he take a hand in the present political situation and try and bring order out of chaos and reunite the sorely divided Republican party. Roosevelt threw himself into the fray, feeling that he could not refuse to help his old party and his old friends. At the earnest solicitation of Governor Hughes of New York he used his influence in favor of the progressive legislation then being championed by Hughes, including the Direct Primary Law, which was bitterly opposed by the most powerful leaders in the state. He took a prominent part in the Republican state convention that met at Saratoga Springs in September, and defeated Vice-President Sherman for temporary chairman, the latter having been put forward by the anti-Hughes faction of the party. Following this victory, he forced the nomination for governor of Henry L. Stimson, secretary of war in Mr. Taft's cabinet at the time, as a man of the same progressive ideas of reform in the state law and policy as held by Governor Hughes. The latter about this time was appointed to the Supreme Court of the United States by President Taft.

Roosevelt was much dissatisfied with President Taft's administration, as he showed by private letters to friends. On October 21, 1910, he wrote to Elihu Root, then United States senator from New York: "I have been cordially helping the election of a Republican Congress, having split definitely with the Insurgents on this point; for though I am bitterly disappointed with Taft, and consider much of his course absolutely inexplicable, I have felt that, as in so many other cases, I had to make the best of conditions as they actually were and do the best I possibly could to carry Congress and to carry the state of New York, with the entire understanding on my part that victory in either means the immense strengthening of Taft. In New York state I deliberately went in to put the close supporters of Taft in control of the Republican machinery, and have done and am now doing my best to elect a man whom, I assume, is a Taft man; because I felt that the one clear duty of a decent citizen was to try to put the Republican party on a straight basis, and now to try to put that party in power in the State instead of turning the State over to Murphy of Tammany Hall." [11] He added the significant words. "Very possibly circumstances will be such that I shall support Taft for the Presidency next time."

In spite of these efforts, the results at the polls in November were a heavy set-back and defeat for the Republicans. The Democrats carried New York by about 67,000, and they elected state tickets in such other important states as Connecticut, New Jersey, Massachusetts, and Ohio. The congressional elections were somewhat like those following the McKinley tariff of 1890. The House of Representatives would contain thereafter 228 Democrats, 161 Republicans, and 1 Socialist, while the Senate would have 51 Republicans and 41 Democrats. But this Republican majority of 10 was apt to vanish at any time, due to the fact that the "insurgent" Republicans would hold the balance of power. The handwriting was plain upon the wall. The question now was, Would the stand-pat element in the Republican party learn their lesson, or would they carry the party to defeat, or even destruction? The answer soon was given. They had learned nothing and forgotten nothing, and down to defeat they went. The only reason the party was not destroyed was the strength of party name and history, its effect upon the loyalty of the rank and file of the voters, and also the mistakes of the Democrats, especially in the second administration of Woodrow Wilson.

During the last two years of Mr. Taft's administration not much legislation of importance could be anticipated. There were, however, several acts looking toward social reform, including the establishment of a Department of Labor with a secretary in the cabinet of the President, and also a children's bureau. A Parcel Post Law also was passed. Mr. Taft negotiated a reciprocity agreement with Canada. The bill dealing with this was forced through the Senate and House of Representatives at a special session called for the purpose and with all the influence at his command, but ratification was refused

[11] The entire letter is interesting. See J. B. Bishop, "Theodore Roosevelt and His Time," II, 304–5.

by the Dominion Parliament. As illustrative of the lack of executive power and force in the Taft administration may be mentioned the gossip prevalent at Washington, D. C., at the time, that Mr. Taft and Mr. Knox, secretary of state, had negotiated this treaty so quietly that Mr. Nagel, in whose department as secretary of commerce and labor lay the main business and effects of the proposed treaty, knew nothing of it until he read the details in the current newspapers. Meanwhile, the Democrats, aided by the insurgent Republicans, passed various lower tariff bills, dealing with certain commodities and schedules, which Mr. Taft at once vetoed. These so-called "popgun" bills were merely for political effect, which was fully felt due to the failure of Mr. Taft to allow them to become laws, even without his signature. This would have been the best sort of political strategy and promptly have forced a "show-down" on all sides, with a possible clearing of the political atmosphere.

And now definite steps were being taken with regard to the nomination for 1912. It was natural that Mr. Taft should seek and expect another nomination, and he at first legitimately used the power of his position in order to secure this. An ominous step was taken on January 21, 1911, when the insurgent elements in the Republican party formed the National Progressive Republican League with the object of furthering progressive policies and legislation. As 1912 drew on, the progressive elements were divided into two wings, those who favored Senator La Follette for the nomination and those who desired a return of Roosevelt. At a business men's banquet in Philadelphia, on February 2, 1912, Mr. La Follette delivered a long, rambling, in part incoherent speech, which proved to be the beginning of a nervous breakdown. This ruined his chances for the nomination. His later erratic and often unbalanced course during the remaining twelve or more years of his life is possibly explained by the lack of a complete recovery from this illness. And the mere mention of the possibility of Roosevelt's nomination caused the major part of the progressive element to swing in his direction. The movement grew with the speed of the proverbial snowball and finally swept everything before it. On February 10 a letter was written, and signed by the seven Republican governors of as many states, urging him to be a candidate for the Presidency. Those governors who signed were Bass of New Hampshire, Glasscock of West Virginia, Hadley of Missouri, Osborn of Michigan, Stubbs of Kansas, Aldrich of Nebraska, and Carey of Wyoming. Joseph Bucklin Bishop, who knew and understood Roosevelt well, remarks:[12] "This letter was ingeniously framed to exert a powerful influence upon Roosevelt. Its authors declared their belief that a large majority of the Republican voters favored his nomination and a large majority of the voters favored his election; that he represented, as no other man did, the principles and policies which must appeal to the American people and which were necessary to the happiness and prosperity of the country; that in making the request the authors of the letter were not considering his personal interests, but the interests of the people as a whole, and that if he were to decline he would show himself unresponsive to a plain public duty." That this statement was true was immediately shown by the vote in the Republican primaries, and a reference to the platform of 1908 was ample support to the statement of Roosevelt's policies and their connection with the welfare of the country, in case any stand-pat element might question its accuracy.

Mr. Taft at once accepted the prospective challenge from Mr. Roosevelt, for in a speech in New York city on February 12 he made veiled references to the latter as a "political emotionalist" or "neurotic." But Mr. Roosevelt, on February 21, made an address before the Ohio constitutional convention in which he took such radical ground that he alienated the votes of large numbers of moderate progressives, who, when the election took place in the following autumn, gave their votes to Woodrow Wilson. It was at this time that Mr. Roosevelt advocated in no uncertain terms the initiative and referendum, further restraints on trusts and large corporations, and the recall of judicial decisions. This was one of the greatest mis-

[12] "Theodore Roosevelt and His Time," II, 316–17.

Photograph by Brown Brothers

A SCENE AT THE INAUGURATION OF WILLIAM HOWARD TAFT

takes of his whole career. Without this speech, there is a great possibility that, in spite of all the efforts of the Taft administration and the stand-pat leaders, he would have received the Republican nomination. As it was, his opponents were barely able to defeat him, and then only by sharp practice which, they claimed, was within the bounds of law but which alienated a large part of the rank and file of the party voters. There is no question that Roosevelt was sincere, for he wrote at the time to Joseph Bucklin Bishop: "Do not get the idea into your head that I am going to win in this fight. It was a fight that had to be made and there was no alternative to my making it." [13]

As a result of recent changes in state laws or constitutions, there were Presidential preference primaries in thirteen states —California, Georgia, Illinois, Maryland, Massachusetts, Nebraska, New Jersey, North Dakota, Ohio, Oregon, Pennsylvania, South Dakota, and Wisconsin. They were to choose all together 382 delegates to the Republican national convention, and both Taft and Roosevelt actively engaged in the canvass of these states, it being popularly understood that they would thus determine who was the actual choice of the rank and file of the voters. Both candidates were on the stump in a way never before known in American politics. Unfortunately, they entered into personalities that did no manner of good, but merely cheapened their canvasses and led to heart-burnings and animosities that are only gradually disappearing to-day. When the vote was cast in state after state, it was found that Mr. Roosevelt had secured 278 delegates, while Mr. Taft, with all the power of a governmental machine that can be used in his own favor by practically any President in office, had secured only 68. Of these, 28 were from Georgia, where there was not a vestige of hope for any electoral votes. In Massachusetts, Roosevelt delegates-at-large had been chosen, but "under a confusing provision of the law a preference for Taft had been adopted by about 3,000 votes."[14] In Ohio, on the other hand,

[13] "Theodore Roosevelt and His Time," II, 319. Mr. Bishop's work is invaluable for the student of this period.

[14] Bishop, "Theodore Roosevelt and His Time," II, 322, from which also the other statistics of the primaries have been drawn.

the Roosevelt preference had been carried by about 47,000 votes. Mr. Taft had announced that he would be governed in the contest by the result in his own state, but, after the ballot, refused to abide by the decision. With the help of the organization and its "steam-roller," the Ohio state convention disregarded this vote and instructed the delegates-at-large for Taft. This was exactly opposite to the action of Roosevelt in the state of Massachusetts, and is a typical illustration of the method used to secure the nomination for Mr. Taft. The whole episode is an unpleasant one from both sides of the case, and shows how both factions were wrought up to the pitch of bitterest hatred against each other, while the Democrats looked on with glee and prepared to profit by Republican dissensions.

The Republican national convention met at the Coliseum, Chicago, Illinois, on June 18, 1912. It was called to order by Victor Rosewater of Nebraska, chairman of the National Committee. This committee had met at the same city on June 6 to decide contested election cases. No matter what may have been the rights or wrongs of the controversy, and the charges and counter-charges are boundless, it had decided the cases of the large number of contested delegates so that the Taft forces could organize the convention. As F. A. Ogg pertinently says: "Whatever the merits of the controversy, a system which gave the southern states and territories more delegates in a Republican convention than were allotted to New York, Pennsylvania, Illinois, Ohio, Massachusetts, Indiana, and Iowa combined, was indefensible." [15]

Among the delegates to the convention were Hiram W. Johnson and Chester H. Rowell of California; J. Henry Roraback and John T. King of Connecticut; Henry A. du Pont of Delaware; Charles S. Deneen, L. Y. Sherman, Martin B. Madden, Fred W. Upham, and Len Small of Illinois; Harry S. New, Charles W. Fairbanks, James E. Watson, and James A. Hemenway of Indiana; Henry J. Allen of Kansas; W. O. Bradley of Kentucky; Phillips Lee Goldsborough and Galen L. Tait of Maryland; Albert Bushnell Hart of Massachusetts;

[15] "National Progress," 190.

Moses E. Clapp of Minnesota; Herbert S. Hadley of Missouri; J. Franklin Fort and Everett Colby of New Jersey; Elihu Root, William Barnes, Jr., Timothy L. Woodruff, William A. Prendergast, William M. Calder, Chauncey M. Depew, Samuel S. Koenig, Job E. Hedges, Ezra P. Prentice, Nicholas Murray Butler, Ogden L. Mills, Herbert Parsons, William L. Ward, Sereno E. Payne, and Alanson B. Houghton of New York; Richmond Pearson of North Carolina; Harry M. Daugherty, Warren G. Harding, Theodore E. Burton, Arthur I. Vorys, and Charles P. Taft of Ohio; William S. Vare, William Draper Lewis, William W. Griest, and William Flinn of Pennsylvania; Henry F. Lippitt of Rhode Island; Newell Sanders and H. Clay Evans of Tennessee; George Sutherland and Reed Smoot of Utah; C. B. Slemp of Virginia; Francis E. Warren and F. W. Mondell of Wyoming.

The chairman of the National Committee placed the name of Elihu Root before the convention for temporary chairman. At once the lines were drawn and a bitter fight developed for the right to organize the convention. The insurgents, progressives, and Roosevelt forces in general put the name of Governor Francis E. McGovern of Wisconsin before the convention, and a bitter contest followed, which resulted in the election of Mr. Root by the vote of 558 to 501. "Twelve of the scattering [votes] were cast for Judge Lauder, of North Dakota, by delegates from Wisconsin, showing the real La Follette strength in that delegation, and its bitter determination not to do anything that might help Colonel Roosevelt." [16] The 74 contested delegates who had been seated by the National Committee were enough to turn the scale in favor of Mr. Root. He assumed the chair amid cries of "Receiver of stolen goods!" A renewed protest against the 74 contested delegates followed, but Mr. Root ruled at once in their favor. Mr. Roosevelt was in Chicago at this time and instructed his followers to take no further part in the proceedings. Most of them obeyed his commands. Mr. Root was elected permanent president and held the convention closely in his power to the end of the dis-

[16] O. K. Davis, "Released for Publication," 298.

orderly proceedings. Following possibly the most united and harmonious Republican national convention ever held, that of 1908, came this most disorderly and disrupted one. By this time the nomination was hardly worth the having, but the "steam-roller" proceeded on its way and the varied business of the convention was carried through more expeditiously.

Charles W. Fairbanks of Indiana, the chairman of the Committee on Resolutions, presented the platform. It was an unusually sane, balanced, and well-written document, moderate in its position on all questions, and evidently drawn up with the intention of bringing together the diverse elements in the party. This attempt was well meant but too late, for there was no question that the Republicans would vote or not vote, as the case might be, on the personalities and records of Taft and Roosevelt. There was a strong stand for the self-imposed restraints of constitutional government. There also was stated the intention of the party "to uphold at all times the authority and integrity of the courts, both state and federal, and it will ever insist that their powers to enforce their process and to protect life, liberty and property shall be preserved inviolate. An orderly method is provided under our system of government by which the people may, when they choose, alter or amend the constitutional provisions which underlie that government. Until these constitutional provisions are so altered or amended, in orderly fashion, it is the duty of the courts to see to it that when challenged they are enforced."

Following this admirable statement in reply to Roosevelt's doctrine of the recall of judicial decisions came the statement "the Republican party is opposed to special privilege and to monopoly." There also was the advocacy of further legislation to supplement the already existing anti-trust laws; of the establishment of a Federal Trade Commission; of a commission to study the causes of the high cost of living, with a declaration that "the fact that it is not due to the protective tariff system is evidenced by the existence of similar conditions in countries which have a tariff policy different from our own." There was the usual reaffirmation of the belief in a protective tariff, with the significant admission that "some of the existing import duties are too high, and should be reduced." There also were the usual indorsements of the civil service, sound banking and currency laws, an adequate navy, conservation, flood prevention in the Mississippi Valley, reclamation, and a specific and favorable reference to the indorsements of Roosevelt contained in the platforms of 1904 and 1908. The Wisconsin delegates made an attempt to include amendments with their own brand of radicalism, but these were tabled and the platform was adopted by the vote of 666 to 53—343 present and not voting.

A national committee was appointed to serve until 1916 and thus control the next convention, if necessary, and then came the nomination of candidates. Warren G. Harding of Ohio presented the name of William Howard Taft. In the course of his speech he spoke of the record of the Taft administration in glowing terms, and added: "Except for the attack of disloyalty in our own ranks, inspired by pap rather than patriotism, the record would rate in current criticism as it will in history, the marvel of progressive accomplishment in one administration." This caused so much disorder that the chairman had to intervene.[17] The nomination was seconded by John Wanamaker of Pennsylvania and President Nicholas Murray Butler of Columbia University, New York city. The name of Robert M. La Follette was placed before the convention by Michael B. Olbrich of Wisconsin and seconded by Robert M. Pollock of North Dakota. The final vote, after repeated challenges and polling of the delegations, was: Taft, 561; Roosevelt, 107; La Follette, 41; Cummins, 17; Hughes, 2; present and not voting, 349; absent, 6.

Mr. Oscar King Davis, in his remarkable and illuminating book entitled "Released for Publication," tells the authentic story of numerous attempts on the part of various members of both factions of the convention to unite on some compromise candidate—as Governor Hadley of Missouri—or possibly to prevent Taft's nomination on the first ballot, which would inevitably lead to a stampede for Roosevelt. The "Old Guard"

[17] "Proceedings of the Republican National Conventions," 380.

was beginning to feel some uneasiness, and even if the leaders would not give way, their followers were becoming worried. Says Mr. Davis: "The Colonel's response to all these feelers was exactly the same, and was of a kind to furnish no reasons for satisfaction or congratulation to the Old Guard. It was that if the roll of delegates were purged of fraud, and the convention honestly organized, he would support the nominee, whoever he might be. The Old Guard, however, had no intention whatever of purging the roll, for they perfectly understood that such action would have two results. In the first place, it would be a public confession of their own guilt, and, in the next place, which was undoubtedly the major consideration with them, it would have been certain to result in the nomination of Mr. Roosevelt." [18]

After Mr. Taft was declared nominated, the name of Vice-President Sherman was placed before the convention, and he was renominated by the vote of—Sherman, 595; Borah, 21; Merriam, 20; Hadley, 14; Beveridge, 2; Gillett, 1; present and not voting, 352; absent, 72. The sinister thing, with regard to any future success at the polls, was the return of the votes from several states as "present and not voting" or "absent." When the convention had adjourned, any common sense observer could see that Mr. Taft was a defeated man already.

Immediately following the adjournment of the Republican convention on June 22 a meeting of seceding ex-delegates and others was held in Orchestra Hall. Here the Progressive party really was launched, when resolutions were passed protesting against the nomination of Taft as procured by fraud, and Roosevelt was declared the nominee for the Presidency. He attended the meeting and addressed it, being received with the wildest enthusiasm. The next day a committee was appointed to decide upon a future course of action.

Mr. Davis is authority for the statement [19] that Mr. Bryan had given the progressive or Roosevelt leaders assurances during the course of the Republican convention, which he attended

[18] Page 302.
[19] "Released for Publication," 316–19.

as a newspaper correspondent, that he was going to the Baltimore convention of the Democratic party to oppose the nomination of Champ Clark, since the latter was supported by Tammany Hall. He added that he expected to be defeated in his opposition, and in that case he would support Roosevelt for President. It always has been the opinion of the present writer, and before he read Mr. Davis' statement, that if Clark had been the Democratic nominee, Roosevelt would probably have been successful. The more conservative and independent Republicans who voted for Wilson by the thousands would in large part have refused to support Clark and have gone for Roosevelt. They doubtless would have swallowed their opposition to the initiative and referendum and the recall of judicial decisions in the hope of later being able to defeat these measures which they opposed, even though Roosevelt might be in office. With the added strength of Bryan's following from the Democratic party, this would have made Roosevelt's success all the more probable. But Clark was not nominated when the Democratic convention convened at Baltimore on June 25. The radical wing resumed control of that party and the nominations went to Woodrow Wilson, governor of New Jersey, and Thomas R. Marshall of Indiana. At that time Wilson was supposed to be a very moderate radical, and stood on a platform of like temper, approaching more nearly to the Roosevelt policies than those formerly championed by the Bryan wing.

The Progressives, seeing that the Democrats would hold together, now went ahead. On July 8 the committee appointed by the Progressive meeting at Orchestra Hall issued a call for a Progressive convention to meet in Chicago on August 5. The call was addressed to all people of progressive leanings throughout the country, irrespective of former party affiliations, and was signed by the Roosevelt leaders at the Chicago convention and many other prominent Republicans. A national committee was organized, headquarters were opened both in Chicago, at the La Salle Hotel, and in New York, at the Manhattan Hotel, and as rapidly as possible organizations were extended to various states.

The Progressive convention met in the Coliseum, at Chicago, the same hall that had seen the bitter fight which resulted in the nomination of Taft, and was more like an old-fashioned Methodist religious revival of frontier days than a political gathering. There was an intensity of enthusiasm and a unity of purpose that were remarkable. The platform was entitled "A Contract with the People" and was based on ideas of social and industrial justice. It was a carefully drawn up document, but included much that people of sane thought have since deemed of doubtful wisdom, and that has not always worked when put in actual practice as the result of state or local law. Such issues as the direct primary, popular election of United States senators, woman suffrage, greater publicity of campaign funds, the establishment of a department of labor, and moderate tariff rates were the least contentious parts of the resolutions. Of course, the initiative and referendum, the recall of judicial decisions, and more extreme measures were sure to arouse greater controversy. Roosevelt was present and made a powerful speech which he called his "confession of faith." He was received with a delirium of enthusiasm by the assemblage. The title of Progressive was adopted as the official party name, Roosevelt was nominated for President and Hiram Johnson of California for Vice-President, and the convention adjourned.

Mr. Taft chose Mr. Charles D. Hilles of New York to manage his campaign as chairman of the National Committee, and he loyally, with the help of the other regular Republican leaders, carried on the fight, seen to be hopeless almost from the beginning. The Progressives organized with Senator Joseph M. Dixon of Montana as chairman of their National Committee, and in reality succeeded in carrying with them most of the younger leaders, as well as the major part of the rank and file of the Republican party, as was shown in the final election returns. Mr. Taft conducted a dignified campaign, not going on the stump, but remaining at work upon the duties of his office. On the other hand, Mr. Roosevelt went upon the stump, and from the latter part of the summer well into October was continually speaking in different parts of the country. Mr. Wilson also did the same, but a sharp change came in the whole aspect of affairs when a maniac attempted to assassinate Roosevelt as he was about to leave his hotel and go to a hall to address a meeting in Milwaukee, Wisconsin. Roosevelt was shot, a bullet penetrating his breast, but beyond permitting a very casual examination of the wound by some physicians who happened to be present, he refused to give up or go to a hospital. Knowing that he might have received a mortal wound, he spoke for an hour and a half, and refused to stop until his entire speech was delivered. No man, unless absolutely sincere, would have acted as he did with the possibility of early death directly facing him.

Two months later Roosevelt wrote to the late J. St. Loe Strachey, editor of "The London Spectator," a characteristic letter, which is quoted in part here from the work of Mr. J. Bucklin Bishop,[20] for it has its especial pertinence at the present day with all the mawkish emotionalism felt by a great many people, who should know better, in connection with capital punishment. Said Roosevelt: "Just one word about the madman who shot me. He was not really a madman at all; he was a man of the same disordered brain which most criminals, and a great many non-criminals, have. I very greatly question if he has a more unsound brain than Eugene Debs. He simply represents a different stratum of life and temperament, which if not more violent is yet more accustomed to brutal physical expression. He had quite enough sense to avoid shooting me in any Southern state, where he would have been lynched, and he waited until he got into a state where there was no death penalty." Roosevelt soon recovered his health, but the bullet never was extracted from his body and he carried it until his death from other causes some six years later. He went home, and was sufficiently recovered to address a monster

[20] "Theodore Roosevelt and His Time," II, 344. Mr. O. K. Davis, "Released for Publication," 371–96, gives a dramatic and first-hand account of the attempted assassination and Roosevelt's characteristic action at the time.

mass-meeting on October 31 in New York city. Governor Wilson, in a public statement, said that he would cease active campaigning, since his principal antagonist was disabled by the attempt upon his life.

In spite of the exciting scenes attending all the nominating conventions of the three great parties, the campaign had a character of listlessness about it, mainly caused by the feeling that the results were already forecast with accuracy. The great question was as to the size of the Progressive vote; also how many members of Congress they might elect, for on this last factor depended in large part the future existence of the party. The minor parties did not arouse much interest. The Socialists were possibly the most prominent of them. They nominated Eugene V. Debs of Indiana and Emil Seidel of Wisconsin. The candidates of the Socialist-Labor party were Arthur E. Reimer of Massachusetts and August Gilhaus of New York; of the Prohibition party, Eugene W. Chafin of Illinois and Aaron S. Watkins of Ohio.

Election day came on November 5, 1912, and resulted in an overwhelming victory for the Democrats. The Republicans carried but two states and those the small ones of Utah and Vermont, which gave Mr. Taft a total of 8 electoral votes. Mr. Sherman died immediately preceding the November election, and the 8 electors cast their votes for Nicholas Murray Butler of New York for Vice-President. Roosevelt carried five states—Michigan, Minnesota, Pennsylvania, South Dakota, and Washington, and also received 11 of the 13 electoral votes of California. This gave him 88 electoral votes in all. Wilson carried the remaining 40 states, with the huge total of 435 electoral votes, the largest number ever given to a candidate up to that time. The popular vote, however, told a very different tale. It was: Wilson, 6,297,099; Roosevelt, 4,124,959; Taft, 3,486,399.[21] This meant that Wilson had a plurality over Roosevelt of 2,172,140, but the significant fact was that Roosevelt and Taft together had a plurality of 1,314,259 over Wilson. If to this latter be added the votes for Debs, 897,011;

[21] Given in "The New York Times" of Dec. 31, 1916, as "official."

Chafin, 208,923; and Reimer, 29,079, it will be found that Wilson was a minority choice by over 2,000,000 votes. More significant still was the fact that if the votes of Roosevelt and Taft could have been added together it probably would have meant the election of a Republican candidate for President. The Taft administration was one of the worst defeated in American history, but it is a great tribute to Mr. Taft himself that he remained extremely popular personally, a popularity that was much increased by his dignified and kindly bearing after the results of the election were known. The public felt that he was a "good sport," and loved him accordingly.

While the Progressives had cast 638,560 more than the Republicans, and thus their claim that they had represented the heavy majority of the rank and file of the Republicans at the time of the Chicago convention was completely vindicated, yet close observers of politics easily could tell that their party was not going to last. This was seen in the future make-up of Congress. They had only 13 representatives and 1 senator. While they had fine leadership and the sympathy of the majority of the Republican voters, yet the organization throughout most of the states and local districts was left in the hands of the "Old Guard" followers, buttressed up by the *name* of Republican, with all that it meant in loyalty and historical association. When the Progressives resigned from the Republican party in such states as New Jersey, Pennsylvania, Ohio, and many others, they gave up the party offices and party control they had won at the time of the Presidential preference primaries in the spring of 1912, when they had routed the Taft forces. The latter quietly came back into office and resumed their old places. It is here that the writer thinks Mr. Roosevelt made the other great mistake of his career. The first was his declaration for the recall of judicial decisions in addition to the still questioned principle of the initiative, referendum, and recall. The second great mistake was one of political strategy. While there was no question that he should have had the nomination at the Republican convention at Chicago, if the plainly expressed will of the people had been observed, yet it was a practical mistake to form the Progressive party. Had Mr. Roosevelt merely stepped aside, restrained his followers, and preserved a strictly negative attitude, there is no question that Mr. Taft would have been most overwhelmingly defeated. But on the day after the election Mr. Roosevelt would have been in as complete control of the old Republican party as in 1904 or at any time in its history. Nothing could have prevented his nomination and overwhelming election in 1916, with the consequent change in the whole history of the world. He would have succeeded to office at the proper time to repair the damage of Wilson's greatest failure, that in foreign affairs, and before the mistakes had gone so far that their results are to-day almost irreparable, as the whole world is beginning to see.

Woodrow Wilson came into office on March 4, 1913. He is the only President, before and since, concerning whom the interesting fact stands that none of his ancestors was in the United States at the time the Constitution was adopted and our national life began. In other words, he totally lacked any colonial American ancestry. This in itself was a sign of the growing age of the country and a change to newer conditions. It is difficult to speak of Mr. Wilson without arousing bitter partizanship, but a brief characterization is necessary. He seemed to be a combination of two different personalities. Highly educated, a brilliant teacher and student, he had worked out the theory of American political leadership, and had the correct workable idea of executive leadership, to cause a unity and driving force in administration. He would correct the divisive and discursive tendencies which were the direct results of the old and mistaken theory of Montesquieu concerning the "separation of powers," and thus do away with the consequent separation of responsibility. He, with Mr. Roosevelt, thus had the correct conception of the office of President, according to the views of the writer, who believes that Wilson's undoubted success in leading his party during his first administration was largely due to this fact. On the other hand, he departed from his own theories in his second term, and his defeat and headlong overthrow at the hands of the Senate, backed by the people, was the result. Furthermore, there is no doubt that Wilson had one of the most fascinating personalities in private life, where his kindliness, warm friendships, good fellowship, and rare power as a conversationalist had full play. On the other hand, and as the result of the other personality, he could be a perfect iceberg when he desired, and as an administrator assert the most ruthless, selfish, and remorseless authority. His greatest weakness was the fact that he considered everything from the personal standpoint, whether of support or opposition, and this led to breaches in friendship and the change of personal loyalties often so hard for the observer to fathom.

Mr. Wilson had well said that he was not a Jefferson Democrat. He believed in popular rights, but his view of the relation of government and individual rights soon developed, while he was in office, to a theory seemingly not far different from that underlying much of recent German state socialism. In other words, he believed in the rights of the people, but the rights were given the people by the government. The Democratic party had gradually resumed Jeffersonian theories of inherent individual rights at the time Wilson assumed its leadership, but he impressed on it the entirely different and theoretically opposed views of his own school of thought, so that the "new freedom" had a very different basis from what at first might be supposed. It thus would seem impossible for one to be consistently a Wilson and a Jefferson Democrat at the same time, although of course any Democrat is at perfect liberty to choose either one of the two types of thought, and with a clear conscience! [22] Finally, it may be said in the words of one of his friends and admirers, "Wilson's intellect was an acrobat, walking the tight-rope of his conscience."

Wilson's cabinet was a strange mixture. It contained two

[22] The problem of Woodrow Wilson may be studied in Henry Jones Ford, "Woodrow Wilson, the Man and His Work"; Robert Edwards Annin, "Woodrow Wilson, a Character Study"; James Kerney, "The Political Education of Woodrow Wilson"; Ray Stannard Baker, "The

men of marked ability, two of incompetence, and the remainder of moderate competence, who could fill their offices as well as did the average official of past years. These appointments were made almost entirely for political purposes. While they caused many failures and a certain breakdown in efficiency of government, yet Wilson did succeed in doing one thing, and that was in uniting the Democratic party to a degree it had not known since the first administration of Grover Cleveland. He gave loose rein to Mr. Bryan in the State Department, one of his conspicuous failures in appointment, with the result that the foreign service of the United States was brought to its lowest state of efficiency and popular respect. There were several outstanding successes in the department, as witness the records of Walter Hines Page at London and Henry van Dyke at The Hague. But so many "deserving Democrats," as Mr. Bryan himself alliteratively called them, were placed in our diplomatic and consular service that a leading newspaper, a strong administration organ, was moved to say that of the first thirty appointments, twenty-eight were obviously unfit.

The greatest Democratic successes came during the first two years of the Wilson administration. He called Congress at once into special session to revise the tariff, and at this time was fortunate in having able leaders such as A. Mitchell Palmer, Oscar Underwood, and Carter Glass in the House of Representatives. The alignment here was: Democrats, 291; Republicans, 124; progressive Republicans, 6; Progressives, 13. The Democratic leadership was weaker in the Senate, and also the party majority was narrower, being 51 Democrats, 44 Republicans, 1 Progressive. It was at this point that Mr. Wilson had to exert his full power of leadership.

When Congress met it elected Mr. Champ Clark of Missouri speaker, and Mr. Wilson surprised every one by reviving the old precedent at the beginning of our Government, set aside by Jefferson in 1801, and addressed the joint session in person.

Life and Letters of Woodrow Wilson." These are by far the best writings yet published on the subject, and Mr. Kerney's book is exceptionally valuable.

This was one of the shrewdest moves of his administration, and focused the attention of the country upon Congress and also congressional activities, with the result that the administration was able to swing public opinion toward the attainment of most of its objectives. The Simmons-Underwood tariff was a fair and honest carrying out of the party platform. The Federal Reserve Banking Act, although it was the work of many men, including Republicans from the time of Senator Aldrich of Rhode Island to Senator Root of New York, should be judged the greatest success of the whole Wilson *régime*. It was passed during his administration, and its passage in large part was due to his insistence and driving force. The creation of the Federal Trade Commission and the Clayton Anti-Trust Act largely "stole the thunder" of the Progressive party, and caused a few of the members of that organization to go over to the Democratic party when their own Progressive organization died a natural death of weakness and reabsorption in 1916.

Wilson went out of his way to deal on the friendliest terms with Latin America. His long patience with the revolutionists, leading to a total disregard of the self-respect or the safety of individual Americans who might be in those countries, no matter how peaceful or law-abiding the mission, was in striking and unfortunate contrast with the firm and enlightened policies of Theodore Roosevelt. These latter policies had resulted in the most friendly and peaceful relations the United States ever had enjoyed. Conditions in Mexico now became so disturbed that marauding bands actually crossed the border and murdered American citizens within the territory of the United States. Only then, forced by an outraged public opinion, would Wilson act, and General John J. Pershing was sent into Mexico, where in a brilliant movement he defeated and scattered the marauding band of followers of Pancho Villa.[23] All this weakness and lack of appreciation of the honor

[23] It was reported in the daily press at the time that General Pershing was ordered to "get Villa dead or alive." This was erroneous, as the copy of the order issued to General Pershing will show. It is printed here in

of the United States was only a forecast of the depths to which the country was brought by the policy of the Wilson administration when the European war burst upon the attention of a startled world. And it is possible that the war saved us from either a renunciation of the Monroe Doctrine and an abject diplomatic humiliation at the hands of imperial Germany itself, or else a war against that fully armed and prepared

---

full out of justice to that gallant officer, and to the soldiers who so finely assisted in carrying out the commands of the War Department.

WAR DEPARTMENT TELEGRAM

Official Business

Washington

Translation

Washington, March 10, 1916.

Commanding General, Southern Department,
Fort Sam Houston, Texas.
Number 883.

You will promptly organize an adequate military force of troops from your department under the command of Brigadier General John J. Pershing and will direct him to proceed promptly across the border in pursuit of the Mexican band which attacked the town of Columbus, New Mexico, and the troops there on the morning of the ninth instant. These troops will be withdrawn to American territory as soon as the defacto government of Mexico is able to relieve them of this work. In any event the work of these troops will be regarded as finished as soon as Villa's band or bands are *known to be broken up.** In carrying out these instructions you are authorized to employ whatever guides and interpreters are necessary and you are given general authority to employ such transportation, including motor transportation, with necessary civilian personnel as may be required. The President desires his following instructions to be carefully adhered to and to be strictly confidential. You will instruct the commanders of your troops on the border opposite the state of Chihuahua and Sonora, or, roughly, within the field of possible operations by Villa and not under the control of the force of the defacto government, that they are authorized to use the same tactics of defense and pursuit in the event of similar raids across the border and into the United States by a band or bands such as attacked Columbus, New Mexico, yesterday. You are instructed to make all practical use of the aeroplanes at San Antonio, Texas, for observation. Telegraph for whatever reinforcements or material you need. Notify this office as to force selected and expedite movement.

(Signed) [H. P.] McCain

---

*Italics mine.

power that most probably would have ended in our defeat. It is stated that the German Government had let it be known that it intended directly to challenge our authority and influence in Haiti, when the war mercifully turned the attention of this aggressive and ruthless force in an entirely different direction.[24]

As soon as the European war began, President Wilson issued a proclamation of neutrality that would have been entirely proper and reasonable had he not adjured American citizens to be neutral in *thought,* which was an utter impossibility for people of any intelligence. Although the conflict became more and more terrible and intense, and showed more and more signs of reaching across the Atlantic and involving us, he made no adequate preparations for necessary national defense, but followed a weak policy of abject pacifism. It was peace at any price, even the price of national self-respect. This had its first great crisis in the totally unjustifiable and barbaric act of the sinking of the *Lusitania* by a German submarine on May 7, 1915, which resulted in the unlawful murder of 114 American citizens, who had been guilty of no offense whatever and had every legal and moral right to be on the ship. Wilson merely attempted to "bluff" Germany by sending a note saying that he would hold that country to "strict accountability." Had he sent the German ambassador home immediately, given an ultimatum with a few days' leeway, and called upon the American people, they would have arisen as one man! Wilson even went further and in an address a few days later spoke of the possibility of being "too proud to fight." For the next two years the whole country was crying for moral leadership, and the one man who was in the position to give it and should have done so was Woodrow Wilson. Even his unctuous and sonorous note to Germany threatening "strict accountability" was too much for his secretary of state, and the country was mercifully delivered from Mr. Bryan's further incompetent conduct of the State Department by his resignation. Robert Lansing was appointed in his place.

[24] See Clifton R. Hall, in "The World Peril," 125–31.

Fortunately for the country, there was one man who was in a position to assume moral leadership, and he did not hesitate to step into the yawning breach. That man was Theodore Roosevelt, who not only had "put the Ten Commandments into practice" while he was in official position, but now as a private citizen recalled the country to its self-respect. With the aid of other courageous and far-seeing men, both Republicans and Democrats, prominent among whom was the late General Leonard Wood, he began to plead first of all for preparedness, and then for a revival of national honor, bringing home to the minds and consciences of the people the fact that there is a worse thing than war—and that is a cowardly and dishonest peace.

This unofficial, and in a sense private, agitation had a remarkable response among the people. On May 13, 1916, there was held a monster preparedness parade in New York city in which more than 125,000 of the city's business and professional men and women marched up Fifth Avenue in a great demonstration in favor of adequate military preparation against war. It was reviewed by General Wood, Mayor John Purroy Mitchel, Admiral Usher, and many others. On May 19, in Detroit, Michigan, considered the center of pacifism due to the influence of its leading business man, Henry Ford, Theodore Roosevelt made an impassioned plea for preparedness with striking results. Training camps were held, and this great popular movement was merely an indication of what undoubtedly would have happened had President Wilson met the emergency in a bold and statesmanlike way. Even he, due to the rise of an overwhelming public opinion, marched at the head of a "preparedness parade," said to number 60,000 marchers, in Washington, D. C., on June 14.

It was just at this time that the election of 1916 loomed before the people. As early as May, 1913, an informal conference of Republicans who came from eleven different states had recommended that the party be reunited and reconstructed on progressive lines, and that a special national convention be called by the National Committee for the purpose. It also referred especially to the need of some reform in the basis of representation for delegates. Following this, the National Committee did meet in Washington, D. C., in December. While it did not judge that a special convention would be expedient, yet it did draw up and submit to the state Republican conventions a new plan of representation based upon the number of Republican votes cast in each congressional district. This would reduce the number of members of the convention from 1078 to 985, and the South would lose 82. The convention of 1916 was made up on this basis, and the change was accepted by the progressive Republicans as a small step in the right direction.[25]

The congressional elections of 1914 were cause for encouragement to the Republicans. The Democrats did gain two senators, but their majority in the House of Representatives was reduced from 147 to 29. The Progressives lost more than half their vote of 1912 and cast only about 1,800,000 votes. It was easily to be seen that the end of the party was near. But right here appeared the bourbon attitude of the "Old Guard" at its worst. They acted in the most high-handed and unrepentant manner, would not amalgamate with the Progressives, and threw away their golden chance to win the 1916 election. Roosevelt undoubtedly was the most popular and influential man in the United States. The Republican party could not possibly win a victory without the return of his followers to their old allegiance. In the light of the great menace to the country from probable European entanglement, which far-sighted people already knew could lead to nothing less than war, Roosevelt was conciliatory and willing to help in a movement toward reunion. When approached with the possibility of his nomination for the Presidency he merely said that the Republican party would have to be in a heroic mood if he should be willing to accept. Conciliatory leaders on both sides used their influence and caused both the Republican and Progressive conventions to be called in the same city and

[25] F. A. Ogg, "National Progress," chapter XX, gives a summary of these events.

on the same day—Chicago, Illinois, June 7, 1916. Also, both conventions appointed committees to confer about some basis of conciliation, but they utterly failed in their task, although the best of feeling was preserved among the larger part of the members. The Republican members of this committee were Reed Smoot, W. Murray Crane, A. R. Johnson, William E. Borah, and Nicholas Murray Butler. The Progressives were George W. Perkins, Charles J. Bonaparte, Horace Wilkinson, Hiram Johnson, and John M. Parker.

The "Review of Reviews" remarked editorially:[26] "The decision to hold the Progressive convention at the same time and place with the Republicans was in effect an abandonment in advance of the Progressive party as such. It meant that the Progressive leaders would make the best terms they could and rejoin the Republicans, with Roosevelt and Taft both out of the running. Even those who are not experienced politicians do not have to be told that a political party which has no real intention of putting its own ticket into the field and making its own fight has divested itself in advance of its influence and its moral power."

The Republican national convention met in the Coliseum, Chicago, Illinois, on June 7, 1916. It was called to order by Charles D. Hilles, chairman of the National Committee, and Warren G. Harding of Ohio was chosen both temporary and permanent chairman. There was little excitement in the convention, as it was smoothly run without a hitch or any real difficulty by a senatorial "soviet" consisting of Reed Smoot of Utah, W. Murray Crane of Massachusetts, James E. Watson of Indiana, Warren G. Harding of Ohio, Boies Penrose of Pennsylvania, and Henry Cabot Lodge of Massachusetts. Mr. Lodge was the chairman of the Committee on Resolutions, which reported the platform. As might have been expected, when coming from such a hand, it was well written, clear, and scholarly in tone, and showed an honest effort to include those policies of the Progressive party that were possible of accept-

[26] July, 1916, page 5 (Vol. LIV, No. 318).

ance by all Republicans of whatever faction.[27] Its main provisions may easily be summarized.

Of course the war and the policy, or lack of policy except pacifism and evasion, of the Wilson administration came in for prompt attention. "We declare that we believe in and will enforce the protection of every American citizen in all the rights secured to him by the Constitution, by treaties and the laws of nations, at home and abroad, by land and by sea. These rights . . . we will unflinchingly maintain." "We believe that peace and neutrality, as well as the dignity and influence of the United States, cannot be preserved by shifty expedients, by phrase-making, by performance in language, or by attitudes ever changing in an effort to secure votes or voters. The present administration has destroyed our influence abroad and humiliated us in our own eyes. The Republican party believes that a firm, consistent, and courageous foreign policy, always maintained by Republican Presidents in accordance with American traditions, is the best, as it is the only true way, to preserve our peace and restore us to our rightful place among the nations. We believe in the pacific settlement of international disputes, and favor the establishment of a world court for that purpose."

To this was added an incisive criticism of Wilson's bungling policy in handling the Mexican difficulties. "We denounce the indefensible methods of interference employed by this administration in the internal affairs of Mexico and refer with shame to its failure to discharge the duty of this country as next friend to Mexico, its duty to other powers who have relied upon us as such friend, and its duty to our citizens in Mexico, in permitting the continuance of such conditions, first by failure to act promptly and firmly, and second, by lending its influence to the continuation of such conditions through recognition of one of the factions responsible for these outrages. We pledge our aid in restoring order and maintaining peace in Mexico. We promise to our citizens, on

[27] The text of the platform can be found in K. H. Porter, "National Party Platforms," 395–402; Republican Campaign Text-Book, 1916, 48–52.

and near our border, and to those in Mexico, wherever they may be found, adequate and absolute protection in their lives, liberty, and property."

Further echo of the war conditions was found in the planks declaring for preparedness and national defense. "In order to maintain our peace and make certain the security of our people within our own borders the country must have not only adequate but thorough and complete national defense ready for any emergency. . . . To secure these results we must have a coherent continuous policy of national defense, which even in these perilous days the Democratic party has utterly failed to develop, but which we promise to give the country."

There followed the usual declarations in favor of protection of American industries and labor, with the added sentence, "Through wise tariff and industrial legislation our industries can be so organized that they will become not only a commercial bulwark but a powerful aid to national defense." The planks dealing with business were wise and sound, stating that "the Republican party has long believed in the rigid supervision and strict regulation of the transportation and of the great corporations of the country. . . . [It] firmly believes that all who violate the laws in regulation of business, should be individually punished. But prosecution is very different from persecution, and business success, no matter how honestly attained, is apparently regarded by the Democratic party as in itself a crime. Such doctrines and beliefs choke enterprise and stifle prosperity." There was a promise to "secure [governmental] economy and efficiency through the establishment of a simple businesslike budget system to which we pledge our support and which we hold to be necessary to effect a real reform in the administration of national finance."

Direct influence of the Progressive party movement was seen in the planks dealing with labor laws and the suffrage. The former stated: "We favor vocational education, the enactment and rigid enforcement of a federal child labor law; the enactment of a generous and comprehensive workmen's compensation law, within the commerce powers of Congress, and an accident compensation law covering all government employees. We favor the collection and collation, under the direction of the department of labor, of complete data relating to industrial hazards for the information of Congress, to the end that such legislation may be adopted as may be calculated to secure the safety, conservation and protection of labor from the dangers incident to industry and transportation." The suffrage declaration was especially significant, in light of the fact that women were to vote for the first time in a Presidential election in twelve states: "The Republican party, reaffirming its faith in government of the people, by the people, for the people, as a measure of justice to one-half the adult people of this country, favors the extension of the suffrage to women, but recognizes the right of each state to settle this question for itself."

On the third day of the convention, June 9, there was taken the first ballot for the Presidential nomination, which resulted as follows: Charles E. Hughes of New York, 253; John W. Weeks of Massachusetts, 105; Elihu Root of New York, 103; Albert B. Cummins of Iowa, 87; Theodore E. Burton of Ohio, 82; Charles W. Fairbanks of Indiana, 72; Theodore Roosevelt of New York, 67; Lawrence Y. Sherman of Illinois, 63. A third ballot, on June 10, the fourth day, resulted in the nomination of Mr. Hughes by 949½ votes, which at once was made unanimous. Mr. Fairbanks was nominated for second place and the convention adjourned.

Charles Evans Hughes was born in Glens Falls, New York, on April 11, 1862. He graduated from Brown University, and from Columbia University Law School, at which he later was a professor and lecturer. He practised law in New York city, becoming famous as counsel for the Armstrong insurance commission of the New York legislature in 1905 and 1906, which led to his election as governor of the state for two terms. He retired from this office in 1910 to become an associate justice of the United States Supreme Court by appointment of President Taft. He was entirely removed from politics during the time of the Progressive split, and had been favorably considered for the nomination by the two wings of the progressives, both those in that party and those who had remained in the Republican organization. As stated at the time, he was "intellectual, virile, industrious, honest and courageous." [28] He had refused to become an active candidate for the nomination, but promptly accepted when nominated, and resigned from the Supreme Court. He sent by telegraph a ringing plea to the party to unite in condemnation of the weak and vacillating policy of the Democrats.

The Progressive convention, meanwhile, was under the presiding leadership of Raymond Robins, who had made a brilliant and persuasive statement of Progressive principles upon taking the chair. It had marked time in the hope that some union with the Republicans might be made. When it found this impossible, it adopted a platform reaffirming its stand for social justice, declared for an adequate army and navy, and nominated Roosevelt and John M. Parker of Louisiana. Mr. Roosevelt, in a letter to the Progressives dated Sagamore Hill, June 22, 1916, declined the nomination, declared that Mr. Hughes met the necessary conditions, and urged his followers to support the latter. He threw himself wholeheartedly into the campaign, went on the stump, and did all in his power to elect the Republican ticket. This meant the end of the Progressive party and the beginning of a final reunion in the old Republican ranks.

Mr. Roosevelt was a big enough man to deny himself and work for the good of the cause. As freely stated at the time, he could have gotten the Republican nomination at least, if not the election, had he started out to work for it. But he thought of the welfare and safety of the country in face of the imminent foreign danger. Furthermore, he was a big enough man to change his mind—a thing many of his less intellectual and able opponents were incapable or fearful of doing. Oscar King Davis tells an interesting story of Roosevelt's later change of opinion with regard to the initiative and referendum, the direct

[28] "Review of Reviews," July, 1916, 11 (Vol. LIV, No. 318).

primary, and so-called "direct government" in general.[29] He wrote Mr. Davis under date of November 10, 1917: "You are quite right, and what you say applies not only to the direct primary, but to the initiative, referendum, and recall. They should all of them be only exceptional remedies. It should be possible to invoke them in exceptional cases to control the bosses and the machines; but they simply do damage if habitually invoked."

Mr. Hughes chose Mr. William R. Willcox to manage his campaign, and he was promptly elected chairman of the Republican National Committee. Whether due to his influence, or to others close to the management of affairs, Mr. Hughes was restrained from a vigorous statement of real Americanism, no matter who might be hit. There was an abnormal and unjustified fear of "the German vote" on both sides in this election. The Democrats, who of course renominated Wilson and Marshall, met this by glibly saying, "He kept us out of war." The Republicans, as was desired by Mr. Roosevelt, one of the ablest practical politicians of his day, should have accepted the issue boldly and aroused the patriotism and moral convictions of the people. The writer firmly believes this would have succeeded and Hughes would have been elected. But his policy of evasion of issues, and one not at all characteristic of the man, is well disclosed in his speech of acceptance which was delivered at a meeting in Carnegie Hall, New York city, on the evening of July 31, 1916. Both "Old Guard" leaders and Progressives, including Mr. Roosevelt, were present. While clever in reuniting the Republican party, after the split of 1912, yet the speech totally failed to rouse public sentiment, and was commonly designated in current slang as "pussy-footing."[30] Furthermore, there still were wounded feelings which the "Old Guard" were not big enough in soul and mind to meet by a generous and conciliatory attitude, especially in such a strategic state as California. On the other

[29] "Released for Publication," 431-3.
[30] The speech can be found in Republican Campaign Text-Book, 1916, 3-18; also a clever analysis by Walter Lippmann, in "Public Opinion," 197-203.

hand, the Americans were mostly busied in money-making, and were enjoying the hothouse prosperity due to war conditions abroad. Their moral fiber had been dulled and their consciences lulled to sleep by the persuasive and eloquent addresses of President Wilson. His policy of peace at any price was very pleasing to the morally lazy, especially when glossed over by idealistic phrases. The trumpet call of a Roosevelt policy would have wakened them, but Mr. Hughes followed the wrong advice and was defeated. Both Mr. Hughes and Mr. Roosevelt went actively on the stump, but their campaign was ineffectual.

The election took place on Tuesday, November 7, and it soon became evident that Hughes had carried the large Eastern states by heavy majorities. The New York city and other newspapers, both Democratic and Republican, promptly conceded or claimed the election of Hughes. But as the returns continued to come in, the prospect began to look more like a very close and doubtful election. It was only after about thirty-six hours that it became an assured fact that Wilson was reëlected by a combination of the South and West against the North and East. New York had voted for the losing candidate for the first time since 1868, and the above combination of sections had carried the country for the first time since the election of Andrew Jackson in 1828. Hughes carried the eighteen states of Connecticut, Delaware, Illinois, Indiana, Iowa, Maine, Massachusetts, Michigan, Minnesota, New Jersey, New York, Oregon, Pennsylvania, Rhode Island, South Dakota, Vermont, West Virginia, and Wisconsin, with 255 electoral votes. Wilson carried the remainder, including New Hampshire, Ohio, and Utah, and received 276 votes. The popular vote was: Wilson, 9,116,296; Hughes, 8,547,474; Wilson's plurality, 568,822. But when it is remembered that the solid South was voting, not on issues of the time, but on those of fifty years before, Wilson's plurality shrinks to insignificance. As pointed out by the "Review of Reviews,"[31] "the South

[31] December 1916, 584 (Vol. LIV, No. 323). For statistics see "New York Times," Dec. 31, 1916.

. . . from Virginia to Texas, was Wilson's from the start, without a contest. In those states where Southern sentiment is strong, but there is a real Republican presidential vote, no great Wilson wave was discernible. Thus in Virginia and Kentucky, Wilson actually lost a good many votes as compared with 1912. His gain in Maryland, Missouri and Tennessee was slight and unimpressive." It is interesting to note that both Wilson and Marshall lost their home states, New Jersey going to Hughes by 57,964 plurality, and Indiana by 16,942. The minor parties cast votes as follows: Arthur Reimer of Massachusetts, Socialist-Labor, 13,922; Allan L. Benson of New York and George R. Kirkpatrick of New Jersey, Socialist, 590,415; Frank J. Hanly of Indiana and Ira D. Landrith of Massachusetts, Prohibitionists, 221,196. Parker, running on the Progressive ticket for the Vice-Presidency, received 42,856 votes. The Democratic majority in the United States Senate was reduced from 16 to 10, while both the Democrats and Republicans had 214 members each in the House of Representatives leaving the control in the hands of a few independents. These later helped the Democrats to organize the House, when it came together in special session in the spring of 1917, in order to declare war against Germany.

And now came a strange and finally inconsistent series of speeches and acts on the part of President Wilson, safely reëlected and with the prospect of another four years in office. On December 18, 1916, he sent an identical note to the belligerents on both sides saying that he suggested a statement by them of their objects in the war, which latter appeared to be the same. He followed this by an address to the United States Senate on January 22, 1917, in which he advocated a "peace without victory." Then came the formal notice by the German Government, on January 31, of unrestricted submarine warfare, which meant a direct menace and ultimate acts of war against the United States. Public opinion was by now so aroused, thanks in large part to Mr. Roosevelt's great campaign, that President Wilson was forced to recall Ambassador Gerard from Berlin, and hand his passports to Ambassador

Bernstorff in Washington. Although there followed a delay of two months, this breach of relations could lead to nothing less than hostilities. On April 2 Congress met in special session at the call of the President. It promptly organized by reëlecting Champ Clark as speaker, and then listened to a stirring and eloquent message from President Wilson, who appeared in person before it. He reviewed the recent course of events and then recommended a declaration of war. He used these significant and true words: "The world must be made safe for democracy . . . the right is more precious than peace, and we shall fight for the things we have always carried nearest our heart—for democracy, for the right of those who submit to authority to have a voice in their own governments, for the rights and liberties of small nations, for a universal dominion of right by such a concert of free peoples as shall bring peace and safety to all nations and make the world itself at last free."

There was general and universal agreement with these sentiments, but at once came the thought in the minds of intelligent and far-seeing people, Why had Wilson been so long in seeing all this? After more than two years of the war had passed, with characteristic German outrages, he had said in December, 1916, that the objects of the belligerents appeared the same; in January, 1917, there must be peace without victory; and then suddenly, in less than three months, this same war is to make the world safe for democracy! The conclusion at once became a conviction with many that President Wilson never would have changed his mind thus suddenly and led the country into war had he not been forced to it by an aroused public opinion. But there was no division of sentiment now. Congress promptly, by nonpartizan action, declared war against Germany. The Senate acted on April 4 with only six dissenting votes, those of Harry Lane of Oregon, William J. Stone of Missouri, and James K. Vardaman of Mississippi, Democrats, and of A. J. Gronna of North Dakota, Robert M. La Follette of Wisconsin, and George W. Norris of Nebraska, radical Republicans. The House of Representatives passed the resolution on April 6 by the vote of 373 to 50. It was significant that the respective administration Democratic leaders, Stone of Missouri in the Senate and Kitchin of North Carolina in the House, voted against war.

During the entire war period the Republican party sank partizan differences and loyally supported the Democratic President and administration. In some cases, as in that of Representative Julius Kahn of California, this was in striking contrast to the actions of the Democratic leaders and committee chairmen themselves. There is a remarkable difference between this Republican loyalty and coöperation both inside and outside of Congress in 1917 and 1918, and the semi-disloyal and partizan opposition of the Democratic party organization throughout the North and West from 1861 to 1865.

The condition of national affairs at the beginning of the war is well described by Professor Charles Seymour, himself favorable to President Wilson.[32] "However firmly united, the country was completely unprepared for war, in a military sense, and must now pay the penalty for President Wilson's opposition to adequate improvement of the military system in 1915 and for the half-hearted measures taken in 1916. . . . No wonder the German general staff ranked the United States, from the military point of view, somewhere between Belgium and Portugal. Furthermore, military experts had been discouraged by the attitude of the administration. The secretary of war, Newton D. Baker, had failed, either through lack of administrative capacity or because of pacifistic tendencies, to prepare his department adequately. He had done nothing to rouse Congress or the nation from its attitude of indifference towards preparation. . . . An extreme liberal, he distrusted the professional military type and was to find it difficult to coöperate with the captains of industry whose assistance was essential. . . . Josephus Daniels, the secretary of the navy, was a southern politician, of limited administrative experience and capacity. During the first years of his appointment he had

[32] "Woodrow Wilson and the World War," 117–8, 144.

alienated navy officers through the introduction of pet reforms and his frank advocacy of a little navy. Resiliency, however, was one of his characteristics, and he followed President Wilson in 1916, when the latter demanded from Congress authority for an expansion in the navy which seemed only prudent in view of international conditions. Largely owing to the efforts of the assistant secretary, Franklin D. Roosevelt, the months immediately preceding the declaration of war witnessed strenuous preparations to render aid to the Allies in case the United States should participate. Thereafter Secretary Daniels tended to sink his personality and judgment in the conduct of the naval war and to defer to the opinion of various officers."

There is no question that there was little popular confidence in the leadership or ability of Secretary Baker and Secretary Daniels. President Wilson took unwarranted chances on a complete downfall of the administration and possible wrecking of the cause of the Allies in retaining them in office, no matter how able and efficient in his personal opinion they may have been. The country was mercifully preserved from the results of his rashness and narrow-minded lack of judgment by the fact that the Allies stood between us and our enemies until we could make proper military preparations, and this latter result was accomplished by the brilliant work of the officers and men of the army and navy, backed by the heavy majority of Congress and the people of the country irrespective of partizanship.

As the war drew to a close in the early autumn of 1918, Wilson more and more took into his own hands the determination of matters of national policy, and more and more the people began to question his judgment and ability to handle them. His celebrated "fourteen points" never were acceptable to a large element among our people, and they looked upon his negotiations with Germany only with serious misgivings. They remembered his efforts for "peace without victory," and feared what happened, a negotiated rather than a dictated peace made more than probable by war-weariness on the part of the Allies.

However, in general the Republican party loyally supported him, criticism was suppressed, and he had such authority in his hands that in reality he was the most powerful ruler in the world. Now began his mistakes in personal policy, which were completely to wreck him.

The first and greatest of these came at the time of the congressional election of 1918. The Republican breach was practically healed for the first time since 1912, only a few Progressive malcontents remaining, most of whom found refuge in the Democratic party just at the moment of its approaching eclipse. The people not only began to remember Wilson's mistakes in diplomacy leading up to the war, but also had lost confidence in many of the Democratic leaders. These latter realized this, and certain of them appealed to the President to issue a statement in behalf of the party. This fell into line with his own feelings and prejudices, for probably his judgment was unbalanced by the intoxication of power, and his impaired health increased the force of his personal peculiarities, arousing his ambitious and dictatorial nature to exert itself to the utmost. One thing Woodrow Wilson never could meet fairly and calmly and that was opposition. The very thought of it now seemed outrageous to him, so on October 25 he issued an appeal to the voters of the country in which he asked them to return a Democratic Congress in the coming elections. He also used the following words: "The leaders of the minority in the present Congress have unquestionably been pro-war, but they have been anti-administration. The return of a Republican majority in either House of Congress would be interpreted on the other side of the water as a repudiation of my leadership."

This fell like a bombshell and, to use a common illustration, blew the cover off the repressed feelings of the Republican opposition. They felt that their loyal and patriotic support of the Democratic President and his administration, often against their own better judgment, or what they sincerely considered to be such, had been met by a virtual "slap in the face." The challenge was at once taken up, and this partizan appeal for a vote of confidence was met by a counter-appeal on the part of the Republican leaders. Mr. Roosevelt, in his clever and acute way, put his finger on the weak point of Woodrow Wilson's character when he replied to the appeal during the course of his own speech at a meeting scheduled in support of the Republican state ticket in New York, at Carnegie Hall on the evening of October 28. Speaking of Mr. Wilson, Mr. Roosevelt said: "He does not ask for loyalty to the nation. He asks only for support of himself. There is not the slightest suggestion that he disapproves of disloyalty to the nation. I do not doubt that he does feel some disapproval of such disloyalty; but apparently this feeling on his part is so tepid that it slips from his mind when he contemplates what he regards as the far greater sin of failure in adherence to himself." [33] Added to this, and better from the standpoint of future Republican prospects, was a joint appeal issued by the two ex-Presidents, Taft and Roosevelt, who had been personally reconciled in public at Chicago on the previous twenty-fifth of May. They repudiated Wilson's plea and accepted his challenge.

Wilson asked for a formal vote of confidence, and it was definitely refused by the people of the United States at the polls on November 5. The Democratic party lost control of both houses of Congress, and had this country had a parliamentary form of government, such as Wilson himself so often had commended in past years, he would have been out of office the next day. The new or Sixty-sixth Congress would stand, in the House of Representatives—Republicans, 239; Democrats, 193; independent and minority parties, 3. In the Senate the Democratic majority was changed into a Republican majority of 2. It is the writer's own opinion that Wilson's appeal actually helped the Democrats in this election, though it made all the more certain the Waterloo of two years later.

Wilson's next great mistake, added to the absolute vote

[33] Joseph Bucklin Bishop, "Theodore Roosevelt and His Time," II, 466–7.

Photograph by Brown Brothers

CHARLES E. HUGHES CAMPAIGNING

of lack of confidence, made a still greater departure from his own ideals and political principles of Presidential leadership of the people. It was his going ahead to negotiate a treaty of peace with a practical ignoring of the United States Senate, not to mention the public opinion of the nation. He did not appoint a single senator on the Peace Commission, and but one Republican, Henry White, who had been abroad in the diplomatic service most of his life and was hardly known to the American people. Mr. White had hardly a speaking acquaintance with the party leaders. The other members of the commission were himself, Secretary Lansing, and Colonel House, both of them proper appointments, and General Tasker H. Bliss, concerning whom the main criticism was the fact that he too was practically unknown to the American people. The inclusion of such men as Senator Lodge, the Republican leader in the Senate, Mr. Taft, Mr. Roosevelt, or Mr. Root would have been not only proper but also should have been looked upon by him as imperative, both from the standpoint of a fair representation of public opinion and from that of political decency.

Not only did Wilson exclude the Senate, but at this time and within a few days *after* the signing of the armistice on November 11, 1918, he announced that the Government would take over the cable lines. This meant that the Democratic administration, just repudiated by the people at the polls, would and *did* absolutely control all news coming from Paris and other capitals abroad while the terms of peace were being negotiated. It not only was entirely wrong from the standpoint of democratic government, whatever advantage it might mean to Democratic government, but also morally unjustifiable. The great political indiscretion is a minor point, for Wilson was rapidly becoming a discredited man in the minds of the rank and file of the American people. He then made another mistake, which made inevitable his future defeat. He went to Paris to negotiate *in camera* and at his own personal dictation a world peace that was to determine the destiny not only of defeated enemies but of victorious allies. This was in striking contrast to the policy of McKinley, at the close of the Spanish War, who had carefully given representation both to the Senate and to the Democratic party on the Peace Commission he sent to Paris, and also had remained in Washington where he was in close touch with the gradual process of crystallization of American public opinion. But McKinley was, as has been shown before, an adept in sensing public opinion. Wilson told the people what they must think, and then deluded himself with the idea that they thought as he did.

Wilson landed in France on Friday, December 13, 1918. He received such a reception in this and other Allied countries as was fitting for the head of the great country over which he ruled, and for the commander-in-chief of one of the greatest of the armies or navies in the world. Also, the people of our Allies expressed through him their friendship for the Ally who had fought by their side. Public opinion abroad was carefully fostered and guided in Wilson's favor by a remarkably well-organized official American propaganda, financed at the expense of the American people who had repudiated its beneficiary at the polls. Nevertheless, Wilson received all these plaudits as personal, and did not seem to perceive that to a great extent they were due to his official position.

When it came to direct negotiations, Wilson was face to face with the most accomplished European and world diplomats. They amused him with his pet scheme of a League of Nations, and meanwhile proceeded to outpoint him on nearly every issue. Instead of settling certain most important things at once and for all time, if possible, the attempt was made to settle everything. Many of the present difficulties in Europe and the world at large are in greater part due to this mistaken policy. The admirable idea of a league of nations or some world organization now fell under suspicion in the United States or actually into disrepute. The Republican leaders were quick to sense this fact, and soon realized, also, that their political enemy had delivered himself into their hands by virtue of all these, his own, mistakes. They promptly took advantage of their legitimate and open opportunities and the downfall of Woodrow Wilson and the Democratic party was the logical result. Events were soon to show beyond the shadow of a doubt which leaders in reality represented the will and desires of the American people.

Chapter XVII

THE REPUBLICAN TRIUMPH

It is probable that the new birth of nationalism and self-respect, the renewed pride in America and all that for which it stands, and from which the Republican party was able to secure such great gains and political prestige, came as a natural result from the work of Theodore Roosevelt. During the war he was able as a private citizen to speak freely and openly, for his prominence and popularity precluded any retaliatory measures on the part of partizan opponents. Roosevelt loyally supported Wilson and the Democratic administration in the conduct of the war, in spite of rebuffs and the cold shoulder. On the other hand, his sound and constructive criticism, backed perhaps unintentionally by the patriotic assistance of such a man as Senator Chamberlain of Oregon, himself a Democrat, caused many inefficiencies to be remedied and mistakes to be repaired. Roosevelt's faith in the people was magnificently justified. He once said to Julian Street:[1] "I am not cynical, because I have observed that just when our people seem to be becoming altogether hopeless they have a way of suddenly turning around and doing something perfectly magnificent."

It was but natural that Roosevelt and Wilson disliked each other—as the writer knows from personal conversation with both men. They were too much alike in their vigor and drive of leadership, and too different in ideals and beliefs, not to mention personal characteristics, to feel otherwise. But at the close of the war it appeared almost certain that Roosevelt would be the Republican candidate in 1920 and lead a move to rid the country entirely of what he called "Wilsonism"—especially the Democratic President's policies in inter-

[1] Quoted in "The Most Interesting American," 94.

national affairs in so far as they portended the involvement of the country in the tangle of world politics. Roosevelt's candidacy was a commonly accepted fact in the private conversation of the political leaders, both "Old Guard" and progressive. He himself remained quiet and bided his time, but he was aware of it. The Republicans in New York desired him to be their candidate for governor of the state in 1918, but he absolutely refused. His health was not good and, as we know now, his final illness was slowly approaching. When one of his closest friends told Roosevelt of regret that he had not accepted the nomination, he replied that he was saving himself—that he had one more fight ahead of him, and only one fight left in him, but that "it was a mighty good fight." He evidently was referring to 1920. Mr. Roosevelt was taken to a hospital in New York city during the month of December, 1918, just at the time that Woodrow Wilson went to Paris. Senator Lodge had several interviews with him at the hospital, and these old and intimate friends worked out certain plans as to what they felt was absolutely necessary to be included in any forthcoming League of Nations, which they knew Wilson purposed to form. These plans later were incorporated in the so-called Lodge reservations when the treaty came before the United States Senate.

Fate willed that Mr. Roosevelt be removed at the time when he seemed most necessary to the welfare of the Republican party and the country, and in fact of the whole world. We can imagine what his leadership would have meant during the trying and tragic years succeeding the armistice and the close of the war. He died on January 6, 1919. The day before, he dictated an editorial article for "The Kansas City Star," in which he used these pregnant words: "It is of course a serious misfortune that President Wilson, through Mr. Creel's misinformation bureau and the control exercised over the correspondents, should prevent our people from getting a clear idea of what is happening on the other side. For the moment the point as to which we are foggy is the League of Nations. We all of us earnestly desire such a League, only we wish to be sure that it will help and not hinder the cause of world peace and justice . . . there isn't a man of sense who does not know that in any such movement if too much is attempted the result is either failure or worse than failure."[2] This was a remarkable and accurate prophecy.

When Woodrow Wilson returned from Paris with his draft of the covenant of the League of Nations and it was found that the League was not a league of consultation alone but also a league of force, it was natural, according to historic American political tendencies in the two parties, that the Republicans should oppose and the Democrats favor such an organization, in so far as the majority of the rank and file of the voters was concerned. The Republican party always has been jealous of national power and prestige, and of course would look askance at any organization that threatened to involve or to diminish these unquestionable things. On the other hand, the Democrats, looking more to local than to national government as important, would not be so jealous of the welfare or safety of the National Government or prestige—and that without the least thought of any disloyalty or lack of patriotism. It merely is a question of direction of patriotism, if it may be expressed in that way.

If it was natural for the Republicans to suspect the intentions underlying the League covenant, as well as the efficiency of its provisions when put in action, it also was natural for them to look to the United States Senate for leadership. In the first place, by constitutional provision the Senate would have the final judgment in the matter of the acceptance of the League, of course subject to the indorsement of their action by the people at the polls; and secondly, a large number of the party leaders were members of that body. They were quick to see that they, and not Wilson and the Democratic party, in reality represented the will of the American people by an overwhelming majority.

Woodrow Wilson was one of the greatest orators and most persuasive public speakers this country ever has produced.

[2] J. B. Bishop, "Theodore Roosevelt and His Time," II, 471.

Warned by a signed statement on the part of the majority of the Republican senators that they could not accept the League covenant as proposed at Paris, he decided to appeal over their heads to the people, and in the early fall of 1919 went on a speaking trip over the country. This was brought to an abrupt and most unfortunate end by his own complete physical breakdown, which developed into a desperate illness. It should be regretted by every fair-minded citizen that this should have occurred. It would have been far better for the whole cause of international peace, and the relation of the United States thereto, that Mr. Wilson should have had the opportunity fully to express his mind and use all his undoubted influence in favor of his policy. And a very dangerous situation developed during his illness, fraught with sinister possibilities to the welfare of the country. His total disability was concealed from the American people by well-intentioned but indiscreet personal and political friends, who proceeded to direct the affairs of the country in his name and without his possible knowledge. It behooves the American people to cause the enactment of such remedial legislation by Congress that a like state of affairs may never again menace the welfare of the whole nation.

Had Mr. Wilson's health continued, it is probable that there would have been no change in the final result, especially since he showed himself, both before and after that time, entirely unwilling to compromise or meet the desires of his opponents in any way. It is also probable that the majority of our people would have been willing to accept membership in the League provided American sovereignty and independence were not involved in any particular. This could easily have been secured through the acceptance by Wilson, and by the Democratic leaders who sympathized with him, of the Lodge reservations, which were well drawn to guarantee exactly these things demanded by the common sentiment of enlightened Americans. Their object was to guarantee that the United States would belong only to a league for consultation and not for force. The celebrated and iniquitous "Article X" was the crux of the situation, for it guaranteed against external aggression the territories of all members of the League, instead of merely containing a guarantee on the part of each member that it would not encroach upon the territory of any other member—an entirely different thing, as Mr. Lansing had wisely pointed out at the time of the negotiations.[3] Wilson, in an arrogant and narrow-minded spirit, would have none of this, and went down to inevitable defeat.

It seems to be the present-day fashion to belittle Mr. Lodge, a movement for this purpose being especially active since the latter's death. Senator Lodge was a man of great ability, of the finest scholarship and patriotism, and at all times a real statesman. His greatest fault was that he never outgrew the provincial and sectional restraints of his New England birth and training. He looked upon President Wilson as a menace to the country, and firmly believed that it was his patriotic duty to use every honorable means to check and defeat him in his objectives. Whether he was right or wrong is another matter. There is no doubt of his honesty and sincerity. There also is no doubt that it was his leadership that did finally result in the overwhelming defeat of President Wilson and the Democrats, and the writer believes that Lodge was right in content and intention of his reservations. The final defeat where the Senate was concerned came on March 19, 1920, when ratification of the partially amended treaty of Versailles was refused by the vote of 57 to 37, thus failing to secure the necessary two thirds favorable vote. Wilson now asserted that he would appeal to the people "in a great and solemn referendum," which meant the approaching national election of 1920, and both parties at once prepared for the campaign thus given an unusual interest and significance.[4]

Mr. Roosevelt's death naturally opened the field to a

[3] Robert Lansing, "The Peace Negotiations," 44–47, 85.

[4] In justice to Senator Lodge, the following should be quoted from his book entitled "The Senate and the League of Nations," 209: "I voted twice for the treaty with reservations and gave to the reservations and to the treaty with the reservations a genuine support; in fact, if I had not given a genuine support I should never have sought for and brought to pass, as I did, the second vote upon the treaty on March 19th, 1920."

number of contestants for the Republican nomination, somewhat loosely divided between those favored by the "Old Guard," or stand-pat elements, and those of the Roosevelt followers. The "senatorial soviet" which had so successfully controlled matters in the 1916 convention and campaign now took things in hand. They followed the clever and, from their standpoint of personal control, the sound policy of using the Presidential preference primaries to block off the success of the popular candidates and then putting forward a candidate acceptable to themselves. They desired a return to what Senator Harding of Ohio ponderously described as "normalcy," thus falling in line with a sound popular desire to get away from war conditions as early as possible. It is an interesting as well as significant fact that before Congress adjourned it passed an act repealing about sixty war-time laws which had conferred exceptional powers upon the executive. The act passed the House of Representatives by the vote of 343 to 3, and the Senate unanimously. Congress at once adjourned and President Wilson kept all his war-time powers by failing to sign the repeal. This allowed him to continue in enjoyment of all his dictatorial authority until after Congress again had met in its final session in December, 1920, for due to the failure of the ratification of the treaty of Versailles we still were technically at war with Germany. President Wilson thus took one more step which decisively alienated the average American citizen.

There was much preliminary activity among Republicans prior to the meeting of the national convention at Chicago on June 8, 1920. The National Committee was under the leadership of Chairman Will H. Hays of Indiana, a man of honesty, integrity, originality, and great executive ability. He put new life into the Republican organization everywhere, and one of the first moves made to attract public confidence was the appointment of a number of prominent leaders to an "advisory committee on policies and platform" in April, 1920, to prepare material for the resolutions to be adopted by the convention. A committee of economic experts was added during the same month in order to give technical advice and assistance to the first committee. Furthermore, there was much activity in the primaries, and as the time for the convention drew near it became evident that the leading candidates would be General Leonard Wood, Governor Lowden of Illinois, and Senator Hiram Johnson of California. A popular demand, not well organized from a political standpoint, existed for Herbert Hoover of California, who had been one of the most prominent and successful administrators and popular leaders evolved as the result of the war. His managers in the main were amateurs who did not know how to capitalize his great popularity, so that later he received but few votes in the convention, although the applause from the galleries was among the greatest for any man whose name was placed before the delegates for consideration. Senator Harding at this time had but a small popular following outside his own state of Ohio.

For the first time in our history there appeared before the startled people a fact that never before had been realized, especially by those who were most ardent and emotional in their sincere devotion to the idea of "direct" government. This fact was the necessary and enormous expensiveness of the direct primary. Speedily sensing the public amazement and dismay, certain elements in both parties in Congress, especially those who had a weakness for a little demagoguery mixed up with their politics, caused the appointment of an investigating committee by the United States Senate which should unearth these "nefarious efforts on the part of moneyed interests" to "buy the Presidency." The committee was composed of Senator Kenyon, Republican, of Iowa, as chairman, and included as its other four members Senators Reed of Missouri, and Pomerene of Ohio, Democrats, and Spencer of Missouri, and Edge of New Jersey, Republicans. There is no question that the committee did good and effective work in disclosing the expensive character of American politics, but the results were used in a most unfair way by cheap demagogues and partizans to hinder or wreck the campaigns of at least two candidates who were most popular with the rank and file of Republican voters, as shown at the primary polls. These were General Wood and Governor Lowden. This disclosure was especially fatal to the latter, due to the discovery of the questionable use of money in Missouri, but which evidently was expended without the knowledge or consent of the governor himself, who was supposed to benefit by it.

The Republican national convention was called to order in the Coliseum, at Chicago, by Will H. Hays, the national chairman, on Tuesday, June 8. Senator Lodge was chosen both temporary and permanent chairman. It was an unusually able and well-conducted body of men and women, and consisted of 984 delegates, chosen on the plan used for the previous or 1916 convention. The Committee on Resolutions was presided over by Senator James E. Watson of Indiana as chairman, who reported the platform. It was a document of unusual excellence, which showed that by now there was little or no difference between the progressive and stand-pat wings of 1912, who were well united on issues, however much they might be apart on personalities or party management. It contained a careful, able, and convincing attack upon the Wilson administration, with a moderate liberal-conservative plan for reorganization of the Government along lines of efficiency for peace-time conditions.

The more significant passages are well worthy of attention. The platform stated, at the beginning, that the party would "resist all attempts to overthrow the foundations of the government or to weaken the force of its controlling principles and ideals, whether these attempts be made in the form of international policy or domestic agitation." It then turned its attention to Democratic shortcomings by the terse comment that "the outstanding features of the Democratic administration have been complete unpreparedness for war and complete unpreparedness for peace." The statement was amplified in the following manner: "This called for vision, leadership, and intelligent planning. All three have been lacking. While the country has been left to shift for itself, the government has continued on a wartime basis. The administration has not demobilized the army of place holders. It continued a method of financing which was indefensible during the period of reconstruction. It has used legislation passed to meet the emergency of war to continue its arbitrary and inquisitorial control over the life of the people in the time of peace, and to carry confusion into industrial life." There is no question that this was an attack upon the before-mentioned policy of Wilson, akin to German socialism, that the Government should determine and give rights to the people. Such a policy, it should be reiterated, is totally opposed to the Jeffersonian principle of inherent rights.

President Wilson had declared that the election of 1920 should be a great and solemn referendum. This became true in a sense. Due to the widespread sentiment in favor of some international organization, but opposed to the specific League of Nations as proposed, the Republican leaders now saw fit to evade the direct issue as much as possible. Their idea was to make Woodrow Wilson and his administration the main issue, instead of a League of Nations—thus capitalizing all the opposition to both Wilson and the Democratic party, yet leaving their hands free to determine later just what form of international organization the country might join. That they succeeded in doing this was largely due to the following platform statement, backed up by adroit handling of the question during the time of the campaign: "We favor a liberal and generous foreign policy founded upon definite moral and political principles, characterized by a clear understanding of and a firm adherence to our own rights, and unfailing respect for the rights of others. . . . Subject to a due regard for our international obligations, we should leave our country free to develop its civilization along lines most conducive to the happiness and welfare of its people, and to cast its influence on the side of justice and right should occasion require." The matter of a League of Nations came in for treatment only on the ground of general principles, although the action of the Senate was specifically indorsed. "The Republican party stands for agreement among the nations to preserve the peace of the world. We believe that such an international association must be based upon international justice, and must provide methods which shall maintain the rule of public right by the development of law and the decision of impartial courts, and which shall secure instant and general international conference whenever peace shall be threatened by political action, so that the nations pledged to do and insist upon what is just and fair may exercise their influence and power for the prevention of war. We believe that all this can be done without the compromise of national independence, without depriving the people of the United States in advance of the right to determine for themselves what is just and fair when the occasion arises, and without involving them as participants, and not as peacemakers in a multitude of quarrels, the merits of which they are unable to judge."

There was a long and detailed statement in discussion of various measures and methods, both political and economic. In this the advocacy of the executive budget, of reform of the levy and administration of taxes, the reorganization of the departments of government, was joined with opposition to the inflationary financial policy of the Wilson administration and to the government ownership of railroads. A definite stand was taken in favor of a protective tariff, as might be expected. More significant still, and of even greater importance at the present time, it was demanded that "to facilitate government supervision, all aliens should be required to register annually until they become naturalized."

The last paragraph or plank of the platform contained a skilful summing up of principles and policies: "We declare that the Republican party has the genius, courage and constructive ability to end executive usurpation and restore constitutional government; to fulfill our world obligations without sacrificing our national independence; to raise the national standards of education, health and general welfare; to re-establish a peace time administration and to substitute economy and efficiency for extravagance and chaos; to restore and maintain the national credit; to reform unequal and burdensome taxes; to free business from arbitrary and unnecessary official control; to suppress disloyalty without the denial of justice; to repel the arrogant challenge of any class and to maintain a government of all the people as contrasted with government for some of the people, and finally, to allay unrest, suspicion and strife, and to secure the co-operation and unity of all citizens in the solution of the complex problems of the day." The retrospect of the past seven years of the Harding and Coolidge administrations discloses a remarkable measure of attainment of these promises, in spite of many mistakes and natural set-backs. The greatest criticism of the platform is its inordinate length, occupying as it does over nineteen pages of small type in a library book of ordinary size.[5] The platform was adopted as reported on Thursday, June 10, the third day of the convention.

When it came to balloting for the nominations, so much hostile feeling had been aroused that no one of the three leading candidates, Wood, Lowden, and Hiram Johnson, was able to win. Wood undoubtedly was the most popular choice, and his name was well presented to the convention by Governor Henry J. Allen of Kansas, and seconded by Mrs. Corinne Roosevelt Robinson of New York, the gifted and eloquent sister of the late President. The balloting did not begin until Friday afternoon, June 11, and much time was frittered away in futile discussion, which is ample proof that the convention was not "bossed," as charged at the time. But there is no question that the self-appointed senatorial "soviet," already mentioned heretofore, was able to block many of the desires of the delegates and finally to take advantage, for its own purposes, of the negative results it had produced. This caused a popular restlessness that has steadily increased until at the present day the United States Senate as a body is at the lowest point of popularity in its history. It still has enormous power, but it can use it only at the peril of the party, or of individual members. It should be mentioned that Chauncey M. Depew of

[5] Text may be found in K. H. Porter, "National Party Platforms," 447–466; also Republican Campaign Text-Book, 1920, 65 *et seq.*

New York, in his eighty-seventh year, made a spirited and felicitous speech worthy of a man fifty years his junior.

Ten ballots were necessary before a candidate was nominated on Saturday, June 12. Wood received 287½ votes on the first ballot, and on the fourth ballot reached his highest vote, 314½. Lowden received 211½ on the first ballot and finally reached the approximate strength of Wood, so these two candidates were a complete set-off. Johnson showed his maximum strength, 148, on the third ballot. The large delegations from New York and Pennsylvania were against Wood and Johnson, as also was that of Ohio, which supported its own favorite son, Senator Harding. While the Wood and Johnson supporters generally opposed Lowden, there is good reason to believe that the latter would have been nominated had it not been for the unfortunate primary developments already stated. It had become evident by the eighth ballot that some compromise candidate must be found, and now the senatorial leaders got in their work and chose their colleague Harding as a sort of least common denominator. He had been much helped by the vigorous and enthusiastic speech of Senator Frank B. Willis of Ohio, and there was a definite trend toward him on the ninth ballot. On the tenth, the Lowden delegates in large part went to him, as did those from other candidates, and he received a heavy vote and the nomination. Had the convention in reality been bossed, it would not have taken ten ballots to register a decision.

The same senatorial clique evidently had decided upon Senator Irvine L. Lenroot of Wisconsin, a man of fine capacity and ability, for the Vice-Presidential nomination, after Senator Hiram Johnson had rebuffed their offer. But the convention already was in a temper of revolt against too much senatorial influence, and turned with a rush toward Governor Calvin Coolidge of Massachusetts, whose name had been placed before it by Speaker Frederick H. Gillett of Massachusetts in an unusually effective speech. He promptly was nominated on the first ballot, and with great enthusiasm. The convention then adjourned.

Warren Gamaliel Harding was born near Blooming Grove, Warren county, Ohio, on November 2, 1865. He came from good old colonial American stock, was a natural healthy country boy with typical American upbringing, and was educated at the village schools. He later graduated from Ohio Central College, at Iberia, a small educational institution of the middle West. He went into journalism and became a successful newspaper editor and owner, later engaging in other lines of business, and then went into politics. He represented his senatorial district in the state legislature for two terms, was lieutenant-governor of the state for one term, refusing to stand for reelection, and was just finishing, at the time of his nomination, his term as United States senator from Ohio. He was a man of charm, personal attractiveness, great kind-heartedness, and absolute honesty and sincerity. He had undoubted ability, and was most often compared to McKinley. Governor Coolidge was of old and original New England colonial stock, and was born on July 4, 1872, in Plymouth, Vermont, a remote village in the hill country of New England. After attending the near-by country school, he prepared in academies at Ludlow and St. Johnsbury, Vermont, for entrance to Amherst College, from which he graduated in 1895. He served in various political offices ranging from city council in Northampton, Massachusetts, where he settled for the study and practice of law, to the state legislature, serving a number of terms in both houses. He became president of the senate in 1914 and 1915; was lieutenant-governor of the state from 1916 to 1918; and was elected governor in 1918. At the time of the Boston police strike he stood firm for law and order, and was reëlected in 1919 by more than 125,000 majority. He was known as a reticent, clear-visioned, able executive, and the "Review of Reviews" remarked at the time of his nomination, "his name strengthens the ticket somewhat as the name of Roosevelt strengthened the McKinley ticket twenty years ago." Strange and unconscious prophecy of what was soon to come! [6]

[6] July, 1920, 14. I have drawn extensively upon this excellent and most reliable magazine for much of my information for this whole period.

Photograph by Brown Brothers

PRESIDENT WARREN G. HARDING AND HIS CABINET

The nomination of Harding was not at once especially popular. The people of the country had become used to striking and outstanding figures in the Presidential office, and General Wood came nearest to their ideal. They had transferred to him much of their old loyalty to Roosevelt, and remembered his brilliant record both in Cuba and in the Philippines, not to mention his services at the time of the outbreak of the World War. The fact that Wilson had acted in a rather condescending way toward him, and that he had been kept out of active service in France, had aroused just and deserved sympathy. General Wood thus personified the bitter opposition to President Wilson which now had become the moving basis of coöperation among a large number of people. It also was known that he was highly esteemed abroad, and America was beginning to realize its position as a world power. It is significant of the foreign estimate of General Wood that Earl Cromer had said openly in Cairo, Egypt, in 1903, that "the regeneration of Cuba had never been equalled in any age or by any race." Later on, when visiting this country, Lord Kitchener, while at West Point, said practically the same thing to Major-General Hugh L. Scott, at one time chief of staff of the United States army.[7] In contrast with Wood, the people had placed before them in the person of Harding a man of honor and respectability, but only fairly well known. He was a typical Presidential candidate of the period of thirty years before, ere Presidential leadership had become the dominant fact in American politics. There was open complaint that the ticket should have been reversed, and that Coolidge and Harding should have been the nominees.

But Senator Harding surprised both his friends and opponents by rising to the occasion in a totally unexpected manner. He conducted a dignified, able, and effective campaign. He chose Will H. Hays as his campaign manager, a choice difficult to excel, and the political "swing" soon began in his direction. The Democrats nominated also a typical candidate

[7] Both quotations were told the writer by General Scott in a conversation on August 31, 1927.

of the type of several decades before, in the person of Governor James M. Cox of Ohio, with Franklin D. Roosevelt of New York, possibly an abler man, for Vice-President. Their platform was a specific acceptance of the Wilsonian policy and indorsement of the League of Nations. This meant that Wilson and his administration was a direct issue, while the question of *the* League was substituted for that of *a* league. The Republican managers were much pleased with this defining of issues, and their political judgment was entirely justified.

Senator Harding was formally notified of his nomination at his home in Marion, Ohio, on July 22, 1920, and he skilfully defined the issues and policy of the campaign along the lines indicated above. His criticism of the League of Nations, as proposed by the Democrats, was acute and sound. He charged that it "was conceived for world super-government, negotiated in misunderstanding, and intolerantly urged and demanded by its administration sponsors, who resisted every effort to safeguard America, and who finally rejected when such safeguards were inserted. . . . It is better to be the free and disinterested agent of international justice and advancing civilization, with the covenant of conscience, than be shackled by a written compact which surrenders our freedom of action and gives to a military alliance the right to proclaim America's duty to the world. No surrender of rights to a world council or its military alliance, no assumed mandatory, however appealing, ever shall summon the sons of this republic to war. Their supreme sacrifice shall only be asked for America and its call of honor." He came out for some international association in the following words: "I can speak unreservedly of the American aspiration and the Republican committal for an association of nations, coöperating in sublime accord, to attain and preserve peace through justice rather than force, determined to add to security through international law, so clarified that no misconstruction can be possible without affronting world honor."

A number of leading advocates of the League of Nations, especially prominent among the intellectual elements of the country, came out in a public statement favoring the election of Harding as the best way in which to secure entry into the League. While many of them later regretted this action, as the years since then have shown no effort to arrange for our entry into the international organization, yet it is probable that their judgment was right in the light of the time. What happened immediately afterward so changed conditions that the Republican leaders did not dare to make any move toward League membership. In the first place, the enormous majority against Wilson and the Democrats, as will be described later, was a warning of hostile public feeling that gave evidence of widespread suspicion of any world organization, so that it was of absolute necessity to go slowly in any such policy. In the second place, and more important still, there is no doubt that there has been a marked change in American opinion since 1920, showing a great growth in the amount of opposition to the League and all forms of such international organization. The League soon ceased to be a political issue in any sense. Even the persistent and devoted agitation and work along the line of propaganda that has been engaged in by its advocates, with great sincerity and personal sacrifice, has been unable to stem the tide flowing so strongly in the other direction.

The campaign of 1920 was one of the best organized and best directed in our history. Mr. Hays, as before indicated, put it upon a plane of marked efficiency and thorough organization. He chose as his chief of publicity a prominent and successful business man, who used the same methods of advertising in the political field that had created great prosperity in his own private business. President Lowell of Harvard some years ago pointed out most truly that the successful politician is a "political broker." [8] Mr. Hays and his able assistants realized this fact and that the advertising business is based upon the science of brokerage. And they acted upon this logical deduction with the greatest success.

Both Mr. Harding and Mr. Coolidge chose to follow a modified form of "front porch" campaign, with a few visits

[8] "Public Opinion and Popular Government," 60–67.

to certain important places, while Governor Cox, the Democratic candidate, followed the precedent of Bryan and made long tours of the country, speaking repeatedly in the most approved but effective "stumping fashion." The minor parties played but little part, although a new party was attempted along the lines of the British Labor party and was entitled the Farmer-Labor party. It nominated Mr. Parley P. Christensen of Denver, Colorado. The Socialists, with consistent fatuity, nominated their old friend Eugene V. Debs, then happily posing as a martyr while serving a sentence in the Federal penitentiary at Atlanta for his unlawful opposition to war measures. The Prohibitionists nominated Aaron S. Watkins, who had been their candidate for Vice-President in 1908 and 1912.

There was remarkable unanimity among the Republicans, and the 1912 breach was entirely healed so far as the campaign was concerned. Senator Harding proved himself a good conciliator, and Mr. Coolidge added great practical strength to the ticket. His speech of acceptance, when notified of his nomination at his home city, Northampton, Massachusetts, on July 27, 1920, was a "masterpiece in form and expression as well as in clarity of thought." [9] He stressed the fact that our institutions had to become autocratic to meet the war crisis, but he now wished the people again to take possession of their government. He also stressed the point that the observance of law is essential to social progress. Senator Watson of Indiana, with his orotund voice, eloquent and emotional periods, not to mention his remarkable gestures, appeared on the platform along with members of the Roosevelt family. Mr. Hays not only secured efficiency but also unity of spirit and effort.

The election took place on November 2 and was a veritable Republican "landslide." The greatest popular majority ever given a ticket was cast for Harding and Coolidge. In part this was due to the adoption of the Nineteenth Amendment to the national Constitution, proclaimed on August 26, 1920, by means of which the suffrage was extended to women through-

[9] "Review of Reviews," September, 1920, 240 (Vol. LXII, No. 3).

out the country.[10] Governor Cox carried only the eleven southern and border states of Alabama, Arkansas, Florida, Georgia, Kentucky, Louisiana, Mississippi, North Carolina, South Carolina, Texas, and Virginia, with a total of 127 electoral votes. Senator Harding carried all the remainder, including such states as Oklahoma and Tennessee, with an electoral vote of 404. In such states as California, Illinois, Iowa, Maine, Massachusetts, Michigan, Minnesota, New York, New Jersey, North and South Dakota, Pennsylvania, and Wisconsin his vote averaged about two and one half times the total of that cast for Cox. The popular vote was: Harding, Republican, 16,152,200; Cox, Democrat, 9,147,353; Watkins, Prohibitionist, 189,408; Debs, Socialist, 919,799; Christensen, Farmer-Labor, 265,411. This gave the Republicans a plurality of 7,004,847, and a majority over all of 5,630,229.

The writer thinks that the results of the election did not necessarily mean an adverse vote against *a* league of nations, but against *the* League of Nations as proposed. On the other hand, there is no doubt of the fact that it was a sweeping condemnation of Wilson and his administration, and the Democratic party in addition. The Republican party was stronger than Harding, for a large part of the vote was a protest vote. We shall find a remarkable reversal of conditions when it comes to the election four years later. While the Eighteenth, or prohibition, Amendment had been ratified and gone into effect on January 29, 1919, it played but little part in the election, and then only in the case of a few local candidates. Both the great national parties entirely ignored it as an issue in every particular.

The "Review of Reviews" ably summed up the campaign

[10] Its adoption had been secured by political influence of doubtful morality in coercing the legislature of Tennessee, and the governor who called it in special session for the purpose, to break their oaths of office, which included the observance of the state constitution. That document forbade action upon any national amendment unless a state election had taken place after the submission of the amendment to the state. This of course had no validity from the standpoint of national constitutional law, and the amendment was in full force and for the first time in this election.

as follows:[11] "The indications throughout the entire campaign period were more clear than in almost any other presidential election of our entire history. The Republican victory was sweeping, decisive, and convincing as respects national opinion. The verdict would have been the same if the balloting had occurred at any time after the beginning of August. Probably, however, the Republicans gained in the size of their majorities as the campaign period dragged along. It is purely a matter of conjecture whether or not the Democrats lost votes as a result of their campaign efforts and arguments. It is proper to say, however, that the attempt to shape the League of Nations issue in such a manner that the Democratic party might be set in direct opposition to the Republican party, as nobler in spirit and more faithful to humanity in its views on our international relationships, was a dire failure."

Senator Harding preserved an attitude of calm dignity following his triumphant election, and remained some weeks at his home in Marion, Ohio. He resigned his seat in the United States Senate early in January, 1921, made a trip to Texas and to the Panama Canal, and later took a holiday in Florida. The necessary interregnum before the fourth of March again caused popular impatience, and a feeling that it was time to change this antiquated and obsolete provision in our Government by means of a constitutional amendment that would provide for a more prompt assumption of office by a President and new Congress following a national election.

Harding and Coolidge were inaugurated President and Vice-President respectively on March 4, 1921, in a simple and dignified ceremony. The announcement of the cabinet in general caused great satisfaction, though there was an undercurrent of dissent at the choice of attorney-general, Mr. Daugherty, a personal friend of Harding, who had managed his pre-nomination campaign, also of the secretary of the interior, Mr. Fall. Events later showed that this dissatisfaction was well justified. The cabinet was made up as follows: Charles E. Hughes of New York, secretary of state; Andrew W. Mellon

[11] December, 1920, 563 (Vol. LXII, No. 6).

of Pennsylvania, secretary of the treasury; John W. Weeks of Massachusetts, secretary of war; Harry M. Daugherty of Ohio, attorney-general; Edwin Denby of Michigan, secretary of the navy; Will H. Hays of Indiana, postmaster-general; Albert B. Fall of New Mexico, secretary of the interior; Henry C. Wallace of Iowa, secretary of agriculture; Herbert Hoover of California, secretary of commerce; James J. Davis of Pennsylvania, secretary of labor. It was a set of men of ability, of whom at least five were outstanding, namely, Hughes, Mellon, Weeks, Hoover, and Hays, President Harding inaugurated the excellent custom of having the Vice-President as a regular attendant upon cabinet meetings. He followed this by inducing Leonard Wood to make a journey for investigation of the Philippine affairs, which had so sadly gone into decadence and inefficiency during the Wilson administrations. Later Wood accepted the post of governor-general, which he filled with such signal ability and personal sacrifice until his untimely death some six years later. A fitting crown of successful work, to end a remarkable life!

Mr. Harding called Congress to meet in special session on April 11, and followed the precedent set by Wilson in going in person to deliver his message the next day. He desired peace with Germany by means of a resolution, and apart from the covenant of the League of Nations or treaty of Versailles. Also, it was understood that Congress would go ahead with tariff and tax revision. The Sixty-seventh Congress was controlled in both houses by the Republicans. The Senate showed a party majority of 22, and in the House of Representatives the alignment was: Republicans, 307; Democrats, 127; Socialist, 1. The lower house promptly organized by reëlecting Mr. Gillett speaker. One of the first acts passed by Congress and signed by the President was that establishing a national budgetary system, which probably will rank in history with the Federal Reserve Act as one of the most important pieces of constructive legislation enacted in the early part of the century. This was followed by an emergency Tariff Act, designed to protect and help the agricultural interests of the country, which were the first to feel the necessary deflation consequent upon a return to peace conditions. This was succeeded by the Fordney-McCumber tariff, designed to put the country upon a permanent high-tariff policy, and it most assuredly accomplished its object.

It is an unfortunate fact that during the time of war and after-war stress and financial difficulty the most important committee in the House of Representatives has been successively in the hands of men who have failed to measure up to the responsibilities and opportunities of the office. Due to our system of promotion to leadership of committees based entirely upon length of service rather than upon ability, during the past decade or more we have had successively Mr. Claude Kitchin of North Carolina, Mr. James W. Fordney of Michigan, and Mr. William R. Green of Iowa, in the position of chairman of the Committee on Ways and Means. No one of them was competent to fill the position. Mr. Kitchin was by far the worst and most inadequate in his attempt to handle the financial affairs of a great nation. The other two were better only by contrast. Under these circumstances an "emergency" tariff was hastily passed, followed by the Fordney-McCumber tariff, which was worked out in a spirit of log-rolling that was anything but edifying to the country. It required a long and bitter fight before this piece of legislation finally passed the two houses of Congress and was signed by President Harding on September 21, 1922. It stands as one of the most ill-drawn pieces of legislation in recent political history. It is probably near the actual truth to say that, taking for granted some principle of protection of American business and industry, the country has prospered due to post-war conditions abroad and in spite of, rather than on account of, the Fordney-McCumber tariff. Mr. Fordney himself was of the vintage of the Republican campaign textbook for 1888, and apparently had learned nothing and forgotten nothing since that time. The attempt to protect agriculture, in a degree utterly impossible of accomplishment, caused the repeated difficulties, political and economic, that now (1927) are troubling the country. The

Photograph by Brown Brothers

PRESIDENTIAL ELECTION RETURNS AT TIMES SQUARE, NEW YORK

McNary-Haugen and other unsound measures of agricultural relief are but a foolish and ineffectual attempt to solve the difficulties caused by this unsound and inequitable piece of legislation.

Republican leaders in Congress rightly claimed for the Sixty-seventh Congress the "saving of two billion dollars in the expenditures of the federal government." This achievement was worthy of note, but also what was to be expected from any efficient legislative body in a period immediately following the close of a great war. Tax revision, pushed through in 1921 and 1922, made an annual reduction of $900,000,000 in war taxes; but the well thought out plans submitted by Secretary Mellon was in large part ignored and stress laid upon those reductions best calculated to appeal to the selfish and unthinking elements in the nation. In fact, the tax revision seemed aimed to leave untouched the unfair and un-American provisions included in the Kitchin tax bill formulated by the Democrats in 1917, and acquiesced in by the people at the time in large part due to loyalty under war conditions. The Democrats then seemed, under Mr. Kitchin's demagogic leadership, intent upon punishing the possession of wealth as a crime, and levied taxes on the urban centers of the country and their tributary population, at the same time penalizing efficiency in business by means of the excess profits and other like measures. Mr. Kitchin actually achieved the supreme absurdity of attempting to levy an excess profits tax upon brains and the results of efficient brain work by professional men! Congress did, however, extend emergency credits to farmers, and also enacted a set of laws regulating and restricting immigration, the last named due to rank with the budgetary legislation as among the most important measures passed during fifty years.[12]

An end was made to war conditions. The House passed the Porter joint resolution on June 30, 1921, by the vote of 263 to 59. This declared peace with Germany and Austria. The resolution was passed on July 1 by the Senate by the vote of 38 to 19, and President Harding signed it on July 2 while

[12] See my article entitled "The Do-Nothing Congress," in "North American Review," October, 1922, 445–454 (Vol. 216, No. 4).

visiting at the home of Senator Joseph S. Frelinghuysen at Raritan, New Jersey.

The outstanding event of the Harding administration, and an achievement that will mark it in the whole of American history, was the Washington conference for the limitation of armament, which met at Washington, D. C., on November 12, 1921, and continued in session until February 6, 1922. Delegates were present from the United States, Great Britain, France, Italy, Japan, China, Holland, Belgium, and Portugal. As the result of its deliberations seven international treaties and twelve resolutions were drawn up. The most important of these provided for the limitation of naval armaments, on a prescribed standard, by Great Britain, France, Italy, Japan, and the United States; related to insular possessions and dominions in the Pacific Ocean; and related to principles and policies to be followed by all the nine powers in matters concerning China. It was one of the greatest practical movements for peace in the world's history, and President Harding and his administrative assistants, especially Mr. Hughes and the other American delegates, were mainly responsible for the conception and accomplishment of the idea. Within about seven weeks after the close of the conference the United States Senate had ratified all the treaties and agreements there formulated.

Had it not been for the skilful political maneuvering of President Harding, a bonus to the soldiers of the World War, later passed over Mr. Coolidge's courageous veto, would early have been enacted into law by a bipartizan movement among the members of Congress. Most of them knew of its unjustifiable character, and admitted their opposition, which they were afraid to translate into votes. As the time approached for the congressional elections, Mr. Harding appeared much stronger than Congress in popular estimation. But there was even then veiled criticism of the social activities of certain officials in Washington, and an acute characterization of the President's part in them as "Main Street in the White House." [13] The

[13] See the first rumblings of criticism in the brilliant, anonymous publication that appeared at this time—"The Mirrors of Washington."

"hard times," business depression, and unemployment, due to after-war conditions, as well as the widespread industrial strikes, caused much restlessness, which naturally was visited upon the President and the party in power. However, the election results showed little more than a normal reaction from the enormous and unusual Republican majorities of 1920. The Republicans would control the Sixty-eighth Congress in both houses, although with reduced majorities. In the Senate their majority was reduced from 24 to 10, so that the membership would stand—53 Republicans, 42 Democrats, and 1 Farmer-Labor. The majority in the House likewise was reduced, 165 to 15, and would stand—226 Republicans, 206 Democrats, 1 Socialist, 1 Independent, 1 Farmer-Labor. A coalition of radical Republicans and Democrats, known as the "farm bloc," later held the balance of power and rendered ineffectual any real party responsibility or program. Mr. Coolidge reaped the results.

As the winter of 1922-23 wore on, the country gradually began to recover from its economic depression. There was renewed confidence, and matters appeared bright from the standpoint both of foreign and domestic policies. The administration, in the persons of such men as Secretaries Hughes, Mellon, Hoover, and Speaker Gillett, received much more of the confidence of the people. On the other hand, criticism of President Harding increased likewise, especially with rumors of graft, favoritism, and excessive partizanship. His appointments had often been above the average, and that of ex-President Taft to the office of Chief Justice of the Supreme Court was welcomed with universal satisfaction. But there were signs of a renewal of congressional attempts in both houses, especially in the Senate, to dominate the direction of governmental affairs, while the natural and historical evolution toward Presidential leadership, which still was continuing unabated, caused criticism of the President that he did not "force Congress" to do his will, and show a more dominating hand. Both by instincts and training, Mr. Harding was more of the "constitutional" or Taft type of executive. But he began to perceive the drift of public opinion, and to appreciate the fact that he must exert himself to regain more of his popular leadership. This was necessary if he not only would secure the renomination in 1924, which should prove a small matter with all the political resources at the control of a President, but also the still more important advantage of a reëlection. It is probable that for these reasons he made his trip through the West and Northwest during the summer of 1923. He even journeyed as far as the territory of Alaska, with an act of graceful and pleasing international courtesy and good fellowship consequent upon a visit to British Columbia. Upon his return to San Francisco, as he turned toward his homeward journey, he suddenly was taken ill. After a few days' sickness he died at 7:30 P.M. on August 2, 1923, "instantly and without warning," as the despatches stated. Vice-President Coolidge was visiting at the time at the farm-house of his father in Plymouth, Vermont. He was awakened to hear the news and took the oath of office about 2 A.M. on August 3. It was administered by his father, Colonel John Coolidge, a local magistrate, in the small parlor of the old family home. He proceeded at once to Washington and took up the cares and responsibilities of his new office of President.

It was announced that Mr. Harding had died of apoplexy, but one is led to wonder whether it was not induced by a broken heart? There is little doubt that he already had discovered the maze of graft, scandal, and, in some cases, of personal dishonesty on the part of certain officials in his administration. The finger of guilt was to be pointed, as later events and investigations clearly showed, at some who were on terms of close and even intimate friendship with the President. Harding, like Grant, was a man of undoubted personal honesty, and also of transparent sincerity. He had trusted certain people to the limit of confidence, and was just finding out how they had betrayed their trust and him also. Like Grant, he too stood by his friends, and probably waited too long before bringing charges against them or dismissing them from office. He would have paid dearly for this loyalty had not death mercifully removed him while still he had the confidence and trust of the large majority of the people of the nation. There is no question that he would have been renominated in 1924. Also, there is every probability that he would have been defeated for reelection. It is hardly an exaggeration to say that his death was one of his greatest pieces of good fortune, both for himself and for his party.

"No President of the United States ever entered the White House with the American people less cognizant of his political beliefs, his stand on important domestic and international questions of the day, than does Calvin Coolidge." These words in a Washington despatch to "The New York Sun" of August 3, 1923, were somewhat of an exaggeration, but yet represented much of the feeling prevalent at the time. Mr. Coolidge came into office at a time most critical for the Republican party, and it is but true to say that he saved it from defeat and gave it a new lease on power and influence. He was known as a quiet, reticent man, a typical New England Yankee, with all the shrewdness and common sense that the term implies. Of the highest rectitude of life and almost Spartan simplicity of tastes and desires, his record in office in Massachusetts had shown him able, courageous, efficient, and adequate. Of course, there at once arose numerous stories of his silence, added to the charge that he was a "human iceberg" and a "cold proposition." Experience since that time has shown that he is kindly, with a sense of humor, a keen insight into people and things, and a warm and abiding faith in American institutions. He is closely allied with the stand-pat elements on the tariff, but in general economic and social matters he is a liberal-conservative. This has been in line with the prevailing mood or temper of the people of his time. Added to this, he has developed a marvelous power of understanding the desires of the people, and would rank with Jefferson, Lincoln, McKinley, and Roosevelt in the ability to sense public opinion. Also, he is one of the ablest politicians that ever has lived in the White House!

Soon after the assumption of office by Coolidge, there came the disclosure of the oil and other scandals of the Harding administration, which would have wrecked the careers of most men. Coolidge came through it absolutely unscathed, for the people trusted him completely. In fact, although there were natural attempts on the part of Democratic and other partizans to bring reproach to him, and involve him in responsibility for these disgraceful conditions, they all failed utterly. As a matter of contrast, the result was a popular feeling that he was the one man above all others who alone could bring the administration and the country safely through a time of storm and moral reproach. He kept intact the cabinet of Mr. Harding until it seemed proved that a member of it, Mr. Daugherty, the attorney-general, was involved in questionable practices, and this official then was replaced. Coolidge moved slowly but surely, and for that reason was unfairly charged with condoning wrong-doing; but idle reproaches of this character merely fell harmless before him.

The President's first annual message to the new Congress was awaited with keen interest, and the country fairly listened with bated breath when, early in December, 1923, he appeared before the two houses in joint session and laid his plans before them and the people. The message was clear-cut, able, and courageous. There appeared prominent the measures of economy, efficiency, reduction of taxation, and square-dealing with both labor and capital, all of which have since become indissolubly linked with his name and reputation. With regard to foreign affairs, he urged membership in the "World Court," a continuation of the policy of non-intercourse with the Soviet *régime* in Russia, and opposed the cancellation of the war debts of foreign countries to the United States. On one of the most contentious problems of the time he spoke briefly and in no uncertain tones, "But I do not favor the granting of a bonus." These ten words of defiance to that minority among the ex-soldiers who wished to legally profiteer at the taxpayers' expense made certain, did Coolidge but know it, his own nomination and overwhelming election in 1924.

Congress, now dominated by the "farm bloc," played into Mr. Coolidge's hands, especially a certain "radical" Republican and Democratic element, by the partizan methods used in the investigation of the oil scandals, which smelled to high heaven, and in the "investigation" of Attorney-General Daugherty and others. These individuals had no real popular sympathy except that aroused by unfair methods which amounted almost to persecution. The ordinary common-law rules of evidence were frequently disregarded, the cheapest and most unreliable sources of testimony were given a solemn and respectful hearing, the accused were given little or no chance to defend themselves, and the public became so disgusted that, although there was little doubt of the transgressions of certain people, in general they were allowed to escape through the consequent popular indifference. Sympathy was aroused in the case of Mr. Denby, secretary of the navy, who was "politically lynched," as one journalist cleverly expressed it. At the same time, Mr. Coolidge issued a statement on February 11, 1924, in which he met by a prompt defiance, a resolution of the Senate "that he dismiss Mr. Denby," and proceeded to put the members of that body in the places where they belonged.

It would seem that there is no office in the United States, social, civil, or ecclesiastical, that so upsets a man's sense of proportion as that of senator, unless it be that of a bishop in any church. Therefore the public greeted with an outburst of applause Mr. Coolidge's cool statement that "the President is responsible to the people for his conduct relative to the retention or dismissal of public officials. I assume that responsibility, and the people may be assured that as soon as I can be advised so that I may act with entire justice to all parties concerned and fully protect the public interests, I shall act. I do not propose to sacrifice any innocent man for my own welfare, nor do I propose to retain in office any unfit man for my own welfare. I shall try to maintain the functions of the government unimpaired, to act upon the evidence and the law as I find it, and to deal thoroughly and summarily with every kind of wrong doing." The President followed this up by permitting Mr. Denby to resign, and virtually dismissed Mr. Daugherty on March 28, 1924.

The net result of all this contest, investigation, and agitation of various kinds was a great popular demand for the nomination of Calvin Coolidge in 1924. There is no doubt that the senatorial soviet, mentioned several times before, or its successors of a later time, never have liked Mr. Coolidge, but they have been compelled to take him, for there is a general feeling that he is stronger even than his own party. In fact, he was forced upon the political organization by public opinion of the Republicans throughout the country. Whenever there was a test of his popularity before the voters the results were overwhelmingly in his favor. Thus in New Jersey there was a Coolidge "sweep" in the preferential primaries on April 22. This was followed shortly afterward by a vote of 4 to 1 in his favor in Ohio, and Hiram Johnson was decisively defeated in his own state of California. When the national convention gathered, it was a foregone conclusion that Coolidge would be nominated without any appreciable opposition.

According to the call of the National Committee, the Republican National Convention met in the Auditorium, at Cleveland, Ohio, on June 10, 1924. It was called to order by Mr. John T. Adams of Iowa, who had succeeded to the chairmanship of the National Committee. Representative Theodore E. Burton of Ohio was presented and accepted as temporary chairman, and delivered the traditional "keynote" speech. Mr. Burton's choice was especially happy, due to his standing as one of the ablest and most respected members of the Republican party, his long experience both in the Senate and House of Representatives, and his wide reputation as a thinker and historical writer of deserved prominence. Mr. Frank W. Mondell of Wyoming was chosen permanent chairman; his turgid and commonplace address made little impression. The whole convention was a "Coolidge" affair, as much as the 1904 convention had been dominated by Roosevelt, and it is interesting to note that while the more conservative wing of the party controlled the proceedings, yet the senatorial clique, as well as the Harding circle of friends, were not at all prominent, even being "frozen out" in some particulars. It was significant that Senator Lodge was placed on no committee, nor did Mr. Daugherty have any such assignment—a strange contrast with 1920.

According to prearrangement, Mr. Charles Beecher Warren of Michigan, then ambassador to Mexico and formerly ambassador to Japan, was chairman of the Committee on Resolutions. He proved himself a capable and efficient harmonizer, for any differences of opinion on planks and policies were well "ironed out" by the time for the submission of the platform to the convention. It was reported that a subcommittee consisting of Ogden Mills of New York, William S. Vare of Pennsylvania, Martin B. Madden of Illinois, and Senator Reed Smoot of Utah performed the major part of the actual work of drafting. Such contentious points as the bonus, and the World Court as advocated by both Presidents Harding and Coolidge, were handled frankly by the acceptance of the bonus as an accomplished fact and the indorsement of the international tribunal. As before noted, present-day platforms are of boring and wearying length, and this one ran true to form, occupying sixteen pages of rather small type in the average-sized book. [14] But as President Lowell of Harvard well remarks, platforms are not to stand on but to get in on! He adds, "In their fervor, generality and vagueness they bear some resemblance to letters of recommendation, in this case written by the body recommended."[15]

The following summary is made as brief as possible. There was first of all an expression of tribute to President Harding, and then a remarkable indorsement of President Coolidge in these words: "He has put the public welfare above personal considerations. He has given to the people practical idealism in office. In his every act, he has won without seeking the applause of the people of the country. The constantly accumulating evidence of his integrity, vision and single-minded devotion to the needs of the people of this nation strengthens and inspires our confident faith in his continued leadership."

[14] See K. H. Porter, "National Party Platforms," 497–513. Also, Republican Campaign Text-Book, 1924, 61 *et seq.*

[15] "Public Opinion in War and Peace," 190–91.

There was additional indorsement of "the firm insistence of President Coolidge upon rigid government economy" and a pledge of "earnest support to this end." A significant statement was contained in the sentence: "Congress has in the main confined its work to tax reduction. The matter of tax reform is still unsettled and is equally essential." Renewed support to civil service was given by the plank which stated a favorable attitude toward "the classification of postmasters in first, second and third class postoffices, and the placing of the prohibition enforcement field forces within the classified civil service without necessarily incorporating the present personnel." There was an indorsement of the debt agreement with Great Britain, upon the general principle that "great nations cannot recognize or admit the principle of repudiation. To do so would undermine the integrity essential for international trade, commerce and credit."

There was a long discussion of the tariff, upon the basis of the statement that "in the history of the nation the protective tariff system has ever justified itself by restoring confidence, promoting industrial activity and employment, enormously increasing our purchasing power and bringing increased prosperity to all our people." There was an interesting discussion of the elastic provisions and the tariff commission idea as "providing for a method of readjusting the tariff rates and the classifications in order to meet changing economic conditions," and that it "furnishes a safeguard on the one hand against excessive taxes and on the other hand against too high customs charges."

Foreign relations were handled with greater emphasis than four years before. "The Republican party reaffirms its stand for agreement among the nations to prevent war and preserve peace. As an immediate step in this direction we endorse the permanent court of international justice and favor the adherence of the United States to this tribunal as recommended by President Coolidge. This government has definitely refused membership in the League of Nations or to assume any obligations under the covenant of the league. On this we stand." This was further amplified by the explanatory statement: "The basic principle of our foreign policy must be independence without indifference to the rights and necessities of others and coöperation without entangling alliances."

Recognition was given to the agricultural difficulties, and to the agrarian political influence, which had been so subversive of legislative efficiency during the past congresses. Pledges and promises were necessarily vague, for the party was not yet ready to grapple with the problem on the basis of its only solution—the reforms of business and methods of cultivation by the farmers themselves, and a frank recognition that a tariff could not much help but could much harm the farmers of the country. The following statement in the long plank on agriculture is typical: "We pledge the party to take whatever steps are necessary to bring back a balanced condition between agriculture, industry and labor, which was destroyed by the Democratic party through an unfortunate administration of legislation passed as war-time measures." As constructive suggestions, there was a promise of "every assistance in the reorganization of the market system on sounder and more economical lines and where diversification is needed government assistance during the period of transition. . . . We favor adequate tariff protection to such of our agricultural products as are threatened by competition. We favor, without putting the government into business, the establishment of a federal system of organization for coöperative marketing of farm products."

Likewise labor came in for a lengthy discussion, with the pledge "to protect labor from undue exactions." With regard to the railroad situation, there was a statement in favor of "the consolidation of the railroads into a lesser number of connecting systems with the resultant operating economy." Furthermore, "collective bargaining, voluntary mediation, and arbitration are the most important steps in maintaining peaceful labor relations. We do not believe in compulsory action at any time. Public opinion must be the final arbiter in any crisis which so vitally affects public welfare as the suspension of transportation." Added to this was the unqualified pledge, "The Republican party stands now, as always, against all attempts to put the government into business. . . . We are firmly opposed to the nationalization or government ownership of public utilities."

There was full indorsement of the recent legislation restricting immigration in a more drastic and sane manner than ever before in American history. "The law recently enacted is designed to protect the inhabitants of our country, not only the American citizen, but also the alien already with us who is seeking to secure an economic foothold for himself and family from the competition that would come with unrestricted immigration. The administrative features of the law represent a great constructive advance, and eliminate the hardships suffered by immigrants under emergency statute."

It was necessary to meet the scandals that had been unearthed during the recent year, and from which President Coolidge had rescued the party in popular estimation. This was done by the statement: "We demand the speedy, fearless and impartial prosecution of all wrongdoers, without regard for political affiliations; but we declare no greater wrong can be committed against the people than the attempt to destroy their trust in the great body of their public servants."

The followers of Senator La Follette, mainly in the Wisconsin delegation, attempted to have included in the platform the radical doctrines which they followed, and which were a compound of the populism of thirty years before, with the socialism prevalent in Europe as the result of after-war disruption. These were voted down, and the platform adopted on June 11 with practical unanimity.

By previous arrangement, an old friend of President Coolidge, Dr. Marion Leroy Burton, president of the University of Michigan, placed his name before the convention in an eloquent and finished speech that partook more of the character of an address than the ordinary type of nominating "oratory." On the third day of the convention, June 12, the nomination was made on the first ballot by the overwhelming vote of Coolidge, 1065; La Follette, 34; Hiram Johnson, 10. Of

Photograph by Brown Brothers

PRESIDENT CALVIN COOLIDGE AND HIS CABINET

course, the votes for the two latter were merely for advertising purposes, as already it was planned to run La Follette on an independent ticket, and this was a convenient way to bring the movement before the country. Former Governor Frank O. Lowden of Illinois was nominated for Vice-President, but promptly declined, and on the third ballot the convention by a vote of 682½ to 243½ wisely nominated General Charles Gates Dawes of Illinois. There was prompt adjournment, the gathering having been marked by unusual dignity and efficiency.

We already have heard of General Dawes as the young man who so cleverly assisted Mark Hanna in swinging the state of Illinois to the support of McKinley in 1896. He was born at Marietta, Ohio, on August 27, 1865, and came from distinguished colonial American stock. He graduated from Marietta College in 1884 and from the Cincinnati Law School in 1886. He was admitted to the bar, and practised law in Nebraska until 1894, when he removed to Illinois and became interested in banking and business. He was comptroller of the currency of the United States from 1897 to 1902. During the World War he was chief of supply procurement for the American expeditionary forces in France, on the staff of General Pershing, with the rank of brigadier-general. In 1921 he became first director of the budget, and during the winter of 1923-24 he was in Europe, where he headed the commission that negotiated the settlement of the reparation claims against Germany. General Dawes is one of the greatest "selling agents" in the world. His energy, cleverness, courage, and method of frank speech are invaluable to any cause in which he is enlisted, and he has a faculty of arousing popular interest and support. His nomination admirably balanced the ticket, although the radicals received cold comfort and were thus induced to go ahead with their plans.

At a convention held in Cleveland, Ohio, and denominated "a national conference of progressives," Senator La Follette was nominated for President, and Senator Burton K. Wheeler of Montana, a Democrat, for Vice-President. The platform contained most of the rejected planks presented by the Wisconsin delegates at the Republican convention, with an additional attack upon the Supreme Court of the United States and a demand that there be a constitutional amendment providing "that Congress may by enacting a statute make it effective over a judicial veto." This was a revamping of the old and exploded demand for recall of judicial decisions. The idea seemed to be that when the Supreme Court should declare an act of Congress unconstitutional, then Congress by a two thirds vote might put the law into effect over the court's veto. This was in reality a practice entirely un-American and opposed to the fundamental principles of the English common law, but prevalent in Continental Europe, where the rights of the individual are entirely dependent upon the fiat of governmental authority. It was a direct repudiation of the idea of unalienable rights as contained in the Declaration of Independence. In fact, it was a return to the principles upon which the Stuart kings had acted in their threat to the existence of popular rights, and which were repudiated and overthrown by the British people in the "glorious revolution" of 1688. To the thoughtful observer of the present day the contention of La Follette, Wheeler, and company that they were "Progressives," as they named themselves, thus was a travesty on words. As a matter of fact, they were the most reactionary party in the country, and desired to go back in American and British history to conditions at a time preceding 1688, about 250 years! They were, so to speak, sitting on the rear platform of a political express train and riding backward at the rate of 100 miles an hour, and all the time they were deluding themselves with the idea they were on the cow-catcher! The Socialist party naïvely indorsed the nominations of La Follette and Wheeler.

The Democrats staged a tragic and almost humorous struggle in their convention which met in New York city on June 24 and lasted until July 9, when it nominated Hon. John W. Davis on the one hundred and third ballot. It was a convention unique in our history. Governor Charles W. Bryan of Nebraska, the brother of William J. Bryan, was named as his running-mate. It is significant that for the first time in history millions of our citizens were enabled to "listen in" upon the proceedings of these conventions, through the instrumentality of the recently invented radio—which probably is going to make a definite change in many of our policies and methods of politics and government. The orderly and enthusiastic proceedings of the Republican convention, which were in such striking contrast to those of the "cat-and-dog fight" of the Democrats, were the best kind of campaign material for the Coolidge and Dawes ticket. It is significant that the Democrats refused to indorse the League of Nations, which marked the definite dropping of this issue from American politics, at least for a time, if not finally.

There was some fear at first on the part of the Republican leaders lest the La Follette ticket might cause such a split in the Republican party that 1912 would be repeated. But as the November election drew near, it was found that all such apprehensions were groundless. Early in May President Coolidge had announced his desire that Hon. William Morgan Butler, a prominent lawyer and business man of Massachusetts, should be chosen chairman of the Republican National Committee, in order to manage the campaign. Mr. Butler is a man of great ability, who has been long interested in politics. For years he was looked upon as the right-hand man of the late Senator W. Murray Crane, himself an unusually acute politician of the old school, and the judgment of the President in this case was entirely justified. It is true that the campaign was in large part managed from the White House, for Mr. Coolidge, as already indicated, has political ability of the highest order, and Mr. Butler was an adequate complement and aid. Soon after the election Senator Lodge died, in November, 1924, and Mr. Butler was appointed his successor as United States senator from Massachusetts. He acted as a personal representative of Coolidge in the Senate during the next two years.

Mr. Davis, the Democratic candidate, went actively on the stump, as did all the Vice-Presidential candidates. Mr. Coolidge remained for the most part busy with the cares of his office, but General Dawes was very effective as a speaker. Senator La Follette was not in good health, so his campaigning was handicapped in an unfortunate manner. It soon appeared that not only was the Republican cause or ticket a strong one, but Mr. Coolidge truly was much stronger than his party. The people looked upon him as "poor and honest," and his typical New England characteristics especially appealed to that large element among our people who have a strain of New England blood in their veins. His quiet, sincere, religious, and homelike family life in the White House was in itself a great asset, and early in the contest the "Review of Reviews" adequately summed up his position and that of his party as follows:[16] "He has declared himself briefly and clearly upon a number of important matters of public policy. He has identified himself with programs of economy and thrift in national finance. He is looked upon as a patient, honest, shrewd, and hard-headed Yankee who naturally aligns himself with the interests of the common people—the people who adhere to old American standards of public and private life. . . . Mr. Coolidge is the present-day leader who will be taken as representing the party in its moral and intellectual convictions. Sometimes one of the great parties finds its character and its views duly expressed by its representation in Congress. But this is not always, or even usually, the case. The President and his administrative group are more likely to stand for the party than is the body of party adherents in one or both Houses of Congress. There are many useful and intelligent men on the Republican side in Congress, but scarcely any who are highly representative of the party in the national sense."

The election day fell on November 4, and the results far out-distanced the most sanguine hopes and expectations of the Republican leaders. Mr. Coolidge carried 35 states, with 382 electoral votes; Mr. Davis carried 12, with 136 electoral votes; Mr. La Follette carried only his own state of Wisconsin, with 13 votes. The Davis states were the solid South, with the border states of Tennessee and Oklahoma, which had voted for

[16] July, 1924, 10–11 (Vol. LXX, No. 1).

Harding in 1920, while Davis lost at this election the state of Kentucky, which had stood by Cox four years before. The popular vote was: Coolidge, 15,725,016; Davis, 8,386,503; La Follette, 4,822,856; Herman P. Faris, Prohibitionist, 57,520. There were four other inconsequential tickets receiving a few votes each. As already stated, there is no doubt that Coolidge was far stronger than his party. In a number of states the business men were fearful of the throwing of the election into Congress through no candidate's receiving a majority of the electoral votes due to the La Follette ticket, so many Democrats cast their votes for Coolidge. This was true especially in such states as Maryland and Missouri. Coolidge carried 22 of the states over the combined votes for Davis and La Follette. The next, or Sixty-ninth Congress would stand—Senate, Republicans, 53; Democrats, 42; Farmer-Labor, 1; the House of Representatives, Republicans, 247; Democrats, 182; Farmer-Labor, 3; Socialists, 2. The so-called Progressive-Republicans, who had more or less followed La Follette, could hold the balance of power in the Senate and were able to do much to check the Republicans and thwart the will of the administration in spite of the clearly expressed vote of indorsement that the people had given it at the polls. Fortunately, the party strength in the House was great enough to give a majority over all opponents, so the La Follette trouble-makers were helpless.

This election proved to be the end of the self-styled "Progressive" party, in spite of its vote of nearly 5,000,000. It had included, in a political Adullam's Cave, all the restless and sorehead elements, with the addition of large numbers who had a real grievance. While it did represent a feeling of legitimate opposition to certain policies and a demand for reform, yet its essentially un-American platform made its defeat and disintegration inevitable. The sound common sense of the people effected a good riddance at the polls in November of 1924. Hereafter, the agrarian elements are apt to work inside the old parties, and their just complaints must be met if they are to be retained by either and their support enjoyed. In the light of this fact, the schism between East and West on the subject of tariff protection holds in it the greatest possible menace to the peace and welfare of the Republican party, unless some formula of tariff readjustment can be found. If the Democratic party ever should return to power, it would meet the same difficulty and danger.

President Coolidge was inaugurated under the most propitious circumstances, his address being heard literally by millions of our citizens through the instrumentality of the radio. He stressed his policies of economy and lower taxes, and also urged the need of party responsibility if our representative government were properly to function. "If there is to be party government the party label must be something more than a mere device for securing office. Unless those who are elected under the same party designation are willing to assume sufficient responsibility and exhibit sufficient loyalty and coherence, so that they coöperate with each other in the support of the broad general principles of the party platform, the election is merely a mockery, no decision is made at the polls, and there is no representation of the popular will." After this sound sentiment and palpable and deserved thrust at the disloyalty of the Republican "radicals" and members of the "farm bloc," he held out the hand of friendship by praising Congress as the necessary and independent part of representative government, and expressed his own personal desire for the closest possible coöperation. Vice-President Dawes shocked the self-righteous and conceited susceptibilities of the Senate by his inaugural address, in which he called upon that body in able and vigorous fashion to reform its procedure, so that one single senator might no longer be permitted at times to hold up the business of over 100,000,000 people by his own "filibustering" whim. The wrath of certain senators was ludicrous, and merely served to accentuate the truth of Mr. Dawes's charges. There is little chance for such reforms to be carried through at present, but they are inevitable at some time in the rather near future, for again the Vice-President has "sold" an idea to the American people, who have accepted its value. A possible reform to meet the condition, and practically the only thing that will delay a change in the rules of the Senate, would be the speedy adoption by Congress and the country of the so-called Norris amendment, which would abolish the "lame-duck" sessions, and move up the inauguration of the President and Vice-President, as well as the meeting of a new Congress, to the January following the November election.

The Senate was called in special session almost immediately following the inauguration in order to ratify new appointments to office. In spite of Mr. Coolidge's olive branch in his inaugural address, this body now saw fit to challenge and defeat his will, and that immediately following his indorsement by the enormous popular plurality of millions of votes. Upon the resignation of Mr. Daugherty in March, 1923, Mr. Coolidge had made the admirable appointment of Mr. Harlan F. Stone of New York as his successor in the office of attorney-general. President Coolidge had recently elevated Mr. Stone to the Supreme Court, and now appointed Mr. Charles Beecher Warren in his place. In spite of the fact that Mr. Warren was a man of the highest integrity and long and distinguished public service, the Senate twice refused to ratify this choice for the President's official family. The refusal of ratification of cabinet appointments is seldom known in our history, yet there were certain Democrats and radical Republicans who challenged the President in this way on the ground that Mr. Warren had been retained years before by large sugar interests in legal matters of importance. Since no lawyer of a prominence and experience sufficient to warrant his appointment to such high office is apt ever to be overlooked by business "big" enough to pay for the best legal services, this act of the Senate, if carried to its logical conclusion, would guarantee semi-incompetence in all legal branches of our public service. Since then this practice has been extended in one or two cases to the Interstate Commerce Commission and other administrative boards of governmental importance. In other words, under the guise of a demagogic care for the public welfare, in future perhaps we must expect competence and experience to be disqualifications for public office. In addition, there was a striking contrast to the action of the Republican opposition in the Senate at the time of one or two appointments of President Wilson which were, in popular estimation, of doubtful propriety. In that case it had been held by Senator Lodge, as Republican leader, that the appointments were personal with President Wilson, especially those to his cabinet, and that an opposition party should accede to them and let the President take all responsibility, unless there were indications of direct dishonesty or lack of moral fitness. These extreme reasons were entirely lacking in the case of Mr. Warren. Mr. Coolidge was ready to fight the matter to the end, but Mr. Warren declined, and the President appointed Mr. John G. Sargent of Vermont, whom the Senate accepted and confirmed with almost indecent haste. This senatorial action in its completeness merely accentuated the popularity of Mr. Coolidge and decreased that of the Senate.

During the summer and autumn of 1925 there was a congressional recess which was very pleasing to the people at large and to business in particular. The dreary succession of "oil trials" and other scandals continued to disgust the people. The strike in the anthracite coal fields dragged its weary way and became a national misfortune, largely on account of the series of mistakes made consistently and for repeated years by the honest but professionally "crusading" governor of Pennsylvania, Mr. Gifford Pinchot. Mr. Coolidge refused to interfere, and the result of the strike was possibly a permanent popular substitution of other fuels, which inevitably will cost the anthracite industry dear both from the standpoint of employer and employee. Congress has refused to pass at this time or since the remedial legislation urged repeatedly upon its attention by President Coolidge, so a large part of the blame for these conditions must rest upon the shoulders, already overburdened, of the national legislators.

The Sixty-ninth Congress met in its first session in December, 1925, and the House of Representatives organized by the election of Mr. Nicholas Longworth of Ohio as speaker. Due to the able leadership and executive ability of Mr. Longworth, backed by the Republican administration majority over

Photograph by Underwood & Underwood

HERBERT HOOVER

all opponents—Democrats and "radical" Republicans combined—the House began to function as a legislative body with greater efficiency and despatch, not to mention party and popular responsibility, than at any time since the "overthrow" of Speaker Cannon in 1910. For this reason it has stood out in striking contrast to the erratic and casual work of the Senate, and has added much to the unpopularity of the latter body, which at the present time stands at the nadir of its popular support and political influence. Mr. Coolidge in his annual message urged renewed tax reduction, which was successfully accomplished, and also our adherence to the court of international justice, or "World Court" as it is popularly known, according to his and President Harding's insistence and the pledges of the Republican national platform. This latter issue came to a decision in the Senate on January 30, 1926, when our adhesion was voted by a ratification of the protocol with a count of 76 to 17. Unfortunately, this was so weighed down by reservations, both good and bad, that there has been no practical result from this policy to which the Republican party has been pledged for nearly a quarter of a century.

Senator Borah of Idaho, who by the absurd principle of seniority now holds the chairmanship of the Senate Committee on Foreign Relations, consistently opposed the administration and the expressed public sentiment of the country on the World Court and most other issues. There is no doubt of his sincerity and honesty, but there always has been a question of his moral right to hold an office to which he never was elected by the suffrage of the American people, and which he has used consistently to block the representatives of their clearly expressed will. The "Review of Reviews" remarked at this time [17] of the senator: "Mr. Borah is self-convinced. He is an impressive public speaker, and independent thinker, and he always commands a hearing. But his opinions do not habitually convince his colleagues nor sway the final judgments of the American people." Or as a British journal shrewdly had remarked: "Senator Borah fights bravely; he

[17] February, 1926, 122 (Vol. LXXIII, No. 2).

is courageous and always goes down with his flag flying. But he always goes down!"

Meanwhile, under the steady and balanced administration of President Coolidge the country was prospering in an almost unprecedented manner. This was on a basis of widespread welfare, which, while it did not apply to the agrarian interests to the same degree that they had a right to expect, yet was of an undoubtedly healthy character. It was under these conditions that the congressional elections of the fall of 1926 were held. The Republicans had reason to expect some reverses, due to the unfailing character of political reaction midway in a Presidential administration. Also, the fact that many members of Congress had not supported in action as they had in speech the popular President, was bound to militate against them. In addition, a number of senators from normally Democratic states who had gone into office upon the crest of the Harding wave were to come up for reëlection.

Under the circumstances, the Republicans did remarkably well. The Seventieth Congress, to meet in December, 1927, was chosen as follows: House of Representatives—Republicans, 238; Democrats, 194; Farmer-Labor, 2; Socialist, 1. This meant a continuation of the services of Mr. Longworth as speaker, and the probability of a further *régime* of party responsibility and coöperation with the Coolidge administration. The situation in the Senate was not so favorable. The results portended an alignment that would give added strength to the "radicals" in the Republican party, and enable them to hold the balance of power. They were: Republicans, 48; Democrats, 47; Farmer-Labor, 1.

The most outstanding feature of the final short, or "lame-duck," session of the Sixty-ninth Congress was the passage, by a combination of agricultural elements in both parties, of the McNary-Haugen bill. This was based upon the entirely faulty principle of using the taxpayers' money to buy up surplus crops, fix domestic prices, and dump surplus abroad at any price it would bring—thus acting as a subsidy to foreign labor in order that the foreign manufacturer might underbid domestic manufacture in spite of the high walls of the Fordney-McCumber tariff! It thus put a premium upon overproduction—the very cause of the situation that demanded a remedy. Through its administrative features it also would put a premium upon "bootlegging" of grain, hogs, and other agricultural crops by the farmers of the nation. President Coolidge promptly vetoed the bill and his veto was upheld. There was a wide expression of support and approval, and his renomination and reëlection in 1928 seemed a foregone conclusion. It was recognized as such by the best political observers of the nation, including even those Republican leaders who were not especially friendly to him. Democratic and "radical" Republican attacks upon the administration policy in Mexico and Nicaragua, which policy had been in large part inherited from previous administrations, both Democratic and Republican, were indulged in during the months of January and February, 1927. The "sniping" and "guerilla" character of this partizan warfare was so apparent that it failed to result in any great popular opposition or to lessen Mr. Coolidge's hold upon the good-will of the country.

In the midst of this state of political apathy and placid acceptance of the inevitable, President Coolidge characteristically threw a bombshell into the political camps of both parties and completely changed the aspect of affairs. On the morning of August 2, 1927 (the fourth anniversary of his assumption of office following the death of Mr. Harding), he handed to the newspaper correspondents who had accompanied him to his summer residence for 1927, in North Dakota, slips of paper upon which were written, "I do not choose to run for President in nineteen twenty-eight." It is at this interesting and uncertain point of political development that the story of the Republican party must be left. Future possibilities, which must be conjectural, depend almost entirely upon the ability of the party leaders to find a basis of coöperation between the capitalistic and industrial North and East with the agricultural West. The tariff may be the great subject of contention for the next decade, as it was during the years from 1887-1896. And prohibition will continue to cut across political lines for many years to come.

Congress at present seems totally incapable of evolving national leaders. Both of the great political parties are overwhelmed by localism. State executives and other officials, therefore, seem destined to continue their hold upon the imaginations and affections of great numbers of people, and their sectional eligibility for the Presidency is almost unrivaled. The task before the citizens of the United States, and especially those who owe allegiance to the historic Republican party, is primarily one of evolving leadership, also principles and policies broad enough for a national application.

INDEX

Index

Index

Index

Index